CHRONICLES OF A NATION

The Founding Fathers, Families, and Patriots

By Joan Wheeler LaGrone

Copyright 2014 by Joan Wheeler LaGrone
Revised May 2015
All rights reserved.
v7.0 r1.0

No part of this book may be reproduced or transmitted in any form or by any means, electronic or mechanical including photocopying recording or by any information storage and retrieval system without permission in writing from the Author. Address all inquires to: WIN Publishers of Colorado, 399 Arroyo Street, Brighton, Colorado 80601 or email the publisher at JoanWheelerLagrone@gmail.com or met2000@frii.com.

ISBN 978- 09679230-2-4

Library of Congress Control Number: 2015908649

Unless otherwise stipulated, the pictures are from the author's personal collection. Pictures of the family crests are found in James Fairbairn's book of family crest written 1892 and published before 1905. Cover Design by nzgraphics.net. Printed by Outskirts Press.

A special thanks to Chris VanSickle for his help with the computer and Sean Irvin for Editing.

WIN Publishers of Colorado
399 Arroyo Street
Brighton, Colorado 80601
Email met2000@frii.com
JoanWheelerLaGrone@gmail.com
www.JoanWheelerLaGrone.com

This book is dedicated to my parents:

Harry Louk Wheeler and Ruth Evelyn Minter
My grandparents
Ralph Bismarck Wheeler and May Winter Evans
And
(Leroy) Roy Minter and Lydia Jordon Edmiston

This book could not be written without the incredible stories of their ancestors who chose to come to America in spite of the appalling hardships and risks in search of freedom and helped to found this Nation. Their descendants who were willing to jeopardize their lives in the War for Independence assisted in establishing these United States of America. I am eternally grateful for their dedication to freedom. The interest in the book by my six sons Mike, Tim, Brien, and Sean Irvin, David and Steven LaGrone, my grandchildren, Kyle, Luke, Maren, Jenna, Jaime and Nicole Irvin, Andrew and hopefully Zachary LaGrone, has helped to give me the perseverance to finish it. My brother Jay Wheeler has equally been a supporter.

About the Author

Joan Wheeler LaGrone is a thirteenth generation American who descends from over sixty direct ancestors who fought in the Revolution. All four of her grandparent's ancestors came to the Colonies before the Revolution, including their related families. These founding families settled in twelve of the thirteen Colonies from Maine to South Carolina. Some held the original grants for founding the Colony. The first ancestor to arrive was Edmond Pearsoll from England in 1613, an investor in the Second Virginia Colony in 1609. He returned to England and his son Thomas came in 1621. Thomas Rogers and his family were next, Pilgrims who came on the Mayflower in 1622 from Dedham, Essex County, England. They founded the Plymouth Colony with the Leyden congregation. Thomas' daughter Elizabeth married Daniel Smith. A descendant, Anne Smith, married Ephraim Wheeler whose family arrived in in Massachusetts in 1639. George Morton, Pilgrim Father arrived in 1623, the ancestor of Lydia Morton who married Joseph Bardwell. The Evans family from Wales arrived in New Jersey about 1730. The Minter's were members of the first Virginia Colony at Jamestown. Through the Edmonstone family, she descends from the Dukes of Flanders, King Robert the Bruce and King Robert III. Queen Elizabeth I, Henry the VIII, King Henry IV of France, and the ancient Kings of Sweden are part of her heritage. The associated families of these immigrants arrived from the 1630's to the 1750's. Only one arrived later in 1780 near the end of the Revolution.

As the only child of Harry Wheeler and Ruth Minter, she is the single combination of these immigrant families with a variety of religions, cultures, and nationalities giving her a unique perspective. Her families have been involved in politics of different political persuasions since they arrived. She views the United States as country for all free and equal independent people regardless of their race, color, creed, politics, or sex, which is the reason for the existence of the United State.

LaGrone is a member of the Daughters of the American Revolution (DAR) through her first documented Patriot, William Butler of the "Fighting Butler Family" of Pennsylvania. His granddaughter Margaret Mariah Butler married Oliver C. Wheeler, her great, great grandparents.

LaGrone is an award winning author of two prior books, "The Edmonstone Chronicles, Royal Knights and Scottish Kings," a Scottish history, and "From Beyond the Veil" connecting the physical and spiritual worlds. She has published several articles in national publications and a founding member of the Rocky Mountain Writers Guild. LaGrone is a past member of the Board of Directors for the Colorado Independent Publishers Association and past Editorial Advisory Chairman of *Connections,* the National Women's Council of Realtors Magazine. She is President of WIN Publishers of Colorado and Broker/Owner of Metro 2000 Real Estate Company. She is also an award winning Designer and Artist. The author is listed in Who's Who in American Politics, Executives and Professionals and an honored member of the International Executive Guild.

LaGrone is the mother of six adult sons, eight grandchildren and is married to Clyde LaGrone, a retired engineer. She lives in the Metro Denver area.

CONTENTS

FOREWORD

PREFACE

INTRODUCTION

CHAPTER I: THE BIRTH OF AMERICA 1

    THE STAMP ACT 4

    THE TEA ACT 5

    THE BOSTON TEA PARTY AND THE SONS OF LIBERTY 6

    THE STAGE IS SET 8

    THE DECLARATION OF INDEPENDENCE 11

CHAPTER II: THE FOUNDING FATHERS 19

    GEORGE WASHINGTON AND THE SCOTTISH PROPHECY 19

    GEORGE WASHINGTON – THE EARLY YEARS 21

    THE FRENCH – INDIAN WAR AND THE INDIAN PROPHECY 22

    WASHINGTON – POLITICS AND RELIGION 24

    THE ROSICRUCIAN PROPHECY 26

    WASHINGTON BEFORE THE REVOLUTION 30

    WASHINGTON COMMANDER IN CHIEF 31

    GEORGE WASHINGTON'S VISION 32

    THE PRESIDENCY 38

    JOHN ADAMS 41

    SAMUEL ADAMS 42

    BENJAMIN FRANKLIN 43

    PATRICK HENRY 45

    ALEXANDER HAMILTON 46

    THOMAS JEFFERSON 47

    THOMAS PAINE 48

    JAMES MADISON 49

    GOUVERNEUR MORRIS 51

    ROBERT MORRIS 52

    FREEMASONARY 53

    ADAM WEISHAUPT 55

CHAPTER III 59

- THE FOUNDING FAMILIES AND PATRIOTS 59
- THE FIGHTING BUTLERS 60
- THE AMERICAN BUTLER DESCENDANTS 62
- WILLIAM BUTLER, PATRIOT 65
- WILLIAM BUTLER, JR. AND ELIZABETH MCMURTY 71
- THE DOUGLAS FAMILY 72
- THE MCMURTRY FAMILY 73
- THE BOONE FAMILY 75
- THE KIRKPATRICK FAMILY 76
- THE GASTON FAMILY IN AMERICA 79

CHAPTER IV 81

- THE PILGRIMS 81
- THOMAS ROGERS, PILGRIM 83

CHAPTER V 85

- THE PURITANS IN AMERICA 85

CHAPTER VI 87

- THE WHEELER FAMILY 87
- THE WOODWARD FAMILY 96
- THE NEWTON FAMILY 97
- THE MILES FAMILY 98
- The GOODNOW FAMILY 98
- THE LOUCK/LAUX FAMILY 99
- THE SCOTT FAMILY 104
- THE CLARENCE FAMILY 105
- THE VANDERWERKEN FAMILY 106
- THE PIERSOL FAMILY 107
- THE BABB FAMILY 113
- THE GHOST OF PHILLIP BABB 116
- THE HUSSEY FAMILY 117
- THE LEWIS FAMILY 119

CHAPTER VII 123

THE EVANS FAMILY	123
THE STYLES FAMILY	126
THE RUDDEROW FAMILY	127
THE DUFFIELD FAMILY	128
THE DILKS FAMILY	131
THE HAWK FAMILY	132
THE WINTER FAMILY	133
THE GROVER FAMILY	136
THE CHEESEMAN FAMILY	138
THE DUTCH COLONIES IN AMERICA	139
THE RYCKEN/SUYDAM FAMILY	140
THE WYCKOFF FAMILY	143
THE VAN NESS FAMILY	145
THE COX/COCK FAMILY	146
THE CLARK FAMILY	149
THE GULICK FAMILY	151
THE VANDENBERG FAMILY	153
CHAPTER VIII	155
THE MINTER FAMILY	155
THE PHILLIPS FAMILY	166
THE HILLHOUSE FAMILY	167
THE LUCKEY FAMILY	170
THE BAIRD/STERRET FAMILIES	171
THE GILLHAM FAMILY	173
THE CAMPBELL FAMILY	175
THE LOVE FAMILY	177
THE LOCKHART FAMILY	179
THE BARDWELL FAMILY	180
MAYHEW AND HEBRON MISSION	182
THE MORTON FAMILY	183
CHAPTER IX	185
THE EDMONSTONE FAMILY	185

- THE EDMISTON FAMILY IN AMERICA 188
- THE THOMPSON FAMILY 192
- THE PATTERSON FAMILY 194
- THE CORY FAMILY 195
- THE SMITH FAMILY 196
- THE GILLILAND FAMILY 198
- THE JORDAN FAMILY 199
- THE MCNEEL FAMILY 201
- THE VAN METEREN FAMILY 203
- THE DAVIS FAMILY 204
- THE DUFORT/TEAFORD FAMILY 206
- THE GRUBER/GREAVER FAMILY 208
- THE ARGENBRIGHT FAMILY 209
- THE HENGERER/HANGER FAMILY 211
- THE KELLER FAMILY 212

CHAPTER X 213
- THE IRVINE/IRVIN FAMILY 213
- THE SPAULDING FAMILY 220
- THE STUNTZ FAMILY 221
- THE DAVIS FAMILY 222
- THE BECKER FAMILY 224
- THE RIMA FAMILY 225
- THE STORM FAMILY 226
- THE GINGRICH FAMILY 227
- THE O'SULLIVAN FAMILY 229

CHAPTER XI 231
- THE LAGRONE/LA GRONE FAMILY 231
- THE KINARD FAMILY 235
- THE HOUSEAL FAMILY 236
- THE STROMAN FAMILY 237
- THE DOMINICK FAMILY 238
- THE GIBBS FAMILY 239

THE BOZEMAN FAMILY ... 242
THE RICE FAMILY ... 244
THE COOK FAMILY ... 246
THE MOODY FAMILY ... 246
THE O'NEILL FAMILY ... 247
THE WHITE FAMILY ... 248
THE TILLMAN FAMILY ... 250
THE BEESON/BEASON/BESON FAMILY ... 251
THE FISH FAMILY ... 254
THE TIPTON FAMILY ... 255
CONCLUSION ... 257
ADDENDUMS ... 259

FOREWORD

This is a book, which all Americans and all those who love the United States must read. Today, when one can cross the ocean by airplane in a few hours, it is almost impossible to comprehend the sheer courage and sense of desperation, which drove those early Founding Fathers (and families) to brave a crossing in sailing ships. If not wrecked or driven off course, the ships would land them on a shore where they had no way of knowing whether they could survive – that is if they landed at all.

Joan Wheeler LaGrone brings the heroic story of these early settlers evocatively to the mind's eye. Her research into the history of these families, who set the pattern of life in that great country of America, as we know it today, is the work of many years. Only someone with a penetrating eye for detail could have achieved a work of such enormous scope. She is greatly to be congratulated by the many readers who will, as I have, find themselves amazed by such a vivid and at times heartbreaking story of the hardship endured by the men and women who had the courage to risk everything in pursuit of their great ideal of a new world, where escaping of all forms of persecution, they could be free.

'No taxation without representation' the incident of the "Boston Tea Party' is one of the illustrations, some painted by the authoress, which bring this book so immediately alive. I hope that on a worldwide scale it will win the acclamation that it richly deserves.

Mary McGrigor,
Upper Sonachan – Dalmally – Argyll, Scotland
Author of "Defiant and Dismasted: The Life and Times of Admiral Sir William Hargood," 2004 "Argyll: Land of Blood and Beauty," 2013, "Anna, Countess of Covenant," 2008, "Rob Roy Country" 2003 and several others at Amazon.com. Her latest book "Lady Margaret Douglas - The forgotten Tudor" will arrive on the shelves in January of 2015.

PREFACE

America was predestined to become a Country and George Washington to be its leader. Our founding ancestors seemed preordained to colonize thirteen states and win the War for Independence. If there is any doubt that America was established under the direction and protection of a "higher influence," the historical documents, prophecies, and stories related here should help lessen any disbelief.

Many of our ancestors were severely persecuted under tyrannical Kings, the Clergy, and Popes in Europe. The American Colonies provided a refuge, the only place left where they could practice their varied religions and raise their families without oppression. For almost a hundred and fifty years, the earlier ancestors lived in moderately agreeable conditions, with the Indians their only major concern. Eventually, the King of England began his relentless malice and interference with the peace and prosperity of the Colonists, forcing them to take action. When it was apparent, King George intended to extend his control through high taxation and intolerable rules, the Colonist went to war.

The American Citizens owe their freedoms to the men and women who suffered severe hardships to cross the Atlantic in overcrowded boats with unhealthy conditions, and lack of food. Thousands died before reaching the Colonies and many did not survive their first winter. Those who did, built our cities, established our churches and schools, and sacrificed their lives in the Revolutionary War for the freedoms we enjoy every day. We owe it to our ancestors and ourselves to remember our true history and see that we never forget their individual sacrifices or lose our freedoms. The following stories and names of a few of these ancestors help to put a face to the many brave men and women who gave us these United States of America.

INTRODUCTION

There was a fundamental difference concerning the meaning of the Revolution between the Founding Fthers. George Washington and the Federalists thought the Constitution and the building of America was the most important act with the Declaration of Independence the beginning. Thomas Jefferson and his party of the Democrat/Republicans, held the liberating act of the Declaration of Independence itself as the most important document. These views were continually debated among them. George Washington predicted that party politics would lead to divisions among the people and the issues of the day would not be debated openly and honestly. He was correct.

The Founding Fathers were liberals and believed in liberal individual rights. Washington did not advocate small government, or a literal interpretation of the Constitution. He believed the Federal Government needed to be stronger and the reason why he supported the creation and passing of the Constitution. All of the Founding Fathers intended the Constitution to be used as *"guidelines and principles to direct the general course of our new nation."*

Today, history is being re-written. Rightwing Christians want us to believe that our founding fathers were all Christians and the basic principles of the Constitution and Declaration of Independence originate from Scriptures. Historical evidence shows that this is not the case. Instead, they were Deists, Theists, and Christians who believed in God and or a higher being. Many were Freemasons who believed in the masonic principals, the brother hood of man, and the Fatherhood of God.

The so-called "Tea Partiers" of today do not represent the original intentions of the 1776 members of the Boston Tea Party or the Founding Fathers. We must keep our true history alive and teach it to our children. We cannot forget who we are. A nation or a people who do not remember where they came from, or their true foundations, can easily be destroyed from enemies without or within.

AMERICA
The Original Thirteen Colonies

CHAPTER I: THE BIRTH OF AMERICA

*"From the aquatic triplicate will be born
One who will make Thursday for its feast:
Its renown, praise, reign, and power will grow,
By land and sea, to the Orients turbulence."*

Whether you believe in predictions or not, there were several prophecies for the founding of the United States and for our founding father, George Washington. The first was by *Nostradamus*, who predicted the birth of America before he died in 1566. He forecast the United States would be formed from three countries, England, France, and Spain, the three major sea powers at the time. These three countries with colonies in America would form the majority of the people and culture. He predicted the United States would celebrate a unique American Holiday on Thursday, our Thanksgiving Day. First celebrated in 1622 by the Pilgrims, it was made official by President Franklin Roosevelt in 1941, three hundred and nineteen years later. The USA is the only powerful country that celebrates Thursday. By 1945, America became the world's first super power with "renown" unmatched and Army and Naval supremacy. The United States became the policy maker for freedom, which resulted in conflicts with the Orientals and communist countries in the middle and Far East.

Nostradamus also prophesied the following for George Washington, which eventually took place on June 15, 1775, the day the Continental Congress appointed him Commander in Chief of the Continental Army. John Hancock had expected to be appointed, but John Adams suggested Washington instead:

"He will rise high over the estate more to the right
He will remain seated on the stone square
To the South facing to his left
Crooked staff in hand his mouth sealed.*

Nostradamus' predicted the following for The Declaration of Independence and Thomas Paine in 1776. Paine became a leader of the Revolution through his publications, "Common Sense."

*"The man will be called by a barbaric name
that three sisters will receive from destiny
He will speak then to a great people in words and deeds
more than any other man will have fame and renown."*

The birth of our Country and its leaders were predicted before 1566. The desire for religious freedom and the need for independence from the oppressive laws and taxes of the European Kings were the primary reasons our ancestors came to America. The desire to own land was another. America was the only place left where freedom and opportunity were possible. By 1650 over 25,000 had reached our

*(An old English meaning of estate, "Social position, or rank, especially of high order." Washington did not pursue the Commander in Chief position or speak out for it)

shores and risked their lives in the small ship crossings with dreadful living conditions. Many did not survive, but those who did were faced immediately with providing shelter and food for their families. They set about establishing towns, churches, farms, and business. In the meantime, they fought hostile Indians, sickness, weather, and shortages of food. However, they were determined. A few were influential and able to obtained grants to establish Colonies. The wealthy were able to obtain large amounts of good farmland. If they were poor, they usually came as an indentured servant and served four to seven years until the cost of passage was paid. By 1750 there were close to two and a half million people in the Colonies from Maine to Georgia.

The Colonies were separated into three regions partly due to the varied climates. In New England, where the climate was cool, there were fewer diseases and deaths. It was easier for the children to survive and the first public schools and colleges were established. The Colonists as a whole were better educated. Shipbuilding and fishing became the primary industries. Since the farms were usually small, people lived closer together and built their homes around a common building where they held town meetings. This provided the opportunity for the people to discuss their concerns and helped to establish democratic thinking. Everyone was required to read the Bible in the Puritan environment. Unlike other colonies, the women were educated. Unfortunately, the early Puritans were intolerant of other religions. They were also intolerant with any disagreement with the church authority and ministers.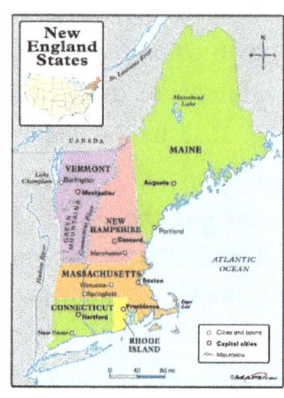
Speaking out could cause expulsion from the Colony as it did for Anne Hutchinson and Roger Williams. In 1692, Puritans in Salem Massachusetts become obsessed with superstitions about the devil and witchcraft, causing them to put twenty of their citizens to death. These people were ultimately cleared of the accusations, the families were given monetary compensation for their loss, and memorials were established. Eventually, new churches were established bringing in a variety of religions.

The middle Colonies provided a better climate with richer soil for farming and many Colonists had sizeable farms. Their primary crops provided food for the people living in the many growing cities. Land ownership was high. Many of the people were religious, mainly Quakers, but by the 1770's the government and society as a whole were not. Innovation was greater here with many new ideas and inventions. They produced the frontier rifles including the Pennsylvania long rifles. The Colonists became the leaders in publishing and printing contributing to America's free press.

The Southern Colonies were populated with a majority of indentured servants, slaves, or farmers. A few became large plantation owners who were wealthy planters with large amounts of land. The main crops were tobacco and cotton. The distance between plantations made it impractical to have schools and limited the number of churches. Maryland began as a Catholic Colony for those members in England who were persecuted after the Protestants took over.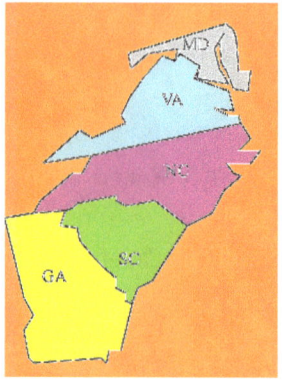

However, the Protestants eventually outnumbered them. Social life revolved around the small plantations towns. They became self-sufficient and built or grew much of what they needed. Life expectancy was lower here than in the other Colonies due to the warm climate, disease and malnutrition. Children often grew up with only one parent. Because there were fewer women, they were prized and after marriage, they were highly protected. Widows did not remain unmarried long. In spite of all the differences, there was still one element in common causing the Colonists great difficulties. The King of England, his Governor's, and proprietors were in charge of the Colonial Government. Taxes could go up and laws could change whenever the King demanded it.

*History and maps sourced from Wikipedia

THE STAMP ACT

The Colonists tax difficulties began in 1765 when the English Parliament passed the Stamp act. The Act was designed to help King George III (pictured) pay for his wars and the troops he kept in America. The Colonists immediately objected, as this was taxation without representation. The Colonists had no one representing them in the English Parliament and to them it was a violation of their rights as Englishmen. John Adams, founding father and member of the Massachusetts Assembly, wrote a response entitled "Essay on Cannon and Feudal Law" which was published in the Boston Gazette. He argued that the Act deprived the Colonists of their basic right to be taxed by consent and tried by a jury of their peers. Since the Colonist elected their own legislatures, they believed raising taxes was up to them not Parliament. Several of the Colonies created "committees of correspondence" to coordinate action between them against the Act. By the end if 1765 all but two of the Colonies had sent formal protests to Parliament and the merchants boycotted English goods. Violent protests erupted in the Colonies and they attacked the Tax distributor's houses, businesses, and government officials. There was a growing network of groups called the "Sons of Liberty" organizing throughout the Colonies and they began communicating with each other. The Massachusetts Assembly sent letters to all of the other Colonies, suggestion they get together to discuss the situation. Nine of the Colonies met in New York calling themselves the Stamp Act Congress. The others latter endorsed their actions. They produced the Declaration of Rights and Grievances, which stated:

1. *Only the Colonial Assemblies had the right to tax*
2. *Colonists possessed the rights of Englishman*
3. *Without voting rights, Parliament did not represent them.*
4. *Trail by Jury is a right*
5. *No Taxation without representation*
6. *The use of Admiralty Courts was abusive*

The Stamp Act was repealed with the help of protests from the English merchants affected by the Colony boycotts. However, the Declaratory Act replaced it the same day. This Act stated that Parliament had the authority to make laws for the Colonists in all matters. The unrest subsided but the taxation issue remained unsolved. The committees established by the Colonists remained in tact and they later used them against future British taxes.

*History and picture sourced from Wikipedia

THE TEA ACT

The Tea Act was the final straw for the Colonist. This Act, passed by Parliament in 1773, granted the British East India Company, who was deeply in debt, a monopoly on tea sales in the American Colonies. This government sanctioned policy and company bail out angered the Americans. It undercut the businesses of the Colony merchants who had previously been able to purchase their tea directly from British markets for resale to the Colonists. At first, the "Sons of Liberty" insisted that the ships in Boston Harbor return to England unloaded. When the British refused, members of the group, who were also Freemasons, met at the Green Dragon Tavern (pictured) in Boston's north end on December 16, 1773. The Tavern, known as the "headquarters for the Revolution," was the home of the St. Andrews Lodge of Freemasons, and the meeting place for both "the Sons of Liberty" and "Committee of Correspondence."

Twenty of the men disguised themselves as Mohawk Indians and along with 155 others; they boarded three British ships in Boston Harbor, dumping 92 thousand pounds of tea overboard. In total, there were 175 participants that day including Josiah Wheeler, a thirty year old from Dorchester Heights who became a Captain in the Revolutionary Army.** In many other Colonial Ports, the tea was unloaded, but left to rot on the docks. In South Carolina, the majority of tea was dumped into the Cooper River, although some of it was stored and later used to help finance the Revolution. The King demanded that the Colonist pay for the loss of the tea. When they refused, Parliament reacted by passing the Intolerable Acts. New resistance arose up and down the Colonies. This set the stage for the beginning of the Revolution.

*History and picture sourced from Wikipedia

**Captain Josiah Wheeler, (DAR #123977) a house wright (builder), commanded a company of minutemen and superintended the erection of forts under General Washington's orders. He later helped build the State House of Boston. He was born in Boston on July 13, 1743 and died August of 1817. His parents were Samuel and Mary Wheeler. Samuel was born 1698 in Rowley Essex, Massachusetts and died in 1747 in Boston. He was a descendant of Thomas Wheeler born 1643 whose father was Obadiah Wheeler born 1610 in Bedfordshire England, one of the original Wheeler immigrant brothers. (DAR #123977 denotes the Daughters of the American Revolution Patriot number).*

THE BOSTON TEA PARTY AND THE SONS OF LIBERTY

The Sons of Liberty was a secret, restricted organization founded first in New York by members of the *Committee of Correspondence* to combat the Stamp Act. The Boston Chapter was organized in 1765. They met in the basement of the Green Dragon Tavern, owned by the Freemasons, the home of St. Andrews Lodge. The Tavern became known as the "headquarters for the Revolution." In the eyes of King George, their actions were treasonous and punishable by death. Consequently, they kept few records. Not all participants were members, but often, sympathetic supporters. The most famous event occurred on December 16, 1773 known as the Boston Tea Party, pictured. Samuel Cooper* gave an eyewitness account of the meeting and the action that followed:

"The duty on tea became a great offence to the colonist generally and in Boston an association was formed in 1770 to drink no tea until the duty was repealed. This course was persisted in 1773 with the arrival of three ships from England laden with tea, which caused great disgust.

No little excitement prevailed among the inhabitants in Boston on account of the arrival of the ships laden with tea from England. Every effort was made to send these ships back but without success and it was soon evident the tea would be landed unless some active measures were adopted by the citizens to prevent it. A town meeting was called on the afternoon of December 16, 1773 to devise measures for getting rid of this annoyance. John Hancock presided at this meeting, held at the Old South Meeting House corner of Main and Milk streets. A little before sundown, an alarm was created among the assembled citizens by the cry of 'fire,' which was suppose to be given by some of the British officers who had attended in citizen's dress and had given the alarm for the purpose of breaking up the assembly. They had nearly affected this object when the town clerk, William Cooper, rose and in a loud voice, told the citizens there was no fire to be apprehended, but the fire of the British and begged them to keep their places.*

Immediately after a detachment of about 20 men disguised as Indians was seen to approach in single file by the west door of the Church. They marched with silent steps down the aisle and so passed by the south door banishing their tomahawks in that direction. The appearance of these men created some sensation. No one seemed to expect their arrival and the object of their visit seemed wholly inexplicable. On leaving the Church, they proceeded in the same order in which they entered, down Milk Street through that part of town, which led to Gray and Taltson's wharves where the tea ships lay. Arrived at the wharves they divided into three troops each with a leader, gained possession of the ships quietly and proceeded to lighten them of their cargo by hoisting out the boxes empting their contents into the dock. No noise was heard except the occasional clink of the hatchet in opening the boxes and the whole business was preformed with so much expedition that before 10:00 o'clock that night the entire cargo of three vessels was deposited in the docks. Many a wishful eye was directed to the piles of tea, which lay in the docks and one poor fellow who could not resist the temptation, had filled the lining of his cloak with about a bushel of the plants. He was soon observed by the crowd and the process of lighten him of his burden was short. He was dragged a little distance to a barrel and was soon furnished with a coat of tar and shavings."

Members of the assembly joined in to help unload the ships. A list of 175 members of the Tea Party has been gathered, documented, and verified. Josiah Wheeler, a Freemason took part.

*Cooper participated in the Battles of Lexington and Concord, Bunker Hill and several others. He became a Major in the Continental Army, DAR # A025802. His wife was the former owner of the Green Dragon Tavern. See list of the names of all of the Tea Party participants at www.oldsouthmeetinghouse.org Boston Tea Party.
**History and Pictures sourced from Wikipedia

THE STAGE IS SET

Founding Fathers John Hancock, Samuel Adams, and John Adams (a cousin) were three of the most prominent Patriots in Massachusetts. Before the Revolution, Hancock was one of richest men in the thirteen Colonies. Born in Lexington, he inherited a successful mercantile business in Boston from his uncle. He was active in politics and was a protégée of Samuel Adams, another prominent Boston politician. His money helped to support the Patriots fight against the British. He became President of the second Continental Congress and was the first to sign the Declaration of Independence with his sizeable bold signature. He later served two terms as Governor. During the crisis that led to the Revolution, he joined the boycott of the Stamp Act. After its repeal, the British passed the Townshend Act, which established new repressive duties on merchandise and designed to curb smuggling. Thinking that Hancock might be engaged in smuggling, his ships, the *Lydia* and the *Liberty* became targets of the British Customs officers.

They boarded his ships without search warrants and Hancock refused to let them go below into the hold. Although charges were filed, both cases were dropped, the first because he had not broken any laws and the second without explanation. The Colonists admired Hancock's stand against the British and elected him to the Massachusetts House of Representatives. He and Paul Revere helped to create the first Minuteman (pictured) companies to be ready for action at any "minute."

In 1768 a "Circular Letter" written by Samuel Adams, also a member of the House was circulated among all the Colonies to coordinate resistance against the Townshend Act. The British then sent four regiments to Boston to try to suppress the unrest and demanded the House rescind the letter. Instead, Hancock, both John and Samuel Adams and the House voted against rescinding the letter and sent a letter to Parliament to recall then Governor Bernard. Even though Governor Bernard returned to England, the British troops remained. This eventually led to the killing of five civilians and the Boston Massacre. Hancock demanded the troops leave Boston and threatened the new Governor stating, *"10,000 colonist troops were ready to march on Boston if the British troops were not removed."* The British officer in charge, Colonel Dalrymple, finally agreed, mainly because his troops were at risk in town. Parliament partially repealed the Townshend act and for a time things were peaceful. However, when the Tea Act followed, it resulted in the Boston Tea Party. The British responded with the Intolerable Acts. There were four parts to the Act:

> 1. *Closed the Boston Harbor until the Colonists paid for the tea,*
> 2. *Cancelled the Massachusetts Charter and made it illegal for the local government to meet unless the Governor called for the meeting,*
> 3. *Moved all Loyal British trials to England to insure a favorable outcome,*
> 4. *Required the Colonist to house and feed the British troops.*

To the Colonists, this legislation was nothing more that an act of vengeance and totally out of proportion with the offense of dumping of the Tea on the harbor. They thought it was a personal attack on each individual's rights. Many of the Colonists, who had not paid too much attention to the growing conflict, now were outraged. Even those who had continued to do business with the British became alarmed.

One wealthy gentleman, a descendant of Puritan ancestors, was chastised in a pamphlet for trading with Britain in violation of the non-importation program. He later related publicly spirits visited him three nights in a row. The first night he states Satan visited him, saying supporting the Stamp Act, The Tea Act, and the Intolerable Acts has made him an enemy of the Country. The third night he was visited by a spirit of an ancestor who lectured him saying, "We did not make the treacherous crossing and fight off Indians and wild beast so that you could commit treason." The Pamphlet, sent to the Gentleman in Boston, was printed, and sold on Marlboro St.

At this point, the Massachusetts House elected five delegates to the First Continental Congress to coordinate the Colonial response including both Samuel and John Adams. The House then resolved itself into the Massachusetts Provincial Congress and John Hancock was elected President.
In 1772, Sam Adams and his colleagues refined the Committee of Correspondence system, which linked the Patriots together throughout the Colonies and drew up their response to the Coercive Acts. This became a shadow government to coordinate their plans. They were instrumental in setting up the first Continental Congress.

Hancock was now a leading Patriot. He was a member of the Boston Selectmen and in 1774, he was elected to the second Continental Congress. Before he reported to the Congress, he was unanimously re-elected President of the state Provincial Congress which was held in Concord in February of 1775. After attending a later meeting of the Provincial Congress in April of 1775, Hancock and Adams decided it was unsafe to return to Boston before leaving to attend the Continental Congress in Philadelphia. Instead, they stayed in Lexington in Hancock's childhood home. By now, Hancock and both John and Samuel Adams were considered by the British to be agitators who were committing acts of treason. As early as January 1774, they had considered arresting them.

In April of 1775, the Governor of Boston, then Thomas Gage, received a letter for the Secretary of State for the Colonies, Lord Dartmouth, advising him to "arrest the principal actors and abettors of the Provincial Congress whose proceedings appear in every light to be acts of treason and rebellion." On the night of April 18, 1775, Gage sent out a detachment of troops whose purpose was to seize and destroy the military supplies the Colonists had stored in Concord. According to some historical accounts, he also told the men to arrest Hancock and Sam Adams. His written orders did not mention this. However, the Patriots believed they intended to do so and sent Paul Revere, hired by the Select Men of Boston (Governing Board) to carry messages, to warn them the British were on the move. Hancock wanted to stay and fight, but Adams convinced him he was more valuable as a political leader and they made their escape.

The first battle of the Revolution began in Lexington and Concord on April 19, 1775. It marked the outbreak of open conflict between the Colonists and the British. The British were not able to destroy the Colonists arms and supplies as the Colonists had received word weeks before that the British were aware of the supplies and they relocated them to other areas. The Militia also received word of the British plans in time to notify the area Militias before the battle. The first battle was fought as the sun came up in Lexington. With only 77 men at Lexington, the Colonists were out numbered. Captain John Parker told his Minutemen that day to

"Stand your ground! Don't fire unless fired upon, but if they mean to have a war, let it begin here."

Suddenly a shot rang out and others quickly followed. At the end of the battle, eight Americans were dead and ten wounded with only one British casualty. The outnumbered Minutemen retreated into the woods and the British moved on to Concord to search for the supplies.

At North Bridge, (pictured) five-hundred Minutemen had gathered. Captain Adam Wheeler**, prominent at both Lexington/Concord and Worchester, a deacon and pillar of his community, led one-hundred of the Minutemen from Hubbardston. Job Shattuck† guided three-hundred of the Minutemen to the green at Concord. Captain Isaac Davis commanded the other one-hundred men. They fought and defeated three companies of British troops forcing them to fall back. As more Militiamen arrived, they were able to cause severe losses to the British as they marched back to Boston. The assembled Militias blocked the narrow accesses to Charlestown and Boston and started the *Siege of Boston*. The War had begun.

* History and pictures sourced from Wikipedia the online free Encyclopedia.
** Captain Adam Wheeler (DAR Patriot number #A123747) was born April 29, 1732 in Shrewsbury, Massachusetts and died August 24, 1802 in Hubbardston, Massachusetts. He descends from John Wheeler born 1661 in Concord who descends from George Wheeler born 1605 in Odell, Bedfordshire, England. George, a founder of Concord, and his brothers were the original Wheeler immigrants. History Sourced Ancestry and *The Wheeler Family in America*.
† DAR Records for Job Shattuck #A103088, and Isaac Davis #A030324. Fifty-two members of the Shattuck family and three hundred members of the Davis family are recorded DAR Patriots. Over two-hundred and fifty Wheeler Family Patriots fought in the Revolution, most from the New England Colonies. See the DAR Records.

THE DECLARATION OF INDEPENDENCE

The Second Continental Congress convened on May 10, 1775 in Philadelphia soon after the War for Independence started. They had delegates from twelve of the thirteen colonies. At the time, Georgia had not sent a delegate. Congress managed the Colonial war effort and moved toward adopting the Declaration of Independence. They acted as a de facto government by raising armies, making treaties, printing money, appointing diplomats, and directing strategy for what later became the United States. Except for two, the delegates were the same as those who attended the first Congress. The new delegates were Benjamin Franklin and John Hancock.

Shortly after the Congress convened the President, Payton Randolph, was called back to Virginia. Virginia delegate Thomas Jefferson replaced him. The delegates first elected Henry Middleton as President, but he declined. John Hancock was then elected on May 24. By July 8, Georgia voted to send delegates and they finally arrived on July 20. On July 14, 1775, Congress voted to create the Continental Army out of the Militia units around Boston and on July 15, 1775 appointed Congressman George Washington Commanding General. The Congress vote to extend an "olive branch" as a final attempt at reconciliation to the British Crown, but it was received too late.

Congress issued the *"Declaration of Cause and Necessity of Taking up Arms,"* which stated:
> *"With hearts fortified with these animating reflections, we most solemnly, before God and the world, declare that exerting the upmost energy of these powers, which our beneficent Creator hath graciously bestowed upon us, the arms we have been compelled by our enemies to assume, we will, in defiance of every hazard, with unbaiting firmness and perseverance employ for the preservation of our liberties; being with one mind resolved to die freemen rather than to live as slaves."*

Congress then formally adopted a resolution for independence and created three committees to draft the Declaration, a Model Treaty, and the Articles of Confederation. The delegates delayed voting on the resolution for several months while the delegates returned to their home Colonies to get approval and consolidate support. The resolution was not approved until July 2, 1776. On July 4, the delegates intensely debated the signing of the Declaration of Independence. Their courage wavered. Signing the document meant they were guilty of high treason. Under British law, they could all be hanged. Then someone in the hall mentioned a scaffold, a gibbet...

Suddenly from the back of the room came the voice of the "Professor," the mysterious Rosicrucian philosopher Counte Saint Germaine, (pictured) friend and teacher of Washington and Franklin. His voice rang loud and clear and propelled the delegates into motion,

"Gibbet" he echoed in a fierce voice. The tall slender man rises. He is dressed in a dark robe, although is sweltering in the hall this hot summer day.

"Gibbet"? He questions. "They may stretch our necks on all the gibbets in the land, they may turn every rock into a scaffold, every tree in to a gallows, every home into a grave, and yet the words on that parchment will never die!

They may pour our blood on a thousand scaffolds, and yet from every drop that dyes the axe, or drips on the sawdust of the block, a new martyr to freedom will spring into birth!

The British King may blot out the stars of God from his sky, but he cannot blot out His words written on the parchment there! The words of God may perish - his Word, never!

These words will go forth to the world when our bones are dust. To the slave in the mines they will speak – hope to the mechanic in his workshop – freedom to the coward-kings these words will speak, but not in tones of flattery. No, no! They will speak like the flaming syllables on Belshazzar's wall.

The days of your pride and glory are numbered! The days of judgment and revolution draw near!

Yes, that Parchment will speak to the King in a language sad and terrible as the trump of the Archangel. You have trampled on mankind long enough. At last, the voice of human woe has pierced the ear of God, and called his Judgment down. You have waded on to the thrones through seas of blood – you have trampled on to power over the necks of millions – you have turned the poor mans sweat and blood into robes for your delicate forms, into crowns for your anointed brows. Now Kings – now purpled Hangman of the world – for you come the days of axes, gibbets and scaffolds – for you the wrath of man – for you the lightings of God!-

Look! How the light of your palaces on fire flashes up into the midnight sky!

Now purpled Hangman of the world – turn and beg for mercy!

Where will you find it? Not from God, for you have blasphemed his laws!

Not from the People for you are baptized in their blood!

Here you turn and lo! A Gibbet!

There - and a scaffold looks you in the face!

All around you death – and nowhere pity!

The executioners of the human race kneel down, yes, kneel down upon the sawdust of the scaffold, lay your perfumed heads upon the block – bless the axe as it falls, the axe you sharpened for the poor mans neck!

Such is the message of that Declaration to man, to the Kings of the world! And shall we falter now? And shall we start back appalled when our feet press the very threshold of freedom? Do I see quailing faces around me, when our wives have been butchered – when the hearthstones of our land are red with the blood of little children?

What are these shrinking hearts and faltering voices here, when the very dead of our battlefields arise, and call upon us to sign that Parchment, or be accursed forever?

Sign! If the next moment the gibbet's rope is around your neck! Sign! If the next moment this hall rings with the echo of the falling axe! Sign! By all your hopes in life and death, as husbands – as fathers – as men – sign your names to that parchment or be accursed forever!

Sign - and not for yourselves, but for all ages. For that Parchment will be the Textbook for freedom - the Bible for the Rights of Man forever!

Sign - for the Declaration will go forth to American hearts forever, and speak to those hearts like the voice of God! And its work will not be done, until throughout this wide Continent not a single inch of ground owns the sway of a British King!

Nay, do not start and whisper with surprise! It is a truth, your own hearts witness it - God proclaims it – This Continent is the property of a free people and their property alone! (There is 17-second applause) God, I say, proclaims it!

Look at this strange history of a band of exiles and outcasts, suddenly transformed into a people – look at this wonderful Exodus of the oppressed of the old world into the New, where they came, weak in arms but mighty in God like faith nay, look at this history of your Bunker Hill –your Lexington – where a band of plain farmers mocked and trampled down the panoply of British arms, and then tell me, if you can, that God has not given America to be free? (12 second applause)

It is not given to our poor human intellect to climb the skies, to pierce the council of the Almighty One. But methinks I stand among the awful clouds, which veil the brightness of Jehovah's throne. Methinks I see the recording angel-pale as an angel is pale, weeping as an angel can weep – come trembling up to that throne, and speak his dread message –

Father, the old world is baptized in blood! Father, it is drenched with the blood of millions - butchered in war, in persecution, in slow and grinding oppression. Father – look, with one glance of Thine eternal eye, look over Europe, Asia, Africa, and behold evermore, that terrible sight, man trodden down beneath the oppressor's feet – nations lost in blood – Murder and

Superstition walking hand in hand over the graves of their victims, and not a single voice to whisper, "Hope to man."

He stands there, the Angel, his hands trembling with the black record of human guilt. But hark! The voice of Jehovah speaks out from that awful cloud, "Let there be light again. Let there be a New World. Tell my people – the poor - the trodden down millions, to go out from the Old World. Tell them to go out from wrong, oppression and blood, tell them to go out from this Old World – to build my alter in the New!   (11 second applause)

As God lives, my friends, I believe that to be his voice. Yes, were my soul trembling on the Wing for Eternity, were this hand freezing in death, were this voice choking with the last struggle, I would still, with the last impulse of that soul, with the last wave of that hand, with the last grasp of that voice, implore you to remember this truth – God has given America to be free! (13 second applause)

Yes, as I sank down into the gloomy shadows of the grave, with my last gasp, I would beg you to sign that parchment, in the name of the God whom made the Saviour who redeemed you, in the name of the millions who's very breath is now hushed in intense expectation, as they look up to you for the awful words – You are Free!" (9 second applause)

The work was done. A wild murmur electrified through the hall. Sign, there was no doubt now. The signers rushed forward to sign. Fifty-six traders, farmers, lawyers, and mechanics signed the Declaration of Independence that day and shook the shackles of the world. (There was another 13 second applause followed by the toll of the Liberty Bell)." (See signers of the Declaration of Independence at google.com)

John Hancock was first to sign his name with a large and bold signature. He professed he wanted the King to be able to read it with out his glasses.

The man, "the Professor," who made that speech was the Count of St Germain, sometimes referred to as the "reincarnation of Sir Frances Bacon."* Most historians fail to mention him, but he certainly existed. A year earlier in 1775 he was a guest of the family who was hosting the committee selected by the Continental Congress to create a design for the American Flag. George Washington, Dr. Franklin, Robert Morris, and Colonel Ross were among members of the group. They invited the Professor to join them. The committee accepted the Professor's design and gave it to Betsy Ross to make into the first Flag. It was unfurled in Cambridge, Massachusetts in 1775, when Washington took command of the Continental Army symbolizing the union of the Colonies. This original flag had the white diagonal cross of St. Andrew and imposed upon it the Red Cross of St. George in a field of blue in the upper left-hand corner. The thirteen stripes, seven red and six white, represented the thirteen Colonies. The design implied a continuing tie to Great Britain, which the Colonists were preparing to break.   When it was unfurled, Washington commented that the British probably wondered

why they did not receive some terms of surrender. Although this flag was used for a short time, it was too similar to the British Flag and a new one was designed in 1776 following the spirit of the original one. The crosses were changed to two triangles, one inverted on the other to form a six-point star**, denoting the designer of the original flag was both a Freemason and a Rosicrucian. General Johnson, Colonel Ross, and Dr. Franklin went to see Betsy Ross and enlisted her aid in making the new flag. Betsy, with her sense of design, thought a five-point star was more beautiful than "the Professor's" six-point star accepted by the committee and thus the flag appeared with the five point stars in a circle in the field of blue. This flag was made just before the Declaration was signed. The Professor, often called the "mysterious Stranger," played an important part in American history.

*According to historical accounts in *"Bacon's Royal Parentage,"* Sir Francis Bacon, born in 1561, was the legitimate son of Queen Elizabeth I (the Virgin Queen) and the Earl of Leicester, Robert Dudley, who were secretly married in 1560. The Queen never recognized him publicly as her heir. In a letter to Francis in 1577, the Queen reveals the secret of Bacon's parentage when she states,

> "You are my own son, but you, though truly royal of flesh and masterly spirit shall rule nor England, nor your mother nor reign o'er subject yet to be."

After his birth, Francis was given to the Queen's Lord Keeper of the Great Seal and Keeper of Wards, Sir Nicholas Bacon and his wife Lady Anne Bacon to raise. Lady Bacon was the leading Lady in Waiting for the Queen at the time. Although Elizabeth had another son with Dudley, she never recognized her marriage to Lord Dudley and died giving James I the reign, son of her beheaded cousin Mary Queen of Scotts. Bacon became Lord High Chancellor, the second ranking office in England, under James I.

The following letters give more evidence of these events.

> "I see you withdraw your favor from me, and now I have lost my friends for your sake. I shall lose you too. You have put me like one of those the Frenchmen call 'Enfans perdu'... (lost children); so have you put me into matter's of envy without Place or Strength"
> – Letter from Francis Bacon to Queen Elizabeth.

In a letter to her son, Anthony Bacon, on April 18' 1593 Lady Anne Bacon asks her son to explain the following to Francis,

> "It is not my meaning to treat him (Francis) as a ward; such a word is far from my motherly feeling for him. I mean to do him good."

This reveals he was a ward of Lady and Sir Nicholas Bacon, not their son.

Among the Spanish State Archives, there is a letter from Robert Dudley begging King Phillip to use his influence with Queen Elizabeth to secure his public acknowledgement as Prince Consort.

In the 1895 addition of the 'British Dictionary of National Biography,' Vol. 16, page 114 under 'Dudley', it is reported that Queen Elizabeth was formally betrothed to him, and that she was secretly married to him in Lord Pembroke's house, and was already a mother.

When Queen Victoria (1837-1901) was staying at Wilton House, home of the 13th Earl of Pembroke, he told her that in the monument room was a document that formed written evidence that in 1560 Elizabeth I married the Earl of Leicester (Dudley). The letter revealed, *"The marriage was preformed in secret oath of absolute secrecy."* At the time of the marriage, the Queen was pregnant by Lord Leicester. The French and Spanish Ambassadors reported this and the death of Amy Robsart, (Dudley's first wife) to their courts. They also told the Queen if she confirmed her marriage to Leicester, France and Spain would jointly invade England to remove the Protestant Queen and replace her by a Catholic Monarch, Mary Queen of Scots. (Elizabeth I did not to confirm the marriage). Queen Victoria demanded that this document be produced and, after she examined it, she put it on the fire saying,

"One must not interfere with history."

(The 15th Earl of Pembroke, who died in 1960, gave this information to Andrew Lyell & Emdash. Pembroke was the great grandfather of the present 18th Earl William Herbert).

The second Lord Pembroke was regarded as a partisan of Dudley, Earl of Leicester, and they were very close friends. Pembroke's aunt, Catherine Parr, was Queen Consort, the last wife of Henry VIII.† (Of interest, Elizabeth's mother, Anne Boylen second wife of Henry VIII, was the Marquees of Pembroke in her own right.)

Sir Francis Bacon was a noted philosopher, statesman, scientist, and author who wrote as Shake-speare. He is said by some to have written many or all of the plays by William Shakespeare. He also wrote the Novel, *New Atlantis,* which laid out his vision for a utopian New World with freedom of religion, separation of church and state and freedom of political expression among other freedoms. These ideas were based on the philosophy of the Freemasons and Rosicrucian's in which he held membership. He believed in reincarnation. (Today over half the population of the earth believes in reincarnation. The concept of "past lives" or "many lives" is older than Christianity. In the sixth century at the Second Council of Constantinople in A.D. 553 it was ruled reincarnation was false and punishable by persecution or death). Bacon invested in the original American Colonies (Virginia and South Carolina). His father, Lord Dudley was a friend and advocate of the Puritans. (Elizabeth I other son with Dudley, Sir Robert Dudley (Jr.), left England in 1605 and lived in Tuscany. Pictures of Francis and Robert show their resemblance to their father Dudley in Hilliard's Miniatures).

In an excerpt from a dictated letter near the end of his life, Sir Francis Bacon described his life,

"Born to the throne of England, but denied its authority, my soul did weep in sorrow and frustration. Stirring within my consciousness was a "seed idea," born of the Father of Light, but not yet nourished and developed to the point where it might be efficaciously utilized by mankind. Yet such is the confusion of the outer consciousness, that often by effort of human will such ideas are aborted or stillborn before their time. This wisdom of abiding in the will of the Father (who will see that the fruit of his seeds mature at the right time) comes with suffering, with illumination and with grace. So I learned the world brotherhood was not to be the outcome of a dynasty of human kings but a spiritual bond of selflessness, impersonal service and shared vision at a later day..."

(It was highly rumored in 1554 the Queen had another son Piers, with her cousin Sir Thomas Butler. The relationship deeply upset Dudley, In Britain today, the above information about Queen Elizabeth I is considered rumor only. The current theory is that Elizabeth I was either a hermaphrodite or unable to bear children because her father, Henry VIII, had syphilis).

*"The Professor,"Counte De Saint Germain, was born in 1712 to Prince Francis II Rakoczi of Transylvania in the central part of Romania and died February 1784. He was a European courtier with an interest in science and arts. He was well educated. He studied a number of rare old books and was very interested in ancient manuscripts. He wrote extensively and seemed at home on any subject. Saint Germain was prominent in the European high society of the mid-1700s. He was a Freemason and Rosicrucian. Some said he was the reincarnation of Francis Bacon "who's fondest hope was the creation of a society of free men in which his Freemason and Rosicrucian principals would govern the social, economic, and political life of the new nation."

**A Masonic symbol of Kabbalistic origin, Kabbalah seeks to define the nature of the universe and the human being, the nature and purpose of existence).

†History, letters and pictures sourced from Wikipedia, Bacon's Royal Parentage by Francis Carr and Lawrence Gerald, *The Great Secret: Count St. Germain by Raymond Bernard,* Americans Weebly free pages.

CHAPTER II: THE FOUNDING FATHERS
GEORGE WASHINGTON AND THE SCOTTISH PROPHECY

About the time of Washington's birth in 1732, a Scottish Prophecy predicted his future. A seemingly insignificant book held in the Library of Congress is one published in 1724 by a Scottish Bart., Sir William Hope, pictured. The book title is the *Vindication of the true Art of Self Defense,* engraved with the badge of the Royal Society of Swordsmanship and written underneath "The Private Library of Sir William Hope." *What makes this book of extraordinary interest is a prediction by Sir William Hope on the destiny of America written on the fly pages, signed, and dated fifty-two years before the Revolution. At the time of George Washington's birth, there was no thought in the Colonies of independence from England. Hope studied astrology and based his poem on this influence.*

He wrote:

> "'Tis Chaldee says his fate is great
> Whose stars do bear him fortune
> Of thy near fate Amerika
> I read in stars a prophecy
> Fourteen divided, twelve the same,
> Sixteen in halfs...each hold a name,
> Four, eight, seven, six—added ten--
> The lifeline's mark of four great men."

The prophecy covers the years from 1732 to 1901. Hope has selected four future Presidents by totaling the number of years they lived. He added four plus eight, plus seven, plus six to equal 25 and then added ten to get 250. At the time of their deaths Washington was 68, Abraham Lincoln was 56, Benjamin Harrison was 68, and William McKinley was 58. The total of these years are 250.

The next twelve lines focus on George Washington and the Colonies struggle for independence.

> "The day is cradled, far beyond the sea
> One starred by fate to rule both bond and free."

The prophecy is dated 1724 but covers the year Washington was born (1732) beyond the sea in Virginia and believed to refer to slavery that existed in the Colonies.

> "Add double four, thus fix the destined day
> When servile knees unbend 'neath freedom's sway"

By double four, we read 44, which if added to his birth date 1732, gives 1776, the year of the American Declaration of Independence.

> "Place six 'fore ten, then read the Patriot's name
> Whose deeds shall link him to a deathless fame
> Add double 4, thus fix the destined day"

There are six letters in
 the name George and ten in Washington, and this Cabala when added to the previous and subsequent descriptions, can leave no doubt as to the man intended in the prophecy.

> *"Whose growing love and ceaseless trust wrong none*
> *And catch truth's colors from the glowing sun!*
> *Deaths door shall clang while yet his century waits*
> *His planets point the way to other's pending fates"*

These lines contain not only a glowing tribute, but also an exact bit of prophecy. Washington died on December 14, 1799, just 17 days before his century passed into history.

> *"Till all the names on freedom's scroll shall fade*
> *Two tombs be built, his loft cenotaph be made"*

Freedoms scroll, the Declaration of Independence, began to fade, and is now preserved under yellow cellophane. George Washington rested in two tombs, his "lofty Cenotaph" is his 555 foot monument, the tallest memorial every constructed in the memory of a man.

> *"Full six times ten the years must onward glide,*
> *Nature their potent help, a constant, prudent guide.*

If six times ten, or sixty years, be added to the death of Washington, the result is 1859 when John Brown raided Harper's Ferry and was hanged for attempting to incite a slave revolt, a circumstance leading directly to the United States of America engaging in the great civil war to preserve the freedom of all it's people.

> *"Then fateful seven 'fore seven shall sign heroic son*
> *Whom Mars and Jupiter strike down before his work is done.*
> *When cruel fate shall pierce, though artless of its sword,*
> *Who leaves life's gloomy stage without one farewell word.*
> *A softly beaming star, half veiled by Mar's red cloud*
> *Virtue, his noblest cloak, shall form a fitting shroud."*

There are seven letters in Abraham, and seven letters in Lincoln. He is the heroic son elected in 1860. (The poem goes on to make a connection to Lincoln, President Harrison, and President McKinley in the next verses).

The prophecy ends with four more lines:

> *"These truths prophetic shall completion see ere times*
> *Deep grave receives the nineteenth century*
> *All planets, stars, twelve signs, and horoscope*
> *Attests these certain truths foretold by William Hope."*

Following this is a statement that the prophecy was 'writ at Cornhill, London in 1732.' At the bottom of the page are four other lines written by some later member of the Hope family as a tribute to the memory of Sir William Hope:

> *"The learned hand that writ these lines no more shall pen for me,*
> *Yet voice shall speak and pulse beat for long posterity*
> *This soul refined for love of kind bewailed life's labors spent*
> *Then found this truth, his search from youth, Greatness is God Accident... William Hope."*

The critics of the Hope Prophecy have tried to disprove it as a forgery but no evidence has been found. The book has been in the Library of Congress for many years. The predictions relating to both Harrison and McKinley took place after the book was placed in the Library of Congress and were true. It is reasonable to assume the Hope Prophecy is a genuine example of fore knowledge concerning the future of the United States of America.

*History and pictures sourced from Wikipedia and "The Secret Destiny of America" by Manley Hall

GEORGE WASHINGTON – THE EARLY YEARS

George Washington, born February 22, 1732, was a third generation American. His great grandfather, John Washington, came to the colonies in 1657 and owned land in both England and the Colonies. His grandfather, father, and half brothers were all educated in England. George's father Augustine married Jane Butler, daughter of Caleb Butler, and they had three sons. Jane died in 1729 and he married Mary Ball. George was the oldest of their six children. The family owned several properties in Virginia. George lived first on Pope's Creek. His father later moved the family to Little Hunting Creek, a Plantation on the Potomac, known as Mount Vernon. In 1738, the family moved again to Ferry Farm near Fredericksburg, Virginia where George spent most of his early years. The family was somewhat prosperous, but after the early death of his father George's mother struggled to keep their home together with the help of her husband's sons from the previous marriage. His mother was very protective and demanding and seldom praised her children.

George became the ward of his older half brother, Laurence, who schooled him and gave him a good up bringing. George was not able to attend school in England as planned and had only an elementary education. Laurence tried to get George into the Navy at age fourteen to get him away from his protective mother, but she would not let him go. At fifteen, George "became personally and professionally" attached to William Fairfax, his neighbor and the prominent English family of his half brother's wife, Anne. Anne helped George learn dancing and the proper etiquette of the day. Before the age of sixteen, George had transcribed the 110 French *Rules of Civility & Decent Behavior in Company and Conversation* and written them in his schoolbook. He followed the rules through out his life including the following:

- *Every action done in Company ought to be with some sign of respect to those that are present.*
- *Sleep not when others speak, Sit not when others stand, Speak not when you should hold your peace, and walk not on when others stop.*
- *Undertake not what you cannot preform but be careful to keep your promise.*
- *Speak not evil of the absent for it is unjust. Think before you speak*
- *Labor to keep alive in your breast that little celestial fire called conscience.*
- *Be not apt to relate news if you know not the truth there of.*
- *Speak not injurious words neither in jest or earnest, Scoff at none though they give occasion.*
- *Strive not with your superiors in argument, but always submit your judgment to others with modesty.*

*History and picture sourced from Wikipedia

THE FRENCH – INDIAN WAR AND THE INDIAN PROPHECY

In 1754, the French and Indian War erupted with England over the territorial right of the Ohio Valley. The Colonies joined with England in the fight. The Virginia Governor appointed George Washington an ambassador to carry his message to the French objecting to their claim. The French did not back down so after his return to Virginia, Washington began to raise troops and was made Lieutenant Colonel. He set out to re-take Fort Duquesne from the French. He built a stockade sixty miles from the Fort called Fort Necessity. Washington received very few reinforcements, but delivered the first strike against the French with only four hundred men. He killed one of the French leaders and ten of his men, taking twenty-one prisoners. He advanced on the Fort again, but was met with twelve hundred troops and had to fall back to Fort Necessity. The French surrounded the Fort and after a brave fight, the French General eventually offered surrender terms to Washington and he was allowed to leave the Fort with all of his men and equipment. Even thought Washington received public honor for his brave stand against overwhelming odds, he was disillusioned with the British over the lack of reinforcements and went home to Mount Vernon.

One of the most experienced officers in England, General Braddock, heard of Washington's velour and asked him to become one of his aids, retaining his former commission. Washington's mother, who feared for his life, tried to persuade him to stay home and not to accept. He reply was,

> *"The God, to whom you commend me Madam, when I set out upon a more perilous errand, defended me from harm, and I trust He will do so now. Do not you?"*

Although Washington tried to convince General Braddock to fight with guerilla tactics like the French and Indians, Braddock did not take the advice from his junior officer. The morning of July 9, 1755, the General moved his army toward Fort Duquesne to try to re-take the Fort. He engaged the enemy 10 miles from the Fort. They were met with a barrage of gunfire. Braddock lined his troops up in the regular British fashion and they cut them down like flies. His troops could not see to shoot their enemy, hidden behind the rocks  and trees. They began to panic and flee the battle. The Virginia men dropped behind the rocks and trees using the same tactics as the Indians and firing only when they could see a target. Braddock, thinking they were cowards, became angry and tried to rally his troops. He raced back and forth across the battlefield. He was finally wounded after having several horses shot out from under him. Washington continued to carry out the General's orders riding back and forth among the troops completely exposed. The picture of the French and Indian War with Braddock's defeat is above.

A friend of Washington's, Dr. James Claik, who was a witness to the battle said,

> *"I expected every moment to see him fall. His duty and situation exposed him to every danger. Nothing but the superintending care of Providence could have saved him from the fate of all around him."*

Washington finally gathered the fatally wounded General, what was left of the Virginia troops and covered the retreat of the army. It was one the most lopsided battles in American history. From then on,

Washington wore General Broderick's red sash at formal occasions in memory of his bravery. (Pictured is Washington in Battle.

After Washington returned to Fort Cumberland, he wrote a letter to his mother and one to his brother. He told his mother he was safe and to his brother, John, he wrote the following:

> "….But by the all-powerful dispensations of Providence, I have been protected beyond all probability of expectation, for I had four bullets through my coat and two horses shot under me, yet escaped unhurt, although death was leveling my companions on every side of me!"

Fifteen years after the battle, Washington and his childhood friend, Dr. Craik, were on an expedition to the west exploring lands. Near the Kanawha and Ohio rivers, a group of Indians came to them with an interpreter. Their leader was the old Chief, Pontiac, pictured. A council fire was started, and when they were all gathered around it, the Chief spoke to Washington:

> "I am a Chief and ruler over my tribes, my influence spreads to the great lakes and the far Blue Mountains. I have traveled a long and weary path that I might see the young warrior (Washington) of the Great Battle.
>
> It was on the day when the white man's blood mixed with the streams of our forests, that I first beheld this chief. I called to my young men and said, mark yon tall and daring warrior? He is not of the red coat tribe, he hath an Indian wisdom, and his warriors fight as we do – himself is alone exposed.
>
> Quick let your aim be certain and he dies.
>
> Our rifles were leveled, rifles which, but for him, knew not how to miss- 'twas all in vain, a power mightier far than we, shielded him from harm. He cannot die in battle. I am old and soon shall be gathered to the great council fire of my fathers in the land of shades, but ere I go, there is something bids me speak in the voice of prophecy.
>
> Listen! The Great Spirit protects that man, and guides his destinies – He will become the chief of nations, and a people yet unborn will hail him as the founder of a mighty empire."

(Dr. Craik, George Washington's life long friend, who was with him and witnessed this remarkable scene, told this narrative to Custis. It was first published in 1828)

Nearly eighty years after the battle, a gold seal belonging to Washington, that bore his initials, was found on that same battlefield. A bullet had shot it off his coat.

*History and pictures source from Wikipedia, Recollections and private memoirs of Washington by George Washington Parke Custis, edited by Benson J. Lossing, Vol. 1, page 248, from the Diary of George Washington, 1788 to 1791, and Chief picture from free download at old pictures.

WASHINGTON – POLITICS AND RELIGION

Washington listed his religion as Episcopalian, which at the time of his birth, was officially the Church of England and the required religion of King George II. As he got older, he seldom attended church. His personal diaries indicate he did not attend regularly on Sunday while at home in Mount Vernon, attending only fourteen to sixteen times a year. Instead, he wrote letters, went foxhunting, and conducted business. However, he engaged in daily morning and evening devotion. He was often seen on his knees with his bible in hand. Although he seldom attended, he was actually a registered member of several churches. He served in the Anglican Church as a vestryman for over a decade, the lowest rung of the political ladder, which was required in Virginia at the time for anyone serving in the House of Burgesses or other government offices.

It was not until 1786 that Virginia enacted the Virginia Statute for Religious Freedom and they were able to break from the Church of England. Before this, anyone desiring to be a vestryman and serve in the House of Burgesses was required to sign the following oath:

> *I, _____, do declare that I will be conformable to the Doctrine and Discipline of the Church of England, as by law established.* - George Washington signed the oath August 19, 1765.

He went to church more often while he was traveling. While serving during the First Continental Congress in Philadelphia, he attended three out of the seven Sundays, attending the Anglican, Quaker, and Catholic Churches. He did not take communion as he stated which is backed by the testimony of several of the ministers of the churches he attended. He did believe that religion was very important for morality in government and that a nation could not be moral long without it. **He was wary of fundamentalism and believed the greatest enemy of religion and freedom was not the devil nor someone else's religion, but fanaticism.** Modern day fundamentalists are no different. In his farewell address, he stated that Religion and Morality are indispensable to political prosperity. Washington believed that all religious practices were beneficial to humans and strongly supported religious tolerance.

In 1752 at the age of 20, Washington became a member of the Freemasons in Fredericksburg, Virginia, as was the custom for young men of means. On March 3rd 1753 he became a Fellow Craft and in August of 1753 it is recorded that he received his 3rd degree that of a Master Mason, *"with the Royal Arch degree being worked four months and eighteen days previously."* He attended Masonic meetings throughout his life and in retirement became Grand Master of the newly formed Alexandria Virginia Lodge No. 22. The record also states he and his future General Lafayette were members of  the same Lodge and shared a great friendship. He received two masonic aprons from Lafayette, both made by the General's wife. One had the Royal Arch Degree embroidered on it, which is the salient, spiritual degree of Freemasonry. The Royal Arch Degree is the essences of mystical teachings and is to give man a glimpse of what lies beyond death and to show him its intimate connection with what lays this side of death.

By the time Washington (pictured) was a master Mason, he was a Colonel and Commander of the Northern Military District of Virginia. Washington expressed his favorable opinion of the Mason on several occasions. In 1792 in an address to the Massachusetts Lodge, he stated that in his opinion "the Masonic Institution's liberal principals are founded on the immutable laws of truth and justice and whose grand object is to promote the happiness of the human race." The Freemason philosophy was the foundation for the religious, educational, political, and social reform that Washington and the founding fathers looked to in forming the doctrines establishing the United States. Some historians site that 50 of the 56 signers of the Declaration of Independence were Freemasons. The Monarchs of Europe and the Church authorities were opposed to these doctrines. Washington's involvement and leadership in Freemasonry gave him the confidence that America's military secrets would be safe among his fellow Freemasons.*

The Lodge's ritual function is to elevate the participant's consciousness and live by the Golden Rule. He surrounded himself with fellow Freemasons and according to General Lafayette, Washington *"never knowingly gave independent command to anyone who was not a Freemason."* Nearly all of his official family and most of his officers who shared his confidence were *"his brethren in the mystic tie."*

At his inauguration as President of the United States, he took the oath of office on a Masonic Bible from St John's Lodge in New York. He believed in the underlying principles and philosophy of Freemasonry, which are *"the Brotherhood of man and the Fatherhood of God."*

*In retirement, Washington became charter Master of the newly chartered Alexandria Lodge No. 22, sat for a portrait in his Masonic regalia ~1798.
**History and pictures sourced from Wikipedia on Google.

THE ROSICRUCIAN PROPHECY

Washington's involvement in the American Rosicrucian Supreme Council is documented in an account entitled "The Fulfillment of the Prophecy, the consecration of Washington, The Deliverer. *(A copy of the Prophecy is in the Library of Congress).*

The Wissahickon Creek* in Philadelphia has a special meaning for members of the Rosicrucian's. To many Americans it is synonymous with a pure mystic religion with the freedom of all religious sects. Here many sectarians established themselves years before the founding fathers arrived. They were a fellowship of noblemen of Europe who came to be free to worship God in their own way, far from the Courts of Kings. The Rosicrucian Order, created in the early 17th century, is devoted to Theosophy, the study of God and the spirit realm. Reincarnation is part of their doctrine. It gives a permanent and forceful basis for ethics and is the most important of all the Theosophical doctrines. Then as today, one does not join the Rosicrucian's, but rather one becomes a Rose Cross through the mastery of Spiritual or Mental Alchemy, which attempts to transmute the evil in man into that which is divine. The secret doctrine of the Rosicrucian's is built on the esoteric truth of the ancient past. Some of these truths are offered in the higher degrees of Masonry. The Masonic Rose Croix, 18th degree of the Ancient and Accepted Scottish Rite and the pinnacle of the French Rite, signifies the rose (Christ) and the Cross.

Famous members and past Masters of the Society include Queen Elizabeth I's friend, poet and philosopher Dante Alighieri, her astrologer, mathematician and adviser Dr. John Dee, lawyer and philosopher Sir Francis Bacon, Robert Fludd theological philosopher who participated in the English translation of the King James Version of the Bible, Robert Boyle and Christopher Wren. The Order aimed to advance the study and application of ancient science, numerology, and cosmic law. It also encouraged the ideals of Egyptian Therapeutate by promoting international medical aid for the poor. The International Red Cross uses their symbol. They preached liberty, equality, and fraternity and saw themselves the challengers of tyrannical oppression of any kind. The Roman Church condemned the

Order. During the time of the intolerant Puritans in England, who called them occultists and heretics, they went under ground and resurfaced after the Stuart Restoration. Famous Americans included George Washington, Ben Franklin, Thomas Jefferson, John Adam, and Charles Thompson.

The early American brotherhood established a Monastery in the Wilderness on the Wissahickon Creek, just outside of Philadelphia at the time. About a mile from the Monastery, another nobleman of wealth and position lived with his two children. His religious beliefs were not tolerated by the churches in Europe so after his wife died he sold his castle and holdings and moved to the Wissahickon. Here he became known as the "Priest of the Wissahickon." He studied the book of Revelations for seventeen years and as the result of his studies, he often affirmed:

"The Old World is sunk in all manner of crime and the New World has been given to man as a last refuge, even as the Ark was given to Noah and his children. The New World is the last alter of human freedom left on the surface of the globe, never shall the footsteps of Kings pollute its soil. It is the last hope of man. God has spoken and it is so. Amen."

On the evening of December 31, 1773, the Priest and his son went to the Chapel to pray as they did every evening. The hunters in the area were familiar with the sounds of prayer coming from the little chapel. This night the Priest broke the silence. He said,

"At the third hour past midnight the Deliverer shall come."

As his son pondered his words, he repeated.

"Tonight he will come. At the third hour past midnight, he shall come through yonder door and take upon himself his great mission to free the New World from the yoke of Tyrants. All is ready for his coming. Behold the crown (a wreath of fresh laurel), the flagon of anointing oil, the Bible and the Cross."

Hours passed as the son knelt in prayer and the father paced back and forth. After midnight, the son tried to prepare his father gently for disappointment. Perhaps it was not the time. His father answered.

"At the third hour past midnight the deliverer will come."

The lad returned to his prayers and the Priest of Wissahickon continued his watch. Finally, the clock in the hall struck three. Then there came footsteps as a tall stranger of commanding presence entered the door of the chapel and spoke:

"Friends, I have lost my way in the forest. Can you direct me to the right way?"
The Priest answered with, *"Thou hast found the way to usefulness and immortal renown."*

Wondering, the stranger stepped closer to see if he were being mocked; but the Priest of Wissahickon rapidly questioned him.

"Did he come from the city?"
"Yes."
"What was the burden upon his heart; was it not his country's welfare?"
"Yes."
"Was he not troubled about the right of a subject to raise his hand against his King?"
"Yes!"

Then said the Priest to the amazed stranger,
"Thou art called to do a great work. Kneel before this alter and here, in the silence of the night amid the depth of these wild woods, I will anoint Thee Deliverer of this great land."

Immediately this peerless stranger, before whom ten thousand might bow their heads, knelt before the white alter and placed his hands upon the Bible.

Then, says the Legend, these words fell from the lips of the Priest of Wissahickon:
"Thou art called to do the great work of a Champion and Deliverer! Soon thou wilt ride to battle at the head of legions – soon thou wilt lead a people on to freedom – soon thy sword will gleam like a meteor over the ranks of war."
The Priest continued.
"Dost thou promise when the appointed time arrives, thou wilt be found ready, sword in hand, to fight for thy Country and thy God?"

"I do," came the solemn answer.

"Dost thou promise in the hour of thy glory, when a nation shall bow before thee, as in the fierce moment when thou shalt behold thy soldiers starving for want of bread, to remember the great truth written in these words. 'I am but the minister of God in this great work of a nation's freedom'?"

Clearly, firmly, came the answer, *"I do promise!"*

"Then in His name who gave the New World to millions of the human race, as the last alter of their rights, I do consecrate thee its Deliverer!"

Then the Priest of Wissahickon dipped his finger in the anointing oil and made the sign of the cross on the strangers forehead and was about to place the wreath of laurel on his head when the Priest's daughter appeared in the doorway. She reached for the wreath placing it on the stranger's head, as the Priest said,
"When the time comes, go forth in victory, on thou brow no conqueror's blood-red wreath, but this crown of fadeless laurel."

Then the lad spoke,

> "Rise the Champion leader of a People. Rise, Sir, and take this hand which has never yet been given to man. I know not thy name, yet on this Book, I swear to be faithful even to death." Then Paul, for that was his name, buckled a sword to the Stranger's side.

When the ceremony was finished, the stranger stood in the chapel in towering strength and said these words:

> "From you, old man, I take the vow. From you, fair girl, the laurel. From you, brave friend, the sword. On this Book I swear to be faithful unto all!"

A moment later, the stranger vanished into the forest. That was New Year's Night in 1774. In the darkest hour of the Revolution, the chapel was burned and the three slept in their graves beside the Wissahickon."**

Years later when America was a Nation and George Washington was the President, he went to the Wissahickon looking for the Chapel and the three that sent him on his mission that New Years Night. He found the ruins of the Chapel and the three graves. That night at a party in Philadelphia, many wondered why the President was sad and thoughtful. Later after his death, it was revealed that Washington had been a member of the Rosicrucian World Council.

It was here in Philadelphia close to the Wissahickon, the American Republic was founded, where the constitution was first conceived and where the Grand Temple of the Rosy Cross was formed. The Wissahickon Creek is now a part of the Fairmont Park system in Philadelphia and the Wissahickon Valley is one of six-hundred National Natural Landmarks in the United States.†

---

*Painting above of the Wissahickon Creek by the Author, Joan Wheeler LaGrone
**Taken from "The Legend of the Wissahickon" from the Library of Congress, Washington, D.C. by Guy W. Ballard, rewritten in 1930. The original Author and publisher are unknown.
†"The stories above are included in The Book of the Rosicrucian" by Clymer 1946.

WASHINGTON BEFORE THE REVOLUTION

In 1758, Washington retired from his Virginia regiment. His experience with the military during the French and Indian war was frustrating due to slow support from the Colonial legislature and the poorly trained troops. He resigned his commission and retired to his home in Mount Vernon. (He acquired the property after his brother Laurence, died in 1752). Shortly after leaving the army, he married Martha Dandridge Custis, a rich young widow with two surviving children ages four and six. They were married in 1759 and had a very contented marriage. Both were twenty-seven years of age. Martha and George did not have any  children of their own, but Washington was devoted to his stepchildren. Washington committed himself to the care and development of his land holdings. Martha brought five plantations to the marriage and over a hundred slaves, which she controlled.

Washington soon entered politics and in 1758 elected to the House of Burgesses. At first, he did not support the colonies seeking independence. However, he changed his thinking after the British **Proclamation Act of 1763,** which banned the colonization of British subjects west of the Appalachian Mountains and ordered those who had already colonized the Ohio Valley to abandon their homes and move back east. Later, Acts that were more repressive were passed including **The Stamp Act of 1765,** which taxed the Colonist without their consent or representation, and **the Townshend Act of 1767,** which put duties on glass, paper, lead, paints, and tea. To him these were fundamental violations by the Crown of the rights of the Colonies. In 1769, he introduced a resolution in the House of Burgesses to boycott British goods until these Acts were repealed. After the **Intolerable Acts of 1774**, passed to punish the Colonist for dumping the tea into Boston Harbor, Washington chaired a meeting where the Fairfax Resolves were adopted calling for the convening of the Continental Congress and use of armed resistance as a last resort. He was selected a delegate to the First Continental Congress in March of 1775. After the Battles of Lexington and Concord in April of 1775, the disputes between the Colonies and Great Britain escalated to armed conflict. Washington attended the Second Continental Congress at Independence Hall in Philadelphia dressed in his uniform and ready for war. He was appointed Commanding General June 15, 1775.

*History and pictures sourced from Wikipedia, original picture of Washington above, reproduction painting by author. Picture of young George Washington in the forest from free pages at genealogy, roots web, and ancestry

WASHINGTON COMMANDER IN CHIEF

On June 15, George Washington was appointed Major General and Commander in Chief of the Continental Army. Washington's experience and training had been, to this point, only in fighting frontier warfare. He did not have the experience in open field fighting like the British or commanding large numbers of troops. However, what he lacked in experience he made up for in courage and determination. He seem to have an uncanny ability to know what the British Generals were planning, some even called it "magical."

At Cambridge, Massachusetts on July 3, 1775, Washington took command of the ill-trained Continental Army in a war that lasted six years. It was here the first American flag was unfurled. The odds were against them from the beginning, but determination was high. He tasted victory in early 1776 in Boston when his artillery, forced the British to withdraw. He withdrew his Army to New York, but in June the British sent over a new commander, General Howe, who defeated Washington and they lost New York. On Christmas Eve 1776, Washington crossed the Delaware and in a surprise attack, defeated the British at Trenton. A few days later, he dealt another blow to the British at Princeton.

General Howe's strategy was to capture the Colonies major cities, thinking if the Americans were deprived of their cities, they would soon surrender. He set out for Philadelphia and defeated Washington at Brandywine. To his surprise, capturing New York and Philadelphia did not unseat the colonial power or government. They simply moved to another location. In the late summer of 1777, the British tried to split off the rebellion in New York, but the strategy backfired and the British lost 6,200 troops at Saratoga. The victory was a major turning point and France allied itself with the Americans.

In the winter of 1777, Washington wintered his Army at Valley Forge. By the spring of 1778, his army was starving. They were camped along the Schuylkill River when dramatically the famine totally ended. Thousands of fat Shad swimming up the Schuylkill to spawn filled the river. The soldiers crowded the riverbank and the Calvary was ordered into

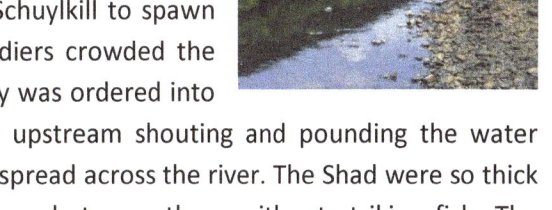

the riverbed. They rode upstream shouting and pounding the water driving the fish into nets spread across the river. The Shad were so thick a pole could not be driven between them without striking fish. The soldiers continued to net the fish day after day until the army was completely stuffed with fish and hundreds of barrels of shad were salted down for future use. Washington received a vision while at Valley Forge that would encourage him to continue the fight for freedom.

*History and pictures sourced from Wikipedia and the online Shad Journal.

GEORGE WASHINGTON'S VISION

Little has been written about Washington's metaphysical leanings, the prophecies about him, and the vision he had at Valley Forge. His vision may have been the deciding factor in holding his rag tag army together despite the many hardships they endured. He often prayed in secret for aid from God for his destitute army. After several defeats, Washington and his army retreated to Valley Forge where he decided to spend the winter of 1777. The following is the recorded testimony of the story of Washington's Vision as given to a reporter, Wesley Bradshaw, by Anthony Sherman, a ninety-one year old former soldier who served with Washington at Valley Forge. He claimed Washington gave him this true story. The interview took place on 4 July 1849 in Independence Hall and first published in the National Tribune in 1859. The latest printing was in 1950. This is the recorded testimony.

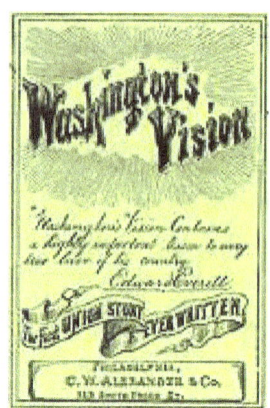

Bradshaw met Sherman in Independence Square on the 4th of July 1849. He was then 91 years of age and had come to see the Hall once more before he died. At 3:30 Sherman said,

> *"Let's go into the Hall. I want to tell you of an incident in Washington life – one, which no one alive knows of, except myself, and if you live you will before long see it verified.*
>
> *From the opening of the Revolution, we experience all phases of fortune, now good and now ill, one time victorious, and another conquered. The darkest period we had, I think, was when Washington, after several reverses, retreated to Valley Forge where he resolved to spend the winter of 1777. Ah! I have often seen the tears coursing down our dear commander's care worn cheeks, as he would be conversing with a confidential officer about the condition of his poor soldiers. You have doubtless heard the story of Washington going into the thicket to pray. Well, it was not only true, but he used often to pray in secret for aid and comfort from God, the interposition whose divine providence brought us safely through the darkest days and tribulation.*
>
> *One day, I remember it well, the chilly wind whistled through the leafless trees, the skies were cloudless and the sun shown brightly, he remained in his quarters all afternoon alone. When he came out, I noticed his face was a shade paler than usual, and there seem to be something on his mind of more than ordinary importance. Returning just after dusk, he dispatched an orderly to the quarters of the officer I mentioned, who was previously in attendance. After a preliminary conversation of about a half hour, Washington, gazing upon his companion with that strange look of dignity which he alone could command, he said to the latter:"*

(Anthony Sherman quotes the vision)

> *"I do not know whether it is owing to the anxiety of my mind, or what, but this afternoon, as I was sitting at this table engaged in preparing a dispatch, something seemed to disturb me. Looking up, I beheld standing opposite me a singularly beautiful female. So astonished was I, for I had given strict orders not to be disturbed, that it was moments before I found language to inquire into the cause of her presence. A second, a third and even a fourth time did I repeat my*

question, but received no answer from my mysterious visitor except a slight raising of the eyes. By this time, I felt strange sentiments spreading through me. I would have risen, but the riveted gaze of the being before me rendered volition impossible. I assayed once more to address her, but my tongue had become useless, even though itself had become paralyzed. A new influence, mysterious, potent, irresistible, took possession of me. All I could do was to gaze steadily, vacantly at my unknown visitor. Gradually, the surrounding atmosphere seemed as though becoming filled with sensations luminous. Everything about me seemed to rarify, the mysterious visitor herself becoming more airy, and yet more distinct to my sight than before. I now began to feel as one dying, or rather to experience the sensations, which I have sometimes imagine accompany dissolution. I did not think, I did not reason, I did not move; all were alike impossible. I was only conscious of gazing fixedly, vacantly at my companion.

Presently I heard a voice say, **'Son of the Republic, look and learn,'** while at the same time my visitor extended her arm eastwardly. I now beheld a heavy white vapor at some distance rising fold upon fold. This gradually dissipated, and I looked upon a strange scene. Before me, lay spread out one vast plain, all the countries of the world -- Europe, Asia, Africa, and America. I saw rolling and tossing between Europe and America the billows of the Atlantic and between Asia and America lay the Pacific. **'Son of the Republic,'** said the same mysterious voice as before, **'look, and learn.'** "At that moment I beheld a dark, shadowy being, like an angel floating in mid-air, between Europe and America, dipping water out of the ocean in the hollow of each hand. He sprinkled some upon America with his right hand, while with his left had he cast some on Europe. Immediately a dark cloud raised from these countries and joined in mid ocean. For a while it remained stationary, and then moved slowly westward, until it enveloped America in its murky folds. Sharp flashes of lightning flashed through it at intervals, and I heard the smothering groans and cries of the American people.

A second time the angel dipped water from the ocean and sprinkled it out as before. The dark cloud was then drawn back in the ocean, who's heaving billows it sank from view. A third time I heard the mysterious voice saying **'Son of the Republic, look and learn.'** I cast my eyes upon America and beheld villages and towns and cities springing up one after another until the whole land from the Atlantic to the Pacific was dotted with them. Again, I heard the mysterious voice say, **'Son of the Republic, the end of the century cometh, look, and learn.'**

At this, the dark, shadowy angel turned his face southward and from Africa, I saw an ill-omened spectre approach our land. It flitted slowly over every town and city. The inhabitants presently set themselves in battle array against each other. As I continued looking, I saw a bright angel, on whose brow rested a crown of light, on which was traced the word "Union," bearing the American flag, which he placed between the divided nation and said, 'Remember ye are brethren.' Instantly the inhabitants casting from them their weapons became friends once more and united around the National Standard.

Again, I heard the mysterious voice saying, **'Son of the Republic, look and learn.'** *At this, the dark, shadowy angel placed a trumpet to his mouth and blew three distinct blasts; and taking* *water from the ocean, he sprinkled it on Europe, Asia, and Africa. Then my eyes beheld a fearful scene: from each of these countries arose thick black clouds that were joined into one. And throughout this mass gleamed a dark red light by which I saw hordes of men, who, moving with the cloud marched by land and sailed by sea to America, which country was enveloped in the volume of the cloud. I dimly saw these vast armies devastate the whole country and burn the villages, towns and cities that I beheld were springing up. As my ears listened to the thundering of the cannon, clashing of swords, and the shouts and cries of millions in mortal combat, I heard again the mysterious voice saying, **'Son of the Republic, look and learn.'** When the voice had ceased, the dark, Shadowy angel placed his trumpet once more to his mouth and blew a long and fearful blast.*

*Instantly a light as of a thousand suns shown down from above me, and pierced and broke into fragments the dark cloud which enveloped America. At the same moment the angel, upon whose head still shown the word "Union," and who bore our national flag in one hand and a sword in the other, descended from the heavens attended by legions of white spirits. These immediately joined the inhabitants of America, who perceived were well nigh overcome, but who immediately taking courage again, closed up their broken ranks and renewed the battle. Again, against the fearful noise of the conflict, I heard the mysterious voice saying, **'Son of the Republic, look and learn.'** As the voice ceased, the shadowy angel for the last time dipped water from the ocean and sprinkled it on America. Immediately the dark clouds rolled back, together with the armies it had brought, leaving the inhabitants of the land victorious.*

*Then once more I beheld the villages, towns and cities springing up where I had seen them before, while the bright angel, planting the azure standard he had brought in the mist of them, cried with a loud voice, **'while the stars remain, and the heavens send down dew upon the earth, so long will the Union last.'** And, taking from his brow the crown on which was blazoned the word "Union," he placed it upon the Standard, while the people, kneeling down, said, 'Amen.'*

*The scene instantly began to fade and dissolve, and I at last saw nothing but the rising, curling vapor I first beheld. This also disappearing, I found myself once more gazing upon the mysterious visitor, who, in the same voice I had heard before, said, **'Son of the Republic, what you have seen is thus interpreted: Three great perils will come upon the Republic. The most fearful is the third, passing which the whole world united will not prevail against her. <u>Let every child of the Republic learn to live for his God, his land and the Union</u>.'** With these words the vision vanished, and I started from my seat, and I felt I had seen a vision wherein had been shown me the birth, progress and destiny of the United States."**

"Such, my friends," concluded (Sherman) the venerable narrator, *"were the words I heard from General Washington's own lips, and America will do well to profit by them."*

Washington had always believed in the Almighty. He was driven by a love of freedom and justice and a deep belief in Divine Guidance. As the Prophets of old were shown the destiny of mankind, so was Washington given a vision of our nation's destiny. Despite the numerous hardships and setbacks, he was determined to persevere and fulfill his own destiny. He spoke of his vision to several of his confidents and fellow patriots over the years during and after the War. History books do not tell the whole story as historians often ignore "spiritual experiences."

The turning point for the Revolution in the south came on October 7, 1780, at the Battle of Kings Mountain in North Carolina. Colonel Isaac Shelby along with Colonel Sevier and their militiamen from North and South Carolina joined forces with Colonel William Campbell's four-hundred Virginia men defeating the British. This was a great victory for the "Over the mountain men," who were independent Militia's and not part of the Continental Army. It stopped the recruitment of Loyalist troops for Cromwell.*

The Battle of Cowpens on January 17, 1881 was another decisive victory for the Continental Army in the retaking of South Carolina from the British. The Continental Army under General Daniel Morgan had only eight-hundred to one thousand troops with most of them veteran Continentals. The rest were experienced militia with some "Over the Mountain men" who had seen service at Kings Mountain and the Battle of Musgrove Mill. Morgan developed a unique plan for the area landscape, which enable him to take advantage of his British opponent, Cornel Tarleton. Morgan's stratagem worked perfectly and won the battle.

Finally, on October 19, 1781, with the French Navy at the back of the British General Cornwall at Yorktown, Washington attacked and defeated Cornwall. This victory would eventually cause the British to evacuate New York. By 1783, the war was over.

In December of 1783, Washington bade his troop's farewell and resigned his commission. He returned to Mount Vernon with hopes of repairing his land and resuming life as a gentleman farmer.

During the Civil War General George McLellan had a vision of the spirit of George Washington. The following account is taken from the National Tribune of December 1880:

In a strategic moment in the Civil War, General George McClellan, who was called by President Lincoln to take charge of the shattered Union forces, fell asleep at his desk. He had scarcely been asleep but a moment, when it seemed that he was awake and the whole room was filled with a radiant light. Suddenly out of the light, he heard a voice, and later saw the face of George Washington, who gave him warning the Confederate Troops were on their way to take the Capitol. Because of this with something akin to a supernatural knowledge, General McClellan was able to pursue General Robert E. Lee and stop the northern invasion by the Confederacy at Antietam, September 1862. The Vision was first reported in the Portland, Maine Evening Courier at the time the tide turned for the Union forces. Since that time it has been written as a warning to the American people again and again because of its reference to the last war, which will be fought near the end of the century…when a great conflict could arise "with the oppressors of the whole earth" in which our land will be involved.

In General McClelland's account of this vision, he relates that the voice of Washington, with penetrating clarity, called out to him: (Note the continuing theme as shown to Washington during his vision at Valley Forge).

"General McClellan, do you sleep at your post? Rouse you, or 'ere it can be prevented, the foe will be in Washington! … You have been betrayed, and had not God willed it otherwise, 'ere the sun of tomorrow had set, the Confederate Flag would have waved above the Capitol and your own grave. But note what you see. Your time is short!"

In this strange dream state, General McClellan was aware of a being that stood beside him, but could only identify as a vapor having the vague outline of a man. As he looked at the living map he saw before him all of the troop positions and he realized his own plans were known to the enemy. With a pencil in hand he began to copy down all that he saw---the position of the Confederate Troops as they marched toward Washington; the maneuvers which they planned in the future. He noted what he saw on the living map and transferred it to the paper map on his table. After the warning of the immediate peril, which faced the Union, the splendor of Washington became even greater as the figure increased in light and glory until it shown as the noonday sun. He raised his eyes and looked into the face of Washington as he spoke of the days ahead in the 20th century, when other perils would befall our nation.

"General McClellan, while yet in the flesh, I beheld the birth of the American Republic. It was indeed a hard and bloody one, but God's blessing was on the nation, and, therefore, through this, her first great struggle for existence, He sustained her, and with His mighty hand, He brought her out triumphantly.

A century has not yet passed since then, and yet the child Republic has taken her position as peer with nations whose pages of history extend of ages in the past. She has, since those dark days, by the favor of God, greatly prospered. And now, by the very reason of that prosperity, she has been brought to her second great struggle. This is by far the most perilous ordeal she has to endure, passing as she is from childhood to open maturity, she is called on to accomplish that vast result, Self-Conquest; to learn that important lesson, self-control, self-rule, that in the future will place her in the van of power and civilization. It is here that all the nation hitherto failed, and she too--- the Republic of the earth, had not God willed otherwise---would by tomorrow's sunset have been a heap of stones, cast up over the final grave of human liberty. But, her cries have come up out of the borders like sweet incense into heaven. She shall be saved! Then shall peace be upon her, and prosperity fill her with joy.

But her mission will not be finished, for 'ere another century shall have gone by, THE OPPRESSORS OF THE WHOLE EARTH, hating and envying her exaltation, shall join themselves together and raise up their hands against her. But, if she is found worthy of her calling, they shall be truly discomfited, and then will be ended her third and last struggle for existence. Henceforth, shall the Republic go on, increasing in goodness and power until her borders shall end only in the remotest corners of the earth, and the whole earth shall, beneath her shadowy wings, become a UNIVERSAL REPUBLIC! Let her in her prosperity, however, remember the Lord her God, let her trust be always in Him, and she shall never be confounded.

Washington raised his hand over McClellan's head in blessing, a peal of thunder rumbled through space; the General awoke with a start. He was in his room with his maps spread out on the table before him, but as he looked at them (to his astonishment, he saw) the maps were covered with the marks and figures he had made during his vision. This convinced him that his dream or vision was real.

He set about immediately...to thwart the enemy's plan, riding his horse from camp to camp to implement the changes at once. The Confederate Army was so close that President Lincoln could hear the rumble of their artillery sitting in the study at the White House.

McClellan's action saved the capitol early in 1862, and saved the Republic from the second peril. The first "peril" had been the Revolutionary War. The Union was saved and General McClellan concludes his account of his Vision with these words:

"Our beloved, glorious Washington shall rest... until perhaps the end of the Prophetic Century approaches, that is to bring the Republic to a third and final struggle when he may once more... become a messenger of Soccer and Peace from the Great Ruler, who has all Nations in his keeping..."

General McClellan never reputed this story from the time of its first publication or any time thereafter. The vision was alluded to in numerous anti-Lincoln articles including one related to spiritualism that is referenced in Chapter 9 of "The Presidents and their Spiritual Advisors." General McClellan tried to trumpet his own stint as General–in-Chief of the union Army in an effort to replace the Commander in Chief, President Lincoln, when he ran against him in the 1864 presidential election where he ran as the Democratic Candidate. Although he failed to unseat Lincoln, he remained in the public eye until his death in 1885. The National Tribune recirculated this story when he was Governor of New Jersey in 1880.

*Eight Edmiston's (Edmondson) and five members of the Buchanan family went out from "Fort Edmiston" in Virginia to take part in that Battle. See Edmiston Family.
**History and pictures from Wikipedia.

THE PRESIDENCY

In 1787, Washington was called again to serve his country. The young republic was struggling under the Articles of Confederation, a structure of government that centered the power with the states. However, the states were not unified and they were fighting among themselves over navigation rights, boundaries and paying off the national War debt. They were also imposing oppressive taxes on their citizens. Washington, although dismayed at the state of affairs, remained noncommittal. Finally, when *Shays Rebellion* erupted in Massachusetts, Washington knew something needed to be done to improve the nation's government.

Shays Rebellion began on August 29, 1786. It was an armed uprising, which took place in central and western Massachusetts in 1786 and 1787. It was named after Daniel Shay, veteran of Lexington and one of the rebel leaders. Adam Wheeler was another participant. Several factors caused it including economic depression, the states fiscal policies and aggressive tax and debt collection. The protestors, many were war veterans, shut the county courts down to stop the judicial hearings for tax and debt collections. After the arrest of some of the leaders, the protest escalated into armed force. Eventually in an armed resistance in Sheffield, the government troops wounded thirty rebels and killed one. Most of these were Veterans who received little or no pay and were behind in their bills when they returned home. Shay was one of these and after being wounded, he return home to find he was summoned to court for nonpayment of debts. He soon discovered he was not alone and many veterans were in the same predicament. In the beginning, veteran Job Shattuck of Gorton organized residents to prevent the tax collectors from collecting taxes. Both Job Shattuck and Adam Wheeler had led the Militias into the first battle of the Revolution at Concord. Governor Hancock refused to crack down on the delinquent taxes and accepted devalued paper currency. However, after the state legislature refused to issue paper money because the merchants and Bankers objected to losing money, Hancock resigned. The new Governor Bowdoin stepped up collections and the legislature increased taxes. John Adams observed the taxes were more than the people could bear. More armed rebellion followed.

Thomas Jefferson, serving as Ambassador in France, was not concerned and wrote to a friend about the rebellion stating,

> *"The tree of liberty must be refreshed from time to time with the blood of patriots and tyrants. It is natural manure."*

In contrast, George Washington, who had been calling for constitutional reform realizing the Articles of Confederations were inadequate, wrote a letter to Henry Lee (pictured), then President of Congress. Lee had been asking for someone with influence to help appease the situation in Massachusetts. Washington wrote back, calling for a convention to correct the problems. He said,

> *"I know not where that influence is to be found, or if attainable, if it would be the proper remedy for the disorders. Influence is not government. Let us have a government by which our lives, liberties and property will be secured, or let us know the worst at once."*

The weakness in the Federal Government under the Articles of Confederation was apparent. The states were debating the need for a stronger central government and in 1786, Congress approved the convention in Philadelphia to amend the Articles. The Constitutional Convention elected Washington President and John Adams as Vice President. Alexander Hamilton, James Mason, Washington, and others determined it was not amendments that were needed, but a new constitution that would give the national government more authority. Washington spoke once and lobbied for major changes in the structure of the government. Finally, the convention produced a plan that would not only fix the current problems, but one that would endure through time. Ratification by the states was next. There were those who were opposed to the new Constitution, including Patrick Henry and Sam Adams, calling it a grab for power. It spite of this it was finally ratified by the last of the thirteen colonies on May 29, 1790.

Although Washington planned to retire to Mount Vernon, he was called again to serve his country. In the Presidential election of 1789, he received a vote from every Elector to the Electoral College, the only President in history to be elected by a unanimous vote. He was very aware that his Presidency would set a precedent for all who would follow. He took his responsibilities and duties seriously and was careful not to emulate any Royal Court. He preferred to be call "Mr. President" rather than any other title. He declined the salary Congress offered, but was persuaded to accept it in order not to give the impression that only the rich could run for the Presidency. Washington believed he was given Divine guidance and acknowledged America was founded on it. Washington believed he was constantly guided by a higher source while directing his troops to out smart the British. He was sometimes called clairvoyant because he seemed to be able to look in the future and predict troop movements. In his first inaugural address he stated, *"No people can be bound to acknowledge and adore the Invisible Hand which conducts the affairs of men more than the people of the United States. Every step by which they advanced to the character of an independent nation seems to have been distinguished by some token of providential agency."*

Washington surrounded himself with the most qualified men, most of them Freemasons. He delegated authority with good judgment and listened to his cabinet's advice before making any decisions. He established presidential powers with integrity, restraint, and honesty, a standard rarely met by his successors. He passed treaties with the Indians, put the nation on a strong financial footing with the help of Alexander Hamilton, lowered the nation's debt, and establish at tax on whisky. This tax caused the Whisky Rebellion, which Washington put down by invoking the Militia Act of 1792 calling on several state militias to help. He personally took command and demonstrated that the federal government would use force if necessary to enforce the law. He took a cautious approach to foreign affairs for the struggling nation and remained neutral in the war between France and Britain, in spite of the French treaty and the objections of Thomas Jefferson, his Secretary of State. He later established a treaty with Britain clearing up some left over issues from the Revolution. The treaty, though controversial, prove beneficial by removing all of the British Forts on the western frontier and setting a clear boundary between the United States and Canada.

Throughout his Presidency, he became increasingly concerned about the growing partisanship in government and the nation. He supported the Constitution and qualified as a Federalist by establishing a federal system of government. He also supported Secretary of Treasure Hamilton's national finance and credit plans over his Secretary of State, Thomas Jefferson's objections. Jefferson desired to keep government small and centered at the state level with the economy based on farming, while Hamilton wanted a strong national government and an economy built on industry. Those who followed Hamilton became know as Federalist and those who followed Jefferson became known as Democrat-Republicans.

Washington despised political partisanship. He did not become affiliated with a party and felt that ideological differences should never be institutionalized. He believed strongly that political leaders should be free to debate important issues without being bound by party loyalty. In his farewell address Washington said,

"The partisan spirit serves always to distract the public councils and enfeeble the Public Administration. It agitates the Community with ill-founded jealousies and false alarms; kindles the animosity of one part against another, foments occasionally riot and insurrection. It opens the door to foreign influence and corruption, which finds a facilitated access to the government itself through the channels of party passions. Thus the policy and the will of one country are subjected to the policy and will of another." He proved to be correct.

His farewell address stated the following about religion:

"Of all the dispositions and habits, which lead to political prosperity, Religion and Morality are indispensable supports. In vain, would that man claim the tribute of Patriotism, who would labor to subvert these great pillars of human happiness, these firmest props of the duties of Men and citizens? The mere Politician, equally with a pious man, ought to respect and cherish them. A volume could not trace all their connections with private and public felicity. Let it be simply asked; where is the security for property, for reputation, for life, if the sense of religious obligation deserts the oaths, which are the instruments of investigation on Courts of Justice? And let us with caution indulge the supposition, that morality can be maintained without religion. Whatever may be conceded to the refined education of minds of peculiar structure, reason and experience both forbid us to expect, that national morality can prevail in exclusion of religious principle."

He stated that, *"not anyone attempting to remove religion from politics could claim to be a true American."*

Washington and the other founding fathers were deeply suspicious of a European pattern of a governmental involvement in religion and sought the separation of church and state. They saw governments corrupting religion with their paid ministers. Washington finally was able to retire for the last time in March 1797. He died two years and nine months later at Mount Vernon.*

*History and pictures sourced from Wikipedia

JOHN ADAMS

John Adams* was vice President under George Washington and served two terms. He became the second President of the United States in 1797, serving one term. He was an early political leader and Patriot and came to prominence in Massachusetts when he was elected a delegate to the first Continental Congress where he advocated independence from Great Britain. He was well educated at Harvard and became an attorney. He played a leading role in getting Congress to declare independence. He helped Thomas Jefferson draft the Declaration of Independence and was the primary advocate in Congress. He and Jefferson later became political enemies. He helped to negotiate the eventual peace treaty with Great Britain.

Adams was from a Puritan background but was an independent thinker in the age of enlightenment and strove for a religion based on common sense and a sense of reasonableness. His forebears where said to belong to a sect of English Druids called the Dragons. Sir Walter Raleigh and John Dee, Queen Elizabeth's astrologer were also members. The Dragons worked to renew the ancient wisdom of earth energies and studied astrological procession of the equinoxes. Adams believed in miracles, providence, and the Bible and believed as Washington, that all men benefited from going to church and belief in God. He criticized the universal authority of the Catholic Church. Although he was in agreement with the principals of Freemasons, he did not become a member. His son, John Quincy Adams became the sixth President of the United States.**

*John Adam's DAR #A000585
** History and picture of Johan Adams sourced from Wikipedia

SAMUEL ADAMS

Samuel Adams* was a true revolutionary, one of the earliest leaders in the movement that became the American Revolution. He and John Adams were second cousins. Thomas Jefferson described him as *"truly the man of the Revolution."* He helped to organize the Boston Tea Party and was a delegate to both the first and the second Continental Congress. He helped draft the Articles of Confederation and fought for the Declaration of Independence. Adams also helped write the Massachusetts constitution and later became the fourth Governor. He was a prosperous merchant and leader in Boston Politics. In 1740, he graduated from Harvard and continued his education earning a  Masters degree in 1743. He pursed a life in politics instead of the ministry, as his parents had hoped. His political views were orientated toward colonial rights. Many of his essays were published in the *Independent Advertiser* emphasizing that people must resist any encroachment on their constitutional rights. *Freemasons, Samuel Adams, and Paul Revere created The Sons of Liberty organization in Boston.* They were the first army of the Revolution. Adams and his colleagues devised the Committee for Correspondence, linking the Patriots throughout the Colonies. Adams was one of the first to argue humankind possessed certain *natural rights* that governments could not violate.

After the Revolution, Adams played an important roll in getting Massachusetts to provide public education for both boys and girls, unpopular at the time. He was one of the charter members of the American Academy of Arts and Sciences in 1780. Adams was a Deacon in The Old South Congregational Church. His parents were devout Puritans and Adams was very proud of the fact. He was married twice and had six children with only two surviving to adulthood. He died October 2, 1803 in Cambridge.**

*Samuel Adams DAR #A000577
** History and picture of Samuel Adams sourced from Wikipedia

BENJAMIN FRANKLIN

Benjamin Franklin* was one of the most influential of the Founding Fathers. He was a political leader, inventor, publisher, writer, politician, scientist, diplomat, postmaster, and civic activist. He eventually became the Governor of Pennsylvania. He earned the title of "the first American" for his early campaigning for unity in the Colonies. His accomplishments were numerous. Franklin came from a Puritan background and believed in organized religion for the good of men. However, he seldom attended church. He was of the age of enlightenment, which reflected his thoughts on Government including the equality and morality of all men. He believed in the freedom of all religions and believed God was partly responsible for American Independence. He was active in Congress and a signer of the Declaration and the Constitution. He was an amazing intellect and a gifted man of all time. He was a Freemason and Deist. He was initiated into the Freemasons in February of 1731. Franklin became Provincial Grand Master of Pennsylvania in 1734. He was a very active member for the rest of his life. He laid the Corner Stone of the Pennsylvania Statehouse (Independence Hall) while he was Grand Master. He was initiated into the Nine Sister Lodge in Paris where Voltaire, Lafayette, and Count de Gebelin were members and friends.

Count de Gebelin was a former protestant Pastor and an advocate for freedom of conscience in Enlightenment France. In Paris, he was initiated into Freemasonry where he welcomed Benjamin Franklin as a lodge brother. He was a supporter of American Independence and contributed to the new theory of economics. His father was a famous religious leader of the *Huguenots*.

Lafayette is called the "hero of two worlds." Lafayette learned of the American Revolution and accepted a commission in the Continental Army as a Major General from an American agent Silas Deane. When he received his commission, it was not dated on the agreed date and he was not assigned a unit. He was about to return to France when Franklin interceded and sent a letter to Washington asking him to accept Lafayette as his aid de camp. He eventually served as a Major General and was on Washington's staff. He joined the Freemasons while in camp at Valley Forge. Lafayette stated, *"Washington was present and acted at Master of the Lodge at time of his initiation."* After becoming a Freemason, he found Washington was more willing to give him a command. He was later made a citizen of the United States and held citizenship in France, as well. His exploits and honors are to numerous to mention.

Voltaire, born in 1694, was a French enlightenment writer who believed in freedom of religion, freedom of expression and separation of church and state. He was an historian, a prolific writer and shared Franklin's ideals. Franklin and Voltaire were brother Freemasons at the Nine Sister Lodge in Paris. He died in 1778.

Franklin published an astrological chart in his *Poor Richard's Almanac.* He wrote and epitaph that suggests he believed in reincarnation; *"The Body of B. Franklin, Printer lies here, food for worms, but the work shall not be lost; for it will appear once more, in a new and more elegant Edition, Revised and corrected by the author."*

Franklin published the books written by Johann Conrad Beissel,** who founded the first Rosicrucian Community (Ephrata) in the New World. The community was a focus for spreading the Ageless Wisdom in America. When it disbanded, most of the metaphysical library became part of Franklin's own library. Both Franklin and Washington were friends of the Community. Franklin often referred to many of the Rosicrucian themes in his speeches and some researchers believe he was secretly a member. Franklin is sometimes referred to as the first President of the United States that never actually became President.†

*Benjamin *Franklin's DAR # A041702*
**Johann Conrad Beissel was a German born religious leader who founded the Ephrata Community in 1732 in Pennsylvania. He came to America in 1720 to join the religious (hermits) group founded by Johann Kelpius who came in 1694. Kelpius' group settled on a ridge above the Wissahickon Creek where they prayed meditated and looked for the coming of Christ. Beissel founded a semi monastic Community called the Camp of the Solitary in what is now Lancaster County. They were influenced by Baptist thought. He was one of the first vegetarians as were the Rosicrucian's.*
†*History and picture of Benjamin Franklin sourced from Wikipedia*

PATRICK HENRY

Patrick Henry* was the Governor of Virginia during the Revolution from 1776 to 1779. In his early political career, he was not afraid to speak out against Great Britain and was often call a radical. He led the opposition against the Stamp Act in 1765 shortly after his election to the Virginia House of Burgesses. In 1773 he led the House of Burgesses to adopt the resolution for the standing Committee of Correspondence which led to the formation of First Continental Congress in 1774 and his election to the Congress. He is famous for his speech *"I know not what course others will take, but as for me give me liberty of give me death!"* He gave this speech before the House of Burgesses on March 23, 1775 in Saint John's Church. The House was deciding whether to mobilize against the approaching British army. Henry's words brought the crowd to its feet shouting, *"To Arms, To Arms."*

After the Constitution passed, Henry fought for the Bill of Rights. He felt the Constitution was too strong on federal powers and endangered the rights of the states as well as individuals. He was a Colonel in the Virginia Militia and fought in the Revolution. He was elected Governor two different times, the last in 1784. Henry eventually owned a ten thousand acre plantation and purchased over seventy-eight slaves. Politically, he was an anti-Federalist; professionally he was a planter and lawyer. A Catholic Christian, he became a protestant and attended the Episcopal Church. He believed religion was conducive to the happiness of societies. Henry had Masonic connections and according to some sources, he was a member of the Freemasons.**

*Patrick Henry's DAR #A063828
**History and picture of Patrick Henry sourced from Wikipedia

ALEXANDER HAMILTON

Founding Father Alexander Hamilton* was one of America's first constitutional lawyers. He became the first Secretary of the Treasury. He was also a soldier, political philosopher, and economist. He was the author of George Washington's economic policies, established the national bank and the tariff system. He served in the Revolution and was an aid de camp and confidant to Washington. He became the leader of the Federalist Party created largely to support his views. He supported a strong central government. He helped to create a new Constitution after he became dissatisfied with the Article of Confederation and then helped to get it ratified.

He was born out of wedlock in the East Indies and orphaned by the age of eleven. He was sent by members of his community to the Colonies to be educated at King's College. He was a Presbyterian of the "new light" and not of the original Calvinists. He was in the habit of praying, but later did not belong to any church. Although there is no prove that Hamilton was a Freemason, he was an aid de camp to General Washington. Washington was known to have primarily Freemasons as his close associates and officers. It is quite possible Hamilton was associated with the military lodges during the Revolution. Hamilton was killed in a duel with Aaron Burr, (Vice President under Jefferson) over their severe political differences. Burr challenged Hamilton to a duel, hoping to revive his political career, but instead Burr was eventually charged with two counts of murder. After his term as Vice President ended, Burr never held political office again.**

*Alexander Hamilton's DAR # A050054
**History and picture of Alexander Hamilton sourced from Wikipedia

THOMAS JEFFERSON

Thomas Jefferson* was the chief author of the Declaration of Independence and one of the principal Founding Fathers. He served in the Continental Congress from Virginia and Governor during the Revolution. He was a lawyer in Virginia and from an elite family. He wrote a series of resolutions against the British Intolerable Acts of 1774 and believed people had the right to govern themselves. He was the first Secretary of State under Washington. He disagreed with Washington on several matters and eventually resigned to establish the Democrat-Republican Party with his friend, John Madison. He wanted the states to govern themselves and thought farming should be the economic basis for the country. He did not want a strong central government. He was a leader in the Enlightenment and very interested in science, invention, architecture, religion, and philosophy. It is believed Jefferson was a member of the Rosicrucian's (often-called The Brotherhood of the Rosy Cross). Among the evidence is a secret code he used, known only to high initiates of the order. He also designed the building of the University of Virginia in a pattern related to a Kabbalistic metaphysical design and was a vegetarian like the Rosicrucian's of that time. He became the third President of the United States and signed into law a bill prohibiting the importation of slaves although he owned over a hundred slaves. He also helped establish the Military Academy at West Point.

Jefferson was a strong supporter of the separation of Church and State and helped to establish laws to prevent state money going to churches. He purposed the Virginia statue for religious freedom adopted in 1786. It declared that the opinions of men were beyond the jurisdiction of civil magistrates. Before the Revolution, anyone desiring to serve in the House of Burgess had to be a member of the Church of England. Jefferson served at a vestryman and after the war became a member of the Episcopal Church though he did not take communion nor was he confirmed. He did not believe in the trinity or miracles. While President, he attended many different churches and believed attendance was good for men and morality. As President, he attended church in the House of Representatives and had every church and denomination preach their sermons. There is no confirmation that Jefferson was a Freemason, but several members of his family and friends were Masons.**

*Thomas Jefferson's DAR # A061895
**History and picture of Thomas Jefferson sourced from Wikipedia

THOMAS PAINE

Thomas Pain* was a political activist, author, political theorist, and revolutionary. He wrote the pamphlets "Common Sense" in 1776 that became the all time best selling American book advocating American independence. According to John Adams, it was so influential *"without the pen of the author of Common Sense, the sword of Washington would have been raised in vain."* He was the subject of Nostradamus' quatrain 1/76, which describes him as a man with a "barbaric" name, remembered along with the Declaration of Independence. He wrote a paper called the "Crisis" during the Revolution to help spur the soldiers to fight. He was an English-American and his ideas reflected the Enlightenment era. Paine became notorious after he wrote his book "The Age of Reason" that promotes Deism, free thinking, and argues against institutional religion and Christian doctrine. He was the author of many books on these subjects. He also introduced the concept of guaranteed minimum income. He believed in God, but not in the creed of any individual church. He wrote several articles on Freemasonry, but there is no actual proof he was a member.**

*Thomas Paine's DAR # A086188
**History and picture of Thomas Paine sourced from Wikipedia

JAMES MADISON

James Madison, known as the "Father of the Constitution," was instrumental in drafting the first ten Amendments of the Constitution. He was a "key champion" and author of the Bill of Rights. He was instrumental in getting Virginia to ratify the Constitution, which was the key to getting the rest of the states to follow. He wrote, *"Every word of the Constitution decides a question between power and liberty."* He favored a stronger national government to fix the problems of excesses by the state governments and redefine the relationship between the states, the national government, and the people. Congress did hot have the power to tax and, as a result, was not paying the debts left over from the Revolution. Shaw's Rebellion in  Massachusetts is cited as forcing the issue. After he became President in 1809, he found the nation needed a stronger military and financial system. He favored a national bank although he had previously been against it.

Educated by Presbyterian ministers, he was an avid reader of the English Deists tracts. His concerns for religious freedom and the separation of church and state are found in his numerous writings. He wrote, **"Religion and Government will both exit in greater purity the less they are mixed together."** After witnessing the persecution of Baptist ministers in Virginia from the established Anglican Church, he worked with the Baptist preacher, Elijah Craig on constitutional guarantees for religious freedoms in Virginia. He and Thomas Jefferson established the *Statute for Religious Freedom for Virginia*, which finally passed in 1786. It disestablished the Church of England and disclaimed any power the state had in religious matters. He excluded Patrick Henry's plan compelling citizens to pay taxes to a church of their choice. Madison's cousin, the Reverend James Madison, President of William and Mary College, worked with both Madison and Jefferson in changes that helped to separate the college from the Church of England and Great Britain. He led state actions that eventually formed the Episcopal Dioceses of Virginia. He attended Saint John's Episcopal Church in Washington while he was President and listed his religion as Episcopal. Historians and scholars sometimes classify him as a Deist.* He and Thomas Jefferson were closely associated in Virginia and both are said to have connections with the Freemasons. The Library of Congress has a letter to James Madison from the Governor of Maryland, John Mercer dated February 11, 1795 while Madison was a member of the House of Representatives. It states, *"I have had no opportunity of congratulating you before on becoming a Freemason – a very ancient and honorable fraternity. – I hold a lodge on your road, pray let me take your hand in it, and let Mrs. Mercer welcome the fair prophetess who has converted you to the true faith.." Mercer is* probably referring to Dolly, Madison's new wife. They were married September 15, 1794.

Madison was well educated and graduated from Princeton. He was the youngest delegate to the Continental Congress, served in the Virginia House of Delegates and eventually in the newly formed House of Representatives. He served as Secretary of State under Jefferson and President from 1808 to 1817. He is credited with numerous policies and treaties and is considered a "workhorse" in establishing the Constitution and the Bill of Rights. He led the Country through the War of 1812, which put an end to British interference with the United States shipping and trade, occupation of the Northwest Territories, and the previous Indian alliances with Britain.

He married the widow, Dolly Payne Todd at age forty-three and had a happy marriage. Dolly was an excellent hostess and help Madison advance his programs while President. She created the role of "First Lady" and directed the furnishing of the new White House. Madison died at his home in Montpelier, Virginia June 28, 1836. Madison was never a very well man and had to protect his health. He was not able to serve in the Revolutionary Army.

In recent years, there have been attempts by right wing Christian organizations to classify our Founding Fathers as Fundamentalist Christians, which they were not. One group has listed Madison as a "Calvinist Baptist," probably because he helped the Baptists with religious freedoms, which Madison did for others, as well. He was not a Calvinist Baptist.

**History and picture of James Madison sourced from Wikipedia

GOUVERNEUR MORRIS

Gouverneur Morris led the idea that a person was not just a citizen of his state but also a citizen of the union. Morris was appointed to the Continental Congress. He signed the Articles of Confederation. He helped write the Constitution, all, or part of the Preamble and called the "Penman of the Constitution." He rigorously defended the right for anyone to practice his chosen religion without interference and fought for the language in the Constitution. An "Aristocrat to the Core, he thought the common people were incapable of self government, because he feared the poor would sell their votes to the rich." Consequently, he thought voting should be allowed only by property owners. He was for a strong central government. He was selected to be on a committee in charge of coordinating reforms in the military with George Washington. After seeing the poor conditions at Valley Forge, he became a representative for the Continental Army with Congress and helped to get reforms and financing.

He lost his leg in an accident and was unable to fight in the Revolutionary Army. He joined a "special briefs club" for the protection of New York, the forerunner of the New York Guards. He was first a member of the New York Provincial Congress representing his family estate in what is now Bronx County. After a dispute with his family over independence, he moved to Pennsylvania. He represented Pennsylvania at the Constitutional Convention in 1787. He later served in the US Senate and Chairman of the Erie Canal Commission in 1810. Morris was probably a Freemason as he gave the address at President Washington's funeral at St Paul's Chapel following the Masonic parade in New York. Some historians described him as a Deist.*

History and picture of Gouverneur Morris sourced from Wikipedia

ROBERT MORRIS

Robert Morris Jr. was a signer of the Declaration of Independence, Articles of Confederation, and the United States Constitution. He was not related to Gouverneur Morris. Robert was elected to the Pennsylvania Assembly. He became the Chairman for the Committee of Safety. He was chosen a delegate to the Second Continental Congress where he served as a member of the Committee of Correspondence and Chairman of the secret Committee of Trade.

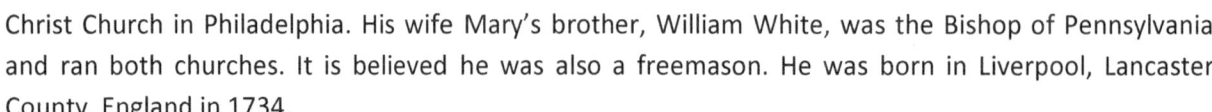

In 1781, he served as Superintendent of Finance managing the economy of the new country. Morris was next to George Washington as the most powerful man in America. His success led him to be called the "Financier of the Revolution." He was also Agent of Marine, and controlled the Continental Navy. He became one of Pennsylvania's original Senators.

Morris, an Episcopalian, was a member of both Saint Peters Church and Christ Church in Philadelphia. His wife Mary's brother, William White, was the Bishop of Pennsylvania and ran both churches. It is believed he was also a freemason. He was born in Liverpool, Lancaster County, England in 1734.

*Robert Morris' DAR #A101304

**The first service at St. Peter's Church was held on September 4, 1761, and the church has been in continuous use ever since. Members of Christ Church living in newly settled Society Hill founded St. Peter's in 1758. Rising on land donated by William Penn's sons, Thomas and Richard, it was designed and built by Scottish architect/builder Robert Smith, who also designed Carpenter's Hall and the tower of Christ Church.

†History and picture of Robert Morris sourced from Wikipedia

FREEMASONARY

"Freemasonry is not a religion or cult, does not have any theology, and is not a path for believers to any divine end. The main requirement is the belief in God or a higher being. Christians are the majority of members, but Jews and other forms of religion are also represented in the Masonic circles. The Lodges around the world share the same belief in universal brotherhood regardless of religion, politics, or national differences, but there is no shared hierarchy and they do not speak with a single voice." *(Brien Handwerk's interview with Masonic Historian Jay Kinney, National Geographic News Sept. 15, 2009)*

Some believe that the Freemasons descend from the Knights Templars, a powerful military and religious order established around 1095 and funded by Kings of many countries to protect medieval pilgrims from Muslims journeying to the Holy Land. In 1312, King Philips II of France influenced Pope Clement V to ban and dissolve the Templars. Phillips was short of funds in his treasury and the Templars were known to have amassed large amounts of money. Their main residence and savings were in France. After the Pope forbids the Knights organization, King Phillips sent his army to take over their money and property, killing or capturing the Templars. The favored view is the few remaining Knights secretly escaped to Scotland and helped King Robert the Bruce to win the battle at Bannockburn. They escaped with part of their treasury and buried it at Rosslyn Chapel. Other Templar treasures legend to be there are the mummified head of Jesus, the Holy Grail, and the Scottish Crown Jewels. The Templar Knights also claimed to have secretly preserved original secrets passages in the Bible, which contained among others, references to reincarnation. In 523, at the Councils of Constantinople, this and other passages were removed. The Roman Church wanted the Masses to believe they had only one life to make their souls worthy to enter Heaven, which was to the Church's advantage. Early Christian writings containing many secrets of the early Christian religion written by Christian Mystics, referred to as Gnostics, were found in Caves in Egypt in 1945 verifying reincarnation was taught by Jesus. These Mystics were called heretics and persecuted by the Roman Church. After the fall of the Roman Empire, the Church emerged as the head of the Christian faith. During the middle Ages, many new cathedrals were built. Every stone was carved to glorify God and the builders found a way to express their faith. They were called free masons. Finding their "craft" strictly regulated including their wages, they joined to form trade unions held in secrecy. By 1360, a law was passed in England forbidding the masons and carpenters to hold secret lodge meetings although the law was eventually ignore.

The philosophy and symbolisms used by the Freemasons are thought to descend from the builders of King Solomon's Temple and the legends surrounding it. The teachings incorporate the three basic religions of the Jews, Christians, and Muslims.

Sir Francis Bacon, born in 1561, was known as the "Father of Modern Science." Some researchers believed him to be the founder of modern Freemasonry and the head of the Rosicrucian Order, which taught the inner laws of nature, spiritual principles for self-transformation and keys for creating a better world. He helped to plant the seeds for the founding of America in his book "The New Atlantis." He was a member of the first Virginia Company that founded the colonies of the Carolinas and Virginia and foresaw America as a land of freedoms. For this reason, as Lord Chancellor of England, he took an active interest in the colonization of America.

Modern Masonry appeared around the 17th century in England, but there is no proof of a connection to the Templar Knights. The Thirty-third degree, called the Scottish rite, is an extension of the degrees of Freemasonry. It builds upon the ethical teachings and philosophy offered in the Craft Lodge, the Apprentice, Fellow craft, and Master Mason degrees.

The Freemasonry philosophy of Brother Hood of man and Fatherhood of God held the foundation for political, religious, social, and educational reform. All the Monarchs and Ecclesiastical authorities of Europe opposed it. Influential Freemasons helped to further the 18th Century intellectual movement known as the Age of Enlightenment that promoted ideas such as freedom, tolerance, and equality. The movement sought to mobilize the power of reason in order to advance knowledge and reform society. It opposed intolerance and abuses in church and state. Philosophers John Locke, Isaac Newton, and Benjamin Franklin were a few of the men furthering these ideas. George Washington and several of the Founding Fathers agreed. At the time of America's founding, the Freemasons had a strong metaphysical orientation, which helped developed common values and purposes among its members and deep bonds of loyalty. The traditional secrecy in the organization made is possible to organize the American Revolution with little fear of being exposed.*

*History sourced from Wikipedia and Freemasons, *Inside the World's Oldest Secret Society*, by H. Paul Jeffers.

ADAM WEISHAUPT

It should be mentioned here that there is no connection between the Freemasons and a group founded in Bavaria by Adam Weishaupt in 1776 know at first as the *Order of the Perfectibilists* and later as the *Ordo Illuminati Bavarensis*. Although Weishaupt had joined the Freemasons, primarily to see how they were organized, he found they did not represent his thoughts for world order and dropped out to form the Perfectibilists/Illuminati in Bavaria. He joined other "secret organizations" to study the organizational methods and procedures to form his Illuminati group. The planned structure of the Illuminati organization came from Weishaupt. He was educated in the priesthood of the Jesuit order and eventually became a professor of cannon law.*

As a Jesuit lawyer, he supported his Jesuit brothers who were persecuted and banned by the Church in 1773. His primary mission was to abolish all monarchial governments and the Vatican for supporting the destruction of the Jesuits Order. In the beginning, the group was established with a small group of wealthy noble and non-noble families to help get revenge on the Catholic Church for their disbandment of the Jesuits. These "Illuminati families" help the Jesuits steal the gold reserves of the Catholic Church and the French State during the French revolution along with important and incriminating documents from the Vatican's secret archives during the capture of Rome by Napoleon's forces. The stolen French gold was placed in the care of the New York bank founded in 1784 and the newly formed bank of Manhattan Company (now JP Morgan Chase Bank). With the help of the secret documents, the Jesuits were able to establish terms with the Church and the Order was restored by Papal order in 1814. The Illuminati families were rewarded for their help with titles, estates, and fabulous wealth on behalf of the Jesuits. The Rothschild's were one of these famous families. The House of Saxe-Coburg and Gotha** was rewarded with the crown of England and remain steadfastly loyal to the Jesuits. Upon the victory over the Papacy and the restoration of the Order, a new Order of power was established, with the Illuminati in an important position under the Roman Pontiff. Although active in the underground in the French Revolution, the Illuminati were not the sole cause.

After the rise of Napoleon Bonaparte, the Illuminati was eventually crushed in France and moved elsewhere. In 1784 the Illuminati was forced underground after they attempted a coop against the Hapsburgs in Austria. Weishaupt died in obscurity in 1830.

In recent years, Clergy members Peter Marshall, David Burton, James Kennedy, and others of the Christian right have questioned George Washington's affiliation with the Freemasonry calling the Masonic principles subversive. Washington answered these same accusations in a letters written to the members of the New Church of Baltimore in 1793, where he defended American Freemasonry and denied the American Masonic societies were contaminated with subversive principles of the Illuminati. His correspondence consistently referred to "the Great Architect of the University."

He further stated:

"We have abundant reason to rejoice that in this land the light of truth and reason has triumphed over the power of bigotry and superstition and that every person may here worship God according to the dictates of his own heart. In this Enlightened Age and in this Land of equal liberty is our boast, that a man's religious tenets, will not forfeit his protection of the Laws, nor deprive him of the right of attaining and holding the highest offices that are know in the United States."

"Your prayers for my present and future felicity were received with gratitude; and I sincerely wish, Gentlemen, that you may in your social and individual capacities, taste those blessings which, a gracious God bestows upon the Righteous. (Signed) G. Washington"

George Washington realized the Doctrines of the Illuminati existed and had spread to the United States but to his knowledge, not to the Freemasons. His was concerned that the Illuminati intended purpose was to separate the people from their Government. He stated his concerns in a letter dated October 27, 1798,** The Library of Congress contains copies of this and others of his correspondence.

There are other warnings of the Illuminati and Bankers in letters from our U.S. Presidents also on file including the following:

"I believe that Banking institutions are more dangerous to our liberties than standing armies. If the American people ever allow private Banks to control the issue of their currency first by inflation, then by deflation, the banks and corporations that will grow up around (the banks) will deprive the people of all property until their children wake-up homeless on the continent their fathers conquered. The issuing power should be taken from the banks and restored to the people, to whom it properly belongs." Thomas Jefferson 1802

"Behind the ostensible government sits enthroned an invisible government owing no allegiance and acknowledge no responsibility to the people." President Theodore Roosevelt. An Autobiography, 1913 *(Appendix B)*

"The real truth of the matter is, as you and I know that a financial element in the large centers has owned the Government ever since the days of Andrew Jackson." President Franklin Roosevelt in a letter to an associate dated November 21, 1933.

Former New York Mayor John Hylan in 1922 summed it up like this:
"The real menace to our republic is the invisible government which, like a giant octopus sprawls is slimy length over our city, state and nation... At the head of this octopus are the Rockefeller Standard Oil interests and a small group of powerful banking houses generally referred to as international bankers (who) virtually run the United States Government for their own selfish purposes."

The Rothschild's and the Rockefellers are closely allied in the creation of a New World Order. David Rockefeller stated the following in his memoirs, published in 2004, page 405:

"Some even believe we (Rockefellers) are part of a secret cabal working against the best interests of the United States characterizing my family and me as 'internationalists' and conspiring with other countries around the world to build a more integrated global political and economic structure – one world, if you will. If that's the charge, I stand guilty and I am proud of it."†

*The Jesuit Order of monks was the first dedicated military order of the Catholic Church formed in 1534 by Ignatius Loyola and approved by the Duke of Grandia, Francis Borja. An earlier version was approved in 1450 by Pope Pius II to help fight the Turks and spread the faith. They were the given official status by Pope Paul III in 1540. Later Pope Gregory XIII gave them the power to engage in banking and commerce. History sourced from World and One Evil: The Jesuits.
**(In 1917, King George V changed his family name from Saxe-Coburg and Gotha to the English Windsor due to the anti-German sentiments in the British Empire during World War I).
†History sourced from Wikipedia

CHAPTER III
THE FOUNDING FAMILIES AND PATRIOTS

The Founding Fathers of America signed the Declaration of Independence knowing they did not have all of the Colonists behind them. The consequences the men would face if they failed to win the war could be death for their treasonous acts against the King. Some Colonists were leery of independence from England and remained loyal Tories. However, the majority of the colonists agreed and gathered arms in preparation to fight for freedom from tyranny, religious freedom, and high taxes without representation. The following are stories of Revolutionary Patriots, the history of their families, and the reasons they came to the Colonies. These are only a sampling of the many brave men who fought for our Country's freedom

THE FIGHTING BUTLERS

Members of the Butler family of Pennsylvania were known as "The Fighting Butlers" during the Revolution. There were five brothers and three cousins, (brothers). During the Revolutionary War, General Lafayette stated when he wanted something done correctly he called on a Butler. General Washington counted on their service and toasted the Fighting Butlers and their cousins for their bravery after the battle of Yorktown.

The progenitors of the American Butler families were Thomas, born 1720 and William, his nephew, born 1743 son of his brother James. James did not come to America. James and Thomas were born on their father's estates in the Parish of Kilkenny (Colkenny), County of Wicklow near Dublin, Ireland. Their father Thomas was the son of Edward, 8th Baronet of Dunboyne. The ancestry goes back to Edmund born in 1440 in Dunboyne Castle in County Meath, Ireland (near Dublin) and to the Dukes of Ormond of Ireland and Scotland.

According to history, the first of the Butlers was Theobald FitzWalter, a subject of the Norman King Henry II. Fitzwalter was one of the invaders who went with Prince John to Ireland landing in Waterford in 1185. The King granted lands and titles to these invaders. FitzWalter was awarded lands in Wicklow, Limerick, and Tipperary. He was given the title of "Chief Butler of Ireland,"

formally denoting he was the King's chief butler in charge of the wine bottles, a title of function. FitzWalter took the name Theobald le Botilier, which later became Butler. The Butlers became one of the most powerful families in Ireland and controlled land from Kilkenny through the Midlands. They also held a British peerage the highest of which is the Earl of Ormond granted to James Butler in 1328 and ceased to exist in 1997 with the death of James Hubert Theobald Charles Butler. In 1391 James Butler, 3rd Earl of Ormond, purchased the Kilkenny Castle, which became the seat of the Butler family and the primary family home. The Baronage of Dunboyne was created June 11, 1541. Edmond, the first Baron married Lady Joan Butler, the 3rd daughter of Piers, 8th Earl of Ormond, and 1st Earl of Ossory.

Thomas Butler, 7th Earl of Ormond, who died in 1515, was the grandfather of Anne Boleyn through his daughter Margaret who married William Boleyn. Anne was the second wife of King Henry VIII. Although Henry VIII beheaded Anne to marry another, their daughter, Elizabeth, became a great Queen and was the great granddaughter of Thomas Butler. In 1543, James Butler, 9th Earl of Ormond and brother to Anne, requested King Henry VIII grant a place at Court for his son and heir, Thomas.

Already at Court were two other cousins of Thomas, Lady Elizabeth Fitzgerald, and Barnaby Fitzpatrick, son of the Baron of Upper Ossory. Henry VIII had selected twelve noble youths to be educated with his son, Edward. Although most of the pupils changed over the years, Thomas and Barnaby remained until the school group disbanded in 1552, five years after Edward became King. Upon the accession of Edward VI, Thomas Butler was made a Knight of the Garter. After Edward died and his sister Mary became Queen, Thomas was retained at Court. He was finally allowed to return to Ireland in 1554 and take over the earldom. His father had died in London in 1546 of food poisoning.

During his long lifetime, Thomas spent many extended periods at Court cultivating his powerful connections. Raised together at Court, Queen Elizabeth considered him a good friend and trusted his opinion. As cousins, they were often companions. Thomas was nicknamed "Black Tom" for suppressing the rebellion against Queen Mary by Sir Thomas Wyatt. Queen Elizabeth called him her "black husband." Although married three times and produced four children, Thomas spent most of his time in England at Court in the presence of Queen Elizabeth. His three boys all died young and only his daughter, Elizabeth, lived to be in her fifties. Thomas (pictured) built a magnificent Manor House for Queen Elizabeth at Carrick-on-Suir. It was in the County of Tipperary in Ireland. He expected her to visit him, although she never did. Besides his four legitimate children, he had at least twelve illegitimate sons and daughters.

After his death in 1614 at Carrick, his will greatly favor his eldest illegitimate son, Piers, suggesting that his mother was someone of great importance. There was a "startling and persistent rumor with enormous circumstantial evidence to support them that the 'Virgin' Queen Elizabeth was the mother of *Piers Butler 8th Earl of Ormond." Thomas was with Elizabeth in late 1553 and she had the opportunity to conceive Piers. In Feb of 1554, it was said she was pregnant at Ashridge. Later in May at Woodstock physicians offered to see her. She "announced *she was not minded to make any stranger privy to the state of her body, but committed it to God.*" Thomas became a highly respected man for his honesty and candor in both Ireland and England. His honesty and the Queen's favor caused him to have many enemies. He was a proficient diplomat and responsible for many treaties of loyalty to the Crown. He held seats on both the Irish and English Privy Councils.

In 1650, the invading forces of Oliver Cromwell attacked Killkenny Castle. In the siege that followed, Cromwell's guns destroyed the front of the Castle and it was never rebuilt. The Butler family continued to live in the rest of the Castle until 1967 when Arthur, 6th Marquis of Ormond gave it to the nation of Ireland who maintains it today as a national treasure.**

*Had Piers Butler been acknowledged as her son, it might have changed the history of events and that of the Butler family. However, it is known the Queen's favor of Thomas Butler caused him the "undying hostility of Robert Dudley, the Earl of Leicester," who was later the Queen's unacknowledged secret husband. Piers daughter, Joan, married James Butler, 10th Baron of Dunboyne.
**History and pictures of Killkenny Castle, Anne Boylen, Sir Thomas Butler, and original Butler crest sourced from Ancestry and Wikipedia, also sourced from "Killkenny, Thomas Butler 10th Earl of Ormond," and "Croft's Peerage."

THE AMERICAN BUTLER DESCENDANTS

The American Butlers descend from Sir Edmond Butler (pictured) who was born in 1440 in Dunboyne, Ireland and died in 1498 and Edward 8th Baron of Dunboyne, relative of Anne Boleyn through her mother Margaret Butler's marriage to William Boleyn. Anne became the wife of Henry VIII, mother of Queen Elizabeth I.

James, the oldest brother of the American descendants, did not come to the Colonies, but stayed in Ireland taking over his father's estates. However, three of his sons and two daughters emigrated. His first son, Thomas, was born in 1740 and died in Pennsylvania in 1832. William, his second son, was born in 1743. He died 1839 in Crawford County, Pennsylvania. The third son, John, was born in 1745 and died in Ohio in 1830. His two daughters, Jane and Sarah came over and married. Jane married William Mahon, but little is know of Sarah. They were born on the Butler Estates in Ireland. The three brothers all served in the Revolution. Thomas was a Private in the Chester Co. Militia (#A017724)*, William was a Private in the Continental line (#A017738), and John was a Private in the sixth Battalion under Captain Samuel Hay and taken prisoner (#A017659).

James younger brother Thomas went to Pennsylvania in 1748 with three of his five sons and settled in Lancaster, Pennsylvania. They left Ireland during the aftermath of Scottish Rebellion. (It is possible he took part in the Rebellion of 1745). His younger two sons and daughters were born in Pennsylvania. The best known and oldest of his sons, was General Richard Butler, who was born in 1743; Colonel William Butler was born in 1744; Major Thomas Butler Jr., was born in 1748; General Percival Butler was born in 1760 and Captain Edward Butler was born in 1762. In 1760, Thomas Sr. moved his family to Carlisle, Pennsylvania and opened a gun shop. William, son of James, joined his Uncle Thomas and cousins in Carlisle. Thomas gave his service in the Revolution as the Public Armorer and gunsmith. (#A017725).* He organized the other gunsmiths in Pennsylvania and provided the Pennsylvania Long Rifles to the Continental Army. His sons all became officers probably in part due to his position. His gun shop still stands in Carlisle and preserved as a historic site. (See picture) He helped to improve, develop, and assemble the Pennsylvania Long Rifle from the early rifles the German gunsmiths brought to Burks, County Pennsylvania in the early seventeen hundreds. The new design with a longer barrel of between forty-

four and forty-eight inches was loaded with a new system, which greatly improved velocity, accuracy, cut down on the amount of ammunition, and cleaned the barrel with each shot. These rifles won the Revolution for the Americans. The riflemen could accurately shoot from one-hundred-fifty to two-hundred yards, greatly out matching the British rifles. (See picture of long rifles).

Richard was a Major General under George Washington. (#A017706).* He served at St. Clair's defeat in Ohio and was at Yorktown. The Battle of Yorktown, the last major battle of the Revolution, was a decisive victory for the Continental Army under Washington and the French Troops under General Rochambeau. Cornwallis surrendered on October 19, 1781. Butler joined the Pennsylvania Line at the beginning of the War as Major of the eighth regiment. He was later promoted to Lieutenant Colonel and transferred to Morgan's rifle command, made up of hand picked men from several Pennsylvania regiments. He took over the command and the regiment became known as "Butler's rifles." He shared in the capture of Stony Point and was at the surrender of Cornwallis. The Battle of Stony Point (fought in July of 1779) was located south of West Point, New York. They captured the British in twenty minutes in a surprise night attack by a select force of infantrymen. He picked his cousin, William Butler to be part of this select group. (See William Butler) This was a key ferry crossing on the Hudson. The British lost nearly an entire regiment. Washington and  General Wayne considered Richard Butler to be one of the ablest partisan officers of the Revolution. He had a long and distinguish career as a war hero and Indian fighter. He was in Washington's circle of Officers.* The County of Butler in Pennsylvania is named after General Butler. During the war, he became a life long friend of General William Irvine, another of Washington's circle. (See Irvine family) After the War in the autumn of 1790, Richard was in a battle with the Western Indians where he lost his life. His brothers, Thomas and Edward were also in this battle, but survived.

William Butler, brother of Richard, was a Captain in the Revolution and later Lt. Col. Commandant in Pennsylvania (#A017737). Thomas Jr. was a first and second Lieutenant in the third Pennsylvania Battalion and later Major. (#A017723) He died in Orleans Parish, Louisiana in 1805. He served under his brother William. Percival was a 1st and 2nd Lieutenant in the second and third Regiment, later promoted to General. After the War, he moved to Carrollton, Kentucky where he became a very wealthy landowner and served in Congress (#A017698).

The youngest son, Edward, was a Lieutenant in the Pennsylvania 2nd Regiment and later made Captain (#A017606). There are many written accounts of *the Fighting Butler Brothers and their Cousins.*

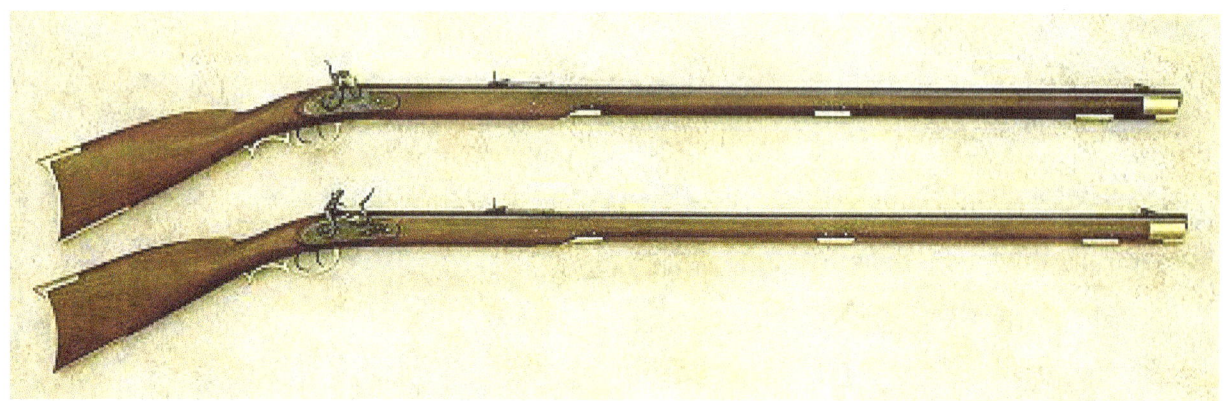

General Richard Butler

*Pictured in the Circle of Officers is General Butler top second line far right next to George Washington. General Irvine is pictured at top left.
** History and pictures sourced from Wikipedia and Ancestry, Butler Gun Shop picture sourced from Pennsylvania Historical Marker

WILLIAM BUTLER, PATRIOT

William Butler, first cousin to the five Butler brothers, was the younger son of James Butler born on his father's estate at Wicklow within two miles of Dublin, Ireland July 6 1743. He was educated in the Dublin schools. In 1760, at the age of seventeen, William was "pressed,"* against his will, to serve in the British Navy during the French and Indian War, which was being fought in America. His ship, a British man-of-war (picture) sailed to America and anchored somewhere off the coast of New Jersey. A squad of marines, including William, went ashore under the command of a Lieutenant to cut wood for use onboard the ship. New Jersey was famous for its hard cider and after cutting the wood, the group went into a farmhouse to get food and especially the cider. The marines stacked their guns in the hall of the house and the Lieutenant placed his sword on a hall table. They all went into an adjoining room to eat and drink their cider.  While the drinking was going on, William slipped out of the room, poured cider in the pans of the old flintlock guns, took the Lieutenant's sword and ran for his life. His departure was not notice for a short time. When his absence was discovered, some of the marines gave chase. Since he had tried to escape before by swimming ashore and been captured after wounding his pursuer with a sword, he knew this truly was a race for his life. Seeing the marines behind him gave him the strength and courage to elude them. The marines finally gave up the chase and William made his way to a wide river (probably the Delaware, which at some points divides New Jersey and Pennsylvania). He buried the sword in the sandy beach, waded into river and swam until he reached the other shore. While he was swimming, he tired from the weight of a heavy double cased watch his father had given him on leaving home and he dropped it into the river. He often regretted its loss.

After crossing the river, Butler made his way into the interior of Pennsylvania where his Uncle Thomas lived with his family of five sons, William's later famous cousins, "the fighting Butlers." He settled with them in Lancaster and later at Carlisle, which became a part of Berks County. Carlisle was a "hotbed" of the Revolution and served as a munitions depot during the War, where his uncle Thomas manufactured Pennsylvania long rifles.

William married Eleanor Douglas in 1769 in Lycoming County, the daughter of John Douglas, (See Douglas family) possibly the son of Lord Archibald Douglass of Scotland and Ireland, also served in the Revolution, and signed the Oath. *(The Oath of Fidelity and Support denying allegiance and obedience to Great Britain).*

William and Eleanor, who was born in 1734, eventually had two boys and six daughters. The sons were James, born 1770 in Chester County and died 1835 in Crawford County and William Jr., born 1772 in Chester County, Pennsylvania and died between 1830 and 1831 in New Orleans, Louisiana where he had taken his barge and was robbed and murdered for his money.

*Impressment or "press gang" as it was commonly known, was recruitment by force and used by the British Navy to combat their shortage of manpower.

As soon as it was evident the signing of the Declaration of Independence was intimate, William volunteered on April 12, 1776, three months before the actual signing, for an enlistment of twenty-two months, until January 1, 1778, (#A017738). He had become an excellent marksman with his uncle's Pennsylvania long riffles. Captain Henry Christ recruited a company in Berks County to join the second Pennsylvania Rifle Regiment commanded by Colonel Samuel Miles. William's cousins also volunteered and he served in several battles with them. After enlisting, his unit proceeded to New York and William received orders to Long Island where he was engaged in battle on August 27, 1776, which was the first major battle of the Revolution (pictured) won by the British. This was the largest battle of the War fought right after the signing of the Declaration of Independence.

His Company retreated in the night to New York City and, upon the evacuation of the City on September 15, 1776, marched to White Plains in Westchester County where he was engage in another battle on October 28, 1776. On the capture of Fort Washington and the evacuation of Fort Lee November 16 and 18, 1776, William along with George Washington and his army retreated across New Jersey into Pennsylvania.

By this time, General Washington had lost the majority of the battles he had fought and the moral of his troops was low. Many of his 5,000 troops enlistments would be up by the first of the year in 1777 and Washington would loose his men. He needed a victory to rally his troops. Poor clothing, the living conditions, and many men without shoes had taken a toll. His troops were encamped on the shore of the Delaware River at McKinley's Ferry, nine miles from Trenton, New Jersey where the Hessian troops, German mercenaries hired by King George III, were lodged. It was Christmas day 1776 and the Hessian Commander, Colonel Rall, and his troops were celebrating with a considerable amount of drinking. The Colonel was so sure no one would be out in the cold raging snowstorm, he had not even sent out the routine patrols and guards. All were enjoying games, food, and drink finally retiring late with most of them intoxicated.

Washington made the decision to attack the Hessian Army out of dire necessity and planned his attack on December 23 with General's Greene, Ewing, and Calwalader to be carried out in the dark on Christmas morning. Ewing was to take troops south, Calwalader was to go further south to cross the river while Washington and Greene crossed to the north. They planned to hem the Hessians in and take them by surprise. Washington called on General Glover's Marblehead's sailors to take the Durham ferryboats across the river. Washington planned to start the crossing at 11:00 pm but due to the blowing snow and floating Ice in the river, they were three hours behind. Washington took the last boat. At 3:00 AM, they started their march on Trenton. About 5 AM, Washington and Greene attacked, surprising the

Hessians. Alexander Hamilton fired his cannons filled with grape shot and the Hessians fell back. The patriots found their rifles were jammed with ice and ran forward with fixed bayonets. After Colonel

Johann Rall was killed, the army finally surrendered giving Washington a much-needed victory. They captured over 900 Hessian troops. William Butler participated in the battle in Colonel Samuel Miles regiment. (Generals Ewing and Calwalader did not make the river crossing due to the ice and snow). Miles' Company suffered severely in the loss of men killed, wounded and missing. His company was reorganized after the battle under Captain Patrick Anderson who remained in command from March to May of 1777.

The victory over the Hessians gave new hope to the Colonists and many of the men stayed to fight. Washington's army found new recruits and the War for Independence gained momentum. It was called a miraculous victory by most and a pivotal point in the Revolution. Washington crossed the river back to Pennsylvania with prisoners and military supplies taken in battle. He later defeated Cornwallis again at Trenton on January 2, 1777 and defeated his rear guard on January 3 before wintering at Morristown, New Jersey.

William served in the Battle of Brandywine on September 11, 1777 with Washington who hoped to meet the British at Chads Ford. Out maneuvered by an unexpected division of the British forces along with confusing reports on their positions, Washington retreated to Chester, Pennsylvania. The exhausted British Army did not pursue him after the daylong battle.

British General Howe was out to capture Philadelphia, the capital of the newly formed country in hopes of demoralizing the American people with the loss of their Capitol. Instead Congress move to Lancaster and then to York with the capture of Philadelphia. Washington lost 4500 troops after the battle. He described the state of the army to Hamilton as "truly deplorable. Finally, reinforcements began to arrive from Congress and the army was ready to fight again. William Butler spent the winter of 1777-78 at Valley Forge in that infamous freezing winter with Washington. Four of his Butler cousins were also there. William served as a guard to Washington and a special Honor Guard for Lafayette, who also served at Valley Forge. He and Lafayette were members of the Valley Forge Freemason military Lodge, which was often presided over by General Washington. William accompanied the detachment ordered to assist in the defense of the Forts at Red Banks and Mud (League) Island (later a navy yard), a short distance below Philadelphia, which was besieged the later part of October and November 1777. The British needed to open communication with their fleet for supplies and were unfortunately successful. William also served in Colonel Patton's Regiment; one of the additional sixteen regiments established on a different footing from the eight regiments apportioned from the States. General Washington appointed the officers of these additional regiments and empowered them to raise men wherever they could. In November of 1777, Colonel Patton resigned.

On January 1, 1778, William reenlisted for three years in Captain John Marshall's Company, the Second Pennsylvania regiment, Continental Line and later commanded by Colonel Walter Stewart. He was at the battle of Monmouth, New Jersey on June 28, 1778 after the British had evacuated Philadelphia on their march to New York City. William remembered the day of the battle as being excessively hot when Washington left Valley Forge to intercept them. By July 1, 1778, William was a corporal and then made sergeant in Captain John Patterson's Company in the Second Pennsylvania Infantry until the close of 1780. In February of 1781, he reenlisted in the Pennsylvania Regiment of Artillery commanded by Colonel Thomas Proctor and Colonel Harris and served until the end of the war. He was at Yorktown, Virginia and the capture of  Lord Cornwallis on October 19, 1781. After Yorktown, his orders took him south serving under General Wayne where he fought in the campaigns of South Carolina and Georgia until the war ended. He was at the last battle and the surrender of Savannah July 22, 1782. Wounded twice, he survived his wounds and was honorable discharged at Philadelphia in August of 1783. He was one of the bravest of soldiers, fighting throughout the entire war. Most men served their enlistment period and went home.

William Butler was frequently drafted, or transferred, into different regiments or companies for special services during his service of seven years and four months. He was at the midnight surprise assault on Battle of Stony Point on the Hudson River with a select group of riflemen on July 16, 1779 under General Wayne, who captured it and made prisoners of the Garrison. He served as a sentinel guarding General Washington's tent and a special bodyguard to General Lafayette. *Lafayette once said, "When he wanted something done and done right, he called on a Butler."* This also included William's cousins, which General Washington praised and toasted for their bravery.

A synopsis of military records in the National Archives of William Butler includes a copy of a small booklet titled, *"William Butler – Soldier of the Revolution – Born in Ireland July 6, 1743 – died in Crawford County, Pennsylvania March 4, 1839."* The book states it was written, *"To perpetuate the memory of one of the bravest soldiers in the Revolution."* The gathered information and material is a true narrative from official documents, old family bibles, and personal recollections of the writer and others with whom the writer conversed. When a boy, the writer said he often spent much time with the *"old hero and listened with intense interest to his descriptions of the battles and the thrilling scenes, through which he had passed. He often drew diagrams in the dirt with his cane to explain the battle positions."* The old copy was poor and mostly illegible. On the last page of the book, there is a note, which says, William McArthur of Meadville, Pennsylvania stated shortly before his death in a letter to the author, the story as follows:

> *"When General Lafayette visited Meadville in 1824 he, (William McArthur) a boy of 13, stood near Lafayette having just shaken hands with him when someone told the General of the old soldier, William Butler, living near. Lafayette remembered his masonic brother, spoke of him, and expressed an earnest desire to see him. The old hero, through failing memory, mistook the appointed day and came to Meadville the day after the General had left. Bitter disappointment grieved the old man and afterwards he often mourned his failure to see the General."*

On July 4, 1824 at a celebration on Independence Day, William Butler was asked to give the toast. His words were the following:
"May the sacred flame, tenacious control, be always burning in the freeman's soul."
May his words forever be remembered.

After the war, William settled in Bald Eagle Township, Northampton, Pennsylvania on ground given to him by the State of Pennsylvania. It was north of French Creek west of the Allegheny River. The site was near the city of Lock Haven on the West branch of the Susquehanna River. He was given 200 acres for his service, which he later sold to James Dunn for 87 pounds sterling in 1796. He and his sons, James and William, worked close by with Colonels Patton and Miles (both Scotch-Irish) at the Center Furnace iron business, which they built in Center County. William later moved with his family to Crawford County where he was a farmer. He owned land, lived in Sudbury Township in 1797, and resided in the eastern part of Summit. In 1798, he executed a deed of four-hundred and one acres to John Irwin (Irvin) assigned November 23, 1804 from tract sixty-nine from the Holland land Company. In 1801, Henry Escher of Crawford County conveyed two-hundred acres in Sudbury Township near Coniott Lake (Conneaut) to William Butler recorded July 15, 1801. He was pensioned in 1823 at the age of eighty. He received both state and national pensions. He was paid $40.00 per year from the State of Pennsylvania. The national pension was $129.83 paid under the US Revolutionary claim Act of April 6, 1838 and paid until his death. He died on March 4, 1839 at the age of ninety-six. He is buried in the old Harmonsburg Union Cemetery in Pennsylvania near his oldest son, James. As of 1962, the Tombstone is tipped over with the base still intact. William and his wife Eleanor had eight children. His sons were James, born in 1770 and died in 1835 and William born in 1772 and died in 1831. His daughters were Jean, Nancy, Eleanor, Sallie, Mary, and Catherine.

In the fall of 1838 at the age of 96, William told a story about threshing buckwheat in the field on a floor made by beating and rolling the ground smooth as they did in the Bible days. He and his grandson, Joseph M. Butler then 13, threshed a complete flooring of buckwheat as it was brought from the field. He is quoted as saying, *"well done for two boys, one 13 and the other 103."* His memory was failing. When he was 90, he walked from his farm to Meadville and back, a total of 16 miles.

William was a strong Protestant and a Freemason. His wife was Catholic and their oldest son, James, and their daughters all followed in their mother's Catholic faith. William Jr. adopted his father's faith and was a Freemason. The *Democrat* and the *Courier Newspapers* both published his obituary on March 12, 1839 in Meadville, Pennsylvania and it is on file in the public library:

> *"Another Revolutionary hero has gone, in the person of Mr. William Butler, who departed this life during the past week at his residence in Sudbury, Township, this County, at the advanced age of 96 years. The deceased is one of those who bore the 'heat and burden of the day' in the struggle for Independence, risked his life amongst the Forlorn Hope at the storming and taking of Stony Point under General Wayne and belonged subsequently to the body-guard of Lafayette. Since the termination of the Revolutionary War he has resided mostly in Crawford County, an upright, honest man, depending on the labor of his hands for a livelihood, until within the past few years, since which he has received a pension from the government."*

William's grandson, William David Butler, wrote a first hand account of his life in his book, "Butler Family in America," from which much of this information is found. His father was William Jr., the second son of William who married Elizabeth McMurtry. His granddaughter, Margaret Mariah Butler, sister of William David, married Oliver C. Wheeler, son of Oliver Wheeler of Massachusetts. They are the great, great grandparents of the author, Joan Wheeler LaGrone. It is through this Revolutionary Hero, William Butler, and his granddaughter Margaret, that LaGrone became a member of the *Daughters of the American Revolution.**

*History and pictures sourced from Wikipedia, also sourced from *"William Butler, Soldier of the Revolution"* in the National Archives, *"Butler Family in America" by William David Butler,* picture of Valley Forge sourced from Britannic. Crawford County, PA Military Records.

WILLIAM BUTLER, JR. AND ELIZABETH MCMURTY

William Butler Jr. was the son of William Butler and Eleanor Douglass. He was born in 1772 in Chester County, Pennsylvania. He married first Sally Dias and had sons John and Samuel, 2nd he married Elizabeth McMurtry in 1823. She was born June 22, 1803 in Harmonsburg, Crawford County, PA, the daughter of Joseph McMurtry and Margaret Kirkpatrick. She was the daughter of Andrew Kirkpatrick. Joseph McMurtry, his three brothers and Andrew Kirkpatrick all served in the Revolution. Joseph McMurtry was from an old Scottish family who settled early in New Jersey, as did the Kirkpatrick's. (See McMurtry and Kirkpatrick families)

William Jr., worked with his father in the iron business in Center County and later moved to Crawford County to farm. He was a Freemason, following his father's example. In 1830, he took a barge or flat boat loaded with supplies from Pennsylvania to New Orleans. He arrived in New Orleans and after selling his supplies; he was robbed of his boat and murdered for his money. For three years, his wife and family were unaware of his fate. In 1833, his brother James went to New Orleans and discovered what had become of him. James returned to Pennsylvania to inform his father and William's wife and children. During his stay in New Orleans, James contacted an unknown disease and died at his father's home shortly after he returned. Elizabeth raised their family of two sons and two daughters with the help of her father-in-law, William Butler. Elizabeth died February 22, 1864.

William Jr. and Elizabeth's children were William David Butler who died in St. Louis, Missouri March 4th 1904, author of the book *"The Butler Family in America,"* Joseph Butler, Adeline Elizabeth and Margaret Mariah. Margaret was born in 1823 in Crawford County, Pennsylvania and died in Fulton County, Illinois 1863. She married Oliver Cleveland Wheeler in 1838 in Crawford County. He was the son of Oliver Wheeler and Elizabeth Woodward of Hubbardston, Massachusetts, the daughter of Daniel Woodward, Patriot (#A129244). Oliver and Margaret died within two weeks of each other suggesting they died of the same disease. They had several children among them were Albert A. Wheeler, born in Crawford County, Pennsylvania in 1842 and died in Prairie City, Illinois in 1915. He married Sarah Jane Louk. The other children were Edwin, John, and William D. Wheeler. Oliver and Margaret are buried in the Virgil Cemetery in Prairie City, Illinois.

THE DOUGLAS FAMILY

The Douglas family is originally from Scotland. They were involved in all the major historic events of Scotland and were a powerful and influential family. The Kings of Scotland gave them large estates, but the original stronghold is about twenty miles south of Glasgow. James Douglas of Drumlanrig was a special friend to Robert the Bruce. The family also held lands in Northern Ireland. James I granted Drumlanrig Castle lands to the Douglas family in 1412.

Lord Archibald Douglass arrived in America with his four sons and family about 1725 on a chartered vessel from Scotland and Ireland. He landed in Newcastle, Delaware. His family included four sons; three were believed to have been engaged in the Rebellion of 1715, supporting the Pretender James Francis Edward Stuart. When his brother, John, was killed, Archibald grew tired of the constant fighting and decided to move his family to America leaving his property to his sister who married Lord Hone. According to historic records, Lord Archibald Douglass was the grandson of Sir William Douglass 9th Earl of Drumlanrig born 1582 and died 1640. He had two sons, Archibald and William Douglas of Kilhead who died in 1773, father of Alexander. The family was Anglican and probably "overseers" hired by the English to manage the vast estate in Northern Ireland, which would account for their wealth and why they were not Presbyterian. Archibald is said to have married Margaret Smith, the widow of David Duncan.

Archibald's sons, Thomas, Archibald, John, and Andrew moved to Pequea Valley in Lancaster County, Pennsylvania where they established homes and bought farmland. Archibald brought several friends and relatives over on his chartered ship. They helped to build the Old St. John Church in 1729 for followers of the Church of England. Many of the family are buried in the churchyard. John Douglas was the father of Eleanor who was born in Ireland. She married William Butler. Several of the Douglas family served in the Revolution including George from Lancaster, Pennsylvania, DAR number (#A033717) and John (#A031748) who died in 1841 in Philadelphia. Five members of the family fought in the Battle of King's Mountain.*

*History and pictures including crest sourced from Wikipedia

THE MCMURTRY FAMILY

According to tradition, the ancestors of the McMurtry family came from the ancient Scottish Kingdom of Dalriada. The name was used to identify a noted  mariner or sea captain. The County of Ayrshire, the Parish of Kirkmichael, and Dalmellington in Scotland were a few of the main settlements of families of the name. James McMurtery was born August 18, 1720 in Kirkmichael, Ayr, Scotland the son of Thomas McMurtery. The picture of the McMurtry home at Maybole Castle, Ayr  Scotland is from the original engraving done in 1837 by W. Bartle.

Many of the families later moved to Antrim, Ireland. The earliest record of McMurtries of Northern Ireland is in the 1630 muster roll around Antrim. In 1620, James I of England created Randall McDonald the first Earl of Antrim. The Earl proceeded to populate his Antrim lands in Dunluce with Scottish Protestants lowlanders. John and Thomas McMurtry are listed as the Earl's British tenants. He also set aside his lands in Cary for Scottish Highlanders.

The Ancient Dunluce Castle in Antrim, Ireland was the home of John, Thomas, and Joseph McMurtry. The castle was built about the Anglo-Norman time. It fell into disuse in the early 1700's.

The McMurtry's were Protestants and by 1715, there were over 200,000 Presbyterians living in and around Ulster. During the 1700's a number of McMurtry families immigrated to America mainly for religious reasons, including three brothers, Thomas, Joseph, and Robert along with their father, Joseph.

Joseph McMurtrie (McMurtry) was born about 1685 in Dalmellington, Ayrshire, Scotland and died May 1762 in Oxford Township, Sussex, County New Jersey Colony. He was the son of Joseph (MacMuirceartach Mackirdie) and Mary McMurtrie. Joseph was a manufacturer of fine Moroccan leather and belonged to the Clan Stuart. He married Ann Boone in 1723 in Philadelphia County, Pennsylvania. She was born in Germantown Philadelphia in 1692 and died in 1781 in Sussex, County

New Jersey. Her parents were Charles and Ann Boone. Charles was born 1657 in Dalmellington, Ayrshire, Scotland and died in Philadelphia, Pennsylvania.

Joseph served in the French and Indian War and was with Braddock at the time of his defeat. Joseph, his brothers Thomas and Robert, and two brothers' in law, purchased a large track of land, 1250 acres, on the Delaware River in Sussex, County in 1730-50, which is now a part of Belvedere. He also lived in Bernard's Township in Somerset, County. Thomas was born in 1725 in Scotland and died in 1788 in Somerset, County, New Jersey. He married Mary (last name is unknown). The Tax list shows he owned eighty-four Acres of improved land valued at four hundred dollars, eight cattle, twenty-seven hogs, six horses, and no slaves. He is buried in Old Roxitcus Churchyard, Ralston, Morris County, New Jersey (no marker).

Thomas served in the Revolution (#A078455) under Captain Jacob Ten Eyck in the First Battalion of the Somerset Militia. He had three sons, James, Thomas, Robert and a daughter. His son Robert born in 1749 served in the Revolution (#A078454) with service in Somerset County. Thomas' brother, John McMurtry born 1738, served in the War by furnishing supplies, (#A078428). John was an organizer of Oxford Township, Sussex County Committee of Safety and a County Delegate. He also served in the New Jersey General Assembly in 1778.

Thomas' oldest son, James, was born in Ralston, Morris County, New Jersey and died before 1785 in Franklin County, Pennsylvania. He died before his father. In his will, Thomas left the children of his oldest son James, seven shillings, and six pence. James' son, Joseph, was born March 8, 1764 in Pluckemin, Somerset County, New Jersey. The dates of his birth and those of his family are recorded in a family Bible transcribed in 1890. Joseph moved from Somerset County to Crawford County in northwest Pennsylvania about 1800 after the creation of the village of Harmonsburg. He built the first house and tavern. He married Margaret Kirkpatrick in 1788 in New Jersey. She was born October 26, 1771 in Mine Brook, Somerset, County, and died in Harmonsburg March 8, 1855. She was the daughter of Andrew Kirkpatrick of Mine Brook and Margaret Gaston, daughter of Joseph Gaston. They had five sons, and five daughters.*

*History sourced from Ancestry and the McMurtry Clane Archives. The picture and crest are from Muircheartaigh.com and used with permission of Clan Chief at McMurtry Archives

THE BOONE FAMILY

The Boone name has been spelled in several ways including Bohun, Bohon, Boon, Bohan and Bound among others. The name originated in France in the town of Bohun in western Normandy. They are found in England in Essex where they were settled on lands given them by King William. They were from France originally and followers of Duke William. Henry de Bohun Earl of Hereford, relative of Godfrey de Manderville, was one of the twenty-five Barons of the Magna Carta. Humphrey de Bohun, Fourth Earl of Hereford was born about 1276. His father was the Third Earl of Hereford and his mother was Maud de Fiennes daughter of Enguerrand II de Fiennes, chevalier, seigneur of Fiennes. Humphrey (VII) was born at Pleshey Castle, Essex. He succeeded his father as the Earl of Hereford and Earl of Essex and Constable of England (later called Lord High Constable). He also held the title of Bearer of the Swan Badge, a heraldic device passed down in the Bohun family, which appears in his personal seal. He married Elizabeth, daughter of King Edward I. He was one of several Earls and Barons under Edward I who laid siege to Caerloverock Castle in Scotland and later took part in several more campaigns there.

Humphrey de Bohum, Forth Earl of Hereford (pictured) was a contemporary of Robert the Bruce and possibly acquainted. Their properties in Essex and Middlesex were very close to each other and they were close to the same age. After Bruce deflected from England and Edward I, Bohun received Bruce's castle of Lochmaben and many of his other properties. After Bruce took the Crown of Scotland in 1306, his Queen, Elizabeth de Burgh, daughter of the Earl of Ulster, was captured by Edward I. Her custodians became Humphrey and his wife Elizabeth. She was freed after Bruce captured Humphrey in the battle of Bannockburn in 1314 and they were exchanged. Edward II who was his brother-in-law ransomed Humphrey. Bruce killed Sir Henry de Bohun, grandson of Humphrey de Bohun the second Earl of Hereford, in the same battle.

The first recorded member of the Boone family to arrive in the Colonies was William Boone in 1642 in James City (Jamestown) sponsored by John Smith. The family of Daniel Boone arrived in 1717. Charles Boone born 1667 arrived in Pennsylvania before 1692 from Dalmellington, Ayrshire Scotland. He died in Philadelphia and buried in the Leverington Cemetery. His daughter Anne was born in Germantown, Pennsylvania in 1692. She married Joseph McMurtrie in 1723 in Philadelphia County. Joseph was also born in Dalmellington in 1685. It is possible the families were acquainted before the McMurtry family move from Scotland.

The DAR lists over fifty members of the Boone family who served in the Revolution. The most famous was Daniel Boone born 1734 in Berks County, Province of Pennsylvania.

Crest and history sourced from at Ancestry and Wikipedia

THE KIRKPATRICK FAMILY

The Kirkpatrick's descend from the tribes of Dalriada in Northern Ireland who went to Scotland around the year 280 with St. Patrick. They settled in Dumfriesshires' in the southwest part of Scotland. St Patrick established several churches, which became know as "kil" or "cell." In Dumfriesshire, one was called "Cella Patricii," which later became Kil Patrick. By 700, there were two religions in the area, one the Roman Catholic and the other the Celtic Church. The Roman church began imposing taxes or tithes on the people and the people rebelled. The Celtic Church believed their sole purpose was to administer the gospel to the people. In 800, the Roman Church moved the seat of the Church to York. The Celtics broke away and made reforms calling the church a Kirk–Patrick and thus the name of Kirkpatrick in Dumfriesshire.

In the 11th Century, King Malcolm of Scotland passed a law giving land to a selected few of his favorites. These feudal Barons were to maximize the income from the lands in any way they wished. Most began taxing the people and charging rent. Malcolm III declared that the Barons must name themselves after the area they lived in and thus the Kirkpatrick family was established in Dumfriesshire Castle (pictured). Ewan Kirkpatrick was written down in 1194 for the first time. Ewan had two sons, Ewan and Rodger, from where the two branches of the family evolved.

Rodger eventually took over his father's land of Auchencas and Ewan was granted the lands of Closeburn in 1232. King Alexander II gave his trusted men lands to guard Scotland from the Norsemen. King Robert the Bruce's grandfather, the Earl of Annandale, granted land in Annandale to Roger Kirkpatrick, another key position. Later Roger's son Humphrey was granted land in Dumbarton from which the family of Colquhoun descends. The family continued to strengthen their position with inter marriages with other landed Barons and Earls. One of the younger sons, Alexander Kirkpatrick, was able to establish himself with land when he captured the rebel Earl of Douglas. The grateful King gave him the estate of Kirkmichael, beginning yet another branch of Kirkpatrick's. They became a very powerful family. Roger Kirkpatrick was with Robert the Bruce (pictured) when he stabbed Comyn at the church. He asked Bruce if Comyn was dead, hearing he was not, he went in to finish him off. He came out with his blood soaked dagger and said "MIC SICCAR" or" Make Sure". This is when the Dagger appeared on the family crest instead of the former swan. Bruce then became the undisputed King of Scotland. Roger and Stephen Kirkpatrick fought with Bruce at Bannockburn. They were knighted for their service. An earlier King sponsored one of the Kirkpatrick family members to fight in the Crusades in Palestine. They were involved in some way in all of Scottish history including the Stuart Kings.

The Kirkpatrick family in America came from Dumfrisshire, Scotland. Alexander was born in Watties Neach. He moved his family to Belfast, Ireland after the birth of his son David in the later part of the reign of George I, about 1725, *"that he might enjoy better liberty of conscience and additional religious advantages."* In the spring of 1736, he and his family left Ireland for America again in search of religious freedom. Alexander's brother, Andrew, and his family came over with him and they eventually lived in Sussex County New Jersey.

Sir Henry Hudson explored the New Jersey area in 1609, but the Swedish and Dutch first settled it. The Colony was not surrendered to the English until 1664 when a British fleet sailed into the Port of New York and New Jersey and forced the Dutch to submit. It was then New Jersey was given its name. The treaty of Westminster was ratified in 1674 and the English controlled the area until the Revolution. King Charles II gave the region between New England and Maryland to his brother the Duke of York. The Duke in turn gave the land between the Hudson River and the Delaware River to his friends, Sir George Carteret and Lord Berkeley, and named New Jersey. To entice more settlers to the area, Carteret and Berkeley granted sections of land and passed the *Concessions and Agreement* document granting religious freedom throughout New Jersey. The settlers paid fees known as quitrents, which were difficult to collect. Lord Berkeley sold his share of New Jersey to the Quakers in 1674.

The Kirkpatrick family had a very stormy trip lasting thirteen weeks and finally landed at New Castle, Delaware. By the time the ship arrived, the passengers and crew had almost starved due to the length of the passage. David told his grandson in later years the first thing he was able to eat on landing was corn. He said he ate it without roasting it he was so hungry. He described his meal as eating the corn until the milk ran down his arms saying he had never tasted anything sweeter. The Kirkpatrick family crossed the Delaware at Philadelphia traveled by foot to Boundbrook and from there went over the mountain. They came to a spring at the side of Minebrook where they built a log cabin and went to work. The spot was about two miles from Basking Ridge (pictured) in Somerset County, New Jersey, one of the oldest Counties in America.

The site was on the south slope of Round Mountain with meadowlands, and an "unfailing spring" with enough water in Mine Brook for a mill. George Washington and his troops marched through the county many times and stay in several of the homes. The battles here were numerous and the families suffered the burden of the battles.

Alexander leased 137 acres in the beginning and planted several apple trees as required in the lease. He later obtained the land title in fee simple granted November 23, 1747 and eventually bought more land. He died at Mine Brook on June 3, 1758. Andrew, his oldest son, inherited the homestead and he eventually sold it to his younger brother David and moved to Washington County, Pennsylvania with his wife Margaret and children. He married Margaret Gaston about 1747 in Somerset County, New Jersey, the daughter of Joseph Gaston. Their children were Alexander, Jennet, Elizabeth, Margaret (who married Joseph McMurtry), Mary Sarah, Anne, and Hannah. In Washington County, Andrew lived on land he thought was public domain and did not apply for a deed. However, in 1759 the Penn brothers, William and Richard, sued him for trespassing on their land. Andrew lost, but the suit was not settled until 1766. He and his family then joined the historic Scotch Colony that migrated to Augusta County Virginia. Alexander Kirkpatrick was the first Sherriff of Augusta County. The family eventually lived in North Carolina and Tennessee. Andrew Kirkpatrick, a descendant, became Chief Justice for the New Jersey Supreme Court in 1798.

Andrew, born 1721 in Scotland, was a Captain in the First Brigade of the Somerset Militia during the Revolution (#A065605). He is listed in Stryker's Regiment of Officers and men of New Jersey. He also fought under Captain Jacob TenEyck. The New Jersey Militia was a vital part of the war effort continually resisting the British movements. They also helped to control the Tory population still loyal to the crown. They helped enforce the "treason acts" and prevent the illicit trade with the British, which continued throughout the war. Andrew died in Washington County Pennsylvania in 1790.

Alexander Kirkpatrick, son of Andrew, born September 3, 1751 in Mine Brook was a Lieutenant from Mine Brook Somerset County (A065602) in the First Regiment of the Somerset New Jersey Militia. He fought under Captains Jacob DeGroat, John Sebring, and Colonel Steven Hunt in Hunt's battalion consisting of three companies from Somerset that defended New York with the "Jersey Line" in the early summer of 1776. He died in Mine Brook September 24, 1827.

David Kirkpatrick (#A065613) born February 17, 1724 in Scotland, brother of Andrew, was a member of the New Jersey Legislature and gave Patriotic Service. He died in New Jersey March 19, 1814.
Hugh Kirkpatrick, born 1735 in Maryland, was a Lieutenant in the Continental Marines in 1780. Another Hugh (#A065633) born 1739 in Scotland, was a Private in the First Battalion Somerset Militia under Captain Ten Eyck. Thirty-five members of the Kirkpatrick family served in the Revolution.

*Crest with dagger, history and pictures sourced from Wikipedia, Ancestry, and Kirkpatrick Family. Kirkpatrick coat-of-arms sourced from www.adeksal.com and gives online permission to print and use picture.

THE GASTON FAMILY IN AMERICA

The Gaston name originates from Gascony, a Provence along the border of Spain and France near the Pyrenees Mountains. In pre-Roman times, the inhabitants were Aquitania's and spoke a language related to the Basque. The Family descends from the Gaston Viscounts of Bearn, a medieval Lordship with the chief seat and stronghold at Pau, which was the capitol of the independent principality of Bearn in 1464. The Pyrenean territory was later united on the person of heiress, Eleanor Countess of Foix to the Kingdom of Navarre where she was Queen Regent of Navarre. In 1441, Eleanor had married Count Gaston IV Count of Foix and Bearn (pictured in the Crusade of 1096). Among Eleanor and Gaston's descendants were King Henry II and King Henry III, who became Henry IV of France. Bearn remained independent ruled separately from France by Henry IV until after his death. In 1620, it became a part of France. The Gaston's are alleged to be connected through marriage with the Grand Dukes of Tuscany of Habsburg-Lorraine. At right is the shield for Gaston IV, County of Foix, and Viscount of Bearn. The crest of Eleanor of Foix, Queen of Navarre is also pictured.

Jean (John) Gaston is the first known ancestor of the American family. He was born in 1600 in Foix, France, perhaps a descendant of John of Foix, Viscount of Narbonne. Jean and some of his relatives were associated with a group of Protestants called Huguenots. In 1598 King, Henry IV of Navarre and France (the first of the Bourbon Kings through his father Antoine de Bourbon) endorsed the Edict of Nantes, which granted rights to the Protestants Huguenots. His mother, Jeanne d'Albret Queen of Navarre, raised him in the protestant faith. However, in 1685 King Louis XIV, who became king in 1643, revoked the Edict and declared France entirely Catholic again. He then pursued a policy of purging the country of Protestants by arresting and killing them.

By 1640, Jean Gaston had fled to Scotland and his estates were confiscated. His brothers and sisters remained Catholic and provided financial aid to him in Scotland until he became established. According to tradition, he descended from royalty. The above history seems to support the belief.

Jean (John) married Agnes who died in Melrose, Roxburghshire, Scotland after 1650. Their children were William, John, and Alexander. Twenty-five years later John and his sons went to Antrim Northern Ireland (between 1662 and 1668) when the Protestants were persecuted in Scotland, moving again for religious reasons. By 1740, there were five Protestant households of Gaston's in Clough in the County of Antrim. John (Jr.) married and had several children, William, Hugh, Mary, Joseph, John, and Alexander. Four of the brothers, John, Hugh, Joseph, and Alexander arrived in America around 1720. They came in through the Port of Amboy and settled in New Jersey. William remained in Ireland.

Joseph Gaston was born in County Antrim, Ireland about 1700 and died in April of 1777 in Bernard's Township, Somerset County, New Jersey. His occupation was listed as farmer and he was a member of the Basking Ridge Presbyterian Church. He married Margaret (?) who was born about 1705 and died August 31, 1795 in Hardwick Twp. Sussex County, New Jersey. She is buried in the Yellow Frame Presbyterian Churchyard in Frelinghuysen, Sussex County, New Jersey. They had seven children, Martha born 1726, Margaret born 1728, John born Nov. 10 (16), 1730, Robert born Jan 28, 1732, Joseph born Nov. 10, 1738, and daughters Priscilla and Ann. Their daughter, Margaret, married Andrew Kirkpatrick. After the death of her husband, Margaret lived with her son, Joseph.

During the Revolution Robert Gaston, son of Joseph and Margaret was a Lieutenant Colonel in the New Jersey Militia, a Captain in the Continental Line and a member of the Committee of Safety (#A0473371). Joseph was the paymaster for the New Jersey State Militia (#A043365). His brother John served as a member and Clerk of the Committee of Correspondence (#A043354). In 1751 John went to Pennsylvania and then to South Carolina. He was a King's Justice and became a leader of the Patriots in his area during 1780-81. Justice John was pursued by the hated British Lieutenant Colonel "Bloody" Tarleton and at one time was forced to leave his home and family. His wife Esther and youngest son Joseph hid in the woods while Tarleton and his troops destroyed all they owned. John returned to find his home completely demolished. His nine sons served as soldiers in the Revolution and four lost their lives. Robert was killed in 1780 at Hanging Rock along with his two brothers, Ebenezer and David. Joseph survived that battle (#A043367). Joseph's wife, Martha, also served (#A043369). An account and history of Patriot Justice John Gaston is found in the book "*Polly of the Pines*." Another related Joseph Gaston served from Pennsylvania and William was at King's Mountain. Twenty-five Gaston's served in the Revolution, including three of their wives.

*History and pictures sourced from Gaston Family History, Wikipedia, and DAR. Gaston crest sourced from doddridgecountyroots.com and gives permission online to use

CHAPTER IV
THE PILGRIMS

The Plymouth Colony was the first permanent New England Colony founded by a group of religious separatists, thirty-five of whom were members of a radical Puritan faction known as the English Separatist Church. Puritanism was a religious reform movement with in the Church of England. After illegally breaking with the Church in 1607, they went first to Amsterdam in the Netherlands and then to the town of Leiden where they lived for over a decade. Economic problems and the fear they would lose their English heritage and language, caused them to make plans to go to the New World. Their intended destination was the area around the mouth of the Hudson River, which they thought was a part of the already established Virginia Colony. Members of the group joined a London Stock Company that eventually financed their voyage on a three masted merchant ship called the *Mayflower*.

In September of 1620, over one-hundred people set sail from Plymouth, England led by John Carver, William Bradford, and a professional soldier, Myles Standish. The ship was blown off course and landed in November on Cape Cod in what is now Massachusetts. A scouting party was sent across the Bay and in late December, they settled on a place they called Plymouth Harbor. While still on board the ship, forty-one of the men signed the *Mayflower Compact*. They agreed to join in a "civil body politic," which became the foundation of the Colony's government. Thomas Rogers, a Leiden separatist, was the eighteenth signatory to the Compact. The Pilgrim settlers lived on the *Mayflower* for several months while they built their settlement. More than half of the Pilgrims died during the first winter including John Carver, the first Governor, due to poor nutrition and insufficient housing. William Bradford was elected to take his place. George Morton, Pilgrim Father and his family arrived in 1623. He was their financial agent, purchased the Mayflower and published the book on the Colony in England. (see Morton Family)

Desire Minter was a young girl traveling with Governor Carver and his household. She was the daughter of William Minter and Sarah Willet Minter members of the Leiden congregation from Norfolk, England. William became a citizen of Leiden on May 3, 1613 and bought a house on September 10, 1614. Sarah was the midwife for the church. Desire's father, William, died in 1617-18 and her mother remarried in 1618 to Roger Simmonson. Desire was placed with another Leiden resident, Thomas Brewer. Brewer was arrested in 1619 by the University of Leidon at the request of the English Ambassador charged with printing and disturbing illegal books in England. Desire was then in the care of John Carver. She was under the age of nineteen during the *Mayflower* voyage. She was not well after the voyage and returned to her "friend" in England about 1621 after she became of age and able to make her own decisions. This was prior to the 1623 division of land at Plymouth. She died not long after her return. Richard Mintrene (Minter) and his son Edward arrived in Jamestown that same year on the ship *Margaret and John.* It is unknown if they were related.

The repressive religious policies toward the nonconformists of James I and Charles I drove many men and women to follow the Pilgrims to the New World. By 1630, a group of over one-thousand Puritan refugees had settled in Massachusetts under Governor John Winthrop who obtained a charter from King Charles I.

*History and pictures sourced from Mayflowerhistory.com/minter, Wikipedia and Britannic

THOMAS ROGERS, PILGRIM

Thomas Rogers (pictured) traveled with his eldest son Joseph on the historic *Mayflower* voyage to the New World. He was born about 1572 near the village of Watford in Northamptonshire, England the son of William and Eleanor Rogers. He later became a member of the English Separatist Church. He married Alice Cosford in Watford parish in 1597, the daughter of George and Margaret Cosford. Their six children were baptized in Watford between 1599 and 1613. Thomas baptized in 1598 and Richard baptized 1599, did not survive. Joseph was baptized January 23, 1602, John baptized April 6, 1606, Elizabeth baptized December 26, 1609, and Margaret baptized May 30, 1613. Another son, James, was born about 1615. His wife Alice and children Joseph, John, Elizabeth, Margaret, and James went to Leiden in the Netherlands about 1614 with the Separatists. Thomas bought a house in Barabarasteeg in 1614 and became a citizen of Leiden in 1618. He was a merchant of *camlet,* a luxury Asian type fabric made from a combination of silk and camel's hair and called silk cashmere.

Thomas left his wife and children behind in Leiden in the household of Antony Clements when he and his eighteen-year-old son Joseph sailed on the *Mayflower*. William Bradford's, leader of the Separatists, account of the *Mayflower* voyage states *"Thomas Rogers and Joseph his son embarked on the Mayflower. His other children came afterwards."* His wife is not mentioned and may have died sometime between 1622 and when the other children came to Plymouth in 1629-30. They arrived with the remainder of the Leiden church members at the Colony's expense. Thomas Rogers died sometime during the first winter leaving his son Joseph to receive his father's allotment of land in the division at Plymouth in 1623. Thomas is buried in the Coles Hill burial Ground in Plymouth.

The *Mayflower* voyage was extremely difficult on the small one-hundred foot ship with one-hundred and two passengers plus a crew of about forty-five. The conditions were very cramped. The ship was battered by strong westerly winds during the second month shaking the ship's timbers so badly, some of the caulking failed to keep the seawater out. The passengers were lying wet even in their berths. This along with lack of food and unsanitary conditions caused many to become ill. Two died during the voyage and left the majority of the women and children unhealthy when they arrived. The harsh winter in Plymouth accounted for the deaths of fifty percent of the settlers including Thomas Rogers.

Joseph Rogers married Hannah Rogers in 1633 and had eight children. Margaret Rogers died in 1622 in Plymouth. Elizabeth Rogers, daughter of Thomas, married Daniel Smith son of John Bland Smith and his wife Isabel. Daniel was born 1610 in Colchester, Essex, England. He went to Watertown, Massachusetts about 1630. He died July 14, 1660. He and Elizabeth were married about 1641 in Watertown. Their son Daniel Smith Jr. was born September 27, 1642 in Watertown and died June 7, 1681. John Rogers married Anna Churchman in 1639 and had seven children.

James Rogers born 1615 in New London, Connecticut, son of Thomas Mayflower Rogers, married Elizabeth Rowland born 1635 daughter of Samuel Rowland. Their son Jonathan, born 1655, married Naomi Burdick, Their daughter Elizabeth Rogers born 1681 in New London, Connecticut, married James Smith, their son Ebenezer Smith born February 4, 1710, married first Lucy Polly Smith and had one child,

Ebenezer born 1745. His second wife was Lucy Hatch born 1720 and they had ten children. Their third child was Anna Smith born 1749 in Montville, New London Connecticut, who married Ephraim, Wheeler.

*History and pictures sourced from Wikipedia, Genealogy, Geni, Roots web, and Ancestry

CHAPTER V
THE PURITANS IN AMERICA

"In the United States, many protestant sects will come and go. Some will be elevated and influence world leaders; others will be abased by scandals.

Expatriate Calvinists will flee from France and will eventually become the Puritans who will bring the reformist movement to the North American Colonies, sustaining and expanding the Christian Church." Translation of Nostradamus' Epistle 14:2.

The infamous Religion Act of 1592 was the beginning of the civil unrest, which stated,
"All persons above the age of sixteen, who obstinately refuse to attend divine service at some established church, shall be committed to prison without bail until they shall conform and make public confession of conformity in terms prescribed by the statute itself."
The Act also denied Queen Elizabeth's authority in religious matters. This Act helped to influence the Wheeler families and many others to immigrate to New England. After James I came to power in 1603, he continued the practice and declared,
"I will make then conform themselves or I will harry them out of the land, or else do more…"

By the end of Queen Elizabeth's reign, the Church of England was firmly in place with three main religions existing within the Church. Some believed the Church was just what it should be, some wanted to reintroduce some of the Catholic practices, and the Puritans wanted to remove anything that was associated with the Roman Church. During the reigns of James I and Charles, I more disputes arose leading to the English Civil War. Religion was only part of the problem but the absolution of the required Prayer Book was a main cause of the conflict. The Puritans were blocked from changing the established church from within. The English laws restricted their religious practices, but they spread their views by preaching and through the educational system. After the Restoration of Charles II, most of the clergy left the Church of England and became non-conformist ministers. The Puritans felt the Church still tolerated too many practices associated with the Catholic Church and wanted greater "purity" of worship and doctrine.*

In 1633, William Laud was made Archbishop of Canterbury. He was opposed to the Puritans and supported by King Charles I. Loud was determined to suppress the Puritans and make them follow the rules of the Episcopal Church of England. The Puritans with their own nonconformist ministers, refused to use the decorations and ceremonies of the English Church.

Reverend Peter Buckley (pictured) became a nonconformist minister in Odell, Bedfordshire England where he was born. After graduating from St. John's College at Cambridge, he received several degrees and succeeded his father as rector in Odell. By the 1630's, there were several complaints about his preaching and he was suppressed by the Archbishop for failing to conform to requirements of the Anglican Church. He refused to read the "Declaration of Spor," the list of limitations on activities on Sunday issued by Charles I, wear a vestment (surplice), or use the Sign of the Cross at a visitation by Archbishop William Laud. He also refused to use them during baptism saying, *"he accounted them ceremonies, superstitions, and "dissenteaneous" to the holy Word of God."* By 1634, he was ejected from the parish for these violations, however his successor was not installed as Rector until July of 1635, over a month after Buckley left England. In May of 1635, he immigrated to New England aboard the *Susan and Ellen.* He was ordained in Cambridge, Massachusetts by 1637 and moved to Concord with several planter families. Peter's oldest son had already arrived in Boston in 1634. His two brothers-in-law, Abraham Mellows and Atherton Hough immigrated in 1633. Together with William Spenser, an early Massachusetts Bay Colony leader, they scouted out a suitable site for a settlement. When Buckley arrived in 1635, they petitioned the Colony governing body, the Court of Assistance for a Township. Concord was incorporated in 1635 but there were no settlers until the spring of 1636. Buckley recruited settlers including many of his former church members in England. The Mill and its dam were constructed in the winter of 1636 in the center of town. (George Wheeler bought eleven acres in the center of town on his arrival in 1637). The church was "gathered" and the elders elected in the spring of 1636.**

Wheeler family members were courtiers during the reign of Charles I and II. On February 9, 10, 11 of 1677, Sir Charles Wheeler, member of the Court of King Charles, carried several Bills in Parliament. A Bill was ordered to "erect a Monument to the late Sacred Majesty King Charles the First to be read on Tuesday morning next." King Charles was beheaded on January 30, 1649. After the Restoration, Parliament eventually approved seventy thousand pounds to erect the monument, which was raised in 1678. Another Wheeler, Captain Francis Wheeler, commanded the sixty-four gun battleship the HMS Rupert in 1689 under Charles II when he help capture a large enemy fleet off the coast of France.

*The English Civil war took place from 1642 to 1652 between the Royalists and the Parliamentarians, which ended with the Parliamentary victory and led to the execution of Charles I for "treason." Parliament then passed a statute prohibiting his son Charles II from taking the throne. Britain became a Commonwealth state, led by Oliver Cromwell, until the Restoration. Although Charles II did not actually begin his reign until 1660, after his Restoration all legal documents were changed and dated as if he had succeeded his father.
**History and pictures sourced from Wikipedia

CHAPTER VI

THE WHEELER FAMILY

A Puritan Family – From the Old to the New World

The Wheeler name is found in England as far back as Thomas B. Wielher, who was born in the year 819 in the new Kingdom of England. He married Mary Ann in 847 and died in 888. He, his wife, and descendants are well documented. King Egbert, who by his own edict, dated at Winchester in 819, commanded the Island be called Anglelond (England) after his Anglo Saxon ancestors. Calling all the leaders of his conquered lands together, with their consent he was crowned King Egbert in 827, the first King of England, (pictured).

The Wheeler family members are found in both the villages Cranfield (dove field) and Odell in Bedfordshire. The Monks of Ramsey Abbey were granted a Manor in Cranfield in 998 by a Saxon. A church was built and the Abbot of Saint Benedict held the land until the monasteries were dissolved during the reign of Henry VIII. (1509-1547). Evidence of Roman occupation in the Odell area before the fourth century includes a farm of two round timbered buildings inside a fenced enclosure. The farm was abandoned about the seventh century. In the eleventh century, Levenot, a subject of King Edward the Confessor, controlled the land. After the Battle of Hastings in 1066, William the Conqueror took over all the land in England. He gave Levenot's land and the title of Baron to Walter Flandrensis a Count of Flanders who fought with him. Walters (sometimes know as Wahul) arrival marked the beginning of a period of centuries when a family with the name Odell continued to hold most of the lands and built their castle. There is evidence of a church building in Odell as early as 1220 when Robert Dunton was minister. The present church of All Saints (pictured) dates back to the fifteenth century. One of its most famous ministers was Peter Bulkeley, who became the rector in 1624. He was suspended in 1635 when he refused to conform to the requirements of the Church of England.

Descending the Wheeler line, Sir John Welere was born in 1348. He married Patty Sue Milk, who was born in 1346. Castlemilk in Scotland was the well know home of Sir William Stewart in 1398. There may or may not be a connection to Patty Sue Milk, but the Sir names often reflect the resident. Their son, John Thomas was born in 1375 the first Wheeler born in Cranfield, Bedfordshire in the reign of Edward III.

Edward IV (youngest son of Edward III) was King in 1472-1482. Henry Wheeler was born in 1482 in Bedfordshire during his reign and died in 1557 during the reign of Queen Mary, (1553-1558) daughter of Henry VIII (1509-1547). His son Obadiah was born 1506 during the reign of Henry VII (1485-1509) in

Bedfordshire and died in 1536 during the reign of Henry VIII.* Henry Wheeler married Elizabeth (unknown last name). John Wheeler, son of Obadiah Wheeler, was born in 1539 in Odell, Bedfordshire, England and died April 15, 1567 in Cranfield, Bedfordshire, England. He married Alice Sayre about 1560 the daughter of William and Alice Square (Sayre), during the reign of Elizabeth I (1558-1603). Alice was born in 1541 and died in 1567. They had ten children, four daughters, and six sons. Their son Thomas was born in 1561 in Bedfordshire and died October 8, 1643 in Bedfordshire. He married first Dorothy Holloway and they had eight children, six boys, and two girls. Their son Thomas was born 1603 during the reign of James I, (James VI of Scotland 1603-1625) and died 1686 in the Fairfield, Connecticut Colony. He married Ann Halsey in 1613. Sons Timothy born 1604-1687, George born 1605 and died 1687 in Concord Massachusetts, Joseph born 1609-1614, Richard born 1614-1676 went to Dedham Massachusetts and died in the Lancaster Indian Massacre of 1775. Ephraim, born 1619, died in 1670 in Stratfield, Fairfield, Connecticut Colony. The girls were Mary Elizabeth born about 1615 and Susannah born 1607 (She married Obadiah Wheeler son of John Wheeler, Jr. and immigrated to New England). Thomas married his second wife Jane Mitchell in 1625 in St. James, Middlesex. They had a son John born 1627 in Middlesex, who went to the Colonies. His third wife was Elizabeth Claye whom he married during the reign of Charles I (1625 to 1649).

Three of the Wheeler brothers arrived in the Massachusetts Bay Colony in 1637 during the reign of Charles I. The King's religious policies and marriage to a Roman Catholic caused the mistrust of the reformed groups such as the Puritans and Calvinists and they left England. The Wheeler family immigrated to Concord, Massachusetts and helped to found the city. Family members later helped found cities in Connecticut. Brothers, George, Joseph, and Obadiah (brother-in-law) are recorded on Concord in 1637 with Ephraim, Thomas and Timothy arriving in 1639 (Timothy returned in to England in 1660), all from Odell, Bedfordshire, England. Their brother Richard immigrated to Dedham, Massachusetts. John (the son of Thomas and his second wife) arrived later in Connecticut. They seem to be a family of wealth and their position and possessions enabled them to assume leadership in their communities. Traditionally, land distribution and favors, including the seating in the meetinghouse were done according to wealth and social position.

Their Puritan ministers Peter Buckley and John Jones arrived in Concord earlier. Reverend Jones left Buckley. He was also a Cambridge University graduate, founded in 1209 the second oldest English speaking University. George Wheeler was a man of influence and was on the city records in Concord as a Selectman in 1660. He owned eleven acres in the center of town at the crossroads of Walden Street and Main Street where he built his house, pictured. He also owned land at Walden Pond among other acreages. He helped build the church and schools. Many of his descendants are still found in the Concord area.

In 1644, after a dispute within the Concord Church, George's brother Ephraim and Thomas Jr. move to Fairfield, Connecticut with the Reverend Jones and about one-eighth of the Concord settlers including James Bennett and his wife, Hannah, who was the eldest daughter of Thomas Wheeler. Thomas Sr. had already moved to Fairfield in 1640 and was the first settler at Black Rock.

The youngest son of Thomas of Bedfordshire was John Wheeler born March 14, 1627 in Middlesex, England and passed away on December 16, 1691 in New London, Connecticut. He married Elizabeth (Ridge) Stanbridge in 1674. She was born about 1635 in Middlesex, England. She died in 1715 in New London. The Stanbridge family is first recorded in Bedfordshire, England where they held a family seat since before the Norman Conquest. They were the Lords of the Manor in the Parish of Leighton Buzzard. The earliest recorded member was Gilbert (Baron) in 1276 with the Estate.

John and Elizabeth had nine children. John is first documented in New London in 1667 as part owner of a ship called the Zebulon. He was primarily in the mercantile business and traded with West India. He later built another ship of his own, which had just returned from England at the time of his death. On May 8, 1690, John delivered at speech to the General Assembly on the "state of the town of New London and the County in regards to the authority therein." He complained that five of the Chief members of the County are related: a Captain Fitch, Captain Mason, Daniel Witherell., L. Bruster and Richard Christopher and they had *"aggrandized themselves to most, if not all, of the office powers and authority."* He then went on to describe the relationships. (It is not known whether this changed the power and authority in town).

John made a brief trip to Philadelphia and built a brick house on the west side of Front Street below Walnut Street near the Blue Anchor Inn. He purchased the lot from William Penn in midsummer of 1684. He sold the property in 1686 to Edward Shippen of Boston who later moved to Philadelphia. Joshua, John's third son, was born in 1680 in New London and was eleven when his father died. In 1725 in a series of deeds, Joshua and the husbands of his sisters, Hannah, Elizabeth and Anna, sold "expeditiously" to the

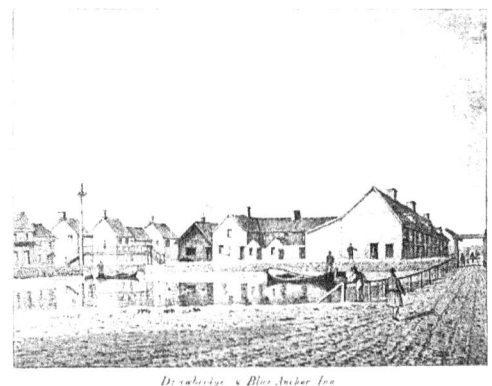

highest bidder or otherwise released their claims for several properties in New York, Pennsylvania, New Jersey, Delaware, and Old London, England. The property in London, according to Joshua, "came to me by descent from my mother Elizabeth Ridge as her only son, the wife of John Wheeler." She derived her right from her father Mr. William Ridge of Newton, Fulgate in the Parish of Saint Leonard, Shoreditch County, Middlesex. Unspecified lands in Philadelphia, Delaware, East, and West Jersey sold for 600 pounds. Joshua Wheeler married Dorothy (?) in Boston and had seven children. He died in 1725 in New London the same year of the land sales.

Joshua's son, Ephraim, was born July 25, 1712 in Boston, Suffolk, Massachusetts and died August 17, 1794 in Montville, New London, Connecticut. He married Mercy Topliff, daughter of Samuel Topliff, (see Topliff) in November of 1737 in Lebanon, New London. The marriage intentions were published on Sunday November 6. She was born in 1717 in Dorchester, Suffolk and died in 1754 in Montville, New

London, Connecticut. They had eight children, Ephraim Jr., born on March 2, 1739 and died 1802. He was born in Boston, Suffolk. William was born September 30, 1739 (1740?) in Willington Tolland, Connecticut. He died in 1782. Samuel was born in New London in 1741-1784. Margaret and the rest of the children were also born in New London. Margaret was born in 1743-1822. (She married Ebenezer Smith descendant of James Smith and Elizabeth Rodgers descendant of Thomas Rogers of the Mayflower). Their other sons were Jerome born 1743, Ebenezer born 1745, Joseph born 1747, and James born 1749 and died1828. Ephraim and Mercy eventually settled on land known as "The Cove" at Montville. (The name is now Horton Cove on the west banks of the Thames River). Mercy died in 1754. Ephraim waited twenty-two years before remarrying. His second marriage was to Mehitable Spaulding on December 31, 1776 in Plainfield, Connecticut. She is listed as Ephraim's wife on his DAR records. They had two children, Sally and Nancy. Ephraim said later after the birth of his daughters, *"they are sometimes confused with his son Ephraim Jr.'s children due to their ages."*

Ephraim Jr.'s Revolutionary War record is also confused with Ephraim Sr.'s (#A123849) record, which has Ephraim Sr.'s birth date and place incorrect. Ephraim Sr. fought with the Johnston Connecticut men and served at the Lexington Alarm in the town of Plainfield. His son Ebenezer, unmarried, died in Schenectady, NY, after the Battle of Saratoga. No date has been found for his death. The battles were fought about two weeks apart. The British technically won the first battle, but they lost two men to every American. The second battle was a turning point in the Revolution. The British General John Burgoyne and his troops thought they had the perfect plan to take over the Hudson River Valley, instead the American troops under Horatio Gates and Benedict Arnold launched a ruthless attack forcing Burgoyne to surrender. After this success, the French enter the war. They provided Washington's army with the needed support and supplies.

Ephraim's son, Joseph Wheeler, (DAR #123968) also fought with Johnston's Men. He was under the commands of Captain's William Stanton, (DAR# 108750) Thomas Wheeler, (DAR # A124049) and Lt. Col. Oliver Smith (DAR # 106582). Ephraim Jr. fought with Col. P. B. Bradley, in the first company of the Fifth Regiment and with Johnston's Men (Connecticut Revolutionary War Records). Jerome was with the 1780 Militia under Colonel Jonathan Dimon. (See Bounties paid the recruits raised for six months, Council of Safety May 30, 1780, CT. Rev. War Records). James is also listed in the Connecticut Revolutionary War Military lists. Ephraim Sr. and all seven of his sons took part in the Revolution.

Lieutenant Colonel Oliver Smith, of the eighth Regiment of the Connecticut Militia may have been related. He was stationed at Stonington, New London County, Connecticut during the Revolution. The Governor and Council appointed him Lieutenant Colonel on July 2, 1776. He ascended from the ranks of Captain and Major. On September 14, 1775, the Governor and Council ordered "the enlistment of fifty men to be placed under the command of Major Oliver Smith for the defense of Stonington and the harbor." (DAR #A106582) He married Mary Denison. His son, Oliver Smith Jr. born 1761 (#A106583) served aboard the Connecticut Privateer Sloop *Hampton Packet* as a Prize Master in March of 1783. He was sent to the prize schooner *Peggy* on March 2, 1783 and brought her into New London on March 6. Oliver's daughter, Anne, married Ephraim Wheeler Jr.

Ephraim's son, William Wheeler (DAR # is A124061) saw duty as a Ferryman. A wharf builder, he was preparing the harbor for the use of the Patriots, when he received word that the British were coming up the river destroying, plundering, and sacking the area. He quickly got his wife and very young children together and took them up the Chautucket River in a canoe to a settlement of Patriots where they had previously assisted in taking care of the sick and wounded. His wife, Hannah French, would not associate with the Tories. She fed and sustained many refugees when the British burned and massacred the town south of the Cove near New London. She later received a Certificate of Service from the state.

On November 22, 1791, Ephraim Sr. sold a parcel of land with a Mansion house and barn to Ephraim, Jr. The land began at the Trading Cove and ran north along the brook to Indian land. (Recorded in the Montville, Ct. land records 2:312). On September 23, 1793, Ephraim Sr. quit claimed two lots of land with a house and barn to Molly, Mercy, and Nancy Wheeler the heirs of his son Jerome then deceased. On March 20, 1794, he warranted twenty-two acres lying next to the heirs of Jerome to Ephraim Jr. for seventy-eight pounds. On March 28, 1794 he warranted another 15 acres to Ephraim Jr. for sixty pounds, (Land records of Montville Quit Claim 3:2, land record 2:304, warranty 2:2:102). On August 6, 1794, Ephraim gave fifteen acres together with the Mansion house (deed 2:108) to Mehitable his second wife for taking care of him in his illness and for the care of their two children, Sally and Nancy. On July 23, 1798, Mehitable quit claimed the right to her dower land to Benjamin Smith with a life lease on three acres of the land and the house on the west bank of the river. (Montville, CT. quit claim 4:5, Estate of Ephraim Wheeler of Montville, New London, Ct., probate 1794, no. 5644).

Ephraim Sr.'s first wife Mercy Topliff, was the daughter of Samuel Topliff and Hannah Trescott. (See Topliff below). Hannah was born in Milton, Massachusetts in 1706 and died 1765, the daughter of Samuel Trescott and Margaret Rodgers born 1664 in Ipswitch, Massachusetts. Margaret's (Rodgers) father was the Reverend John Rodgers born 1630 in Essex, England. He came with his parents, the Reverend Nathaniel Rogers and Margaret Crane, to Ipswitch in 1636. He married Elizabeth Denison, the daughter of General Daniel Denison and Patience Dudley. Patience was the daughter of Thomas Dudley, the first Governor of Massachusetts. Reverend John Rodgers became the fifth President of Harvard College in 1682. The Trescott, Rodgers (Rogers), Denison and Dudley families were very early immigrants to the New England Colonies from England.

Ephraim Wheeler Jr., born March 2, 1739, married Anna Smith, daughter of Oliver Smith. She was born in December 13, 1749 Montville, New London, Connecticut. Ephraim and Anna had five sons, Joshua, Jerome, Oliver, Topliff, and Ebenezer. The two girls, Sally and Nancy listed as their children, were actually the children of Ephraim Sr. Ephraim Jr. died in December 1802 in Montville. It is unknown when Anna died. (See Smith Family and Thomas *Mayflower* Rogers**)**.

Oliver Wheeler, son of Ephraim Jr. and Anna Smith Wheeler, was born in 1784 in Montville, New London. He married first Elizabeth Woodward, the daughter of Patriot Daniel Woodward. She was born in 1785 and died in 1817. Her sister, Lucy, married James Harvey Wheeler whose father was Silas Wheeler of the Concord Wheeler branch. (*See Woodward, Newton, and Miles Families*).

Samuel Topliff was born 1695 in Dorchester, Massachusetts to Samuel Topliff, born in 1652 in Gloucester, Massachusetts, and died in 1742 in Dorchester. Samuel's father was Clement Topliff born November 17, 1603 in Ipswich, Essex County, England. Samuel married Patience Somes born 1653 in Gloucester daughter of Morris Somes and Elizabeth Kendall. Morris was born in Bedfordshire, England in 1610. Elizabeth Kendall was born in Cambridge, Middlesex, England in 1628 to John Kendall and Elizabeth Sacherell.

Four members of the Somes family fought in the Revolution from Gloucester, Massachusetts, descendants and relatives of Morris. Abraham (#A107063) was a first Lieutenant, David (#A107065) was a Town Officer in Newcastle, Maine, and Isaac Somes was a Lt. Commander of the *Tempest*. He died at sea in 1782. John Somes, son of Morris was listed as the owner of the *Tempest*. He was Commander of the Massachusetts Privateers during the War. Nehemiah *Somes was also listed as owner and Commander of the Tempest.* (Sourced from *The American War of Independence at Sea).*

During the Revolution, the Wheelers were at almost every major battle in the Northern Colonies including the first battle at Lexington and Concord. Benjamin Wheeler fought in the south at King's Mountain. They were members of the Freemasons and took part in the original Boston Tea Party. The Daughters of the American Revolution (DAR) has over 249 records of Wheeler patriots who fought in the Revolution. After the War, Adam Wheeler was involved in Shaw's Rebellion resisting the high taxes in Massachusetts. This incident compelled George Washington to call for a meeting of Congress, which helped establish a new Constitution. The Wheeler family made significant contributions to the founding of America.

Oliver and Elizabeth Wheeler were married in Montgomery, Hampden, Massachusetts August 18, 1807. They had five children: Amos Maynard born March 23, 1808, Elizabeth Erminia born July 15, 1810, Zilphanna Wheeler born September 5, 1812, Chorodon Nelson born September 4, 1814, and Oliver Cleveland born February 4, 1816 and died 1863. Elizabeth died March 14, 1817, the year after Oliver Cleveland was born.

Oliver married a second wife, Sarah Freeland born 1795 and died 1872. They had six more children, three unknown, Louisa, another Ephraim born 1828-1920, and another Oliver M. born 1838-1909. His son from his marriage to Elizabeth, Oliver Cleveland, accompanied him and his second family to Pennsylvania about 1830/31. The other children from his first marriage seemed to have stayed in Massachusetts. It is possible Oliver moved to Pennsylvania to work on the Erie Canal as construction began there in 1831. He was a mason by trade. (From the Crawford, Pennsylvania archives) The canal starting point was in Beaver, Pennsylvania and ended in Erie. The Conneaut branch of the canal was in the middle and went through both Crawford and Mercer counties where they lived. Oliver died in 1840 in Salem, Mercer County, Pennsylvania.

Oliver Cleveland was born in Montgomery, Hampden, Massachusetts February 4, 1816. His residence in 1840 was in Sadsbury, Crawford County, Pennsylvania. He married Margaret Mariah Butler in Sadsbury that same year. Margaret was born in Crawford County in 1823, the daughter of William and Eleanor Butler. By 1850, Oliver Cleveland and Margaret had moved to Salem in Mercer County. It is possible he was also employed on the Erie Canal although the census says he was a farmer. They had six children: Edwin born in 1841, Albert Alonzo born March 16, 1842 and died in 1915, John A. born 1845 and died in 1920 in Davenport, Iowa, Elizabeth Ann born 1848, William D. born 1851 was married and living in St. Lewis in 1910, and Edgar who was born in 1859 was living in Illinois. All but Edgar were born in Crawford County, Pennsylvania. By the 1860 census, the family had moved to Lee, Fulton County, Illinois. The census listed Oliver as a farmer. He was probably a Freemason. Both Oliver and Margaret died less than two weeks apart, possibly due to the small pox epidemic in Illinois from 1861-64. Margaret Mariah died on March 22, 1861 at age of forty-two and Oliver Cleveland died on March 31, 1861, age forty-eight. They are buried in the Virgil Cemetery, Lee Township, Fulton, County, Illinois. It is unknown where the younger children went after the death of their parents. The youngest child, Edgar, was only two. Edwin, the oldest, was nineteen and a student. Albert eighteen enlisted and served in the Civil War.

The same month and year that Oliver and Margaret died, President Lincoln left Illinois and took office in Washington, DC. Lincoln was able to lead the United States through its greatest constitutional, military, and moral crisis in history, preserving the Union and abolishing slavery. The Civil War began with the Confederate attack on Fort Sumter April 12, 1861. The War finally ended with General Lee's surrender at Appomattox Courthouse in Virginia on April 9, 1865.

Albert Alonzo Wheeler was born March 16, 1842 in Georgetown, Crawford, Pennsylvania. He was thirteen when his family moved to Fulton, County, Illinois, and eighteen when his parents died and the Civil War began. He married Sarah Jane Louck on July 30, 1863. She was born November 25, 1844 in Lee, Fulton County, the daughter of Jefferson Louck and Anna Piersol. (See Louck and Piersol families) They had five children, three of whom reach adulthood. Esther Ann was born in 1864 and died in 1920. (She became a member of the DAR). Maggie Mariah was born 1866 and died in 1875. Ralph Bismark was born in 1870 and died in 1924. Charles Floyd was born in 1872 and died in 1938 in Greeley, Colorado. Don Pedro was born in 1878 and died in 1884.

Albert joined the 38th Illinois Infantry, organized under Colonel William Carlin during the Civil War, and mustered into the Federal service August 15, 1861 at Camp Butler, Springfield, Illinois. He was in Company K of his Regiment. The 38th Infantry took part in many battles under Generals Grant and Sherman primarily in Tennessee and Georgia. The Regiment was mustered out December 31, 1864. Albert received a pension for his service. Among those who were killed from Prairie City was C. E. Wheeler. It is possible this was Edwin, oldest son of Oliver and Margaret Wheeler. No other records are found on Edwin.

The 10th Calvary was mustered into the service of the United States November 25, 1861 at Camp Butler under the command of Colonel James A. Barrett. It was called **"Lincoln's own."** The Regiment was mounted on horses owned by the individual members until 1864 when the government by purchase and supply became owner. In January of 1865, the 10th Cavalry was reorganized to include the Illinois 15th Cavalry. On March 16, the Regiment was on their way to New Orleans when they received intelligence of the assassination of President Lincoln. The Regiment was ordered to New Orleans as a police force and given complete control. Their actions prevented confusion and bloodshed and made the City one of the quietest in the Union during that fateful time. On November 22, 1865, the Regiment was mustered out of the service and sent back to Camp Butler for final pay and discharge on January 6, 1866.

Albert was a farmer and ran the local grain elevator built in 1855/56 in Prairie City. The railroad depot was completed the same year along with the frame schoolhouse known as the Academy and started under the orders of the Free Will Baptist Church. Albert was an active member of his community, serving on the school board, and as the Township Collector and Clerk. He was also a Freemason, a Baptist, and a Democrat. Albert was a member of the Golden Gate Lodge No. 248, Ancient Free and Accepted Masons organized June 2, 1857. The charter is dated October 1, 1857. Among the Officers in 1885 were J. B. Pearsoll (Piersol) and A. A. Wheeler, Treasurer. (Joel E. Piersol was the brother of Albert's mother-in-law, Anna). By 1879, Albert owned 80 acres on section 16 next to his father-in-law, Jefferson Louck. He and Sarah Jane celebrated their fiftieth wedding anniversary on July 30, 1913. Their three surviving children, Ester Ann, Ralph  Bismarck who married May Evans and Charles Floyd attended with their spouses and family. Albert died March 1915 in Prairie City. Sarah Jane died in Greeley, Colorado at the home of her son, Charles, November 8, 1918. They are buried in the Wheeler plot in the Prairie City Cemetery. The Fiftieth Anniversary is pictured, Left to Right Back row: Blanche, Charles, Ester, Ralph, May, second Row: neighbor, Sarah and Albert, Frank Meade (Husband of Ester), neighbor, third row: neighbor girl, Harry, Rollin, and Russell. (See Wheeler Addendum for descendants)

- A bit of history found in the Prairie City Notes from the Village of Prairie City News in 1896 gives a glimpse of the life of the Wheeler family in the Village during the late 1800's:
"The telephones are now in working order…" "The first service was from Frank Mead's store."

"The editor of the newspaper was definitely an anti-license party and referred to the six taverns in Prairie City as variously gin mills, licensed murder mills and cited some incidences of the effects of liquor on some of the younger generation." "The Women's Christian Temperance Union was first organized in September 1877 by Mrs. Reed. Mrs. Vaughn, wife of the Baptist minister, was elected President and Mrs. Salmon wife of the Presbyterian minister was elected Secretary."

March of 1892 – "Women are now entitled to vote for the candidate for school trustee to be elected April 5, and for a member of the school board at the election April 23. They should all see that they are registered. The new law gives them the right to vote for all city and township officers." "Out of the 150 votes cast, there were seven ladies brave enough to go out into a man's world and vote, but to bolster up their courage, they met at the Methodist parsonage and were accompanied by Rev. Brink and his wife to the schoolhouse where they cast their vote." (Cornelia and May Evans Wheeler may have been among of them).

August 27, 1887: A.A. Wheeler has purchased the apples in the City Park and anyone caught carrying them off will be prosecuted."

August 1885: NOTICE: "On and after this date cattle will not be permitted to run the streets after 9 p.m.
May 1st, 1890: "An ordinance was passed that all owners muzzle or kill their dogs."

July 1893: "Cats are selling for 20 cents a bushel. "September 1892:

"A neighboring Doctor advertises: "I will pay half of the funeral expenses where I am not successful."

*Wheeler family members were courtiers during the reign of Charles I and II. On February 9, 10, 11 of 1677, Sir Charles Wheeler, member of the Court of King Charles, carried several Bills in Parliament. A Bill was ordered to "erect a Monument to the late Sacred Majesty King Charles the First to be read on Tuesday morning next." King Charles was beheaded on January 30, 1649. After the Restoration, Parliament eventually approved seventy thousand pounds to erect the monument, which was raised in 1678. Another Wheeler, Captain Francis Wheeler, commanded the sixty-four gun battleship the HMS Rupert in 1689 under Charles II when he help capture a large enemy fleet off the coast of France.
**History and pictures sourced from Wikipedia, author, and Wheeler Family History. Crest is from family and Ancestry.

THE WOODWARD FAMILY

The first recorded name of Woodward was in Normandy. Commander Wadard assembled the army for William in preparation for the invasion of England. King William granted Commander Wadard lands in Essex for his aid at the Battle of Hastings. By 1290, the family had branched north to Warwickshire. The name was then spelled Waudard, meaning "warden of the wood." In the fifteenth century, the family claimed to descend for John Wodeward, ranger of Arden Forest.

Daniel Woodward was a soldier in the Revolution born 1760 and died 1853 in Hubbardston, Massachusetts. (DAR # A129244). He was in the Continental Army at Saratoga and at the surrender of the British General Burgoyne. He married Keziah Newton in Hubbardston, Massachusetts in 1784. He was the son of Daniel Woodward and Mary Stone. His great, great, great, grandfather, Richard Woodward was born in Ipswich, Suffolk, England and died in February 16, 1664 in Watertown, Middlesex, Massachusetts. He married Rose (?) in Ipswich and had twin boys, George and John. The boys were thirteen when they came over on the *Elizabeth* of Ipswich bound for New England the last of April in 1634. Richard was a freeman in on September 2, 1635. In 1648, he bought a windmill from Edward and Anna Holiock of Boston. He sold it December 26, 1648, to William Aspinwall of Boston. In 1654, Richard was documented as serving on a jury. His wife, Rose died in 1662. He married secondly, Anne (Veare) Gates April 18, 1663, the widow of Steven Gates, son of Thomas from Norwich, England.

One hundred and twenty six members of the Woodward family served in the Revolution. Josiah Woodward (#A129304) born 1746 in Norton Massachusetts was at the Lexington Alarm.

*History and pictures sourced from Wikipedia, Woodward Family History, and Geni. Crest from www.adeksale.com, permission to use crest granted online

THE NEWTON FAMILY

The Newton name is originally from Normandy. Members of the family aided King William in his invasion of England in 1066. He granted them lands in Cheshire for their help. Newton is now found in many locations in England and a commonplace name.

Keziah Newton was born February 16, 1759 in Shrewsbury, Worchester, Massachusetts. She married Patriot, Daniel Woodward. She was the daughter of Elisha Newton and Sarah Miles. Sarah was born in Shrewsbury January 29, 1731. Elisha was the fifth generation descendant of Richard Newton born between 1601 and 1609 in Suffolk England and died August 24, 1701 in Marlboro, Massachusetts. He was one of the original founders of Sudbury and was allotted land there in 1640. In 1647, he was a freeman and on June 27, 1647. He was the owner of the estate of Nathaniel Sparrowhawk. He owned a cider mill, tannery, and a blacksmith shop. In 1664, he petitioned for the building of a church. He married Anne Loker August 9, 1636 in Bures, Saint Mary, Suffolk and they immigrated to Sudbury, Middlesex, Massachusetts. (Sudbury town records) She was born in England about 1612, the daughter of Henry and Elizabeth (French) Loker. Henry, a Glover, died in 1631 in England and Elizabeth joined the Puritans and immigrated to Sudbury before 1638. She and her family were among the first settlers.

Over one hundred members of the Newton family served in the Revolution, most from Massachusetts. Paul Newton born 1751 (#A083231) was a Minute man from Southborough, Moses (#A083225) and Nathan (#A083228) were fifers.

*History and crest sourced from Wikipedia, The family Roost, and free pages at genealogy, Ancestry, Rootsweb

THE MILES FAMILY

Sarah Miles, the daughter of John Miles, was born March 20, 1706-07 in Concord, Massachusetts. John Miles who was born in England, son of John, born in 1618 in Bedfordshire, England, immigrated to Boston about 1637 and settled in Concord, one of the first settlers. He died there August 23, 1693. He was a blacksmith. He married first Sarah (?) and had one child, Mary. His second wife was Susanna Goodnow and they had three children John, Samuel (born February 14, 1681 in Concord), and Sarah. John may have come on the same ship as the Wheelers and been a member of Reverend Buckley's former congregation in Bedfordshire.*

THE GOODNOW FAMILY

The Goodnow families in America (also spelled Goodenow, Goodenough among others) descend from the Goodnow ancestors who lived in southern part of England. Five members of the family immigrated to America in 1638, three brothers, John, Thomas, and Edmund and their sisters Ursula and Dorothy. They left England after being persecuted for not attending the required Church of England. The families, found in several close Parishes of Sutton Mandeville, Donhead, St. Andrews, and Donhead St. Mary, were related. They became members of non-conformist groups. Edmund, Edward, Ralph, and Simon were called before the Archdeacon for "wandering from their parish church" and "going to Shaftesbury to church on Sundays and Holy days." They were required to do public penance and levied a heavy fine. Although the Goodnow's obeyed, they made plans to leave England. The Goodnow families and several others sailed from Southampton bound for Boston on the ship *Confidence* in 1638. They help to established the town of Sudbury, Massachusetts where they became strong leaders.* Susanna Goodnow, born 1647 daughter of Thomas Goodnow and Jane Ruddick, married Samuel Miles.**

Fifty-eight members of the Miles family served in the Revolution along with twenty-seven members of the Goodnow family.

*History sourced from the Miles family home page of Roy Gilbert Tripp, Worcester County documents and *Concord's First Settlers*, crest from Ancestry.
**(The family is mentioned in the Pulitzer Prize winning book, *Puritan Village* by Sumer Chilton Powell and *The Goodnows Who Originated in Sudbury Massachusetts* by Carol McWain Goodenough).

THE LOUCK/LAUX FAMILY

The origin of the Laux family (also spelled Louck or Louk) is recorded in the ancient chronicles of both sides of the Pyrenees region in the extreme southeast of France. The head of the family is traced to Inigo Lupe du Laux, Seigneur de Biscaye (the Bay of Biscaye) and Count of Alava, who had two sons. They came from the ancient Lord of Alava, a Province of Spain. One of them, Guillaume Sanche de Laux, is the founder of the house or family of all those bearing the name of Laux. He was born before 1055 in Spain. He crossed the Pyrenees in 1075 and established himself in the Viscount of Bearn, or Basque, Providence in Spain and France near the City of Pau in what was the ancient Kingdom of Navarre, the birthplace of Henry IV in 1553. Laux was made the Grand Ecuyer (Squire) of Garcais, member of the King of Navarre's household, and Governor of the Town of Navarre. He married Sancia Vaca, Souveraine (Sovereign) of a small town close to the Pyrenees. She was born in France in 1055. The  family was very wealthy and powerful in the area and held important, high offices of state. (In 1188, Count Gaston VI*, Viscount of Bearn, descendant of Gaston IV, son of the ruling Viscounts Mary and William I of Bearn, established his Court here and the Sovereign Council equivalent to the House of Lords). Jean Du Laux, a staunch Huguenot, was born about 1553 and was a devout friend and Prince de Conde (military general) for King Henry IV of Navarre, (pictured). He married Marie in 1573, the daughter of Francois Comte de la Rochefoucault. Jean received the following letter from King Henry:

> *"I write you with haste, to pray you join me in Bergerac to meet the Queen, my wife, en muilleur equipage that the shortness of time will permit. There you will be most welcome, Mr. du Laux, and received most cordially. Your affectionate friend, Henri."* (Preserved in the Laux family archives).

Gaston IV was Viscount of Bearn and Foix from 1090 to 1130, was called the Crusader, and participated in the First Crusade (pictured). He was one of the lessor Knights, but carried his own Standard and commanded his own men. Gaston joined Godfrey of Bouillion and marched with him to Jerusalem. He was in charge of the siege engines and the first man to enter the City on July 15, 1099. Gaston had learned from his experience in the Reconquista in Spain, Muslims could live under Christians and tried to protect some of the Muslims in Jerusalem by sheltering them  in the Temple. He preferred negotiations and dialogue to senseless massacre. However, they were soon killed by other Crusaders, which infuriated Gaston. After the victory in the Battle Ascalon, he returned home with his men. His descendants include, Gaston VI and Gaston VII who participated in the Seventh Crusade. Henry III (IV of France) was also a descendant through Eleanor Queen of Navarre. Guillermo II was the father of the first Gaston, who succeeded him in 1229.

Although baptized a Catholic, King Henry was brought up a Calvinist by his mother Jeanne, Queen of Navarre, who was the leader of the French protestant (Huguenot) movement. When Henry IV (also Henry III of Navarre) inherited the throne of France, Navarre became part of France. King Henry (1553-

1610), the first Bourbon King, became the leader of the Huguenot Army. Many members of the French Nobility and the social middle class practiced the new reformed religion, based on a belief of salvation through individual faith without the need for intercession of the church hierarchy and on the belief of an individual's right to interpret scriptures for themselves. Although Catholic at the time, members of the Laux family became protestant during the enlightenment, age of Luther and Calvin and later suffered the consequences. *(See Henry III and Margaret Valois marriage and St. Bartholomew's Day Massacre).*

The grandparents of Philip and Nicholas Laux moved from the Kingdom of Navarre to the Palatinate of the Rhine in Hesse-Darmstadt and Hesse Nassau sometime before the Revocation of the Edict of Nantes. The Edict, established by Henry IV in 1595, granted the Protestants religious freedoms. (Henry IV was born at Pau Castle, pictured). Unfortunately, King Louis XIV, the grandson of Henry IV, revoked the Edict in 1685 starting the "Thirty Years War," known as the religious "War of King Louis XIV of France." Pope Innocent XI, who commissioned Louis XIV to eliminate the Protestants, financed the wars.

After the Revocation, hundreds of thousands of *Huguenots* fled into the German Palatine (and other countries) where for a time they found freedom to practice their religion. Later the French entirely devastated the Valley of the Rhine. The Palatinate, on both sides of the Rhine River, was one of the most severely affected and life became a horror for the protestant residents. The Catholic French King ordered his Generals to destroy the Palatinate to rid the area of his protestant subjects. They burned villages, towns, and cities to the ground and ten thousand people were killed. (In 1687, a feud erupted between Louis XIV and Pope Innocent over the French Papal Territories and the French elite military forces of 800 entered Rome and took possession of the Papal Palace).

Thirty thousand Palatinate *Huguenots* fled to London after the sympathetic English Queen Anne (1702-1714), invited them to make a new home in her American Colonies. Queen Anne was the second daughter of James II, a Catholic. (Pope Innocent XI also financially supported James II in his violent attempt to reintroduce Catholicism in England). Although James wanted to raise his daughters as Catholics, both Anne and Mary were raised with Protestant religious instructions at the insistence of the Bishop of London. After his death, James first daughter, Mary, became Queen with her Protestant husband William of Orange, whom she allowed to reign. She and William died without heirs, giving the throne to Anne. Interestingly, Catholic Louis XIV of France secretly sponsored Anne's marriage to Prince George of Denmark, who was also a Protestant. Louis XIV was in hopes of an Anglo-Danish alliance against the Dutch and William of Orange, which never materialized. Anne was the last of the Stuart Monarchs and the first married Queen of England.

Among those who left the Palatinate with their families were the brothers Philip and Nicholas Laux descendants of the ancient Laux family of Pau. While in London, Philip and Nicholas met a delegation of Mohawk Indians who were there to meet with Queen Anne. The Queen conveyed the land in the

Schoharie Valley in New York to the Indians, with the intentions of helping the Huguenots, which the Indians offered to the Laux brothers.

On Christmas Day of 1709, four thousand Huguenot emigrants left London on ten ships, including Philip and Nicholas Laux. The voyage took six dangerous months. During that time, seventeen hundred passengers died from lack of food and fever. Some perished during the landing in New York June 14, 1710. The remaining twenty-three hundred passengers where camped on Nutting Island (now Governor's Island) in New York Harbor. In the late fall, fourteen-hundred of the Huguenots were taken a hundred miles up the Hudson River to Livingston Manor. The agreement made with the Queen for payment of the cost of passage and parcels of land was to raise hemp and to make tar and pitch for the British Navy for a certain period. The men were quite willing, however, the forests and the soil proved unsuitable for the production of either. A third of the men, including Philip and Nicholas enlisted with the British in the Canadian Expedition of 1711. They were in the Haysbury Company formed in Livingston Manor. They were to receive the same wages as the soldiers, their wives were to be taken care of by Governor Hunter and his associates, and they were to keep the arms given to them for the Expedition. Many of them lost their lives and when the survivors returned, they found their families starving. Not only had the Governor not provided the promised food, he took their arms away, as well.

At this point, they remembered the offer made to them by the Indians and petitioned the Governor to allow them to move to that land. The Governor refused stating,
> *"Here is your land, and where you must live or die."*

Many, including Philip Laux, were determined to move away from the injustices and made plans in late 1711 to go the Schoharie Valley. They had no wagons, horses, or transportation to make their way through sixty miles of wilderness. Instead, they strapped their belongings to their backs and harnessed them selves to rudely constructed sledges to carry the children, infirmed, and pregnant women over the snow. The trip took three weeks of suffering from cold and hunger before they reached their destination. With the help of the friendly Indians, they survived the winter. A year later, they had built their homes and cultivated the land. The vindictive Governor still pursued them and after spending ten years in the area, Philip, his family, and some of the others left to find permanent homes in the more hospitable area of the Mohawk Valley where they became very prosperous. Numerous men of the Laux families served in the Revolution. Many of Philip's wealthy and influential descendants are still found in the area today.

Philip Laux bought land in Middleburg and in the town of Sharon in Schoharie, County. He had four sons, Peter, Cornelius, Andrew, and William. Andrew was a well-known musician and Chorister of the Lutheran Church at Schoharie. William Laux settled in Middleburg. He married Margaret Vanderwerken born 1758 and died in 1846. Her parents were Johannes Vanderwerken and Marytje Devoe. His father,

Johannes Roelof, had a farm above the fourth fork of the Mohawk River as early as 1677. The Vanderwerken family came over from Holland on the ship De Rosebaum. The passenger list dated March 15, 1663 names Roelof Gerritse Vanderwerken, Johannes, John, William, and Thomas Vanderwerken. During the Revolution, their descendants served in the Second Regiment of the Tyrone County Militia of New York. (See Vanderwerkin Family)

William Laux and his son Andrew were the only Tories in the family. When General Johnson of the British Army and his troops invaded the valley in 1780, they burned all of the Laux buildings except William's, which was used to house supplies and as a resting station. William was married twice. His children by his first wife were Andrew, Peter of Sharon, Jeremiah of Middleburg and a daughter who married John Ingold of Schoharie. The children by his second wife were John W., Jacob, Henry, William, David, and two daughters, Mrs. Storm Becker and Mrs. William Borrt.

Peter Laux, born about 1755, was the son of William and his first wife. He was a farmer and *"energetic business man and had a clearer view of political matters than his brother, Andrew, especial during the struggle for liberty."* Peter was a Patriot and soldier in the Revolution. (#A071745). His brothers, Jeremiah of Middleburg were also a patriot (#A071739), as well as Jacob (#A071738), and John (#A071741). Jacob, Peter, and Henry were in the Second Regiment of the Tyrone County, Militia. There are twenty-four DAR records for the Laux/Louck family. Peter's sister was the wife of Storm Becker Jr., Ensign (#A008330), whose father was Captain Storm Becker (#A008329) who served under Colonel Peter Vrooman of the 15th Regiment of Albany, County, and member of the Committee of Safety. The Vrooman family has over twenty-five document Patriots.

Jacob was born in 1765 in Batavia, Genesee, New York and died in Stafford, Genesee in 1810. He married Catherina Lorina Clarence born in 1765 and died in 1830. (Her parents are unknown but the Clarince/Clarence name is of Scottish origin. (See Clarence Family). Their son, David Louck, born April 10, 1789 in Genesee County, New York, married Clara (Clarissa/Clarry) Scott in 1810-11. She was born June 4, 1796 in Vermont.* (see Scott Family). David appears in the 1810 censes in Cambria, Niagara County, New York with three adult males and no females in the family unit. He served in the military in 1812 in New York. He enlisted June 29, 1812 as a private in Captain Rufus Hart's Company in Churchill's 164th Regiment of the New York Militia. He was wounded December 30, 1813, in the defense of Buffalo, by a musket ball in the left shoulder. The ball entered near the center of his shoulder blade and lies near his backbone. He was discharged January 5, 1814. His pension application made on May 31, 1814 states,

> "He is no longer able to do manual labor, and any exercise gave him 'great pain.' He is a farmer by profession, is thirty years of age, and has to provide for his family."

He was put on the pension roll July 2, 1819 and he received forty-eight dollars per year. He appears in the 1820 censes in Stafford Township, Genesee, New York with one boy and one girl. In the 1830 censes he is in LeRoy Township with two boys and four girls. In 1833, he lived in Perrysburg, Cattaraugus, New York, the owner of improved land and building on lot 28. In the 1840 censes he is in

Fulton County, Illinois. Fulton County awarded him seventy dollars per year under the Index of Awards and Claims for soldiers in the War of 1812. The Fulton County Atlas states that David, Clarry and his sons Benjamin F., Jeremiah (Jefferson) and four daughters, Caroline, Lucy Ann, Lorina, and Clara Jane arrived in Fulton County before 1838. Daughter Mary Jane was born in Fulton County in 1835. David and Clarry Louck are buried in the Virgil Cemetery in Lee, Township, (pictured).

Jefferson Louk (Louck/Laux) was born June 6, 1822 in Genesee County New York. He was about twelve years old when he moved with his family to Fulton County, Illinois. He was listed as a farmer in the 1850 Fulton County censes. By 1870, he was a lumber merchant and lived in Prairie City. He married Anna Piersol February 1, 1844, the daughter of Peter Piersol, (see Piersol Family). She was born January 3, 1824 in Middletown, Butler, Ohio. The Jefferson Louk Dry Goods store was opened in Prairie City in the late 1800's. They also owned a Grocery Store. Jefferson was a member of the Golden Gate Masonic Lodge. He and his wife Anna had seven children, Sarah Jane born November 25, 1844, David, Benjamin Franklin (Frank), Hestor Ann, John Piersol, Charles F., and Julia. The Louk family was very active in Prairie City for many years. Jefferson Louk was a member of the Fiddler's Union, treasurer of the Masonic Lodge, and elected President of the Village in 1935. He was the Postmaster in 1921. David was a member of the Telephone Committee in 1899, Fred Louk was a member of the City Band, and John P. Louk served as a school director in 1880. According to the 1890 Prairie City Village News, Gertrude Louk was a member of *"the newly organized Dumbbell Club, a women's exercise group who all wore black bloomers."* Jefferson died July 13, 1901. He is buried in the Virgil Cemetery in Fulton County. Anna died June 29, 1906. She is buried beside Jefferson. Their daughter, Sarah Jane Louk married Albert A. Wheeler in Prairie City July 30, 1863.

*History and pictures sourced from Louk family, Wikipedia and *Mohawk Living*, a free magazine, artist is unknown. The crest is that of Counts of Alava and Kings of Castile sourced from Wikipedia.

THE SCOTT FAMILY

The family name of Scott is found early in Scottish history beginning with Uchtred "Filius" Scott in 1120. The name is recorded witnessing many charters including that of David of Strathearn and the Bishop of St. Andrew. The family became one of the most powerful border clans in Scotland. Four generations after Uchtred, his descendant Sir Richard married the heiress of Murthockstone and acquired her estates. The new laird built his residence at Buccleush, which today is the largest private landowner in the United Kingdom and the art collection of the Duke of Buccleush is international known. Anne Scott, the second daughter of the 2nd Earl of Buccleush, was considered the greatest heiress in the Kingdom. King Charles II arranged for her to marry his illegitimate son James the Duke of Monmouth and they were created the Duke and Duchess of Buccleush. During the many wars between Scotland and England, members of the family moved to England.

Clarry Scott's ancestry appears to date back to Henry Scott of Ipswich, Suffolk, England and eventually to his son Thomas Scott of Ipswich, Massachusetts and Stamford, Connecticut. Thomas and his wife Elizabeth sailed to America on the ship "*The Elizabeth*" in April of 1634. His widowed mother accompanied them. His son Thomas Scott was born in 1744 in Ashford, Connecticut. He and his wife had several children. The first child was born in Connecticut in 1767 and then they moved to the Green River Valley in West Halifax, Vermont. Clarry Scott and members of her family later moved to New York.

Henry Scott born 1763, (#A101478) was a Sergeant from the Rhinebeck in Duchess County, New York. He served beneath six different Captains during his service. William Scott born 1748 was also a Sergeant from Rhinebeck, Duchess County, New York. He served under Colonels Van Shank and Wincoop, Captains Ten Neck and Van Sanford. Thomas Scott (#A101833), born 1753 in Hartford Connecticut, served with the Johnston Connecticut Men. William Scott born 1743 in Ulster, Ireland was a Major and served in both New Hampshire and Massachusetts. He served with Colonels Paul Sargent and Joseph Cilley. He died in New York. His father, William Sr. of New Hampshire, born 1713 in Coleraine, Ireland, gave Patriotic Service (#A101871).Two hundred and seventy-two members of the Scott family served in the Revolution, thirteen were in the Battle of King's Mountain.

*History and picture sourced from Wikipedia and Geni, Crest from Ancestry free pages

THE CLARENCE FAMILY

The ancestors of the Clarence Family come from the ancient Scottish Kingdom of Dalriada. The family name comes from the personal name of Lawrence. (Mac Labhran in Gaelic). The Clan is believed to descend from Ferges MacErc who landed in Argyll about 503 AD. Although the linage before the twelfth century is hard to prove, it is proven that the Clan held vast territories called the Braes of Balquhidder. They were documented as being "all grand, strong men" and when the Kirk of Balquhidder was restored, Clan members supervised the exhumation of some of the bodies of ancient members of the Clan for reburial. It was said they found very large boned men even for today's standards.

The Clarence's are found first in Argyllshire near Lock Lomond where it is said, "they were so powerful, that no one could take their place in church until the MacLaren Clan was properly seated." They were related to the Celtic Earls of Strathearn and their branches were at Balquhidder, Strathearn, Auchleskine, Stank, Druach, and Lochearnside. They were a fighting Clan and involved neighboring Clans in vigorous disputes, but always remained faithful to the Royal House of Stewart. They were hereditary Celtic Abbots of Achtow. They derive their name from Abbot Lawrence. Their gathering place has been at Creag and Tuirc, the "Boars Rock at Achtow" in Balquhidder, (pictured) for Centuries. The name also is derived in England from the Duke of Clarence. The name may originate from the town of Clare in Suffolk, which was owned by George, the first Duke of Clarence in 1449-1476.

The first immigrants to America and Canada bore the name of Clarence and the variant spelling MacClaren. Members of the family may have come to America after losing the battles in Scotland for the Stewart Kings in 1715 (Sheriffmuir) and 1745 (Culloden). John and Patrick MacLaren settled in South Carolina in 1716. Others immigrated to New York, the New England Colonies, and Canada. Caterina Lorina Clarence married Jacob Louck in Genesee, New York about 1788. Her parents are unknown. Members may have been in the Militia, but there are no DAR records.

*History, pictures and crests of Scotland and MacClaren sourced from Wikipedia, Ancestry, and MacClaren Clan

THE VANDERWERKEN FAMILY

The Vanderwerken family was among the first settlers of Albany, New York, (New Amsterdam Colony). Roelof Gerritse was born about 1645 in Meppelen, Drenthe, Holland. His father was Garrit Van Der Werken born in 1616 and died 1695. Roelef left Amsterdam, Netherland March 15, 1663 aboard the ship *De Roosenboom (The Rosetree)* under Captain Pieter Reyersz Van Der Beets. He arrived in New Amsterdam (Albany) between May 11, 1663 and August 17, 1663. He worked four years as a farmhand for Symon Groot. By 1667, Roelof had a farm at Halfmoon on Cohoes Island in Saratoga County above the fourth fork of the Mohawk River. In 1683, he lived outside of Albany's Northgate. He was a farmer in Marte Gerritse's company. The 1697 census shows him as a resident of Albany with a wife and six children. His wife was Geetruy Jacobse Oostrant born 1651 and died 1695. They were married in 1676 and were members of the Albany Dutch Church where nine of their children were baptized. They had fourteen children, five of them sons. Roelof died in Half Moon, Saratoga September 3, 1728.

Roelof's third son, Johannes, was born in 1688 and died in 1767. His wife was Margaretta Baar born in 1695. Her parents are unknown but they were probably Dutch. Roelof and Margaretta had fifteen children. Their son Johannes born 1734 married Marytje Devoe on December 26, 1754 in Albany. Her family may descend from Frederick Devoe who arrived in New York in 1675, or Nicholas Devoe who arrived in New Jersey the same year. The Devoe name is first found in Burgundy in the town of Volney, France. Three members of the Devoe family from New York served in the Revolution, Anthony born 1783 from Albany (#A005442), Able born 1755 from New Rochelle (#A032173) and Jeremiah born 1757 from Ulster, Ireland. Johannes was in the second Regiment of the Tyrone County Militia and served under Captain Jellis Fonda. He and his wife, Marytje, had ten children. Their daughter Margarita Vanderwerkin born 1758 married William Louck September 25, 1774 in the Dutch Reformed Church. Johannes was a Patriot who survived the war and died August 10, 1810 in Waterford, Half Moon, New York. Several members of the Vanderwerken family fought in the Revolution, but there are no DAR numbers listed. They are only listed in New York State Militia's.

*History and picture of the Vanderwerkin family and Dutch immigrant ship from free pages at Ancestry

THE PIERSOL FAMILY

The Piersol/Pearsoll family name is from ancient French origin. The family arrived in England from France with the Norman Conquest of 1066. They lived in Staffordshire where they had family estates. They were established on lands given them by Duke William for their support at the Battle of Hastings. Gilbert D. Corbiel a descendant of Rollo, the first Duke of Normandy in 912, acquired the Manor called Pershale where his son Robert Fitz Gilbert Pershale took the name Robert de Pershale. King William also descends from Rollo. The Normans were Scandinavian invaders who settled in Normandy in 820. Supposedly, Rollo descends from Adam. (See The Descent of Adam at, members.core.com/sharprm/library/rollo.htm).

"Male members of the family have inherited an ancient heirloom: a Y-chromosome that traces its roots to the Kings of Sweden over 2,000 years ago. The male Y-chromosome is unlike other types of DNA in that it is a non-recombining, thus it does not change except by the odd chance of a mutation every several hundred years." (From Pearsall Family DNA surname project). The Pearsoll family is a rather small family with about five-thousand members worldwide. It increases to about fifteen-thousand when the varied spellings are added. Over the centuries, members of the family migrated to Norway, France, England, and America. In 1928, Clarence Pearsoll wrote a three-volume book on the History of the Pearsoll family. He traced the ancestry back to the Viking Era. His information is referenced here.

Members of this ancient family in France became protestant Huguenots in the seventeenth century. They were persecuted for their religious beliefs. They fled France with thousands of others. One family found asylum in the mountains of Wales. In 1717, members of this branch of the family left Wales and settled in Chester County Pennsylvania. Earlier in 1683, another branch, three brothers, also came from England to the province of Pennsylvania and were natives of Pennsylvania for several generations. One of the brothers was Thomas Pearsall born in 1650 in London. His son, Thomas, was born in Pennsylvania in 1670 and married in 1690. His son John was born 1694 in Chester County and died in 1776.

The earliest London Branch of the Pearsoll/Pershall family in America stems from Richard Pershall born in 1530 in Staffordshire, descendant of Rollo. He married Isabelle Rolleston. They had eight children, Robert, Edmund born about 1531 who married Maria Bathurst born about 1555 in Bathurst, London, and Thomas born 1535 in Horsley, Staffordshire, James, Humphrey, Bridgett, Constantia, and Elizabeth. Pershall Manor is pictured.

Edmund Pearsall, born 1531, became a leading merchant in London and very involved with the woolen trade in Lancashire. He eventually held a patent from the King giving him a monopoly on the tobacco trade in Virginia. He and his family and friends were major contributors to the second Virginia Company in 1609. "The Historie of Virginia, New England, and the Summer Isles" a book by Captain John Smith published in 1634, lists the names of the "The Adventurers of Virginia" and includes Edmund Pearsall and Timothy Bathurst, a member of his wife Maria Bathurst's family. She was the daughter of Lancelot Bathurst, Lord Mayor of London.

Captain John Smith, pictured, sailed from London in 1606, and arrived in what became Jamestown, Virginia May 24, 1607. The voyage was funded by the first Virginia Company formed with a charter from James I in 1606 and charged with the settlement of Virginia and making a profit for the investors. Unfortunately, the first Company of one hundred-forty men and boys did not fair well. After picking the future Jamestown site, the men's first concern was survival and building a fort. They were provided food and clothing and after seven years were to receive land of their own. However, with sickness, Indian attacks, poor food, water, and poor leadership they had only minimal success. When Captain John Smith became their leader in 1609, industry and relations with the Indians improved. It was then the Second Company received a charter and six-hundred colonists sailed for Virginia between 1608 and 1609. The new deputy Governor, Sir John Gage appointed by the King also set sail but was ship wrecked in Bermuda along with supplies and did not arrive in the  colonies until 1610. When he arrived, he found only a fraction of the settlers had survived the infamous "Starving Time." The investment was by now a financial disaster. The Company then incurred further debt when they were forced to send more colonists and supplies. They continued to fight to succeed and a Third Charter was issued which added more incentives for investors including three hundred leagues of sea and Bermuda was included as part of Virginia. However, it was not until John Rolfe's successful experiment with growing tobacco that a way was provided to recoup financially. Edward Pearsall became a big investor in growing tobacco.

By 1616, the original settlers were to receive their land and stock shares and the investors in England were due the dividends. The Company had to renege on the cash payments and instead distributed fifty-acre lots. They also instituted the "head right" system as a way to get more colonists to Virginia. Investors and residents were able to acquire land by paying the passage of the new settlers. The new settlers usually spent time working on the land of the investor before purchasing their own land. This approach worked for a while.

By 1621, the Company was in debt by nine-thousand pounds with unpaid dividends and debts. In 1622, the Indians staged an uprising and killed over one fourth of the settlers. By 1624, King James changed the status of Virginia and made it a royal colony administered by a Governor appointed by the King. It stayed this way until 1776 when the colonists went to war.

Edmund Pearsall and Maria Bathurst were married June 9, 1567 during the reign of Queen Elizabeth I. They had four children, Edmund born 1570 in Staffordshire, Thomas born about 1571-80 in London, Mary born about 1583 in Bromley, Kent, and Robert born about 1590. Edmund's occupation was listed as a Merchant of the Staple. Their sons were the fifty-seventh generation of the Pearsoll (Piersol) family.

Thomas Pearsoll, first arrived in Virginia in 1621. He had assumed the management of his father's tobacco business about 1613 in London, Holland, and Virginia. In 1615, he took over when his father retired from the active participation as a trader and member of the London Grocers Guild. The fortunes of the world became concentrated on the tobacco business in America and Edmund Pearsoll and his son were leaders in the industry. In the beginning, Chesapeake Country beyond the Delaware River was the center of the planting. Their tobacco enterprises continued to grow in America. However, by the time of Edmund's death in 1629 there was very little left of his estate in England. The Staffordshire family lost most of their lands due to their loyalty and devotion to the Catholic Church and the Stuarts Kings when the Protestants took over Parliament. Edmund was arrested for taking part in a meeting of Loyalists and put into the Fleet Prison in London where he died March 26, 1629. After King Charles I was beheaded and Cromwell took over from his exiled son Charles II during the Commonwealth Era, two thirds of the land of Edmund's cousin, John Pearsoll, Bart, was also seized for "holding a meeting of loyalist in his home in Staffordshire." A warrant for his arrest was issued and he was committed to the tower of London. After Charles II was restored to the throne in 1660, Sir John's property was restored and he became Keeper of the Justice of the Peace for Staffordshire. A relative, Henry Pearsoll, a prominent English composer and musician was a member of the Royal Chapel and sang at King Charles II coronation in 1649.

During the civil unrest, Thomas lost several of his merchant ships sailing under the English flag, but he continued to sail under the flag of Holland until England declared war on Holland and declared the Colonists could only trade with British ships. After 1630, Thomas Pearsoll spent most of his time in America. He married Mary Brent in 1597 in London, Middlesex, England, and the daughter of William Brent. She was born about 1584 in Gloucestershire. Thomas' first residence in America was in the Isle of Wight in Virginia. He also bought land in Maryland. Thomas later moved his family to the Long Island Dutch Colony where his enterprises were protected from the British and the family continued to prosper. Thomas and Mary had five known children. Thomas was born in London, Middlesex England in 1609 and died in Long Island, New York in 1667. Henry was born in London about 1611 and died 1664 in Hempstead, Long Island, Nicholas born in 1613 death unknown. George was born 1615 in London, Middlesex and died about 1687 in Nantmeal Township, Chester County, Pennsylvania. Samuel was born about 1620 in London and died in Virginia in 1643. Thomas Sr. died in 1642 in Virginia and Mary died in 1657.

George Pearsoll born in 1615 married (wife unknown) and had two known children. John Piersol was born about 1630 and Jeremiah Pearsoll/Piersol who was born about 1635. George moved from Long Island to New Jersey with a group of settlers under Luke Watson, a land promoter. He then moved to the Delaware Peninsula and finally to the area around the head of the Brandywine River in what he and his fellow settlers thought was Maryland, but eventually decreed to be land owned by William Penn in Pennsylvania. Penn incidentally was from an old Staffordshire family. It was not until years later the title controversy to the Colony land was finally settled and George's sons and grandsons accepted a Pennsylvania title in what became Chester County Pennsylvania. The family traditions states that George was killed by Indians near Philadelphia. He died about 1682 in Nantmeal Township, Chester County, Pennsylvania near the foot of Welch Mountain. Jeremiah, born about 1635, son of George Pearsoll, married Elizabeth (last name unknown). They had two known sons, Richard born about 1660 and Edward born about 1685 in Chester County. Jeremiah and his brother helped to found a congregation of seventh Day Baptists

in Nantmeal Township. They moved to the upper end of the county to the falls on French Creek (pictured) to get away from their more orthodox neighbors. Jeremiah died before 1700 in Nantmeal, Chester County.

Jeremiah's son Richard Pearsoll married Elizabeth (last name unknown) about 1680. They had two known children, Richard born about 1681 and John born 1682 in New York City the original home of his grandfather. Richard's wife was possibly of Dutch ancestry and from the New York Dutch Colony. Richard and his brother John co-owned property in Chester County. Edward Pearsoll was born in 1685. His will, dated August 1717 in Chester County, names his mother Elizabeth and gives her half of his estate. He also mentions his brother Richard. Richard Pearsoll was one of the last of those who accepted the proprietorship of the Penn brothers over the land controversy south of the fortieth parallel in the Chesapeake colony.

John Pearsoll born 1682, married Sarah (last name unknown) born 1675 and had six children. He died in Chester County, Pennsylvania. Their children were Edward born 1700, Job born about 1707 in Nantmeal, John born 1710, Jeremiah born 1712 in Honeybrook Township, Chester County, and Richard born 1714. Jeremiah's, born 1712, resided in West Nantmeal Township in 1722. He married Mary Jerman born 1715 who died 1755. She was the daughter of the widow Mary Jerman and Jeremiah Jerman born in 1663. Jeremiah's father John Jerman, was born in Somerset, Maryland about 1650. John and Mary had five known children, John Piersol born about 1735, Jacob born about 1739 in West Nantmeal, David born 1740, Abraham born 1741 and Isaac born about 1742. Jeremiah died in 1769.

Jacob Piersol, born 1739, owned fifty acres of land in Nantmeal Township in 1765, which was left to him by his father. He evidently sold this land and in 1769, purchased one-hundred and thirty acres. He married Ann Babb, the daughter of Peter Babb of West Caln Township, Chester County. Peter was born in 1695 on the Isle of Shoals in the Gulf of Maine, part of the Massachusetts Bay Colony. The Babb family was originally from St. Dustan, London, England. Ann was born about 1747 in Brandywine, New Castle, Delaware. (See Babb Family) Jacob and Ann were married about 1760. She was "disowned" by a Quaker meeting for "marrying outside the faith by a Priest" according to early Quaker records. The Priest was probably a member of the Episcopal Church. At the time, members of the Piersol family attended the Episcopal Churches in the area. The 1762 and 1763 tax records show Jacob and Ann living in West Caln Township. Jacob and his family then moved to the Pittsburg area and he appears in the Virginia Military records, so it appears he staked a land claim through that Colony. The Colony claimed the area, which is now southwestern Pennsylvania. Jacob did not appear in the Pennsylvania records until after the boundary dispute had been resolved in 1780. Jacob and Ann had four children, John born about 1761, Simpson born 1764 in Beaver County, Jacob, and Peter born about 1780.

On March 22, 1777, Jacob enlisted in the Army to serve for three years during the Revolutionary War. He first appears in the muster rolls of Captain James O'Hara's Independent Company of Regulars, which was raised by Virginia in the Pittsburg area. Jacob is listed as an "artificer" in muster rolls for September 16 and December 28, 1777 at Fort Pitt. On the muster roll of October 1, he is listed as "at the S.P. Hospital." He evidently stayed in Captain O'Hara's Company as the next mention of Jacob in the military records at the National archives is June 1779 when he appears in the records of the 9th Virginia

Regiment. While he was with O'Hara, he is listed in the merchant's records in June 1778. The Company was sent to Fort Kanawha in 1778, which was provisioned and protected by O'Hara's Company. The equipment supplied to O'Hara's Company included boats, which were used to carry articles for trading with the Indians. The Company was sent west to the Ozark to fight the Indians who were being supplied by the British. They marched several days to the British Fort Sackville, which they attacked and forced to surrender. The Company went from there to Fort Randolph and eventually back to Fort Kanawha after most of the Company had been killed by Indians attacks. The Garrison was reduced to twenty-nine men, too small to protect the area and the Fort was evacuated. Colonel Broadhead annexed the Company into the ninth Virginia Regiment around October 1779. Jacob already appeared in the muster rolls covering June to December 1779 as Private Jacob Persol serving under Colonel John Gibson at Fort Pitt. The Regiment was formerly the Virginia 13th and served under General Washington in the Philadelphia Campaigns. The Regiment was reassigned to the Western Frontier to protect the Frontier from Indian raids. Jacob was discharged in March of 1780 at Fort Pitt after his enlistment was up. He appears in these Militia records, but there is no DAR record.

Ironically, in April and May of 1780, Indians attacked the area several times and killed a number of settlers. Jacob was in the field working during one attack. Two of his sons who were with him ran for help. Jacob was able to hold them off for a short time, killing several, but the Indians eventually killed him before help could arrive. His wife, Ann rode to the neighbors to warn them of the Indian attack and to get help. His estate papers filed April 17, 1783 stated he was "killed by Indians near Pittsburg." Among the papers was a merchant's account, which ended in April 1780. The papers also indicated he had a young child, (Peter). John handled his father's estate after his death and paid for his father's coffin. Ann died April 12, 1834 in Somerset County, Pennsylvania.

Jacob's son, Sampson Piersol/Pearsall, born 1764, served in a Company of Indian Spies in 1781 and 1782 under Captain Sissney (Sipeney), Captain Hood, and Colonel Crawford. He was seventeen at the time. He received a Revolutionary War pension # S.22937 (DAR #A086972). Jacob's son, John also served as a private in Captain Hood's Company. In June of 1782 at age nineteen, he was in Colonel Crawford's ill-fated expedition against the Indians at Sandusky who were believed to be the source of the raids against the settlers in western Pennsylvania. The army marched against the Indian settlements, but was defeated after the Indians were warned of their approach. The Indians were re-enforced by the British and the next day Crawford decided to withdraw. The Indians attacked the retreating troops, scattering and capturing many of them. Colonel Crawford was captured and killed. John returned with the survivors and continued under Captain Sipeney (Sissney) until October of 1782. Sampson was also in this battle. John and Sampson did their best to avenge their father's death. After the war, the Indians were still a threat to the settlers and they both continued to serve in the fourth Company, 1st Battalion of the Allegheny Militia. Sampson was appointed Lieutenant on May 1, 1792. In August of 1793, he was elected Captain. President Washington called his unit into duty during the Whiskey Rebellion when the settlers rebelled against the high taxes. Sampson became a leading citizen in District Pitt and later in the newly established Beaver County in 1800. He was a Justice of the Peace and acted as business attorney for many of his neighbors throughout the years. He became counselor and advisor for the whole community. He built a small church on his farm called Mount Pleasant Bible Class and is buried there. He died in 1842.

There were several members of the Pearsall/Piersol Pennsylvania families in the Revolution. Benjamin Pearsall born 1760 (DAR #086954), was a Guardsman on the Pennsylvania Frontier under Captain Wilson and Colonel Broadhead. He was in the eighth Pennsylvania Regiment and fought in the Battle of Brandywine, Paoli and other skirmishes. Jeremiah Pearsall (#A086964) was a Lieutenant under Captain John Graham in the Pennsylvania 1st Battalion, Mordecai Pearsall (# A086965), brother of Jeremiah, served in the 1st and 2nd Battalion under Lieutenant Colonel John Gardner of the Militia, Richard Pearsall; (#A086971) was also in the Pennsylvania 1st Battalion under Colonel John Graham.

Peter Piersol was born in 1780 after his father's death. His brothers John and Sampson took care of him until he became an adult. In the 1820 censes he is shown living in Salt Creek Township in Wayne County, Pennsylvania, with five males and seven females. He moved to Holmes County, Ohio about 1820 and to Fulton County, Illinois in 1836. He married Sarah Lutton about 1802. She was born September 8, 1782 in Alleghany County, Pennsylvania. She was the daughter of Robert (Warburton) Lutton and Shawanos Lutton. Her father was born in 1760 in Moria, County Down, Northern Ireland and died in Alleghany County. His father was William Lutton born 1709 in Moria, County D'Argenbrightown and died there in 1801. The Lutton name is found in England in the days of William the Conqueror with Sir Robert de Lytton and as far back as 939 when Hugh de Lytton married Alice. A James Lutton, born 1759 gave Patriotic service in Maryland and signed the Oath of Allegiance in 1778. He was a brother to Robert Lutton.

Peter and Sarah had thirteen children; twelve of them lived to adulthood. Their children were, Elizabeth born 1803, Joel born 1804, Prudence, Nancy, Sally, Sampson, John H., Hannah, Mary, Peter, Anne born 1824 who married Jefferson Louck and two not named. In the 1850 censes Peter is listed in Lee, Fulton County, Illinois age seventy and his wife Sarah is sixty-eight. He is listed as a farmer and lives next to his son Joel age forty-six, a farmer. Joel was an active participant of the Prairie City Village and member of the Masonic Lodge. He was involved in the Community politics and held several offices. Sarah died in 1858 and Peter in 1859, both buried in Virgil Cemetery in Fulton County Illinois.

Anne Piersol, daughter of Peter and Sarah, was born in Middletown Butler, Ohio on January 3, 1824 and moved with her family to Fulton County, Illinois in 1836. She married Jefferson Louk/Louck in Fulton County on February 1, 1844. The 1870 censes shows Jefferson and Anne living in Prairie City. The Louk family owned several businesses in Prairie City and were very active in the Village. Jefferson and Anne had seven children, Sarah Jane born 1844, David L., Hester Anne., Benjamin F., John P., Charles F., and Julia E. Anne died June 29, 1906 and buried in Virgil Cemetery in Lee County beside her husband Jefferson. He died January 3, 1884. Sarah Jane Louk born 1844, daughter of Jefferson and Anne, married Albert A. Wheeler in 1865. Their son, Ralph Wheeler married May Evans in Prairie City, Illinois in 1885. They had three sons, Russell, Rollin, and Harry, who married Ruth Minter. (See Wheeler and Minter Families).

*History and pictures sourced from Wikipedia, History of the Pearsoll family, Ancestry, Pacheste-L Archives at Rootsweb, PA tourist and the National Park Service Historic Jamestown, crest from free pages at Ancestry

THE BABB FAMILY

Thomas Babb was born about 1570 in St. Dunsten, Cranbrook, London, England and died in 1620 in Linehouse, Middlesex, England. He married Mary (last name unknown). They had two know children, Phillip born 1604 in St. Dunsten, Stepney, London, England, and Thomas also born in St. Dunsten in 1608. Thomas became Captain of the immigrant ship *Hopewell*. The ship's second voyage left England in mid September of 1635 and landed in Massachusetts Bay after a safe voyage. On October 12, 1641 Captain Thomas Babb, referred to as the former Master of the ship "*Hopewell*" out of London, came ashore at Norfolk in the Virginia Colony. He received a patent for one-hundred acres of land on the West Branch of the Nansemond River. After Thomas and his widow Eleanor died in 1665, the land was granted to their only child, Mary Babb.

Phillip, brother of Thomas, was the father of Phillip II born 1634 who settled on Hog Island (now Appledore Island pictured) in the Isles of Shoals. At the time, the Islands were under the government of Massachusetts. They consisted of eighteen small islands ten miles off the coast of Maine and New Hampshire. They were recorded in Captain John Smith's findings while he was exploring the coast of Main in April of 1614. He described the islands as *"a heap of many barren rocks with such scrubs and sharp 'whins' you can barely pass through them. They are without grass or wood except four three or four shrubby old cedars."* There was a pond of fresh water on Hog Island. Sir Christopher Levett stopped on the Islands in 1623 and described them as *"a great fishing place for six ships ---the harbor is but indifferently good. There are no savages at all."*

The fishing may have been what drew Phillip to the Islands. His name first appears November 24, 1652 when he was elected Constable for the Isles at the age of eighteen. He was a respected member of the small community and held the position for the rest of his life. He became a fishing master, a local magistrate, and the operator and owner of a butcher shop. *"He was able to amass a fortune of over three-hundred pounds in his short life time by producing dunfish, a world renown product made of thinly sliced salted cod dried on the island then shipped to Europe and Spain on a regular basis. This market lasted for over one-hundred and fifty years."**

The children of Phillip and his wife Mary are listed as the following: Thomas, Phillip III, Peter, William, and Sampson. Phillip died March 31, 1671 at the age of thirty-seven in the Isle of Shoals leaving five small children. His wife died three years later in 1674. Neither of them left a will. An inventory of the estate totaled three-hundred and twenty pounds, six shillings and eight pense. Some of the children were indentured to families on the mainland. *(History from David R. Babb's history on Phillip Babb).

Thomas Babb, son of Phillip and Mary, was born about 1664 on Hog Island. After the death of his parents, he was indentured in 1675 to Henry Green of Hampton, New Hampshire until he was eighteen years old. He met and married Bathsheba Hussey prior to 1700 while living in Hampton. She was born September 21, 1671 in Hampton, New Hampshire, the daughter of John Hussey and Rebecca Perkins of Hampton and Delaware. The Hussey's were Quakers and persecuted in Hampton. Thomas Babb and the Hussey family moved first to Nantucket Island and in 1695, moved to Delaware where there was greater religious tolerance. Thomas obtained one-hundred acres in Brandywine Hundred, New Castle, Delaware. In November of 1735, Thomas received a patent for six hundred acres on Apple Pie Ridge in Fredrick County Virginia. He sent his sons Thomas and Phillip to occupy it and carry out the provisions of the patent. Three acres out of every fifty had to be cleared and cultivated with yearly payments to the King's agent. The old Thomas and Bathsheba Babb house is pictured.

Thomas and Bathsheba had eight children: Peter, Thomas, Phillip, Lydia, Sampson, Mary, Hulda, and Rebecca were all born in Delaware. Bathsheba died in 1713 in Brandywine Hundred, New Castle. After her death, Thomas announced at the church meeting he was in need of someone to care for his young children. On March 25, 1720, he married Elizabeth Conway Booth, widow of Charles Booth.

In an election in Fredrick, County, Virginia in 1758, Thomas Babb, Thomas Babb, Jr., Phillip, Thomas Babb (son of Phillip) Peter Babb, and Joseph Babb all voted for George Washington for a seat in the House of Burgesses. (See 1899 Virginia Historical Magazine).

Thomas died August 13, 1751. His will dated August 17, 1748, was proven on August 13, 1751. He left his homestead in Delaware to his oldest son Peter and the Virginia holdings to his son Phillip and son Thomas Jr. Other bequests were left to his daughters and his granddaughter, daughter of Hulda.

Peter Babb was born about 1695 in New Castle, Delaware. He and his brother Phillip moved just across the state line to Chester County, Pennsylvania and moved his membership from the Newark Quaker Monthly Meeting to the Concord Monthly Meeting. He married Mary Lewis December 11, 1728 at Cain, Chester County, Pennsylvania. She was born about 1697 in Cain, the daughter of Evan Lewis. She was the descendant of William Lewis the immigrant from Wales in 1686. (See Lewis Family) Peter received a grant of four-hundred acres in West Cain Township, Chester County from the Penn brothers for which he initially paid fifteen pounds, ten shillings per hundred acres plus one-half penny sterling yearly rent per acre. He was Captain in the local Militia. Peter and his wife Mary had eleven children: Mary, Content, John, Thomas, Peter, Susannah, Elizabeth, Bathsheba, Ann born 1738, and Sampson. Peter died October 27, 1773 in Chester, Pennsylvania. His son Peter, born 1735, a Captain in the Revolution, married Mary Beeson (See Beeson Family-LaGrone). His daughter Ann Babb married Jacob Peirsol, born 1736. They were married outside of the Quaker religion.

Eighteen members of the Babb family fought in the Revolution, including several from Peter's family. John Babb born 1749 (#A206755) gave Patriotic service, paid the supply tax. Mary Babb born 1737

(#A004175) furnished forage and provisions for the Militia, Sampson Babb born about 1740 (#A004179) served in the Chester County Militia under Captain William Withrow and Colonel Bell, Thomas Babb born 1729 (#A004181) served under Captain Joseph Marshall and Colonel Thomas Duff, Thomas Babb born 1740 (#A004182) furnished supplies for the Continental Army. Peter born 1735 (#A004178) was a Captain in the Frederick County Militia. He qualified on November 5, 1776 and served until June of 1777 when he resigned because of his age. In March of 1777, his Company was sent to Fort Pitt to relieve the Twelfth Virginia Regiment, which joined George Washington in New Jersey. During his time at Fort Pitt, he had several skirmishes with the Indians. At the same time Jacob Piersol, who married Ann Babb (daughter of Peter Sr.) was also serving at Fort Pitt. Peter Babb and his brother Thomas Babb, both had sons named Peter and both were born in 1735. According to the DAR records, Captain Peter Babb of the Revolution was the son of Thomas Babb, Sr. Other documents say he was the son of Peter.

*History and pictures sourced from Wikipedia, genforum, Ancestry, and free crest from www.jebabb.us

THE GHOST OF PHILLIP BABB

During the Revolution, most of the families from the Island of Shoals were evacuated to Rye, New Hampshire for safety. The Islands were abandoned until the middle of the nineteenth century when Thomas Laighton, a lighthouse keeper on one of the islands, and Levi Thaxter built a popular summer hotel on Appledore Island. Laighton's daughter, Celia who married Levi, became a popular American poet. She hosted an arts community on the Island, which was frequented by famous authors and artists. Ghost stories began surfacing at the hotel about pirates and their buried treasurer, the ghost of a ship wrecked off Smuttynose Island in 1813, and the ghost of young women who was washed away by a high wave as she sat on a rock viewing the ocean. The ghost of Phillip Babb, the first inhabitant of Hog (Appledore) Island is said to wear his butcher's apron and carry a butcher knife. Pictured is the famous map of the Isle of Shoals by Captain John Smith.

Nathaniel Hawthorne visited Appledore in 1852 and wrote the following in his journal:

> *"Mr. Thaxter once had a man living with him who had seen "Old Babb' the ghost. He met him between the hotel and the sea and described him as dressed in a sort of frock, and with a very dreadful countenance."*

Phillip Babb died a very successful young man, leaving his fledgling family. He would hardly fit the description of an "old man with a dreadful countenance." If his spirit came back at all, he was probably looking for his wife and young sons. It is not known why he died so early in life. Perhaps his fishing boat wrecked. However, after the Hotel burned down 1914, the ghost stories went with it. "Old Babb" has no longer been seen. He now rests in peace.

*History and picture sourced from Wikipedia

THE HUSSEY FAMILY

The Hussey family in England descends from Hubert, son of Hugh Hussey and the daughter of the third Earl of Normandy France. Hubert may have fought in the Battle of Hastings in 1066. Henry Hussey was born 1547 in Slynfold, Sussex, England to John Hussey. In 1662, Henry was enrolled in Queen's College at Cambridge University. He married Judith Pagent. He was the Clerk of Spicery for Queen Elizabeth and James I. He lived in the Court for thirty-five years. He died May 23, 1611 and buried in the south isle of the Hussey Battersea Church of Middlesex, England.

The children of Henry and Judith include John Hussey born April 29, 1659 who married Mary (Marie) Wood (Moor) on February 5, 1593-4. John was one of her Majesty's Commissioners for Surrey and Sussex, (pictured). Christopher Hussey, baptized February 18, 1598 in Dorking, Surrey England, was the son of John Hussey and Mary Wood. Christopher married first Theodate Bachilor and second Ann Capon. Christopher and his family immigrated to America aboard the William and Francis in 1632 along with his widowed mother Marie Wood who was an original grantee of Hampton, Norfolk, Massachusetts in 1638, now in Rockingham County New Hampshire. In 1650, seats in the Meeting House were assigned to "ould mistres Hussey." She died in 1660 in Hampton.

Christopher served as a lot layer, town clerk, selectman, juror, representative and Lieutenant in the Militia. He was appointed by the King as one of the Councilors of the newly formed Colony of New Hampshire. He purchased land on Nantucket in 1649, which he later gave to his sons Stephen and John. Christopher and his sons were inclined to the Quaker doctrines. In 1664, he was admonished for attending a Quaker meeting and later fined in 1663 and 1664 for not attending church. They were fined again in 1668 for working on a fast day. (These were Puritan observances). Christopher died March 6, 1685 in Hampton.

Christopher's son John was baptized on December 31, 1635 in Lynn, Essex, Massachusetts. He married Rebecca Perkins September 2, 1659, the daughter of Isaac and Alice Perkins, and settled in Hampton, New Hampshire. (Isaac Perkins was from Hillmoton, Warwick, England). John and Rebecca had seventeen children. He was appointed a Representative in 1692 but refused to take the oath of office (taking oaths were against the Quaker tenets). He and his family later moved to New Castle, Delaware where he owned the *Nonesuch Plantation,* a six hundred and forty acre tract and became a Quaker preacher. (Alice Perkins, mother of Rebecca, moved to Delaware with her son Ebenezer after the death of her husband). In 1696-98, John served as a Representative and a member of the Pennsylvania Assembly. Quakers were not required to take the oath in Pennsylvania. He died in 1707. John's will was dated May 8, 1707. Bathsheba, his seventh child born September 21, 1671, married Thomas Babb. They moved with her family to Delaware.

Eleven members of the Hussey family served in the Revolution and loaned money to the cause. George Hussey (#A061204) born 1738 in Nantucket, John Hussey (#A061209) born 1737 in Nantucket, Joseph Hussey (#A134049) born 1740 in Nantucket, Christopher Hussey (#A061203) born 1724 in Nantucket and Batchelor Hussey (#A061201) all loaned money to the Government. Stephen Hussey (#A061216) a member of the Committee of Safety, supplied shoes, and was muster master. Mary Hussey (#A061211) from North Carolina furnished supplies.

Part of the northeast half of the Hussey tract is now part of the Wilmington, Delaware Airport. The one hundred fifty acre Cedar Hill Cemetery was also formerly part of the tract know as the Nonesuch Cemetery in what is now Suitland, Maryland (pictured). It is a short drive from Washington D.C.

*History and picture sourced from Wikipedia, Hussey Millennium Manuscripts of the Gowen Research Foundation, and crest from Britannia

THE LEWIS FAMILY

Members of the Lewis family of Wales are said to descend from Phillip Llywelyn, the youngest son of Llywelyn of Saint Pierre near Chepstow around 1300. Part of this 14th century Manor House is now a Marriott hotel and country club. Others trace the Welch Lewis family to Gwathford, a Leon representative of the linage of the Princes of Britain who lived in the fifth century. There is a similarity in the arms borne by the Lewis family in Glamorgan. William Lewis of Glamorganshire and his family immigrated to America in 1686.

Another progenitor of the Lewis (Llywelyn in Welch) family in America was Evan Lewis born 1610 in Wales. His father, Evan, was born in 1585 in Yspytly Parish Denbighshire, Wales. Evan was in his seventy's when he and one of his sons, Henry Lewis emigrated from Wales in 1682. Henry was born in Narbeth, Pembrookeshire, South Wales where the family had long held a prominent position. He married Margaret (Protheroe) Philpin on January 12, 1671 in Landewy, Pembrookeshire (Landewi Velfrey). Henry was a carpenter In Narbeth. He came to America with his wife and three children, two sons and a daughter. Henry and fellow immigrants, Lewis David, and William Howell were received into the Philadelphia Friends Meeting on a certificate from the Redstone General Meeting, Pembrooke County, Couth Wales dated August 6, 1682.

Members of the Society of Friends were persecuted in the 1680's and large numbers of both English and Welch immigrated to the Colonies under the leadership of William Penn, pictured. Penn was issued a Patent on March 4, 1681 by King Charles II for the Province of Pennsylvania. This was in payment for a debt of 16,000 pounds loaned to Charles II by Admiral Sir William Penn, father of William Penn. On June 21, 1681 Justices of the Peace, magistrates and other offices were notified of the grant to Penn. Pennsylvania was originally set up as a Quaker Colony.

In 1681 three ships sailed from England, two from London and one from Bristol with the Evan and Henry Lewis family aboard. The *John and Sarah* left first followed by the *Bristol Factor,* which arrived in Chester December 11, 1681, and the *Amity*. The *Amity* was blown off course. The ship did not arrive until the spring of 1682. Penn did not sail until August 30, 1882. He left from Deal on the ship *Welcome*, with one-hundred passengers, most of who were members of the Society of Friends, and arrived in New Castle, Delaware October 27, 1682. Penn took possession of the territory around New Castle known at the New Castle grant. He landed in (Upland) Chester, the seat of his government, on October 28 or 29. The first legislative assembly was held December 4, 1682 with several representatives of his counties. Penn returned to England in 1684 and made one more visit to Pennsylvania in 1699 staying until 1701. This was his last visit to America. He died in Berkshire, England in 1718 and his sons took over the grant.

The Welch had bargained for a separate Barney of forty-thousand acres (the Welch Tract) before they left Wales. This land was mostly in the wilderness, but was eventually settled as more and more Welch emigrants arrived. About one-fourth of the tract eventually became part of Delaware with the rest in Pennsylvania.

William Lewis, another prominent member of the early Lewis family in America was from Eglwysilan, parish of Llantrisant, County Glamorganshire, Wales. His family moved to Haverford, Pennsylvania in 1686. William was the son of Ralph Lewis of Llanishen, a landholder in Eglwysilan in 1683 and the son of David Lewis. David was the son of Edward of Llanishen who was the son of Edward Lewis a large landholder and Sheriff of Glamorganshire in 1548. Ralph Lewis married Ann Prichard of Glamorganshire, the sister of Thomas Prichard, and had two sons. In a letter to his brother Ralph Lewis written in 1684, William tells him his "uncle Thomas Prichard has died." Thomas is documented as being a Member of Parliament when he died in 1683. The Prichard family is well documented. They descend from King Edward III through Edmund, Duke of York, who was the son of Edward III. Ralph Lewis is traced through his mother Ann Prichard to eight Magna Carta Barons.

Many members of the Prichard (Pritchard) family move to America in the late 1600's. Twenty-two served in the American Revolution. George Pritchard (#A093419) built ships for the American Navy. James (#093424) was a Sheriff and Court Clerk in South Carolina and furnished supplies for the Army. Several were soldiers in New England.

William was a Freeholder of a large plantation in Haverford, Delaware Colony, Pennsylvania. He and his wife Ann had four know children, their son William married in 1704 to Gwen the daughter of William John of Gwynedd. Lewis married Mary Howell of Bristol, Evan born August 2, 1677 in Eglwysilan, Glamorganshire, married Mary Hayes, who was born about 1675 in Eglwysilan and son David married Ann Jones of Merion in 1695.

Evan and Mary Hayes were married about 1696 in Chester (now Delaware County, Pennsylvania) and had several children including daughter Mary Lewis born in 1697. She married Peter Babb. Their daughter Ann Babb married Jacob Piersol. Their daughter Ann Piersol married Jefferson Louck, and their daughter Sarah Jane married Albert Wheeler. Evan died February 11, 1731 in Newtown Township, Chester County, Pennsylvania. His will provided for his wife Mary. He gave ten pounds to the poor of Newtown and to his eldest son Mordecai he gave his plantation containing about 700 acres. To his son Jonathan he gave his plantation of 200 acres in Ridley, also 259 acres in Whiteland. His will stated

> "Mordecai is to release to Jonathan all that tract of land in Hatfield Township, which descends to me and my wife from my brother-in-law Jonathan Hayes."

Three hundred members of the Lewis family served in the Revolution, twenty-eight from Pennsylvania, nine from Chester County. Henry Lewis' grandson, Isaac Lewis (#A069967) born 1725 in Haverford was a Lieutenant in the Chester County Militia Third Battalion under Captain Pitt and Colonel Pierse. Two Evan Lewis' served in the Chester County Militia, Evan born 7-10-1740 (#A069894) under Captain Hugh Jones and Caleb Davis, and Evan born 4-13-1740 (#A069895) under Captain Mordecai Morgan. Others in the Chester County Militia were David born 1714 (#A69839) Alexander (#A069711), James born 1748

(#A069989), Jehu born 1723 (#A069996) Phillip, Sr., born 1751 (#A070104), Samuel born 1726 (#A070126) and his son Samuel born 1754 (#A070125), ten fought at the Battle of Kings Mountain. It is probable one or more of the above were related to Evan of Newtoun.

On June 18-25 1776, the Eve of the Revolution, a Provisional Conference was held at Carpenter's Hall (pictured) in Philadelphia where a provision was made to form a "flying camp" of ten-thousand men in the middle of the colonies. Pennsylvania's quota was forty-five hundred men. The Militia was to be ready to march any place the Congress ordered. They were called up to help Washington when he crossed the Delaware, at the battle of Brandywine and the flanks at Germantown. They were used to augment the Continental Line on many other occasions.

*History and pictures Wikipedia, Crest is free to use from genform, Pritchard crest from Pritchard family genealogy

CHAPTER VII
THE EVANS FAMILY

The Evans family name comes from Elystand Gledridd, Prince of Fferleys who founded the Fourth Tribe of Wales. The name itself means, "Well born." Ieuan, born 1155 in Ystard, Glamorgan, Wales, was a Knight of the Holy Sepulchre. His ancestry goes back to the sixth century. There are legends of early Celtic Voyages to America in the twelfth century (before Columbus) led by Madoc, son of Owain Gwynedd Prince Gwynedd of Wales, which are usually dismissed. However, a letter written in 1810 from John Seiver, first Governor of Tennessee to his friend Major Amos Stoddard told of a conversation he had with the old Cherokee Chief, Oconastota, about ancient fortifications built on the Alabama River. The Chief told him that a white people called "Welch" had built Forts to protect themselves from his Cherokee ancestors, who drove them away. In 1799,  Seiver wrote about the discovery of six skeletons wearing brass armor with breastplates bearing the Welch Coat of Arms. They were found near Jeffersonville, Indiana on the Ohio River. There are other references connecting Madoc to sites such as Devils Backbone along the Ohio River. A plaque, pictured, on the public strand of Mobile Bay put there by the Daughters of the American Revolution that reads,

> "In memory of Prince Madoc, a Welch explorer, who landed on the shores of Mobile Bay in 1170 and left behind, with the Indians, the Welch language."

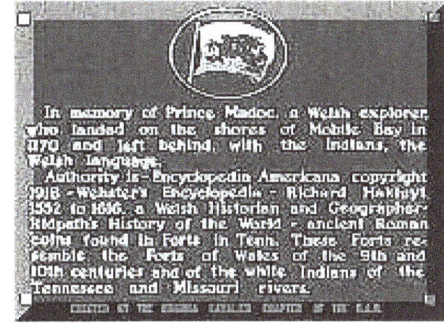

There is another plaque to Madoc ap Owain Gwynedd on the wall of the *Fine Arts Center of the South* in Mobile, Alabama. Visitors can view a map, which points out where Madoc, the Welch explorer of America, arrived with his three ships.

The Welsh migration to the American Colonies began as early as 1622 when Christo and Laurence Evans landed in Virginia looking for religious freedom. Many of the Welsh emigrant's religion did not conform to the Church of England. Some of the early British settlers, including the Pilgrims were Welch or Anglo-Welch.

According to family tradition, the Lott Evans family sailed from Liverpool. Lott's father died aboard ship  on his way to America. He was buried at sea. Lott Sr.'s son, Lott Evans Jr. was born in Wales about 1717 and died in 1784. He is buried in Whaler's graveyard in Blackwood town, New Jersey. He married Lydia Taylor, who was born August 23, 1725 in Wales. The Taylor family is first found in Kent, England where they held a family seat given to them by King William for their assistance at the battle of Hastings in 1066. Lott and Lydia had seven known children, two sons and five daughters, David born 1737 in Wales, John born in Wales August of 1738 and died December 6, 1817 in Eaton Luzerne County Pennsylvania, Elizabeth, Grace, Polly, Rachel, and Sallie Ann.

John served in the Revolution as a Private in Colonel Somers 3rd Regiment of the Gloucester County, New Jersey, Militia, (DAR #037572). David also served in the Militia. The Militia men were called up for particular campaigns and they voluntarily left their plows and followed Washington in the defense of freedom. Their tour of service was sometimes as short as six weeks at a time. The Gloucester County Militia and Atlantic County men under Colonel Somers were involved in the battles of Trenton and Princeton helping to provide diversions for General Washington while he attacked the Hessians Christmas Day at Trenton. Colonel Griffin helped with the diversions by keeping his Troops near Mount Holly, New Jersey who with the help of a beautiful young widow (Betsy Ross), kept Colonel Von Donop and his Hessian Troops engaged while Washington crossed the Delaware on Christmas, attacked, and defeated Colonel Rall. Von Donop, who, according to the diary of one of his officers Captain Ewald, *"was exceedingly devoted to the fairer sex,"* and was permitted to set up his headquarters in the Ross home. Captain Ewald further stated,

> *"Colonel Donop was led by the noise to Mount Holly by Colonel Griffin and kept there by love. This great misfortunate surely caused the utter loss of thirteen splendid provinces of the Crown of England."*

The "embarrassed" Von Donop retreated with his troops from Mount Holly to Princeton on December 27, 1776.

A few days after the victory at Trenton, Washington attacked Princeton and won another victory. These successes essentially turned the American War for Independence around and freed New Jersey from British occupation. Washington and his army then went to Morristown for the winter. The Gloucester Militia divided and went in three directions to protect New Jersey. Part of Somers Regiment under Captain Estell returned to their farmsteads to prepare for spring planting. One hundred and sixty one Evans' family members who fought in the Revolution, seven were in the Battle of King's Mountain.

David Evans married Sarah Stiles born 1738 in Moorestown, Burlington, New Jersey. Her father was Robert Stiles III born 1681 in Philadelphia and died in Moorestown, New Jersey. Her mother was Sarah Stiles Rudderow born 1689 in Philadelphia and died 1728 in Moorestown. Sarah's father, John Rudderow, was born 1660 in Hairant, Montgomeryshire, Wales.

David and Sarah were married February 13, 1786 in Woolwich, Gloucester, New Jersey at the Trinity Episcopal Church. They had nine children, Tamson born 1780, Job born 1790 and died in 1870, and Thomas born Oct 15, 1794 in Gloucester, New Jersey, and died 1877 in Upper Alloways Creek, Salem, New Jersey. The others were John, Polly, Rachel, Betsy, Sally Ann, and Grace. David and his wife are buried in the Stiles cemetery in Cross Keys, New Jersey. (See Stiles Family)

Thomas Evans married Lydia Duffield December 24, 1815 in Gloucester. She was born June 21, 1795 in New Jersey and died January 6, 1878 from a tumor in the throat. She is buried in the Freasburg Lutheran Church Cemetery in Upper Alloways Creek. Her father was James Duffield born 1764 in Gloucester and her mother was Susannah Hawks born 1765 in New Jersey. (See Duffield and Hawks families). Thomas bought a twenty-eight acre farm from the

Griffith family in 1840 on the border of Salem and Cumberland Counties. A sign on the farmhouse identified it as the "Thomas Evans House," pictured.

Thomas and Lydia had ten children, nine boys, and one girl. James Duffield Evans was born 1816 died 1891. He was in the mercantile business and Postmaster of Cohansey, Cumberland County. David, a shoemaker, was born 1819 died 1883, Isaac was born 1821 died 1903. He was an engineer in Alloways. Josiah Duffield Evans was born 1823 died 1900. He and his brother Johnathan were in business together as proprietors of a foundry and agriculture implements in Smyrna, Delaware. Hezekiah was born in 1826 and died the same year. Thomas Jr. was a mechanic and patternmaker for a large foundry in Millville, New Jersey. He was born 1827 and he died 1877. William Reynolds was born May 22, 1830 in Upper Alloways Creek, New Jersey and died in 1910 in Prairie City, Illinois. John Evans was born 1832 and died in 1900. He was in the mining business in Colorado. Lydia Susannah was born 1835 and she died 1854. She married Theophilus Remster. Jonathan Burr was born 1838 and he died 1920. Thomas died April 28, 1877. He is buried in the cemetery at Freasburg Lutheran Church in Freasburg, New Jersey beside his wife Lydia.

William Reynolds born May 22, 1830 in Upper Alloways Creek was baptized there on June 4, 1837 at age seven. He married Cornelia Winter born July 10, 1839 in Franklin, Sumerset, New Jersey and she died July 10, 1916 in Prairie City, Illinois. In 1850, Cornelia was living in Fairview, Fulton County Illinois at the age of eleven. (See Winter and Suydam family). William and Cornelia were married March 27, 1858 in Fulton, Illinois. He was a stockman, farmer, and carpenter. He built several houses in the area including his own. In 1880, they were living in Prairie City. They had four children, baby Evans and John Bernard born 1868 died young. Charles Winters Evans born 1863 in Fairview, died in 1900 in Fulton, Illinois. May Evans was born June 16, 1872 in Fairview and died in Flagstaff, Arizona September of 1935. She is buried in Prairie City, Illinois beside her husband William. (See Winter Family) May Evans married Ralph Bismark Wheeler in 1885 and had sons Russell, Rollin, and Harry. Pictured are William Reynolds Evans and Cornelia Winter Evans.

*History and pictures sourced from Author, Evans Family History, and Ancestry, crest is from Ancestry free pages

THE STYLES FAMILY

The Styles family comes from old Bedfordshire, which was once a part of the Angle-Saxon Kingdom of Mercia. They also lived in Somerset where William de Stiless is recorded in 1229 and 1234. Robert Stiles Sr. was born in Yorkshire, England in 1634 and died July 30, 1690 in Boxford, Essex, Massachusetts. Robert Sr. fled England for religious reasons during the reign of Charles I. He married Elizabeth Frye born 1637 in England. Robert Stiles Jr., born in Staffordshire, England in 1666, came to America in 1683 with his father, Robert Stiles Sr. and his sister Lucy.

Robert Jr. married Priscilla Howell, daughter of Thomas and Catherine Howell of Staffordshire. She was born in 1664 in Tamworth, Warwickshire, England and died November 2, 1690 in Gloucester, New Jersey. Her great grandfather Thomas Howell was born December 8, 1599 in Lincolnshire, England and died there. Robert and Priscilla were married about 1681 in Philadelphia, Pennsylvania and settled first in Bryn Mawr. In 1695, Robert Jr. purchased 415 acres of land on the branches of Pennsauken Creek three miles west of Morristown, New Jersey. Priscilla's father gave her one hundred acres of homestead property when he died. Besides farming, Robert made rosin and was consider an excellent "artist" in that capacity. Early records show he was active in the affairs of Chester Township. They had three children that reached adulthood, Robert III born 1681-1728, John born 1683-1694, and Martha born 1687. In 1684 his sister Lucy, married John Rudderow and they lived in Chester, Burlington County, New Jersey.

Robert Stiles III was born in 1681 in Philadelphia. He married his cousin Sarah Stiles Rudderow the daughter of Lucy and John Rudderow in 1705 in Morristown. She was born in 1689 in Philadelphia. They had five children, Robert VI born 1720-1770, Ephraim born 1723-1771, Nicholas born 1727-1812, Sarah born 1728 who married David Evans, and Isaac born 1729-1806. Upon the death of Robert Jr., they inherited the Pennsauken Creek Farm.

John Stiles, Jr. was a Quartermaster during the Revolution. He died in Stiles Town, New Jersey in 1830. His DAR Patriot number is (#A109951). Aaron Stiles, born in Morristown August 28, 1761 was a private in Captain John Ward's Company (#A109874). He died in 1843 in Stiles Settlement. David Stiles born in 1760 in Morristown was in the Morris County Militia, Patriot (# A109913). Fifty-two members of the Stiles family served in the Revolution. Captain James Styles fought in the Battle of King's Mountain.

*History sourced from Ancestry, and Nelson S. Hollingshead family history. Styles crest is from the Styles family.

THE RUDDEROW FAMILY

There is little known history of the early Rudderow family in Wales. John Rudderow was born in Wales in 1634. He married Ann Jones. Their only son John was born in Hernant, Powys, Montgomeryshire, Wales in 1660. He was educated in law and planned to be a lawyer in England. He was appointed surrogate to the Crown and assigned duty in the Colonies when William Penn and the Quakers started the settlements in West New Jersey and Bryn Mawr, Pennsylvania in 1680-1683. The Government sent John to the Colonies as a "Crown Surveyor." It was his duty to report the surveys made by the Proprietors to the Crown. He arrived in Philadelphia when there was only one home built, (Penn's home in Bryn Mawr pictured). William Penn gave him "one square," a front lot, to entice him to stay. He was also Superintendent of the layout of the City of Philadelphia. When he had finished his work, he was about to return to England when a ship arrived with a company of Welch colonists, including his father and mother and the Robert Styles family,  (See Styles Family). William Penn had granted a Charter to them in Bryn Mawr. In 1684, John surveyed a six-hundred and forty acre track of land in Chester Township Burlington County, New Jersey between the forks of Pennsauken Creek. The original survey was in the names of John Rudderow and John Clark. Four-hundred and seventy-five acres located at the forks of the Creek later resurveyed for John Rudderow. He subsequently purchased all the land between the Forks and a mile back.

John married Lucy Stiles and lived on a large plantation. They had five daughters and one son, John, who lived to adulthood. His daughter Sarah Stiles Rudderow, born in 1689, married Robert Styles III in 1705. John was active in the community and served as Town Clerk for several years. He was also appointed Judge of the Courts in 1706. Since there was not a church in the area, John held services in his home until a church could be built. He left ten pounds in his will for that purpose. His will was proven May 12, 1733. He died in Chester, Burlington, New Jersey. He belonged to the Church of England, as required by the King. Later when St. Mary's Church was built, (pictured) his son, John paid the legacy. Between 1690 and 1700, John was engaged in the shipping trade between Philadelphia and the West Indies with his co-partner Captain Howell. In this way, he imported the bricks from England to build his house. The house was later torn down, but his descendant, John Rudderow, still lives on part of the original track of land. John died May 12, 1733 in Chester Township, Burlington, New Jersey.

John's grandson John, born February 17, 1759 of Gloucester County New Jersey, (#A099540) joined the British Army during the Revolution according to DAR and his property was confiscated in 1778. However, ancestry records claim he was a minuteman and fought in defense of Philadelphia in 1777-78 along the Cooper and Delaware rivers. His name does not appear in Stryker's records since he was under age. No other war records for members of the Rudderow family have been found.

*History and pictures sourced from Wikipedia, Ancestry, and Philadelphia history, free picture upon request.

THE DUFFIELD FAMILY

The first recorded spelling of the Duffield name is Rodger de Duffeld in 1190 in the Poll tax records in Yorkshire during the reign of King Richard I known as "Richard the Lionheart" 1189-1199. The spelling is traced to the Old Norse word "dufa" for dove and the old English word for field "feld" thus Dovefield or Duffield. There are two Duffield townships in Yorkshire. The Duffield Castle was an old Norman Castle in Duffield, Derbyshire. Its ruins are part of the English National Trust, pictured.

Duffield

Robert Duffield, born in Yorkshire in 1610, married Bridget (last name unknown). He evidently died there. His son, Robert Duffield, born August 24, 1634 in Leeds, Yorkshire, died November 15, 1692 in Philadelphia. He married Bridget Hart born in 1635 who died in 1682 in Philadelphia. Robert and Bridget's children was Robert Jr., born in 1657, Mary born about 1659, Benjamin born about 1661-2 and Joseph born September 29, 1661 and died May 1, 1741 in Philadelphia. They were all born in Yorkshire, England. In 1678, the ship "Shield" from Hull, England arrived in Burlington, New Jersey with passengers Robert Duffield, his daughter Mary Duffield (who married Allen Foster) and sons Benjamin and Joseph Duffield. It is possible Robert, Jr. came over earlier on the ship Kent in 1677 with several Yorkshire passengers who settled in

Burlington. Robert Sr., Joseph, and Benjamin Duffield first made their home in New Jersey in 1678 and later moved to Pennsylvania on William Penn's land grant. Joseph was a member of the Pennsylvania Assembly in 1711-12 and again in 1715 to 1721. His wife and children are unknown. Benjamin and his wife, Elizabeth Watts had fourteen children, most lived and died in the Philadelphia area. Members of that family were very involved in developing the state of Pennsylvania. The earliest member of the family to arrive in the Virginia Colony in 1622 was John Duffield, a boy of fourteen.

In the year 1682, King Charles II made laws that became intolerable for the Dissenters, Ministers, and members of the Non-Conformists churches. Every member of the House of Commons was compelled, under pain of expulsion, to take the Sacrament according to the form prescribed by the Liturgy. The hangman burned the covenant in the Palace yard and it was made a crime to attend a dissenting place of worship. A single Justice of the Peace could convict a person for this offence without a jury, and for a third offence pass sentence of "transportation beyond the seas for seven years." A convicted person was not allowed to go to New England where he might find sympathy. If he returned for the same offence, he was subject to capitol punishment. In Besse's "History of the Sufferings of the Quakers," he speaks of William Duffield of Isfiled, Sussex,

"(

"Who having been seen at a meeting, was, at the motion of Henry Hallywell a priest, taken the next day from his employment and carried before the Justice. The Justice tendered him the oath of allegiance, and on his refusal to take it, committed him to Horsham Gaol (prison)."

About the same time in 1681, William Penn obtained the land grant of Pennsylvania. He also purchased a portion of land from the Indians. He established *"wide and perfect toleration in matters of worship."* This motivated the dissenters, non-conformist and members of the "Friends religion" to follow Penn. Ship after ship carried the settlers to Pennsylvania many landing in Burlington, New Jersey. Several of the settlers were people of wealth and intelligence who left the oppressions of Charles II. Members of the settlement in Pennsylvania wrote to their relatives in England telling them of their large estates and the fertile land. They spoke of the abundance of wild game and fish, the fruit trees that were breaking under the weight of the fruit and the beef, sheep, and hogs that grew fat on the land. In a letter from Mahlon Stacy to his brother in 1679, he stated he had no desire to return to England.

"All of our people live better than they did and are able to provide well for their posterity." He wondered at those in Yorkshire who would rather, *"live in servitude, work hard all year, and not be three pence better at years end."*

John Duffield was born in 1740 in Gloucester County, New Jersey and died April 12, 1807 in Deptford Township, Gloucester. He is buried in Bethel Methodist Cemetery in Hurffville, Gloucester, (pictured). He married Amy Dilks March 3, 1760 in Gloucester. She died in 1811. John and Amy had six children, James, born between 1764-68 in Gloucester, Nancy, Jonathan born 1772 and died 1870, Edward born 1772 and died 1855, Josiah born 1777 and died 1856, and John.

James Duffield, son of John, was born in 1764 and died May 7, 1814 in Gloucester. He married Susannah Hawks born in New Jersey in 1765. They were married September 14, 1790 in the Pittsgrove Baptist Church in Salem, New Jersey. She died May 7, 1814. She was the daughter of Benjamin Hawks. James Duffield and Susanna Hawks had three children James L. born 1790 and died 1862, Lydia born 1795 and died 1878 in Upper Alloways Creek, Salem, New Jersey of a throat tumor, and George born 1796 and died 1872.

Lydia Duffield married Thomas Evans December 24, 1815 in Gloucester, New Jersey. They lived in Upper Alloways Creek for over thirty years. Lydia is buried in the Freesburg Lutheran Cemetery in Alloways Creek. They had ten children; James Duffield Evans born 1816 died 1891, David was born 1819 and died 1883, Isaac born 1821 and died 1903, Josiah Duffield Evans born 1823 and died 1900, Hezekiah born 1826 and died 1826, Thomas Jr., born 1827 and died 1877. William Reynolds was born 1830 and died in Prairie City, Illinois in 1910, John was born 1832 and died 1900, Lydia Susannah was 1835 and died 1854, and Jonathan Burr born 1838 and died in 1920.

William Reynolds Evans married Cornelia Winters born 1839 in New Jersey. William and Cornelia lived in Illinois. Their daughter May Evans married Ralph Wheeler. (See Winters and Suydam families)

Ten members of the Duffield family are recorded with DAR as serving in the Revolution. Among them were John Duffield from New York, a Surgeon in the Third Artillery (#A034384), Benjamin Duffield from Pennsylvania who was also a Surgeon (#A034380), Edward Duffield gave Patriotic Service in Pennsylvania (#A034381) and Thomas Duffield was a Corporal in the Fourth Artillery (#A034387). George Duffield was a Chaplin from Lancaster, Pennsylvania (#A034382). The New Jersey Duffield family members served in the New Jersey Militia.

*History and picture from Wikipedia and Ancestry, crest from Ancestry free pages

THE DILKS FAMILY

The ancient Dilks family name is recorded in Warwickshire, England before 1066. Members of the family arrived in America in the area of Dilksboro, New Jersey in 1699. James Sr. emigrated from England in in 1714 and was the founder of the South Jersey town of Dilksboro in old Gloucester. He purchased a thousand acres from John Ladd. The deed is dated May 31, 1714. James married Ann Barker December 2, 1710 in the old Coles Church in Moorestown, New Jersey. James was the son of Edward Dilks and Elizabeth Gamble of Staffordshire, England. His ancestry goes back to Thomas Dilks born in 1632 in Longford, Derbyshire, England. James was born November 12, 1679 in Litchfield, St. Mary's Parish, Staffordshire England, (pictured).  James and Ann's children were James, Joseph Aaron, John, Isaac, Abraham, Rachael, and Sarah. Each of his children received a "patrimony" farm, part of the original tract. Their son James (Jr.) married Sarah Jane (?) and their daughter Amy married John Duffield in March of 1760.

 Samuel Dilkes (#A132706) born 1753 in Gloucester, New Jersey, was a private in the Gloucester Militia. He was the son of Isaac. He served under Colonel Richard Somer. Isaac Dilks born 1762 and died 1833 in Hurffville, Gloucester is listed as a Revolutionary soldier in the New Jersey Library archives file number 14971. He was also the son of Isaac born 1739 and grandson of James Sr. The 1776 New Jersey Flag is pictured.

*History and picture sourced from Wikipedia, crest, and flag from Ancestry free pages

THE HAWK FAMILY

The name Hawk comes from the old English Heafoc meaning a person who raised hawks. He was usually a tenant who held land by providing hawks for his Lord. The name is recorded in Cromwell and in Lincolnshire in 1273. They owned a family estate in Lincolnshire in feudal times. The most famous Hawke is Edward (1705-1781) an Admiral of the Fleet that saved England from a French invasion in 1759. He was created the first Baron Hawke of Towton in 1776 for his service.

Members of the family immigrated to the Colonies. Richard Hawks arrived in Maryland in 1668 and Jeffery Hawks landed in Baltimore, Maryland in 1720. Adam Hawks is a Mayflower descendent. Several members of the Hawks family served in the Revolution.

Susanna was the daughter of Benjamin Hawks, who was born 1740 in Gloucester, New Jersey and died March 18, 1814. His will dated, March 18, 1814 mentions his children from both his first and second marriages, son Benjamin from first wife, and three sons from his second wife Sarah. Their children were Josiah, Hezekiah, and John, daughters Susanna Hawks who married James Duffield, Mary Day, Johannah Bishop, and Elizabeth Hawks. The parents of Benjamin Sr. are unknown.

Nineteen members of the Hawks family are recorded in the DAR records that fought in the Revolution, most from Massachusetts. Henry Hawks (#A053759) born before 1740 gave patriotic service and furnished supplies in Augusta County, Virginia. Isaac Hawks (#A053581) born 1759 served under Captain Hutton and Captain Bell in Virginia.

Robert Hawks was a pirate in the Caribbean and South Atlantic during the early part of the eighteenth Century and received a pardon in South Carolina in 1718. He was possibly from Virginia. His descendants have been traced to Kentucky, Illinois, and Iowa. It is unknown if he is related to the above families.

*History and crest sourced from the Hawks Family, Archives, and Ancestry

THE WINTER FAMILY

The Winter (Wynter) name is found in Gloucestershire, England where they held family estates before the Norman Conquest. They descend from David Wyntour born 1160 in Wales. The Rodger Winter family is found in Gloucestershire where Rodger was born in 1275. He married Margaret Nee in 1294. The Winter families continued to live in Gloucester for generations. A descendant, Sir William Wynter was born 1534 in Brecknock. He married Lady Maria Langston in 1563. He was an Admiral in the British Royal Navy and was Surveyor (head) of the Navy for Queen Elizabeth from 1559 until his death February 20, 1589. His father, John was born about 1500 in Gloucestershire. He was a merchant and sea captain of Bristol and Treasurer of the Navy. He was friends with Sir Thomas Cromwell and William Tirrey of Cork who's daughter Alice became his wife. The Winter family later survived the religious politics of the day.

Admiral William Wynter, pictured, was schooled early in the navy. He took part in a two-hundred-ship expedition in 1544 to Scotland under King Henry VIII, which burned Leith and Edinburgh. This was during the "rough wooing of Mary" after King Henry's marriage proposal for the infant, Mary Queen of Scots, for his small son was rejected. In 1547, he took part in Lord Lisle's channel fleet under the Duke of Somerset and the English victory at Pinkie at Edmonstone Edge, land owned by Sir Edmonstone, five miles from Edinburgh, Scotland. The Scots pitched their camp here before the battle of Pinkie where ten thousand Scots were killed. The victorious army's shouts could be heard in Edinburgh.*

Later, after King Edward's death, William was appointed by John Dudley Earl of Northumberland, an extreme protestant, to assistant in a plot to put protestant Lady Jane Grey on the throne and later in Sir Thomas Wyatt's plot for Elizabeth to prevent Edward's Catholic sister Mary from succeeding. Lady Jane became Queen for nine days, but lost to Mary. Even though Jane was beheaded and Elizabeth went to the Tower, William was not punished. William's wife was a secret Catholic and a statute of the Virgin and a stone font were found hidden in his warehouse after he died.

In 1558, William sat in Queen Elizabeth's early Parliament. In 1559, he commanded a fleet to guard against French landings in Scotland while diplomatic efforts were being made to aide the Scottish Protestants during the Scottish Reformation. The French were supporting the Catholics. He was given orders by the Duke of Norfolk to hinder any French landings in the Firth of Forth, but to avoid battle, pretending he came up river by chance without any official commission. His blockade was successful. In 1561, he purchased Lydney Manor in Gloucestershire for his residence. In 1588, as Lord Admiral, he was granted the Manor for his services against the Spanish Armada.

He proposed the fire-ship plan to drive the Spaniards from their anchorage. Pictured is the painting of Admiral Winter's ship the *Vanguard* from the *Spanish Armada* dated July 25, 1581. In 1561, he helped to save the Palace of the Bishop of London from fire by advising the Mayor of London to demolish the roof of the adjacent north aisle of Saint Paul's Cathedral when the church caught fire after being struck by lightening. William was knighted in 1577. Over the years, he was successful in many naval battles and expeditions for the Queen. William and his brother George invested in Sir Francis Drake's 1577 voyage around the world and received a handsome return. Sir Francis Drake was Vice Admiral and second in Command of the English fleet against the Spanish Armada. Drake and Wynter were friends and associates for many years. Sir Walter Raleigh was another of their acquaintances and fought in the Spanish Armada.

Admiral Sir William Winter in the Vanguard,

William and his wife Maria had eight children: Edward, William, Nicholas died fighting the Spaniards. His descendants came to America, James (died young), Mary, Elizabeth, Eleanor, and Jane. William died in 1589 at age sixty-eight. His eulogy written by William Patten was published that year.

The first members of Winter family found in the American Colonies were John Winter who settled in Maine in 1616, Robert who settled in Virginia in 1616 and Edward Winter who settled in Maryland in 1634. A descendant of Admiral Winter, William Winter born 1654 in England, arrived in Chester County Pennsylvania in 1685 on the ship the Bristol Merchant from Gloucester County. A shoemaker, he married Hannah Grover in 1688, a widow with two sons, Richard and Joseph Gardiner. She was the daughter of James Grover. (See Grover Family) William and Hannah had five children, John born 1688 died 1758, Andrew born 1689 died 1760, James born 1693 and two daughters, Rebecca Applegate and Zeruiah Borden. William's will dated July 3, 1722 was proved June 13, 1733 in Middletown, New Jersey. Andrew Winter was the surviving Executor. William's father was John Winter born 1641 at St. Peter and Paul Wharf in London. His father was Francis Winter II born 1610 in Reading Berkshire, his father was Francis Winter born 1581 in Reading Berkshire, his father was Nicholas born 1558 in Lydney, Gloucester, and his father was Admiral William Winter born 1534.

Thirty members of the Winter Family served in the Revolution, eight from New Jersey. John Winter (#A128937) born in Sussex County in 1755 served in Captain Jacob Winters Company in the Sussex County New Jersey Militia. Other Winter family members of the New Jersey Militia were James, Isaac, Henry Jr., Peter, and three by the name of Jacob.

The New Jersey Militia was a vital part of the war effort. It was their job to keep the roads open, defend against the British attacks, guard certain strategic posts, control the Tory population, and harass and keep the British expeditions from finding fresh food, wood and animal fodder. Washington called on them for help in numerous battles. Half of the Militia served each month leaving the other half at home to work their farms. They were eventually paid a good wage of one shilling and six pence per day of service. However, there was little consequence for not showing up for duty, which made the Militia unreliable in the beginning of the war. This was later changed to a full month of service with stricter penalties for not turning out. In contrast, the Continental Army had to serve a minimum of one-year enlistments with much more severe consequences if they did not show up. All men between the ages of sixteen and fifty were expected to serve unless their religion prevented it. The Militia chose their officers from among themselves and commissioned by the Continental Congress or the Committee of Safety. Each County was to form one or more companies, depending on the population. The Counties also had minute men companies serving four-month terms with their officers chosen by the Congress. They were to be ready for action at any minute.

The Militia kept a steady threat to the British, harassing them from all sides, keeping them from using their full army against the Continentals. A Hessian Officer Johann Ewald wrote the following about the New Jersey Militia:

> *"What can you not achieve with such small bands who have learned to fight dispersed and to use every molehill in their defense, and who retreat as quickly when attacked as they advance again and will always find a space to hide. Never have I seen these maneuvers performed better than by the American Militia, and especially by that of the Provence of New Jersey. If you were forced to retreat against these people, you could certainly count on constantly having them around you."*

John Evans Winter was born in New Jersey about 1792. He died 1875 in Illinois. He married Jane, daughter of Peter Suydam, born 1805 and died 1860 in Illinois. (See Suydam Family) In the 1840 census, John and Jane were living in Franklin, Somerset, New Jersey. They had eight children, Theodore born 1834, Peter born 1837, Cornelia Suydam born July 10, 1839 in Franklin, Somerset, New Jersey, Sarah born 1840, Catherine born 1842, James born 1844, Sophia born 1845 and Jane born 1847 in New Jersey. In the 1850 census, John had moved his family to Fairview, Fulton County Illinois.

Cornelia Suydam Winter married William Reynolds Evans March 27, 1858 in Fulton, Illinois. They had four children with two surviving to adulthood: A baby girl, Charles born 1863, John born 1868 who died young, and May born 1873. William died in 1910 and Cornelia in 1916. Both are buried in Prairie City, Illinois. May Evans married Ralph Wheeler in 1885 in Prairie City.

*History and pictures sourced from Wikipedia, *"Edmonstone Chronicles, Royal Knights and Scottish Kings"* by this author, Ancestry free pages and New Jersey Militia records For further information on Sir William Wynter, see the Dictionary of National Biography, 22 volumes London 1921-22.

THE GROVER FAMILY

The Grover name is recorded in Sussex, England before the Norman Conquest. It comes from the family living in an area called the "grove." In the seventeenth century members of the family immigrated to the Colonies to escape the religious chaos they were experiencing in England.

James Grover was born July 1621-23 in Chesham, Buckinghamshire, England. His parents were John Grover born 1597 in Chesham and Martha Monk also born in Chesham in 1600. (Several Monk family members immigrated to the Colonies). James arrived in New York in 1646. He was one of the first settlers of Kings County, Long Island of New Netherland Colony. He was apprenticed in 1643 to James Hubbard of Lynn, founder of Monmouth County and was granted land at Gravesend February 20, 1646 in the first division of land. In 1669, he was living in Middletown, New East Jersey. He married Rebecca Cheeseman in Gravesend, Long Island before 1650. She was the daughter of William Cheeseman, born 1606 in Beeston, Saint Lawrence, England and Martha Dorset born 1607 in England. Rebecca was the oldest of nine children. Her father died in Monmouth, New Jersey in December of 1653. Her mother, Martha, died in 1644. James and Rebecca had five children, James who died in 1715, Joseph died 1689, Safety died 1658, Abigail and Hannah. (See Cheeseman family).

James was evidently a devout Baptist and one of the followers of the Lady Deborah Moody, who founded Gravesend in 1645 after she was "booted out" of Salem, Massachusetts for her beliefs on adult baptism. He seems also to have been an ardent English Patriot although he lived in Gravesend in the Dutch Colony of New Netherland for many years. The English and Dutch were trade competitors and by the mid 1600's, the English set their sights on New Amsterdam after the Colony became prosperous. Consequently, the two countries were often at war. In 1655, James Grover and James Hubbard of Lynn raised the flag of rebellion. Oliver Cromwell had planned to attack New Netherland with the help of the New England Colonists, but the plan was never carried out. It was about this time that the Director General, Peter Stuyvesant, of New Amsterdam issued an order for the arrest of James Grover after he intercepted a message James was carrying from Oliver Cromwell urging the English settlers to rise up and revolt against the Dutch. James escaped to New England, but later returned to Middletown. The English eventually took control of the Dutch Colonies.

On March 21, 1667, James sold his farm in Gravesend Long Island to Thomas Delvall and moved to East Jersey where he was one of the first settlers of Middletown, Monmouth County. He was one of the men who purchased Middletown from the Indians. He had lot 16 assigned to him December 30, 1667 and farm lot 15 in the first division of the Middletown land. He was the first Town Clerk and one of the founders of the Baptist Church in 1668. James and his son James Jr., were constituent members of the Baptist Church along with William

Cheeseman. He received a commission as Lieutenant of Foot Company June 13, 1672. James died in 1685 and his will was proved January 28, 1685. He left a Manor House, Mill, meadowland beside Mill

creek and livestock including cattle, horses, and swine. His possessions were divided between his wife and three surviving children, James, Abigail, and Hannah, who married William Winter.

Twenty-nine members of the Grover family served in the Revolution. John Grover, born about 1732 served in New York (#A101805) and gave patriotic service. He was an Assemblyman and served in the Militia. The majority of the Grover family members who served were from the New England colonies.

*History and picture sourced from Wikipedia, Ancestry, Roots web, Grover Family History, and DAR. Crest from Grover family.

THE CHEESEMAN FAMILY

The Cheeseman family is another ancient English family. The family descends from Edward born 1390 in London. His descendant Robert Cheeseman, pictured, born 1485 was a politician and Falconer to Henry VII. He was a Member of Parliament for Middlesex from April 28, 1539 to July 24, 1540. He married Eleanor Owlett. He was the son and heir of Edward Cheeseman, born 1460, who was Cofferer and Keeper of the Wardrobe for Henry VII and succeeded to the family estates in 1517. Edward was a Justice of the Peace in Middlesex in 1528 and served on a number of commissions. He was on the juries for many famous trials including that of the Thomas Wosley inquirer, the trials of Godfrey Pole, Thomas Culpeper, and Francis Dereham for treason in 1541. He supplied troops in 1534 to the army combating the rebels of the Pilgrimage of Grace. He married Alice Dacres of Mayfield, Staffordshire, the daughter of Henry Dacres, son of Humphrey Baron of Dacres. He was a Merchant Tailor and Aldermen of London. When Edward died, he held the neighboring manors of Southall and Norwood/ Naworth Castle through his marriage to Ann. It is now a part of greater London. A monument is held in the Chapel of Norwood in his honor.

William Cheeseman was born in 1606 in Rutherfield, Sussex. Other charts show him born in Beeston, Saint Lawrence England. He married Martha Dorset born 1608 in Kent, daughter of James Dorset born in 1586 in England and Elizabeth Polling born 1685. Martha and her parents immigrated to Monmouth, New Jersey. William's father was John Cheeseman born in 1575 in Sussex, England and his mother was Constance Horsley born 1575 in Chislet, Kent. Both parents died in Monmouth, New Jersey. His ancestors were John born 1559 in Sussex and Margaret Swainton born 1563 and traced on back to Robert born 1485 in Kent, England who died in Middlesex in 1547.

William and Martha had nine children. Rebecca, the oldest child, married James Grover before 1650. William was one of the men who purchased Middletown, Monmouth County, New Jersey from the Indians in 1667. James Grover was also one of these men. William was assigned lot eleven and farm lot twenty-two. He was one of the founders and first members of the Baptist Church. He was active in the town and served on the Middletown Grand Jury numerous times. He died in 1711 and Martha's death is unknown.

William Cheeseman (#021288)) born 1753 in Monmouth County New Jersey was a Sergeant in the New Jersey Militia. Thomas Cheeseman (#038166) born 1734 fought under Colonel Somers in the Gloucester County Third Battalion. They are the only recorded Cheeseman patriots.

*History, picture, and crests sourced from Wikipedia and Ancestry.

THE DUTCH COLONIES IN AMERICA

In 1602, the Republic of the Seven United Netherlands chartered the Dutch East India Company with the mission of finding a passage to India and claiming any unchartered areas for the United Provinces, which led to the Province of New Netherland. In 1609, they commissioned the English explorer Henry Hudson to find a passage. Hudson entered the Upper New York Bay and sailed up the Hudson River (named after him) thinking he might find a northwest passage. He claimed parts of the United States and Canada for the Company. The first Dutch settlement was founded in 1615 and called New Nassau, which was located on Castle Island in the Hudson near Albany. It was named in honor of the House of Orange-Nassau. In 1621, a new company called the Dutch West India's (WIC) was established with a trading monopoly in America. Beaver Pelts were one of the main items of trade. They wanted recognition for New Netherland as a Province, which was granted in 1623. That same year, another Fort Nassau was built on the Delaware River near Gloucester City, New Jersey.

In 1624, the first colonists arrived on Governor's Island and dispersed to other areas. In 1626 Peter Minuit, Director of the WIC purchased the Island of Manhattan from the Lenape (also called the Delaware Indians) and started construction of Fort Amsterdam, which became New Amsterdam the capitol and main port. The Colony expanded to the outlying areas of Long Island, Bronx, Brooklyn, and Panovia. The Territory changed hands several times during the Anglo-Dutch Wars and finally went to the English in 1674 at the Treaty of Westminster. New Amsterdam then became New York named after the Duke of York.* Freedom of religion was one of the main reasons for the Dutch immigration. Members of the Dutch families mentioned here helped to found the cities, churches, and schools in New York and New Jersey. The New Jersey settlement of Elizabethtown in 1664 was made primarily by people from Long Island and is considered the period of colonization.

*History sourced from Wikipedia

THE RYCKEN/SUYDAM FAMILY

The progenitor of the Suydam family is Hendrick Rycken born 1640 in Arnhem, Gelderland, Nederland. His father was Henrick Rijcken born 1615 and died 1665 in Holland. The family originally bore the name of Rycken and resided in the lower part of Saxony, Germany before moving to Holland. Hans Von Rycken and his cousin Melichior were 11th century Knights and were in engaged in the Holy Land Crusades under Richard Coeur de Lion A.D. King of England. Melichior survived and became the founder of the Holland branch of the family.

Hendrick Rycken, the founder of the American Branch of the family, emigrated from Suyt-dam or Zuyt-dam (meaning south of the dam) Holland in 1663. He married Ida Jacobs. It is unknown to which of the New York Jacobs families she is related. However, Hans Jacobs of Flatbush may be her father. There were fifty-five members of the Jacobs family with registered DAR numbers in the Revolution. Ida was born in 1644 in Nederland and died in Flatbush, Queens, New York. Hendrick and Ida had nine children: Jacob Suydam born 1666 in Nederland and died 1738 in Brooklyn, Cornelius born 1668, Hendrick born 1670, Ryck Suydam born 1675 and died 1741, Ida Suydam born 1678 and died 1777, Abraham born 1683, Jannetje born 1685, Gertrude born March 2, 1691, and Hendrickse birth date unknown. His first three sons Jacob, Hendrick, and Ryck, who were born in Suydam, adopted the name of their birthplace as their surname in 1710. The rest of the children followed.

Hendrick Rycken lived first in New Amsterdam, New York and moved to Flatbush in 1679 where he acquired a large estate. He joined the Flatbush Church, which became the Flatbush and Brooklyn Dutch Reformed Church. Jacob Suydam inherited the family farm after the death of his father. He combined farming, smithing and later became a Supervisor in the local government. The Cornelius Suydam Homestead is a historic farmhouse representing the 18th and 19th century construction, located in Centerport, Long Island. By 1989 the home (pictured) was on the Local, State and National Registers of Historic Places.

Suydam House, c1991

James S. Suydam, a Deacon of the Flatbush and Brooklyn Church (pictured), was a descendant of Hendrick. He bought a two hundred acre farm at Bedford, which is now Bedford Street in east New York. Another descendant, James Schoonamaker Suydam was also a Deacon and involved in the Banking Business with the firm Matthew Morgan and son. He was elected Secretary of the Atlantic Trust Company. Three of the Church Memorial windows are dedicated to the Suydam family.

During the Revolution, the family was known for their patriotism and loyalty to the cause of freedom. The battle of Golden Hill was fought July 18, 1770 on their farm. It marked the first bloodshed of the Revolution. However, historians state Lexington as the first bloodshed. (See Ancestry) There were ten related members of the family fighting in the War for

Independence. Johannas (John) Suydam (#A111436) signed the Queens County Declaration on January 19, 1776. Hendrick Suydam (#A111430) pledged money for the American Army. Captain Lambert Suydam (#A111437) advanced money to support the state government. He was in King's Company troop of Horse. The younger Hendrick Suydam (#A111429) served in Captain Lambert's troop of Horse. Six others were Privates in various Companies.

Jacob Hendricksen was born October 10, 1666 in Flatbush, King's New York. He married Sytie Hanse Jacobs July 29, 1688 in Flatbush. Sytie was born about 1674 in Flatbush. Her father was Hans Jacobs. They had fourteen children: Ada, Johannes, Gertie, Adriantje, Jan, Jacob, Hendrick Cornelius, Seytie, Aeltje, Isabella, Ryck Suydam born 1703, Jannetje, and Dowe.

Ryck Suydam born 1703 in Flatbush, died in Franklin Park, Somerset, New Jersey in 1798. He was married twice. He married first Elizabeth Barkalow in 1735. She was born in 1712 and died in 1740. They had two boys and two girls, Hendrick, Elizabeth, Ryck, and Jannetje. He married second Maria Fonteyn in 1741. She was born in 1707 and died in 1784. She may have been related to the Charel Fonteyn family who arrived in Kings County from Marne, France. He was born in France about 1630. His son Charel was born in 1666 in King's County and died in Somerset in 1734. Ryck and Maria had seven children: Peter Suydam born 1736 and died 1788, Jacobus born 1738 and died 1778, Isaac, Abraham, Ryke, Mary, and Ida.

Jacobus Suydam was born in 1738 in Somerset County, New Jersey and died in 1778. He married Marie Wyckoff born in Somerset County in 1738 and died in 1794 in Somerset. Jacobus and Marie had six children: John, Peter born 1766, Ryke, Joseph, Jane, and Abram. Marie's parents were Pieter Wyckoff born 1675 in King's County New York who died there in 1759 and Ann Elizabeth VanPelt born August 9, 1696 in Long Island, New York. She died about 1760. They were married September 5, 1716. She was the daughter of Aerte T. VanPelt born 1664 in New Amsterdam. Aerte's father was Anthonius Laenen born May 5, 1622 in Overpelt, Liege, Belgium. He married Grietje Antinos born before 1620 in the Nederland.

Pieter and Ann Elizabeth moved to New Jersey about 1710 and bought ninety acres in Middletown. His children were all baptized in the First Dutch Church (pictured) in Freehold, New Jersey. Pieter Wyckoff's parents were Cornelius Wyckoff born 1656 in Flatbush, New York and Charity Van Arsdalen born 1660 in Flatbush. Her parents were from Belgium. His parents were Pieter Wyckoff born January 6, 1625 in Bode, Oland Island, Sweden, and Grietje Van Ness born 1627 in Holland. (See Wyckoff Family).

Peter J. Suydam was born October 11, 1766 in Middlesex County, New Jersey. He married Cornelia Cox May 15, 1793 in Somerset, County. She was born in 1777 and died in 1851. They lived in Hillsborough Township until 1797 when they moved to Franklin Township. Peter died November 12, 1840 in Three Mile Run, Somerset. They had seven children, Henry born 1794-1851, John born 1797-1856, Jacob born 1799-1850, William born 1803-1861, Jane born 1805 and died 1860, Maria born 1807-1861, and James Voorhees born 1812-1837.

Jane Suydam married John Winter. Their daughter Cornelia Suydam Winter married William Reynolds Evans and their daughter May Evans married Ralph Wheeler in 1885.

Twenty Van Pelt family members served in the Revolution including Jacob Van Pelt (#A118799)) born 1754 from Middlesex who served in Captain Jockum Gulick's Third New Jersey Regiment. (See Gulick Family). Fifteen members of the Fonteyn/Fontine family also served, including Becket De Roche Fontaine, (#A040400). He was Captain in the Engineers of the French Contingent part of the 1778 French and American Alliance. The Van Arsdalen/Van Arsdale family had twenty-six members fighting including John Van Arsdale (#A117099) born 1722 who assisted refugees to escape up the Hudson River when the British took possession of New York.

*History and pictures sourced from the Suydam Family and Wikipedia, crest from Ancestry

THE WYCKOFF FAMILY

Claes Corenlissen van Schouwen was born April 3, 1597 in Boda, Oland Island, Sweden. He married Margaret van der Goes from Middleburg, Walechern of the Dutch Islands. She was born in 1601 and died in 1631. He owned a ship called the *Svenska Kronan*. He was from a family of Scandinavian traders who lived in Borgholm on Oland Island. His father was Cornelius Peterson and his mother was Johanna van der Goes. They carried on trade in the Dutch Islands, Baltic, North Sea, and Zuydersee to Nordinge and east Friesland and as far as Middleburg, Walehern, and Zeeland. By 1631, the Thirty Years war was making trade both dangerous and unprofitable, and after his wife Margaret died, he sold his ship and migrated with his son, Pieter, to America. He died in 1674.

Claes and Margaret's son, Pieter Claesen (Wyckoff) was born Jan 6, 1625 on Bode, Oland Island, Sweden. He died June 30, 1694 in Long Island New York. Pieter, founder of the Wyckoff family in America, came to Fort Orange Province of New Nederland April 7, 1637 with his father on the ship *Rensselaerwick*. (Pictured is a Dutch Sailing ship). Pieter described the trip:

> "The ship sailed from Amsterdam, Holland on September 26, 1636 and reached New Amsterdam, New Nederland March 13, 1637. Tuesday April, 7, 1637 about 3 o'clock in the morning we came to anchor before Fort Aernice (Arnica), the end of our journey upward."

The ship was outfitted by Killian Rensselaer, a diamond merchant of Amsterdam, who had a speculative contract with the West India Company for the grant of a large body of land near the headwaters of the Hudson River under which he was required to transport men and animals to the new country. Among the passengers listed on the ship were Pieter Corenlissen from Monnickendam, North Holland, Pieter Clasen Van Nordon, and Simon Walisebez. The three did not remain in New Amsterdam but went on to Fort Orange. Here Pieter Corenlissen became prominent in the affairs of the Colony. According to the records, Pieter was one of thirty-eight laborers assigned to farmers on the Rensselaer estate. He was assigned to Simon Walisebez. He was to receive fifty gilders per year for the first three years and then seventy-five per year for the last three of his contract. About the time the lease was up, Simon's lease was canceled on the grounds he was an "unsatisfactory tenant" and the Rensselaer Estate made final settlement.

Pieter was eighteen years old when the contract with the Rensselaer Estate ended. He then rented a farm and married Gerritje Van Ness, who was born between 1627 in the Netherlands. (See Van Ness Family). She was the daughter of a prominent citizen of the colony. He moved his family to New Amsterdam in 1649 and became one of their leading citizens. Pieter became a local judge and helped establish the Dutch Reformed Church (pictured) at the corner of Flatbush Avenue and King's Highway. He and seven other men obtain a patent from the first Governor of New York,

Richard Nicoll, to establish the town of Flatland (Flatbush). He bought land in 1652 and continued to buy more land over the years. He built the house on what is now 5816 Clarendon Road in the Flatbush area of Brooklyn, pictured. It is the oldest surviving example of a Dutch Salt Box frame house in America. The New York Department of Parks and Recreation, operated by the Wyckoff Trust Association, now own the house. The house is a museum and a member of the Historic House Trust of New York City. A photo of the house is also in the Library of Congress. Successive generations of the Wyckoff family lived in the house for 237 years.

Peter Clasen was the only one of Pieter Corenlissen's sons to take the name of Wyckoff. In 1644, the English government required citizens to have a family name and Pieter chose the name Wyckoff. The Dutch and German surname of Wyckoff was a topographic name for someone who lived in an outlying settlement dependent on a larger village.

Pieter and Gerritje had two known children, Nicholas born 1646 and Cornelius Pieter Wyckoff born 1656 in Amersfoort, Kings, New York. He married Geertje (Charity) Van Arsdalen in 1678 in New York. Cornelius died in 1746 in Middlebush, Somerset, New Jersey.

During the Revolutionary War and the Battle of Brooklyn, Pieter and Gerritje's great, great, grandson, Peter A. Wyckoff and his wife Heyltie Remsen live in the Wyckoff House with three small children and several slaves. Several similar buildings are found in the surrounding landscape. Peter Wyckoff (#A126155) was Quartermaster for Captain Lambert Suydam's Troop of Horse.

John Wyckoff, son of Cornelius and Geertje Wyckoff, born August 25, 1758, served in the Middlesex County, New Jersey Militia throughout the Revolutionary War and was in the battles of Trenton, Princeton, and Monmouth. Another Peter Wyckoff (#A126140) was a Captain in the Second Regiment, Monmouth County, New Jersey under Colonel David Forman's State Troops. Simon Wyckoff gave Patriotic Service. (#A126170). Cornelius Wyckoff (# A126109) born in 1760 in Middlebush, Somerset, New Jersey was a private in the Fourth Regiment, Light Dragoons of the Continental Line. Twenty-five of the twenty-seven Wyckoff family members who served were from New Jersey and New York. The other two were from Maryland and Pennsylvania.

*History and pictures sourced from Wikipedia and free pages at genealogy

THE VAN NESS FAMILY

Cornelius Hendrickse Van Ness and his wife Maryken Hendrickse Van den Burchgraeff were the progenitors of the Van Ness family in America. He was born about 1594 in Noordeloos, Holland, the son of Hendrick Gerriste and Geritje Van Ness. Maryken was born about 1600-1602 in Lavereld, Holland the daughter of Hendrick Adreaensz Van' De Burggrave/Burchgraaeff. Cornelius and Maryken were married July 31, 1625 in Harvendijk, Zeeland, Holland. They came to America on the ship "Oaktree" in 1640. They settled first in Rensselaerswyck near Albany, New York. By 1643, he owned a farm in Greenbush across the Hudson River from Albany. In 1652, he was elected Counselor for Rensselaer and held the position until 1658. He was re-elected in 1662-1663. He owned and operated the first known Brewery in Greenbrush. He purchased fifty acres of farmland in the Flatlands area and owned twenty-one acres in Schenectady. He led an expedition to Fort Christina, Delaware under the direction of the Governor, Pieter Stuyvesant to re-capture the Fort from the Swedish Colony who had taken it from the Dutch. The siege was over in two weeks when the Swedish surrendered.

Cornelius and Maryken had two daughters, Grietje Hendrickse and Hendrickje Cornelese born about 1626 in Holland. Grietje Hendrickse Van Ness was born between 1624-1630 in Vianem, Nes, Holland. She married Pieter Clasen Wyckoff about 1646 in Fort Orange, Albany, New York. Maryken died March 24, 1663/64 in Rensselaerwyck, Albany, New York. Cornelius died about 1685 in Fairfield, Essex County, New Jersey.

Seventeen members of the Van Ness family served in the Revolution. Abraham Van Ness (#A118517), born 1750 in New Jersey, served as a Captain in the Militia under Colonel Neilson's Regiment. David Van Ness (#A118519) born 1745 from Albany was a Major in the Duchess County Militia. John Van Ness (#A118568) born 1731 in Hunterdon County New Jersey was a Lieutenant in the Second Regiment of the Sussex County Militia and listed in Stryker's Regiment of Officers.

*History and crest sourced from the Van Ness family History and Ancestry

THE COX/COCK FAMILY

James Cock, the Cocks/Cox family Quaker ancestor came to the New York Colonies in the late 1650's. He was born 1630 in Norfolk, Bukaram in England, the son of Thomas, and died December 11, 1699 in Killingworth upon Matinecock, New York. His wife Sarah Clarke, the daughter of John Clarke, was born in North Sea Southampton, New York in 1637. They were married in 1654 in Killingworth. The Cock family was active in many professions in England. They were Lawyers, Bishops, Aldermen, Mayors, Merchants, Priests Rectors, Sheriff's, members of Parliament, and Yeoman. James' ancestors were found in 1401 in Buckenham (Buckingham) at Cromwell's Manor. John Cock was buried in the new aisle of St. Martins Church in 1479.

The town records in 1648-58 of Southold, North Fluke at the east end of Long Island lists James Cock as a member of the Village Plot. The names of Captain John Underhill, John Bayles, Thomas Mapes, and Thomas Terry are also listed as all coming from Bermuda. In 1659, Captain Underhill, James Cock, James Prior, and William Frost were together in the plantation of Setucket. They appear to have been on the same ship from England. The ship was attack by an extremely large swordfish, which broke off in the side of the ship causing it to leak. They were forced to put in to Bermuda for repairs. They also appeared on the records of Oyster Bay in 1662 and finally settled in Killingworth upon Matinecock in the township of Oyster Bay, Long Island, New York. There was an area in Long Island in 1720 called Buckeram, a territory occupied by James descendants including Sampson, Hezekiah, and Joshua Cock. The Cock family and their neighbors were engaged in trade with the West India's where they sent salted meats and pipe staves to construct barrels for the return of sugar, molasses, and rum which was delivered to the Dutch at New Amsterdam free of duty. They joined the Long Island Dutch Colony in 1659. The Cock family lived in this area for over two-hundred and thirty years. The Society of Friends meetings and marriages were performed at the homes of James Cock, Underwood, Prior and Fekein in Killingworth and in Oyster Bay at the home of Anthony Wright. James was active in the community and was often witness for his neighbors for land sales, wills and other documents.

James Cock/Cox will of 1699 is on the records of Oyster Bay. He and his wife Sarah had nine children: Mary born 1665, Thomas born August 15, 1658, Martha born July 1661 died at nine months, John born November 22, 1666, Hannah born June 5, 1669, Sarah born July 20, 1672, James born February 4, 1674, Henry born February 1, 1678. Sarah died October 15, 1715. Sarah died October 15, 1715. All of their children were born in Killingworth. She and James are buried in the Underhill burying ground in Killingworth.

Henry's second marriage was to Martha Pearsall, daughter of Nathaniel and the brother of George Pearsall. They had two children, Thomas born September 15, 1718 and Samuel born about 1720 in Killingworth. Martha Pearsall was born December 13, 1680.

A second member of the Cox family to arrive in the Colonies in 1665 was Thomas Cox born 1620, in Herefordshire, England. He was one of the first settlers in Mespath Kill, Long Island, New York. His brother John came over with him. On December 30, 1667, Thomas bought land from the Indians in Middletown, New Jersey. He was one of the founders of the Middletown Baptist Church. He paid in full for the portions of land guaranteed him under the Governor Nicolls patent. He was a Monmouth Patentee and assigned lot number eight (#8) in Middletown and lot number twenty-one (#21) in the Poplar Field December 31, 1667. He and three others were chosen that same year to make practical laws for Middletown. In 1668, he was also named "rate maker" for the town. He became an extensive landowner and leading citizen of Middletown. He married Elizabeth Blashford, a Quaker, on April 17, 1665 in Mespath Kill and had four sons and two daughters: James Cox born August 18, 1672 in Monmouth, New Jersey and died there in 1750, Thomas, John, and Joseph. The daughter's names are not listed. Thomas and Elizabeth died in Middletown, he in 1681 and she in 1691. His grandson, Thomas born 1700, son of Thomas Cox born February 1, 1668 and Mary Wright, gave patriotic service in the Revolution.

Cornelia Cox, born in Middlesex, New Jersey February 1, 1777 was the daughter of Henry Cox and Jane Jannetje Gulick, daughter of Jochem Gulick and Cornelia Vanderberg. (See Gulick Family) Her brother, Judge John Cox, was born Jan 6, 1774. Henry was born 1756 in Readington, Hunterdon, New Jersey. He was baptized in the Readington Church, pictured, on February 18, 1756. Jane Gulick was born in Somerset, New Jersey. They were married in New Jersey about 1776. Their daughter, Jane Cox, married Peter J. Suydam. Their daughter, Cornelia Suydam, married John Winter, their daughter Cornelia Winter married William Reynold Evans, and their daughter May Evans married Ralph Wheeler.

The North Branch of the ancient Dutch Church was established in 1719 and moved to Readington Village, Hunterdon, New Jersey in 1738 where Henry Cox was baptized. Dr. Jacob Hardenburgh was the Pastor of the Readington Church all through the Revolutionary War. His inflammatory and patriotic sermons caused the British to put a fine of one-hundred pounds on his head. He also advised George Washington regarding local conditions. He later became the first president of Queen's College, which is now Rutgers.

Cornelia's father, Henry Cox, born 1756, served in the Revolution (#A027006) under Captain James Moore in the Somerset County Militia. Other Cox family members from New Jersey were Richard Cox born 1755 in Burlington, Monmouth County (#A027071) who was a major in Stryker's Regiment of officers and in Brigadier General William Maxwell's Second Regiment of the New Jersey Line. He was also a Lieutenant in Captain Ross's First and Third Regiments. Richard Cox (Sr.) born 1727 in Upper Freehold Township, Burlington (#A134728) gave Civil and Patriotic Service, signed the New Jersey

Petition May 12, 1781 and the petitions for depredations and supply tax and gave supplies to the Army. He was a Judge in 1783 in Monmouth County. Thomas Cox, (father of Richard Sr.) born 1700 in New Jersey (#A134795) gave Patriotic Service, signed the New Jersey Petition on May 12, 1781 and signed the petitions regarding depredations and supply tax. He also gave supplies to the Army in 1781. Jacob Cox from Gloucester County born 1754 (#A027014) was a private under Colonel Richard Somers Third Battalion. William Cox born 1750 from Sussex County (#A027096) served in the Second Regiment under Captain James Dillon. Phillip Cox born 1763 in Somerset, New Jersey (#A027066) served in the Militia. Nicolas Cox born 1742 (#A027063) was a Chaplin in the First Battalion 2nd Establishment. Gershom Cox born 1755, (#A027008) Somerset was a Corporal in the New Jersey Militia. Isaac Cox born 1743 in Somerset served in the New Jersey Militia. Captain William Cox was in the Battle at Kings Mountain.

General James Cox, (pictured) a Revolutionary War hero, (#A027019) was a descendant of the Thomas Cox family of Middletown, Monmouth County. He was the son of Judge Joseph Cox and his wife Mary. He was born in 1753 at Cox Corners and died in 1810 in Upper Freehold, New Jersey. He enlisted as a private and became a Lieutenant in the New Jersey Militia. He was at the battles of Brandywine, Germantown, and Monmouth. James was promoted to Brigadier General and Commander of the Monmouth Brigade when the Monmouth Militia was reorganized. James was later a Speaker of the New Jersey Assembly and was a Congressman at the time of his death in 1810. He and his wife Ann Potts had thirteen children. He is buried in the Old Yellow Meeting House Cemetery in Upper Freehold Township, New Jersey. One-hundred and sixty-six members of the Cox family served in the War.

*History, pictures, and crest sourced from Wikipedia, Ancestry, Geni, DAR, and *The Cock, Cocks, Cox Family in America by George William Cocks and John Cox*

THE CLARK FAMILY

John Clarke was one of the first members of the Clarke family to arrive in the New England Colonies. He was born in Westhorpe, Suffolk, England October 8, 1609 from Quaker parents. He was one of eight children, six of whom moved to America. John was a medical doctor and a Baptist minister. He was well educated and could read the Old Testament in Hebrew. He arrived in Boston in 1637. He was married three times, first to Elizabeth Harges, second to Jane Fletcher and third to Sarah Davis by whom he left a long line of American descendants. He was co-founder of the Rhode Island Colony and Providence Plantations.

In 1638, John conferred with Roger William, Anne Hutchinson, William Coddington, and Phillip Sherman other religious dissenters and together they settled on Aquidneck Island (Rhode Island), which was originally purchased from the local natives. In 1644, the settlements of Providence, Portsmouth, and Newport united for their common independence as the Colony of Rhode Island and Providence Plantations governed by an elected council and president. The Colony received a liberal Royal Charter from King Charles II in 1663 after John Clarke and Roger William went to England for twelve years on matters concerning the Colony. Clarke wrote the charter and it became their Constitution, securing the freedom of everyone in maters of conscience concerning religion. John became the third and fifth Deputy Governor of the Colony in 1669-70. Although the King suspended the charter, Rhode Island managed to keep possession of it until William of Orange came to power in 1688 and the charter was resumed. The Charter was used as the State Constitution until 1842. In 1639, the First Baptist Church was founded in Newport and Dr. Clarke (pictured) became the teacher/preacher for many years. He died April 4, 1676 in New York.

The Colony refused to allow Catholics to join them until after the Revolution. During the Revolution, the French Army made their base on Rhode Island and the people were so impressed with the good manners and deportment of the Catholic troops, they changed their laws concerning Catholics. John Clarke's daughter, Sarah Clarke, born in 1637, married James Cock (Cox).

Thirty-seven members of the Clark family from Rhode Island served in the Revolution including two Majors, seven Captains and Willet Clark a Fifer born 1759 (#A202114) from Hopkinton. Major Thomas Clark was born in 1743 (#A022720). He was from North Kingston and served under Colonel Charles Dyer. Major Samuel Clark born 1754 (#A022666) served in Rhode Island, Captain Walter Clark born 1738 (#A022737) from Newport was in the Third Company, Second Battalion. Captain Simeon Clark Jr., born 1742 (#A022687) from Richmond was the enlisting officer for Richmond, was Captain of the First Company Militia and Justice of the Peace. Captain Oliver Clark, born 1743 (#A022597) served in both the First and Ninth Regiments of the Continental Army. Others were Captain Ethen Clark born 1745 (#A022287) from Newport, Captain John Clark born in 1738 (#A022467), from Westerly Kings County, served under Colonels Dyer and Maxon. Captain Joseph Clark born 1728 (#A 022518) from Westerly gave patriotic service and was Commissioner of the Loan Office for Rhode Island in 1776. A Sargent Major, a Lieutenant and several others gave patriotic service. There were a large number of leaders from the smallest of the Colonies. Three-hundred members of the Clark family are recorded in the DAR records serving in the Revolution; five were in the Battle of King's Mountain.

*History, pictures, and crest sourced from Wikipedia and Ancestry

THE GULICK FAMILY

The Glick name is discovered before 1066 in Berkshire, England where they were Lords of the Manor. The name Gotlac is recorded in the Cheshire Domesday book. The name is also recorded very early in Holland.

The Gulick family descends from Hendrick Van Gulick born 1625 in Holland and married Gertrude (Geertruyt Jochem) Willekins born about 1625 in Hamburg, Germany. They were married September 11, 1643 in Buren Gelderland. They had two children born in Holland, Jan born 1647 and Jochem (John) born 1649. They arrived in New York before 1650. Hendrick died in 1653 in Gravesend, Long Island, New York. Pieter Gulick, son of Jochem, was born September 4, 1689 in Gravesend, Brooklyn, Kings, Long Island, New York and died December 4, 1774 in Somerset, New Jersey. He married Eva Van Sycklin. She was born 1697 in Franklin Park, Middlesex, New Jersey. They had fourteen children.

Their son Peter was born December 18, 1732 in Six Mile Run, Franklin Park and died April 8, 1798 in Cranbury, New Jersey. He married Willempje Johnson, born January 25, 1735-36, the daughter of Nicklaus Johnson and Ann Wyckof. She died in Cranbury November 25, 1795. Johannes Gulick was born about 1695 in Somerset New Jersey. He married Rensje Van Sycklin born in 1692 daughter of Ferndandus Van Sycklin and Gertruyt Johannes. Their son Jochem Gulick was born in 1724 in Middlesex, New Jersey. He married Cornelia Van Den Berg born April 16, 1726 in North Church, Sussex, New Jersey, pictured. They were married before 1743. Cornelia died March 22, 1792 in Somerset. Their daughter, Jane Gulick married Henry Cox. Their daughter Cornelia Cox married Peter Suydam and their daughter Cornelia Suydam married John Winter.

Jochem Gulick was a Captain in the Third Regiment of the Somerset, County Militia. The Regiment was raised on January 1, 1776 at Elizabethtown, New Jersey for service in the Continental Army. They saw service at Brandywine and Germantown before wintering at Valley Forge. They were one of the finest Regiments in the Continental Army and known

as the "Jersey Blues." Fourteen members of the Gulick family served in the Revolution, twelve of them from New Jersey. Two Jochem (Joachim/John) Gulick's are mentioned in the DAR records. Captain Gulick's (#A048299) DAR record incorrectly states he was born in 1650 and died in 1711. The New Jersey record Roll gives his birth as 1724 and he died in 1803. He was born in Somerset, Middlesex, New Jersey. He was Captain of the Second and Third New Jersey Regiments. The other Joakim Gulick Jr. (#A048300) born 1764 in Somerset, a Sergeant in Captain Jones second Regiment, is probably Captain Gulick's son.

He died in 1840. Ferdinand Gulick (#A048288) born 1756, was either another son who served under Gulick and named for his grandfather or was the son of a brother. James Gulick (#A048297) born 1758, was Captain Gulick's brother and served under him at the battle of Monmouth. James widow, Elizabeth, owned an Inn and Tavern in the Township of Amboy. He had two other brothers, Abraham and Cornelius who served under Captain Gulick in Neilson's Second Regiment. There are no established DAR records for them.

*History, pictures and original crest of Julich/Gulick family sourced from Wikipedia and Ancestry. New Jersey Blues picture from unknown doner at Facebook

THE VANDENBERG FAMILY

The Vandenberg family is from the Netherlands and had long been influential in Gelderland. Herman van den Bergh (1558-1611) had been the King's Stadholder (Steward) and continued to be Stadholder, which developed into a hereditary head of state under King Albert, the brother of the Emperor of Hapsburg. Herman and his three brothers, Fredrick, Oswald, and Henrick were the Counts of van der Bergh. Their father Count Willem IV (pictured) had been one of William the Silent's, (Prince of Orange and leader of the Dutch revolt against Spain), principal military commanders against Phillip II the sovereign of the Hapsburg Netherlands. He had responsibility for Upper Gelderland. Their mother, Maria of Nassau, was a sister of William the Silent and a committed protestant. Their ancestral seat was in Huis Bergh with the lands of Gelderland and the Castle Ulft. Henrick was later to be the Hapsburg Stadholder of Gelderland in 1620 and became Spain's second in command and the most senior Netherlander in the army of Flanders.

Willem and his sons were among the best soldiers of their compatriots and all held positions of prominence. They were involved on both sides of the Eighty Year War (1568-1648) that eventually resulted in the formal independence of the Dutch United Provinces in 1648. The war was caused by heavy taxation and Spain's strict religious uniformity within the Roman Catholic Church enforced by the Inquisition. The reformed teachings of John Calvin and other protestant leaders had gained followers in the Netherlands. Tired of the constant war and religious persecution, Gysbert Cornelise van den Bergh landed in New York in 1645. He was born in 1620 in Gelderland and died in America in 1717. He married Lysbet Cornelise VanVoorhout, born 1627 in Lieden, South Holland. They had eight children.

Their son (Willem) Gerrit Gysbertsen was born in 1645 in Albany, Albany County New York. He married (Catryn) Cornelia Wynantse Vanderpool in 1684 in Albany. She was born 1644 in Albany and died March 3, 1753 at age one-hundred and nine. Her father, Wynant Gerritse Vanderpool was born 1620 in Mappel, Drenthe, Netherland. Her grandfather Garrit Vanderpoel, born 1590 in Gorcum, died in Amsterdam, Holland in 1632. Garrit and Cornelia had twelve children, their youngest son Goosen Van Den Bergh was born about 1696 in Rensselaerswyck, Albany County, New York and died in 1728 in New Brunswick, Middlesex, New Jersey. He married Annatje Pieter Van Nest born 1705 and died 1728 in Somerset, New Jersey. She was the daughter of Pieter Van Neste and Tryntje Janes born in Holland. Pieter Van Neste, born 1600 was from Nes Ameland Friesland, Holland. Goosen and Annatje had two children, their son Goosen Van Den Berg was born in 1728 and died in 1811. Their daughter Cornelia Vandenberg was born April 16, 1726 in North Church Sussex, New Jersey and died in Somerset. She married Jochem Gulick. Their daughter Jane Jannetje Gulick born 1756 married Henry Cox.

Twenty-two members of the Van Den Bergh family served in the Revolution. Among those were Gerrit G. Van Den Bergh (#A117533) born 1725 in Albany New York, a Colonel in the Fifth Regiment of the Albany County Militia, Cornelius Van Den Berg (#A204264) born 1710 in New York, was a Member of the

Committee and gave Patriotic Service. Cornelius Van Den Berg (#A117527) born in 1726 and baptized 5-13-27 was a Captain in the New York Militia. Gysbert Van Den Berg (#A117534) born 1748 from Rensselaer New York served under Lieutenant Colonel Henry K. Van Rensselaer Regiment New York Militia. Evert Van Den Berg (#A129299) born 1738 from Albany gave Patriotic Service. His home was burned at the battle of Saratoga. Henry Van Den Berg (#A117539) born 1759 was a Captain and Lieutenant Colonel in the Second, Third and Fifth Regiments of the New York Line of the Continental Army and listed in the History of Regular Officers. Another Henry born in 1756 (#A117545) was a Captain serving with Captains Van Wyck, Johnson and Lee in New York. He was promoted over a period from Sargent to second and first Lieutenant.

Several of the family later served in the Civil War. Among them was Jacob Vanderberg, a private in Company K in the Seventh Regiment of the New Jersey Infantry, Union Army.

*History, pictures, and crest sourced from Wikipedia and Ancestry

CHAPTER VIII
THE MINTER FAMILY

The ancient Minter family history stems from the County of Kent in the northeast section near Canterbury, England. They may have lived there as early as the year 449. Cliff Minter of Canterbury has done much of the research on the family. The Minter family members are recorded in the 1300's living in Canterbury. Geoffrey Chaucer, a courtier, wrote his Canterbury Tales in the late 1400's, published in 1483. The tales were a critical portrait of English society at the time and especially of the Church. Chaucer first presented the tales to a group of pilgrims as they traveled to the shrine of Saint Thomas Becket at the Canterbury Cathedral. Becket was murdered in 1170 by King Henry II's knights for refusing to give the King power over the church. Perhaps a Minter was among the travelers. It was not until Henry VIII became king in 1491 that the church lost control.

George Minter born in Kent about 1577 was the father of Henry Minter. Henry was born in 1610. He married Elizabeth of Ash in Kent. The Canterbury Minters are traced to Thomas Minter who married Hannah Merchant on January 14, 1699 at Saint Paul's Canterbury. Members of the family were blacksmiths, coachman, butchers, surgeons, mariners and several became freemen.

The first to arrive in the American Colonies was Desire Minter, orphaned daughter of William Minter, who came with the Pilgrims in 1620, in the charge of John Carver the Governor of Plymouth. She returned to England to "her friend" a year later and died of ill health.

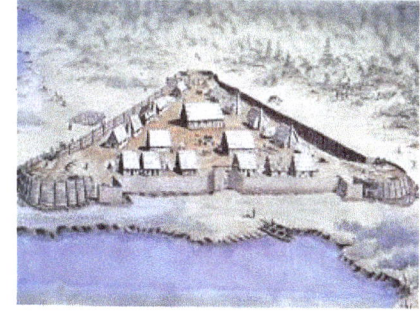

Next were Richard Mintrene (Minter) age forty and his son Edward age twelve both listed on the ship "*Margaret and John*" arriving in Jamestown Colony in 1620. They appear on the muster rolls of Elizabeth City, Virginia in 1624. It is unknown if they were related to Desire. Edward Minter in 1635, probably his brother, brought over Jon Minter on the ship "Paule." William Barker and his Associates paid the passage for Jon (John) age sixteen (passenger #7), Elizabeth Phillipps (passenger #15) and twenty-three other passengers. Barker and his Associates received fifty acres of land for each person they paid passage for giving them a total of 1250 acres. The land transfer was recorded November 26, 1635, on page 320 of the James Colony (pictured) land patent records. Edward Minter is recorded with three hundred acres May 30, 1638 on the upper Chipppoecks Creek with fifty acres transferred to his wife Grace. This entrée is made on page 353. Richard and David Minter arrived in Jamestown Colony Virginia in 1635. They are recorded in the James Colony books of land patents, David on page 331.

The Minter family is listed among the original colonists in the Historic Register of the First Families of Virginia who settled primarily in Jamestown. Most of the immigrants settled along the James River and other navigable waters.

Jon Minter and his wife Elizabeth Phillipps are recorded living in Charles City. Jon died in 1655 and his wife was granted her dower right by the Charles City County Court. John Minter II, born about 1645 in Charles City, married, but his wife's name is unknown. Their son John III was born about 1685 in Gloucester County, Virginia. His residence was in the Parish of Petsworth. His son John IV was born about 1715 in Gloucester. He married Frances Phillips daughter of John Phillips, who was born in England in 1650 and buried in North Farmhand Parish in Virginia. They had ten children. She was born in Powhatan, Virginia. John, Frances and children moved from Gloucester County to Essex County about 1739 and he is recorded as purchasing one-hundred and fifty acres from Richard Beale. In 1740, he purchased an additional fifty acres from James Presnall (Pearsall?). John died in 1743 leaving his widow and ten children: John, Josiah, Elizabeth, and Sarah were of age. James, William, Phillip, Joseph, Thomas, and Lucy were minors and were appointed guardians by the court. Josiah was guardian for James, John Phillips (Uncle) was guardian for William, Phillip, and Joseph, Frances was guardian for Thomas and Lucy with her brother John as surety. By March 1747, both Phillip and Thomas had died and John Phillip was appointed Administrator of their estate. For some reason, William, who was only eleven years old when his father died, was only given one shilling sterling "barring him from the rest of my estate" as stated in his fathers will. It is curious what an eleven year old might have done to anger his father to the point he would leave him out of his will. However, William received his brother Phillip's share of the estate after Phillip died. Frances died in 1780 in North Carolina.

John III's son, John IV born 1715 lived in Essex County until about 1761 when he, his brothers Joseph and William and daughter Lucy sold their shares of the land inherited from their father. John IV lived in Middlesex County. Josiah and Joseph were the only sons to continue living in Essex. Joseph joined the Essex County Militia and served under George Washington during the French and Indian War. He was described in the Militia records, as being five foot six inches tall. His occupation was a tailor, he married Ann (?) and they had four sons.

Josiah born 1718 became an inspector of Tobacco appointed by Virginia Governor Patrick Henry and later by Governor Edmund Randolph. He served in this position from 1785 to 1792 when he died. He married Mary Baker in the South Farnham Anglican Church and they had six children. He own a "middling plantation" (under 800 acres) where tobacco was his main crop.

William was born July 5, 1731-36 Gloucester County. When he was sixteen, on February 21, 1748, he signed apprenticeship papers to become a millwright and Carpenter. He was apprenticed to Caleb Lindsey. He went with him to Augusta County, Virginia where he served in the Augusta County Militia during the French and Indian War. William had a land patent of two hundred and twelve acres on Mossy Creek in Augusta County dated September 9, 1760. On May 18, 1762, he bought two-hundred and seventy acres on Linvells Creek from John and Hannah Miller for forty-five pounds. On June 21, 1763, he sold the same property to Skidmore Mosley for one-hundred and five pounds. He bought two-hundred and forty-five acres on Linvells Creek on October 18, 1762 for one-hundred and twenty-five pounds from Samuel and May Harrison who were from Craver South Carolina. On September 4, 1767, he sold the same two-hundred and forty-five acres to John Curry. By this time, William had already moved to Cavern County, South Carolina. He continued to buy and sell land on and around Turkey Creek in York County, South Carolina. In 1767, he married Martha Hillhouse born April 3, 1746, in Salisbury, Rowan, North Carolina, the daughter of Samuel Hillhouse and Ann Luckey. (See Hillhouse Family)

William and Martha had ten children: John born May 10, 1769, William born May 25, 1770 (DAR records give William's birth date as 1741), Margaret born October 17, 1772, James born August 9, 1774, Josiah born May 25, 1776, Mary July 6, 1778, Joseph born May 1, 1780, Jacob born February 11, 1783, Sarah born December 15, 1785, and Jonathan born June 1, 1789. William owned a plantation where their main crops were tobacco and cotton. He died in York, South Carolina July 3, 1809. His will was dated September 6, 1806 and probated July 3, 1809. He left his children the following:

John received the two-hundred acres where he was living, William received one-hundred acres, Joseph received $50.00 and five pounds, Josiah and Jacob received the acreage with grist mill and the cotton machine, Sarah received three-hundred dollars, and Mary (Moor) received five pounds. The youngest son Jonathan was left the Plantation house and land were William and Martha lived. He was to receive it after Martha died. His other children were not mention in his will and perhaps had died.

William gave civil service and was on the Jury list of 1778-79 during the Revolution. His grave is marked with the DAR Revolutionary Marker and his patriot number is #A080373. Nine members of the Minter family are recorded in the DAR list of Patriots. Joseph Minter born about 1743 (#A208713) paid supply tax in 1783, John Minter born about 1730 (#A206869) furnished supplies. They are probably related to William.

John, son of William and Martha, was born May 10, 1769 in the Camden District (York County) South Carolina. He married Jane Gillham born April 21, 1773 in Bullocks Creek, Chester County of the South Carolina Colony. She was the daughter of Thomas Newton Gillham Jr., and his first wife Susannah McDow. (See Gillham Family). Thomas Jr.'s mother was Margaret Campbell daughter of William Campbell of Augusta County Virginia. John and Jane were married January 18, 1791 and had six children: Martha born May 20, 1793, Isaac born February 15, 1795, William born May 13, 1797 married Eliza (beth) Lucinda Love, John Thomas born May 13, 1800, Mary Ann born March 15, 1804 and Jesse Jackson born 26, 1806 and died May 16, 1834.

John owned land on both sides of the Chester and York county lines, some of which he inherited from his father William. The County and State lines both changed during his lifetime and Carolinas were divided into North and South. He was well educated and owned a small library of books including a set of Encyclopedia's, Ferguson's Astronomy with plates, Euclid's Elements, Moore's Geography, and Walkers Dictionary. When he died, his moveable property amounted to two-thousand, two hundred and sixty-seven dollars. His will stated that the money received from the sale of the personal property was to be divided into four equal amounts and one fourth was to go to Jesse Gwinn and his wife Mary. The will states, "one half of this bequest is to go to the sole and separate use of said Mary A. Gwinn if the said Jesse Gwinn continues in his present deranged state of mind." (York County Estates Records, Case 7, File 281).

Jane died September 24, 1834 in Blairsville, South Carolina. She is buried in Bullocks Creek Presbyterian Church Cemetery, York County. John died December 16, 1836 in Blairsville. He is buried in Bullocks Creek Presbyterian Church Cemetery. (Pictured Bullocks Creek Cemetery)

Their son John Thomas married Adeline Love March 28, 1824 in Chester County. She was born May 4, 1804 in South Carolina possibly the daughter of Richard (1768-1842) and Elizabeth Love. Eliza (beth) Lucinda Love, the wife of William Minter, may have been related to Adaline. (See Love Family). John and Adeline had the following fifteen children born in Chester County:

Elzy Davis born February 4, 1825, died 1907 in Lowndes, Mississippi,

Thomas Jefferson born June 17, 1826 and died 1859 in Lowndes, Mississippi,

Julia Ann born May 28, 1828 died 1885 **in** Hutchinson, Kansas,

Joseph Monroe born February 17, 1830, died 1908 in South Carolina,

Clarissa Adaline born January 6, 1832, (no further information)

Jesse Blairs born November 24, 1833, died 1886 in Burrton, Kansas

Infant died 1835,

Mary Jane born September 2, 1836 and died in Newton, Harvey County Kansas 1918,

John Neely August 14, 1838,

Martha Amelia born May 8 1840 (no further information),

Nancy Ellen born January 12, 1842,

Loronto(Larann) Dow born September 26, 1843,

Infant died 1845,

Lee Roy (Leroy) born October 2, 1846,

Henrietta born December 18, 1847.

By the 1850 census, John and Adaline were living in Choctaw County, Mississippi with seven of their children in the household, Mary Jane, John Neely (also shown at age twenty-one in the 1860 census), Martha A., Nancy E., Laronto D., Leroy, and Henrietta the youngest. Jane Love, age eighty born in South Carolina, mother of Adeline is living with them. John is listed as a farmer with a personal estate of three-thousand dollars and real estate at twenty-six hundred. Cotton was "King" in Mississippi at the time and was probably his main crop. Their son Jesse Blair and daughter Clarissa Adaline also moved with the family to Choctaw but seem to be living elsewhere. Nothing more is known about Clarissa. Elzy Davis, their oldest son moved to Mississippi and married Nancy Klob in Caledonia, Lowndes County in 1851. He died there in 1907. Joseph Monroe either stayed, or went back to Chester South Carolina and died there in 1908. Julia Ann and her husband Thomas Fair went with the family to Mississippi from South Carolina and eventually moved to Hutchinson, Kansas where she died in 1885. Thomas Fair died June 17, 1897 in Hutchinson. Thomas Jefferson died 1859. John Thomas' wife, Adeline, died July 13, 1866 in Choctaw, County. She is buried in the Mount Moriah Baptist Church Cemetery four miles from the town of Weir.

Five of John and Adeline's sons served in the Confederate Army during the Civil War: The oldest son Elzy D. served in the First (Patton's) Mississippi Infantry. He was thirty-six years of age and a Sargent in Company C of Reube Davis' Rifles. Joseph Monroe served in the Lindsey's First Regiment of the South Carolina Cavalry Battalion, first in Company D and then in Company K. The Cavalry was organized October 31, 1861. After June 25, 1862, it became part of the First South Carolina Cavalry Regiment. The men were from Charleston, Abbeville, Allendale, Chester, and Georgetown. They fought at Chambersburg, Fredericksburg, Brandy Station, Upperville, Gettysburg, Bristoe, Kelly's Ford, and Mine Run. Of the three-hundred and ninety members of the Regiment, only forty-six were present at Gettysburg in February of 1865. Ordered south, they were prominent in the defense of Savannah and the campaigns of the Carolinas. The Regiment was included in the surrender of the Army of Tennessee in 1865. Joseph married Mary Ann Harden in 1854 and they had eight children. He survived the War without injury and died in Chester County October 11, 1908.

Jesse Blairs (J. B.) Minter was a member of the Fourth Regiment of the Mississippi Infantry, C.S.A. (Confederate States of America) and served as a Private in Company H of that Regiment. This Company was known as the Carroll County Rebels and was mustered into State Service at Carrollton on August 24, 1861. They fought at Fort Henry, Tennessee and were captured, but later exchanged. They were captured at Vicksburg (pictured), again exchanged, and attached to General Baldwin and Sears Brigade. The Brigade crossed the Tennessee River November 20 and marched against Schofield's Federal Command at Columbia. On the twenty-ninth, they moved to Spring Hill intending to cut off Schofield's retreat. They led the pursuit of Schofield at Franklin and took part on the assault of Stewart's line. The battle  raged from four in the afternoon until after dark. Skirmishes continued until two in the morning. After carrying the outer line, the men advanced across an open field with a deadly crossfire of artillery. General Sears published a list of those who made it across to the trenches of the main Federal line. Listed in Company H was J. B. Minter. The casualties in Sears Brigade were thirty killed, one-hundred sixty eight wounded and thirty-five missing. By December 15 at the Battle of Nashville, out of twenty-three hundred men on the brigade roll, only two-hundred and ten took part in the battle. The rest were wounded, taken prisoner or otherwise not available. After the battle the few remaining crossed back over the Tennessee River with the army and wintered at Tupelo. There were few left of the Company at the surrender at Mobile in April of 1865. Jesse Blair must have been one of them.

Both Lorenzo Dow born 1843 and Leroy born 1846, John Thomas' youngest sons were also in the Confederate Army. They were Privates in Company I of the Thirty-First Mississippi Infantry, (Jacksons Rifles from Choctaw County). It was organized in March of 1862 using the Sixth (Orr's) Mississippi Infantry Battalion as its basis. It was part of the Garrison at Vicksburg, fought in the Battle of Baton Rouge, and at Jackson. Later they served under General Featherson in the Army of Tennessee. The Garrison lost ten men killed and thirty-seven wounded at Baton Rouge. Of the two-hundred and fifteen men engaged at Peach Tree Creek, Georgia in 1864, seventy-six percent were disabled. By the end of 1864, there were eighty-six men present for duty and only a few surrendered in April of 1865. Lorenzo and Leroy served under Captain Drane. Their father, John Thomas is also listed in Captain Drane's

Company of the Choctaw Silver Grey's. Nothing more is found about Lorenzo after the War. Leroy married Sarah Minter in 1880 and moved to Hill, Texas. Pictured are John and his sons, back row – Jesse and Leroy, front row – Elzy and John Thomas. Seventeen members of the Minter family served in the Civil War from Mississippi.

The Civil War was devastating to the people of Mississippi. The State was one of the largest producers of cotton in the country with a large slave population for harvesting. Many had become wealthy plantation owners. When President Lincoln was elected to office in 1860 determined to free the slaves, Mississippi followed South Carolina and seceded from the Union in 1861. They were concerned about the threat of abolition, but had decided the cotton states could secede from the Union and organize their own country if need be and expand to the south into Mexico and Cuba. Eventually eleven southern states succeeded. In February of 1861, Jefferson Davis, a Senator from Mississippi, was elected President of the newly formed Confederate States of America. They did not expect a war. In April of 1861 when the Confederate Army attacked Fort Sumter in South Carolina, held by the Union, they demanded its surrender and the war began. The war shattered the lives of all the southern classes. Women found their lives devastated as they lost their husbands, sons, brothers and their incomes. They found themselves faced with shear survival. They took on the chores of the slaves and held on to the end. After the war, many championed the "lost cause." During reconstruction, secession was repealed, new laws were written, and new state constitutions penned to include freedom for the black slaves. President Andrew Jackson appointed a temporary government in Mississippi; several of the representatives were former army officers. Many Mississippians remained committed to circumventing the legal rights of the freed people. Congress responded by refusing to seat the newly elected Mississippi delegation and in 1867 they put the State under Army rule until the legal status of the former confederates and freed slaves could be resolved. They finally adopted a constitution in 1868 and Mississippi was re-admitted to the Union on January 11, 1870.

By the 1870 census, John Thomas was still living in Choctaw at age seventy with children Nancy Ellen age twenty-seven, Leroy age twenty-four, and Henrietta age twenty-two. There were two additional household members, Mariah born in Mississippi and Miner Minter born in South Carolina, both age thirty. They were former black slaves listed as a farmer and housekeeper.

By 1872, John and several family members decided the conditions in Mississippi with reconstruction were no longer acceptable and the life and land offers in Kansas seemed more promising. The Osage Indian lands became available in 1872, and John Thomas, his daughters Nancy Ellen, Henrietta, Juliann, and husband Thomas Fair from South Carolina, all moved north to Hutchinson, Reno County, Kansas. Juliann died in 1901. John's nephew, William E. Minter, son of John's brother, William Sr., also moved to Hutchinson with them. William Sr. stayed in Mississippi and died there August 23, 1781. The City of Hutchinson was founded in 1872 when Clinton Hutchinson, Indian Agent, contracted with the Santa Fe Railroad to build a city at the railroad crossing over the Arkansas River. The Community was known as "Temperance City," incorporated in August of 1872.

John Thomas' daughter, Mary Jane who married Francis B. Campbell, also moved to Newton, Kansas, twenty-five miles north of Wichita. In 1872, Newton became the end of the line for the Atchison, Topeka and Santa Fe Railroad and the railhead for the Old Chisholm Trail cattle drives. There was a gunfight at Hyde Park in 1871 between two local lawmen that killed eight men and the city became known as "Bloodiest and wickedest City in the West." In spite of the lawless city, Mary Ann lived until 1918 and Francis died in 1915.

John's son Jesse Blair and family moved to McPherson, Kansas to farm about thirty miles east of Hutchinson. Twelve members of the McPherson Town Company founded McPherson in 1872. It was named after General McPherson, a Union General of the Civil War. In 1878, Marion and McPherson counties chartered the railroad from the Atchison, Topeka, and Santa Fe. The cities were all within a short distance of each other and accessible by train after 1878. All three of the cities were founded in 1872, the year the Minters arrived in Kansas, and they were among the early settlers.

The 1880 census shows John Thomas, age eighty, head of the household a widowed farmer with daughters Nancy Ellen (Nannie) age twenty-six and Henrietta age twenty-four as housekeepers living with him in Hutchinson. He died six years later in 1886. His obituary below was published in the Hutchinson Democrat April 3, 1886, page five.

"DIED – At his residence on Fifth Avenue, at four o'clock, Thursday morning: Mr. J. T. Minter, age eighty-six. Mr. Minter was among the first settlers of this place (Hutchinson) having come from Mississippi in 1872. Rev. Stewart preached the funeral sermon yesterday afternoon at two o'clock." He is buried in the East Side Cemetery, City of Hutchinson (marker pictured).

Nancy E. (Nannie) Minter is also buried in the East Side Cemetery in Hutchinson. Her headstone reads, "Nancy E. Minter, born 1842, Death 1918." She lived thirty-two years after her father died. Henrietta married Albert Herriman, age forty-one, of New Tacoma, Washington on July 30, 1884 two years before her father died, and moved to Puyallup, Washington. They had one son, Frank, born in 1886. She died September 17, 1916 in Seattle. W. E. Minter, nephew of John Thomas, died in 1911. He is buried in the East Side Cemetery next to John T. Minter. Little is known about him or his life in Hutchinson.

Jesse Blairs born November 24, 1833 in Chester, South Carolina, married Mary Aurelia Bardwell in November 20, 1867 in Oktibbeha, Mississippi. She was born December 12, 1841 in Mississippi, the only daughter of Elijah Bardwell and Sarah D. (Hillhouse) Bardwell. Her mother was born in 1818 in South Carolina. Her father was born 1812 in Massachusetts and died February 2, 1844 at age thirty-one in Starkville, Oktibbeha,

Mississippi. Sarah was twenty-five. He was a Presbyterian Missionary to the Choctaw Indians. (See Bardwell Family). Pictured are Mary Aurelia Bardwell Minter and Jesse Blairs Minter.

Jesse and Mary's first child, Sarah (Sallie) Adaline, was born March 6, 1869 in Choctaw. Their daughter Josepha was born June 13, 1874 in Kansas. Their sons Leroy (Roy) born December 10, 1876 and Glen William born April 7, 1881 were born in Superior, McPherson Kansas. In the 1880 census, Jesse, Mary, and three of their children were living in Superior, McPherson, Kansas. He was listed as a farmer and had John Stalker, age thirty-one, living with the family, possible helping on the farm. A year later their son Glen was born.

When John Thomas died April 1, 1886, Jesse went to Hutchinson to attend his father's funeral on April 3, 1886 and to pick up his inheritance money. On his return home to McPherson, he was shot in the back and robbed near Burrton, Kansas where he is buried. He died April 3, 1886, the same day of his father's funeral. His wife, Mary, suspected a member of the family shot him for the inheritance money, possibly his cousin W. E. Minter, or a brother/brother-in-law. However, there is no record of a brother living in the area or one attending the funeral. No one was arrested for his death. Jesse left a widow and young family without funds.

According to the 1895 census, Mary was living in Burrton, Kansas with the Sheperd family, possibly helping with their large family. She had moved from McPherson. The 1895 Census show Glen at age thirteen living in Burrton with the Paine family. It is obvious Mary was not able to keep her family together. Roy (Leroy), the oldest son, learned to be a telegraph operator on the railroad in McPherson at age twelve. The family lived close to the railroad station and he spent many hours watching and learning from the station operator. He eventually became a telegraph operator and went on to become a Railroad Station Master in Oregon and Washington. For a short time after his father died, Roy was sent to live on one of his Aunts farms. However, the experience was not a good one. The youngest son, Glen, became a Fireman in Tacoma Washington and was eventually Fire Chief of that City. He married Elsie Marie Simmons December 23, 1911 and they had one daughter, Mary Louise, born February 23, 1913. She had a daughter, JoAnn born about 1929.

Jesse and Mary's oldest daughter Sarah (Sallie) married John William Smith on October 11, 1888 at age nineteen. In the 1890 census, they were living in Burrton, Kansas with two children, Myrtle and Ada (Adaline). In the 1910 census, they were in Phoenix, Arizona with three children, Mary Myrtle, Ada Ruby, and Clair Minter Smith. Myrtle married Lindsey E. Thomas. Jesse and Mary's grandson, Robert McComb, son of Ada became a Phoenix Veterinarian, graduating from Colorado A & M during World War II. Their youngest daughter Josepha may have gone to live with her sister Sallie after she moved to Phoenix. There is no record of her as an adult. Mary Aurelia eventually moved to Tacoma, Washington. She is shown in the 1910 census in Tacoma, Ward 3, Pierce, Washington at age sixty-eight as head of the household with her son Glen W. (George incorrect) Minter age twenty-nine and Emily Garrette, a widow age fifty-three living with her. After Glen married, she moved to Phoenix, Arizona and is listed in the 1913 City Directory, address 744 W. Fillmore. She may have been living with her daughter, Sallie. She died about 1916 in Phoenix. The family story handed down through her son Roy, is that Mary and her daughters moved to Puyallup to be near her sons Glen and Roy who were both living in Washington in the early nineteen hundreds. When Josepha came down with Tuberculosis, she moved to Phoenix for her health, which may be why her sister Sallie and her husband also moved to Phoenix. It is alleged Josepha died in a Tuberculosis sanitarium.

Roy, born 1876, eventually became a Western Union Telegraph Operator on the Railroad. The 1900 Census indicates he was a boarder living in Towanda Village, Butler Kansas were he owned and operated a Creamery. He met Lydia Edmiston in the creamery. She was in town from Nevada, Missouri visiting her Aunt. Several of her cousins and local young ladies frequented the establishment for ice cream. They

wanted to meet Roy, who was known as a "young business man" and a great "catch." According to Lydia "she set her cap" for Roy and they were married January 29, 1902 in Towanda, Kansas. Lydia was the youngest daughter of Abram Edmiston and Jennie Teaford. (Pictured are Roy Minter and Lydia Edmiston Minter). She was born March 24, 1881 in Clear Creek Township near Nevada, the youngest of their six living children. Her older sister died of Tuberculosis at age twenty-five. Her father owned a large farm outside of town.

Roy and Lydia had six children who lived to be adults. Roy and Lydia's first child, a boy born about November of 1902, did not survive. Grace was born in Missouri in 1904 and Paul was born in 1907. They moved to Dallas, Oregon about 1907 where Roy was Assistant Station Master for the Railroad. Their daughter Ruth was born in Dallas in 1909. He was transferred to Castle Rock, Washington by 1910 where he was Station Master. Daughter Pearl was born 1911 in Castle Rock. He retired from the Railroad and moved to Seibert Colorado were Roy Jr. was born in 1918 and Carol was born in 1921. He farmed for a few years until about 1930 when a flood wiped out their home and destroyed the crops. He moved to LaSalle, Colorado where he traded his land for a restaurant where the cliental was primarily from the railroad. With the loss of business after the railroad station closed, the restaurant failed and he was able to make a partial trade for a home in Fort Collins, Colorado. They moved to Fort Collins in 1933 and Roy worked for the Ideal Cement Company until he retired. Their home for many years was the historic Arthur House at 334 East Mulberry built in 1883. (Pictured) It was also home to several college students over the years who boarded with Roy and Lydia including John R.P. Wheeler, cousin of their son-in-law Harry. Roy built two more houses before he retired. He died in 1967. He is buried in Grandview Cemetery. Lydia, who died in 1969, is buried beside him.

Their daughter, Grace, was born in Towanda, Kansas October 28, 1903. (See Picture). She attended Greeley State Teachers College and became a schoolteacher in Idalia, Colorado. She met Joe McCommon from the near by town of Joe's who had attended Yale. He became a mechanic and they were married July 5, 1927. She died of pregnancy complications on November 5, 1927.

Paul was born in 1907 in Missouri. By 1910, the family was living in Castle Rock, Washington where he went to grade school. His father was a Station Master on the Railroad in both Dallas and Castle Rock. By 1920, his father retired from the railroad and decided to try farming. The family moved to Seibert, Colorado where Paul went to High School. At age sixteen, Paul had an argument with his father, left home and went to Denver. He first worked for a mortuary in Littleton where he tried to learn the trade. He then received his Chauffeur's license and stayed in that industry the rest of his life. He married three times, the second time to a divorced red head named Gates with a drinking problem of which Paul was unaware. She had a daughter named Donna Kay Gates born about 1930 who spent the summer of 1939 in Fort Collins, Colorado with his sister Ruth's family and his mother. Paul and his wife had a daughter, Lydia Sue, (named after Paul's mother) born in the summer of 1939. Shortly after the birth, his wife filed for divorce. Unknown to Paul, she gave the baby away for adoption to her friends, Laurence and Jewell Workman, who lived in Idaho Springs. Paul and his sister Ruth hired an attorney and went to court to try to get the baby back. Unfortunately, the small town Judge was a friend of the Workman's and they lost the case. The Workman family moved to Chicago and Paul only saw his daughter once. He never got over the loss. In 1935, he was living in Grand Junction, but had moved back in Denver by 1939. Over the years, he developed a drinking habit, but his smoking causing him to develop emphysema and he died at age seventy-two in 1979. He was a kindhearted person and very fond of his mother and family. He is buried next to his parents in Grandview Cemetery in Fort Collins, Colorado.

Ruth (pictured) was born in May 23, 1909 in Dallas, Oregon. By 1920, she was in school in Siebert, Colorado. She graduated with honors from Siebert High School in 1927 and went to Greeley State Teachers College where she graduated with a teaching degree. She was  a teacher in the rural Seibert area until she married. She met Harry L. Wheeler in college and they were married in 1930 in Pasadena, California. Harry and Ruth (pictured) had one daughter, Donna Joan, born March 29, 1931 in Pasadena.  They moved to Flagstaff, Arizona to be near the Wheeler family and 1936 moved to Fort Collins, Colorado where Harry became a State Highway Patrolman. During the War in 1943, Harry joined United Air Lines and they were transferred to South San Francisco where he worked until he retired. Ruth died in California from an operation in May of 1954. She is buried in Grandview Cemetery in Fort Collins.

Pearl born May 31, 1911 in Castle Rock, Washington, married Bert Floman about December 31, 1939 and moved to Culbertson, Montana. Before her marriage, she was a housekeeper in Billings, Montana for an engineer who had lost his wife. She also cared for his two children. Her brother-in-law, Harry Wheeler, was instrumental in getting her the job. Pearl was very shy and stayed close to her home and parents. Harry was afraid she might die an "old maid." She met her husband while living in Montana. Bert owned and operated a general store with a butcher shop in Culbertson. Bert and Pearl had twins,

Lee and Lillian born in February of 1941. They lived in Culbertson until her husband retired and then moved to Fort Collins. They owned a butcher shop for a few years in Fort Collins. She died in March of 1998. She is buried beside her husband in Resthaven Memorial Gardens in Fort Collins.

Roy Jr. (pictured) was born February 28, 1918 in Castle Rock, Washington. By 1933, his father had sold the farm in Seibert and moved the family to Fort Collins, Colorado where he went to work for the Ideal Cement Company. Roy graduated for Fort Collins High School in 1938 and attended Colorado A & M College. He served in the Army Air Corp during World War II. His high school sweetheart, Bonita, married while he was serving in the Air Corp. After the War, he went back to college and eventually married Maxine (Max) Mitchell October 5, 1948. They had four children, twin boys, Patrick and Michael born October 11, 1949. Michael died within a few days. Daughter Shannon was born November 13, 1953 and son Michael was born 1955. Roy and Max divorced in 1956. He later married Marilyn and had a daughter  Nancy born in 1964 in Loveland, Colorado. They were divorce and he married Carol, a girl he knew in High School. Roy spent his entire career in the automobile business. He died October 18, 1986 of cancer. He is buried in Loveland, Colorado.

Carol was born September 25, 1921, in Seibert, Colorado and graduated from Fort Collins High School in 1939. She graduated from Beauty School and attended Colorado A & M where she met Fred J. Clark. They were married November 29, 1942 during the War. He was a Lieutenant in the Army and served in Burma. After the war, they returned to Fort Collins where Fred continued his education and graduated from Colorado A & M (CSU). He received a master degree in mathematics from the University of Illinois. They had three children, Janet born March 1, 1944, Kenney, born November 22, 1947, and Barbara born May 25, 1954. Fred was with the Atomic Energy Commission in Berkley, New Mexico and in Washington, DC. He died in 2012. Carol lives in Santa Rosa, California.

*History and pictures sourced from Wikipedia, Britannic, bbc.co.uk, and Minter family, crest from Ancestry free pages

THE PHILLIPS FAMILY

An old Phillips family legend says the family descends from Maximus, the Briton, who was the Roman Emperor and King of Britom in 383. The family was forced into Wales by the invading Saxons. They also claimed "decent from Tudwell (c. 528-564) 'of the wounded knee' a descendant of Rhodri Mawr, the first King of Wales." Picton Castle in Wales was their ancestral home. One of the first recorded spellings of the Phillips name is Alicia Phillippes in Huntingdonshire England during the reign of Edward I.

Members were signers of first and third charters of Virginia and the progenitors of the Virginia families. A Thomas Phillips arrived in the Virginia Colony in 1618. By 1625, he was the head of a wealth household at the age of twenty-five. He was a tobacco planter and owned three-hundred acres of land.

On September 22, 1622, Eleanor Phillips paid for the transportation of Daniel Francks a convicted criminal, to the Virginia Colony. Elmer Phillips accompanied him on the ship *Southampton,* indicating he may have been related to Eleanor. Francks was killed by Indians in 1623. In 1629, Elmer patented land in Jamestown. By June 5, 1633, Elmer had moved to Elizabeth City where he patented one-hundred acres on Fox Hill.

Henry and Eleanor Phillips of England arrived in the Virginia Colony about 1623 and lived in Charles City. In February 16, 1624, Henry was living at Warresqueak, on the Bennett Plantation. Edward Bennett was a wealthy London Merchant who had interests in Holland and Virginia. He was one of the Virginia Colony's largest investors. He received a patent in 1621 for land where he and his associates founded the Warresqueak (tobacco) Plantation, with the condition that they move two-hundred settlers to Virginia. Fifty of the people on the plantation were killed in an Indian attack in March of 1622. By 1625, the Plantation was well populated with a large supply of provisions including food and weapons. Among his associates were his brother Robert Bennett and nephew Richard Bennett. He placed his land in the hands of his tenants who paid their rent with money and labor. His indentured servants were required to serve four years. Two-hundred members of the Bennett family served in the War, twenty-five frim Virginia.

Richard Minter and his son Edward arrived in the Colony in 1620. Jon/John, who landed in Virginia in 1635, was brought over by Edward Minter when Jon was sixteen. He was passenger number seven and his wife Elizabeth Phillips was passenger fifteen. Jon Minter died in Charles City in 1653 and Elizabeth was granted her dowry. (See descendants of John and Elizabeth at Minter Family).

Two-hundred and thirty-two members of the Phillips family served in the Revolution.

*History and crest sourced from Wikipedia, Genealogy, Ancestry free pages, DAR, and Roots web

THE HILLHOUSE FAMILY

The family of Hillhouse is originally found in Buckinghamshire, England in very ancient times. Members of the family moved very early to Scotland. They are found in the Parish of Kilmarnock in 1547 where they resided in Ayrshire for several centuries. They were shipbuilders in Glasgow on the river Clyde. They were prominent in city and national government, University professors, solicitors and Masters of the Merchants Ventures Society of ship owners. Years ago James Hillhouse, a Solicitor of Ayre, Scotland provided much of the information on the Hillhouse family. He died September 14, 1938. His daughter Muriel provided further information on the family, which is traced back to Adam Hillhouse in 1684 in the Village of Fail.

Abraham Hillhouse and his wife Janet moved from Scotland to Artikelly, County Derry in Northern Ireland during the "Plantation of Ireland" which began with Henry VIII and accelerated by James I and his son Charles I. They were part of the Protestant landholders and built the "Freehall" manor house on Freehall road, area pictured. They were also trade merchants. In 1689, Captain Hillhouse was involved in the siege of Londonderry during the struggle for power between James II and William of Orange. He was cited as in arms against the crown, declared, and adjudged a traitor. The religious conflicts were prevalent in England and continued in Ireland. Several family members immigrated to the American Colonies.

The Reverend James Hillhouse immigrated in 1719 to Montville, Connecticut and was the founder of the New England Branch of the family. There are many distinguished family members from this branch including a US Senator and Treasurer of Yale University.

The southern branch of the family lived in the Province of North Carolina. The border between North and South Carolina was established west of the Catawba River in 1772. A large portion of land previously claimed by North Carolina became part of South Carolina and called the "New Acquisition."

The progenitor of the family in the south was established by Samuel, the son of John Hillhouse of Ireland born in 1667 and his wife Rachael born in Scotland. Samuel was born at Freehall in County Derry, Ireland about 1707 and arrived in Pennsylvania around 1744 with his brothers William and Charles. He married Anna Luckey sometime before 1754. She was born about 1707, the daughter of Robert Luckey Sr. and Isabel Baird of Lancaster County. (See Luckey and Baird Family). After Ann's father died in 1757, Samuel, Ann and other members of the Luckey family left Pennsylvania and by way of the Shenandoah Valley and settled in the Scotch-Irish community near the Thyatira Presbyterian Church in Rowan County, North Carolina. He purchased six-hundred and forty acres in Rowan County in 1761. He died in 1782. He is buried at the Thyatira Presbyterian Church cemetery (gravestone pictured) along with his wife, Ann. In his will Samuel left his

three sons, Sampson, Samuel Jr., and Robert each a third of his plantation. His daughters were also mentioned. John and Palser left Rowan in September of 1779 with Daniel Boone who led a group of emigrants to Kentucky. After Samuel died, the family sold the farm and moved to Kentucky about 1786. Samuel and Anna had eight children, Martha who married William Minter, (see Minter family) Elizabeth, Robert born 1755, John born 1758, Sampson born 1759, Samuel Jr. born 1760, Palser born 1762, and Ann born 1780. All five of Samuel's sons Sampson, Robert, John, Samuel Jr., and Palsar fought in the War. Samuel fought in the Continental Line, Robert fought with Company B under General Griffith Rutherford's Army of North Carolina and under Cornel Francis Locke regular commission and with Captain William Wilson. Samuel Jr. fought under Griffith Rutherford's Tenth Regiment of the Continental Army at age sixteen. John served under Captain Bell and was present when Cornwallis surrendered. He also fought under Captain Hyskill. Palsar also served in the War. The Scotch-Irish families were for freedom almost to the man and did not hesitate to take up arms against the British. They had suffered considerably for generations under the British and were ready to fight for their freedoms. The Scotch-Irish Presbyterians of the lowland hills of North Carolina issued the Mecklenburg Declaration, which pre-dated the Declaration of Independence by more than a year.

William Hillhouse arrived in South Carolina around 1772 from Pennsylvania when he obtained a land grant of three hundred acres in the Parish of Saint Mark on Turkey Creek. He was born in Ireland in 1715, was the brother of Samuel and the great grandson of Abraham. He was too old to serve in the Revolution, but his sons, William Jr. and John were both Captains. His son James also served. He gave patriotic service, furnished supplies, and was a wagoner under Colonels Neel and Watson. (#A207591) Eight members of the Hillhouse family from South Carolina served in the Militia. Only James has a DAR number.

William Hillhouse Jr., born in 1760 owned a Plantation on a hill overlooking the Catawba River south of what is now the town of York, South Carolina. This area is home to some of the most important battles in the southern campaign of the Revolution, including Cowpens, Kings Mountain, and Williamson's Plantation. During the battle of Cowpens and Tarleton' defeat in January 1781, Cornwallis was camped at William Jr.'s Plantation. He used his house for his headquarters. When he left, his soldiers stripped William's home and took his possessions. William was quoted as saying, "they took everything I had but the land." The family fled to Old Anson County in North Carolina, which was later in the Bullock's Creek area of York County. William was made Captain during a battle where the commanding officer was killed and he was elected to take charge. He served a total of two years and one month and lost two horses during that time. A partial paraphrased description of his Revolutionary War service in a letter to the War Department is as follows:

"During my tour of duty from May 1780 to October of 1781 I entered as a Sergeant and was soon elected a Lieutenant under Brigadier General Thomas Sumter and Colonel Andrew Neil. We marched through both North and South Carolina and it was at the battle of Williamson's plantation in the District of York where we gloriously defeated the Tories. That same month we faced the enemy at Rock Mount where my "brave and beloved Colonel Neil was slain." Eight days later, I was in the battle of Hanging Rock where my Captain was severely wounded and unable to command. In the heat of the battle, I took command of the Company, which, I held until April, when I resigned. In August, I was in the battle of

Camden Ferry where our troops captured a British Guard and a number of wagons. William also fought at Granby Fort and The Big Savannah where they captured a large Guard and a great quantity of military stores. He fought in several other battles. William also states, "British Commander in Chief Lord Cornwallis on his march to Virginia in January 1781, made my plantation his place of rendezvous from Tuesday until Friday stripping me or all my possessions except my land, which he could not destroy." (Information sourced from the War Department records).

After the War, William and his family moved to Alabama. From there they moved to Starkville, Oktibbeha County, Mississippi where he died April 28, 1848. He is buried in the Odd Fellows Cemetery. The Minters, Hillhouse and Love families seem to move in groups and were found living together again in Mississippi.

* History and pictures sourced from Wikipedia, Find a Grave and *Hillhouse Kinship* by Billy Hillhouse

THE LUCKEY FAMILY

The surname Luckey comes from the Clan Lamont of Scotland. The family originated in Scotland and moved to Northern Ireland during the religious persecutions in Scotland. Three brothers, Robert, John, and Samuel immigrated to the American Colonies around 1732. Robert Luckey was born in Londonderry, Ulster, Ireland around 1690, the son of Robert. He married Isabel Baird born in 1690 in Londonderry. (See Baird Family) They had twelve children, seven boys, and five girls. Their daughter Ann, born about 1707 married Samuel Hillhouse. Robert died in 1757 in Pennsylvania. His will was proven in Lancaster County, Pennsylvania November 21, 1757.

At least seven members of the Luckey family served in the Revolution. Robert born February 6, 1760 in Rowan County was in the North Caroline Line under Captains Johnston, Armstrong, and Cowan (#A072297). John born 1735 in North Carolina served in the Western Militia (#A072295), Robert from Pennsylvania served under Captains Moorhead, Brady, Askey and Strain in the Cumberland Militia (#A072298), Samuel born 1733 in Rowan gave Patriotic Service and signed the Oath of Fidelity in 1777 (#A205021), Private James from North Carolina gave Patriotic Service (#A072294). Joseph born in 1750 in Pennsylvania was a Captain (#A 072296) and William Sr. born 1736 in Pennsylvania was a Ranger on the Frontier under Captain Nelson (#A205926).William born about 1757 in Rowan served in the North Carolina Line but there is no DAR number. Hugh Luckey of North Carolina applied for a pension.

Little more is known about the family in Ireland.

*History and crest sourced from Ancestry and Genealogy free pages

THE BAIRD/STERRET FAMILIES

The Baird name is found in 1190 in Italy. Ugone (Hugh) de Bard, Val de Aosta in Turin was first Lord of the Valley and ranked next to the Viscount of Aosta. His home was Castle Bard. He made his allegiance to Tomaso I of Savoy. He had three sons, Ugone (Hugh), Anselmo (Andrew), and Guglielmo (William). Hugh the elder gave his youngest son the Signoria de Bard, which caused jealously among the other sons. These sons eventually incurred the wrath of their sovereign for their radical actions. They were deprived of their lands and they left the Valley. The Duke of Savoy took the Castle and gave it to his brother the Count of Flanders and Heinault and it became a state fortress guarding the Saint Bernard Passes. The Signoria de Bard (Family of Bard) descends from the ancient family of Lorraine in France.

Seigneur de Bard was with William the Conqueror in 1066. Hugo de Bard was witness to the "Safe conduct granted by King Richard to King William the Lion in 1194." Ugone (Hugh) who left Aosta in 1191 may have been Hugh of England in 1194. It is also thought that Ugone and his brother Anselmo went to Scotland. There were many Bards or Bairds in England after 1066. Godfrey Baird held a Barony in Northumberland in 1165 and George Washington descends from this line. Sir David Baird, the noted general, descends from a branch in Scotland. Robert the Bruce granted Robert Baird a charter in 1310 on the lands of Cambusnethan.

Henry Baird was a student at King's College, Cambridge. During the reign of Charles I, he was a Colonel in the King's royal army, was knighted in 1643, and created a baronet in 1644, Baron of Drombey and Viscount of Bellamont in the peerage of Ireland. The American Baird's, Francis, and Christopher, sons of Richard were cousins of Henry Viscount of Bellamont. Robert Baird was a ruling elder in the Presbyterian Congregation of Taughboyne in County Donegal a few miles from the city of Derry. He died about 1714. He had three sons the youngest a Robert.

John Baird, son of James of Strabane, County Tyrone, Ireland, immigrated to America soon after his father died. He had been a Lieutenant in the British Army. He settled in Christiana, Newcastle, Delaware and then moved to Chester County, Pennsylvania about 1729. John's wife Rebecca and his oldest son Robert returned to Ireland to settle James estate and executed deeds under a letter from an attorney dated 1728. Robert returned to America with his mother, Rebecca Sterrett. John and Rebecca's children were Robert, John, William, James, Hannah, and Thomas, who eventually went to Staunton, Virginia. Robert was born in Londonderry Northern Ireland and died in Lancaster, Pennsylvania in 1755. He married Jane Lindsay in Ireland. Their daughter, Isobel, was born 1690 in Londonderry, Ireland. She married Robert Luckey in Pennsylvania. John Baird of Lancaster was a member of the Pennsylvania Convention, which ratified the Federal Constitution.

Forty-four members of the Baird family fought in the Revolution from Massachusetts to North Carolina. John Baird born 1737 in Lancaster, Pennsylvania, (#A004822) gave Patriotic service as a Juror and Grand Juror in Lincoln County. James Baird born 1750 in Tyron, North Carolina (#A004818) was a Captain in the

Militia in 1776 and member and signer of the Committee Safety of Tyron County. Adam Baird born 1745 in North Carolina (#A004809) was a Captain in the State Troopers. Absalom Baird born 1755 in Chester County, Pennsylvania (#A004808) was a Surgeon. Francis Baird born 1759 in Ireland (#A004816) served under Captain Jameson and Pugh in Pennsylvania. Robert Baird born 1756 in Conestoga Township in Lancaster, Pennsylvania (son of Robert) (#A004828) served under Colonel Crawford and Boyd.*

Rebecca Sterret, wife of John, was born 1674 in Ireland where they were married about 1700. Her parents are unknown. The Sterrett family is found in Ayrshire Scotland where they held lands before the Norman Conquest. Members of the family later moved to Ireland. A James Sterret landed in New England in 1718. Another James settled in Boston in 1768. A James Sterret Sr. (#A108567) was born in 1723 in Lancaster, Pennsylvania and was in the Militia. He married Sarah Montgomery and had at least three sons. His father was John Sterrett of Scotland who married Martha Work in Ireland in 1720. He and eleven members of the family fought in the Revolution. Fifteen members of the Sterret family fought in the war.

*History sourced from Wikipedia, Baird Crest sourced from Don Baird family history page. He sent his high-resolution picture to the author with permission to use it and from *"The Baird and Beard Families"* by Fermine Baird Catchings

**History and Sterret Crest sourced from Ancestry free pages

THE GILLHAM FAMILY

It is believed the Gillham name comes from the Comte Deguillaume who came from Normandy, France and went to England with William the Conquer. The Peter Gillame family name was recorded in the Calander of Names in 1276 during the reign of King Edward I. They were granted a coat of arms about 1679. William Gillham appears on the hearth money rolls in 1699 in Ballyconnell in the Barony of Antrim, Northern Ireland. The first know ancestor of the Gillham family in America is Thomas born about 1710 in Ulster County, Ireland. He arrived in the Port of Philadelphia in 1730 with his wife Mary Meade and one child Charles. He came with John Patton and James Lewis. They were part of a very large land grant in Virginia of Scotch/Irish immigrants. He had seven sons and four sons in law who all fought in the Revolution.

Thomas and Mary had three more children before she died in 1740. They were Ezekiel, Mary, and Nancy. He then married Margaret "Peggy" Gay Campbell born in Scotland in 1725, a member of a prominent Scottish family. They were married in Calf Pasture, Augusta County about 1742. She was the daughter of William Campbell and his wife Sarah (Gay) Campbell of Augusta, County Virginia. Her father was a cousin of the General William Campbell of Revolutionary fame, the Commander at King's Mountain. Thomas was Captain of Foot in 1752 during the French and Indian War. Margaret and son in law Thomas are mentioned in William Campbell's will of October 5, 1754 of Augusta County (see Campbell). Thomas and Margaret had seven more children, Sarah, Thomas Jr. born 1749, James, William, John, Isaac, and Susannah. Thomas secured a land grant in Mecklenburg County from Governor Tyron of North Carolina, which eventually became Union County, South Carolina. They sold their land in Augusta County Virginia and moved. Thomas died around 1789-90 in York County, South Carolina and buried in Bullocks Creek Cemetery. Margaret died in 1776. He served as a Sergeant in South Carolina's Militia in Grandon's Regiment before and after the fall of Charleston. In September of 1785, he was issued five pounds plus a horse, saddle, and bridle, replacements for loses he incurred in 1780.

Four of Thomas' sons, four of his-sons-law and at least one grandson served in the Revolution. Two of his sons-in-law were killed. Thomas Jr. served two-hundred and ten days in Captain Barnett's Company of Hill's Regiment, and fifty-four days in Captain Thompson's company in Bratton's Regiment. The South Carolina State Treasurer paid him. The General George Rodgers Clark Chapter of the SAR (Son's of the American Revolution) has memorialized all four brothers, Thomas, Jr., John, Isaac, and James. They are buried in the Wanda Cemetery.

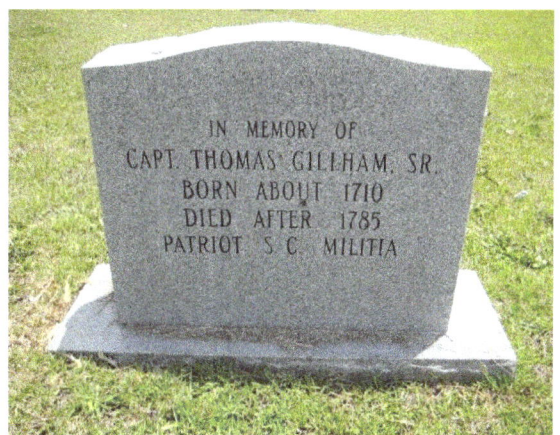

Thomas' son, Thomas Gilliam Jr., was born May 17, 1749 in Virginia. He died 1828 in Madison County, Illinois. He married Susannah Rutherford about 1795. She was born around 1750. Her family was also of Scotch/Irish descent. They had ten children. Their daughter Jane, born April 21, 1773 married John Minter in South Carolina and they had six children. Their son, John Thomas born May 13, 1800 married Adaline Love March 28, 1824. (See Rutherford Families)

*History and pictures sourced from DAR, SAR, Sir Name database, and Ancestry

THE CAMPBELL FAMILY

The Campbell family is from Argyllshire in the western region of Scotland. It is part of the Council Region of Argyll. The Campbell Clan is one of the larger of the Highland Clans. The Chief of the Clan became the Earl and later The Duke of Argyll.

During the Jacobite rising in the eighteenth century, Clan Campbell supported the British. They owed their position in Argyll to the British King. However, some members still supported the Scottish Stewart King. In November 13, 1715, the Campbell's fought with the British at Sheriffmuir and Argyll claimed the defeat of the Jacobite's. However, it was really a draw and had the Earl of Mar, the incompetent Jacobite leader, pursued the British after he found his troops in possession of the battlefield, the Jacobite Army might have won and changed the Scottish history. However, both General Mar and Argyll made severe mistakes. Sir James Edmonstone carried the Restoration Standard for the Jacobite's in the battle. Argyll claimed he captured the Standard, but it was untrue. Sir James was in possession of it and he gave it to his brother Patrick to keep. Patrick (secretly a Jacobite) later gave it to Bonnie Prince Charlie and the Standard flew again in 1745 at the Battle of Culloden where it was captured and destroyed. Here four companies of the Campbell Militia from Argyll, helped the British finally defeat the Jacobite Army, which was the end of the last Scottish attempt to regain their county from British rule.* The Campbell family of Argyll became very prominent in the history of Scotland. Inveraray Castle in Argyll (pictured) is the current seat of Clan Campbell. It is used today in the TV series of Downtown Abby. Members of the family later moved to Ireland.

Colin Campbell was one of the first to immigrate to the Colonies. He landed in New Jersey in 1685. A relative, Duncan Campbell was born in 1645 at Invearary, (Inveraray) Argyllshire, son of Andrew and grandson of Hugh and Lady Mary Campbell. They were descendant of Colin. Campbell was the first Earl of Argyll born September 10, 1433 in Argyllshire, Scotland. He married Isobel Stewart, Countess of Argyll. Colin descended from Sir Duncan Campbell, born 1390, first Lord Campbell.

Duncan born 1645 was the father of John Campbell of Donegal, Ireland who was the original Irish emigrant to Augusta County Virginia where he died in 1741. His son William was born about 1674 in Donegal and died in Augusta County 1754/59. He married Sarah Gay also born in Ireland. He was a distant cousin of Captain William Campbell, hero at King's Mountain. Their daughter Margaret born about 1704 in Ireland married Thomas Gillham Sr. also born in Ireland. She died in 1785 in York County, South Carolina. She was the mother of Thomas Gillham Jr. who married first a McDaw and second Susannah Rutherford. Their daughter Jane Gillham born 1773 married John Minter. (See Minter Family)

Two-hundred and thirty-eight members of the Campbell family served in the Revolution, fifty-eight from Virginia. Captain John Campbell (#A018654) born 1748 in Augusta County served under Major William Edmondson (Edmiston) and Colonel William Campbell. (Brigadier General) Captain William Campbell (#A018793) was born September 1, 1745 in Augusta County. He is pictured on the next page. He led the

First Virginia Regiment at King's Mountain to defeat the British, turning the tide of the Revolution. He died in 1781 in Virginia.

*History sourced from Edmonstone Chronicles by this author, Joan Wheeler LaGrone
** History and pictures from Wikipedia, SAR, Ancestry, Geni, and Roots web

THE LOVE FAMILY

The Love family dates back to very early British history to the days of the Anglo-Saxon tribes. The name is derived from an Old English personal name of Lufu. It was change to Love after the Norman Conquest in 1066. They were first found in Suffolk were they held family estates well before the arrival of Duke William in 1066. Members of the family eventually moved to Scotland and Ireland. Several members of the family came to the Colonies including Thomas Love, who arrived in Virginia in 1636. A Jon Love arrived in 1637 and a Richard Love settled in Virginia in 1642. Religion and the quest for freedom was the main cause for going to the Colonies, but later in 1688-89, the Willamette Wars known as the War of two Kings, (between the Catholic Stuarts Kings and the Protestant William English King), caused much of the Scotch and Irish immigration.

Robert Love was born 1688 in County Antrim Ireland at the beginning of the Wars. He grew up in the turmoil of the aftermath. The Jacobite Wars between Scotland and England continued until 1745 with many of the Irish taking part. Growing tired of the constant Wars, many families immigrated to the Colonies. Robert, son James Love and his wife Martha were emigrants. They came in through the Port of Baltimore about 1725 and settled first in Pennsylvania. His brothers, Robert, Alexander, and William also came to the Colonies. Robert is believed to be the progenitor of most members of the Love family in America. He had ten children.

James and Martha moved to South Carolina about 1755 and resided at Love's Ford on Broad River in what was then Carven County North Carolina, which became Chester County South Carolina. Some members of his family eventually moved to Alabama and Mississippi. James was a Weaver by trade and sometimes identified as James "the Weaver" Love. His birth is listed as April 27, 1705 in County Antrim Northern Ireland, the son of Robert Love born about 1688 and Margaret Miller. The family was originally from Scotland. James wife was Martha (Mattie) Harvey, born about 1708 in the Province of Ulster, Ireland. She died April 27, 1760 in Craven County, South Carolina. Martha and James were married in Antrim in 1722. James died in 1760. His will was dated April 8, 1760 in Chester County, South Carolina distributing 3500 acres among his children. Benjamin, born 1723-1795, married Jean Gaston daughter of Hugh Gaston, Robert born about 1728, William born about 1730 in Pennsylvania, John (the Taylor) born about 1732 in Pennsylvania, Thomas born 1733-1760, (Captain) James Love II born 1735-40, Jean born 1736, Joseph born 1740 and Jennett (Jane) born about 1746 in Chester County South Carolina. She married William Gaston about 1760.

James is buried in the Irish Graveyard in Chester County. James II received one-half of his father's land on Turkey Creek, three tracks on Broad River and the land where his father was living. The remaining land was divided between his three unnamed younger children. John (the Taylor) carried on his father's clothing mill

business, which continued in South Carolina for generations. The smoke stack still survives, pictured. The Lockhart Clothing Mills began with James the Weaver's weaving looms, and then passed to John the Taylor and then to his son William who married Marjorie Lockhart. His son James married Jane Lockhart.

Several members of the family fought in the Revolution. Alexander Love (#A071802) was born 1718 in Ireland. He was the son of Robert and the brother of James. He lived in York County, formerly Camden County, and was one of the fourteen-member delegations to the Provincial Congress of South Carolina. They assembled on November 1, 1775 to protest the British treatment of the Colonies. After his election in August, he wrote to his brother John in Pennsylvania stating,

> *"I don't like it. It is two hundred miles off and very expensive, but I cannot get clear. I doubt it will hurt me, but anything is better than Slavery."*

He was responsible for naming York County after his former home in York, Pennsylvania. His son Andrew Love (#A071805) became a Captain of the local forces. He was wounded at the Battle of Kings Mountain. He was later elected to the Legislature. His son Robert Love (#A071841) also served in the Revolution under Colonel James Martin, who was the model for the movie ***"The Patriot***." Benjamin Love (#A071806) Chester, South Carolina was the oldest son of James, born 1723 in Antrim. He provided patriotic service and furnished provisions, a wagon and team. Others were Captain James Love (#A071817) born about 1735 in Camden South Carolina, Captain James Love Jr. (#A071818) born 1763 in Camden District, son of Richard, who served in the Militia under Colonel Thomas Brandon, First Lieutenant John Love (#A071823) born 1745-50 in South Carolina served under Colonel Marshall. William Love (#A071844), born 1746 in Ireland, was from the York District in South Carolina. He was a Lieutenant under Colonel William Thompson's Third Regiment of the Continental Army and was at King's Mountain. Fifty members of the Love family served in the Revolution, five were at King's Mountain.

James Love II born 1735-40 married Jane Lockhart. Their son Richard Love, born 1768 married Elizabeth (Jane) Love daughter of Benjamin Love. Their son James Harvey Love born 1803 eventually moved to Choctaw, Mississippi with other members of the Love family including Adeline Love born 1804 wife of John Thomas Minter, Eliza Lucinda Love, born about 1795, and her husband William Minter, brother of John Thomas. Jane Love, born 1770-1772, probably the widowed mother of Adeline went with them.

*History and pictures sourced from Wikipedia, Love family history, DAR, and Ancestry

THE LOCKHART FAMILY

When Duke William disposed the Lockhart family of their lands in England, they moved to Scotland. They settled Ayrshire and Lanarkshire where they lived for over seven hundred years. In Annandale, the town of Lockerbie is said to be named after them. The earliest record of the family name is a charter in 1323 found in the family archives binding them to pay rent from their lands. Symond Locard fought beside Robert the Bruce against the English. He was knighted for his loyal service. Symond later accompanied Sir James Douglas when he took the heart of Bruce on the Crusade in 1330. Symond carried the key to the casket. He rescued the casket after Douglas was killed in Spain and returned it to Scotland. From that time the heart and fetterlock was included in the Lockhart arms and motto.

Lieutenant James Lockhart, born January 4, 1640, was the son of Robert Lockhart and Anna Fleming. He arrived in Jamestown Virginia in 1677 as part of a Regiment of soldiers of Charles II to fight in "Bacon's War" the first uprising by the discontented Colonists. The rebellion, led by Nathanial Bacon, was against the Jamestown Governor Berkley for not protecting the people from the Indian attacks and for playing favoritism. The rebellion was put down before James and the troops arrived. Since there was no return passage, the troops were forced to stay. James remained in America in charge of one hundred of the Royal Troops and soon promoted to Captain. He was in the Royal Colonial Army until his death in Bertie, North Carolina in 1711. He had two know half brothers, William and John. He married Margaret Burnett in Edinburgh Parish Midlothian Scotland December 26, 1672. They had at least four sons, James Jr., Joseph, Benjamin, and John. On October 20, 1689, James Lockhart was granted one-hundred and seventy eight acres in the lower parish of Nansemond County giving him a total of three-hundred and thirty eight acres. It was located near the head of the Mill Run of Bennett's Creek. By 1702, James was Justice and by 1704, he owned eight hundred acres in Nansemond listed on the rent rolls. His sons inherited the land, granted to them at the time of his death, April 28, 1711.

James Jr. married Elizabeth Moss Craske about 1708, the widow of Captain John Craske and the daughter of William Moss Sr. She was born about 1665 in Old Rappahannock, Virginia and died October 8, 1724 in Essex, County. A descendant, Jane Lockhart born 1772 married Captain James Love II.

Twenty-one members of the Lockhart family served in the Revolution. Captain James Lockhart (#A071015) born 1730 in Virginia was a member of the North Carolina Court Martial Board, Lieutenant Aaron Lockhart (#A071013) born 1748 from Craven County, South Carolina was in Colonel Winn's Militia and furnished supplies. James Lockhart (#A071017) born 1740 in Bertie North Carolina was a Lieutenant Colonel in the eight Regiment under Colonel James Armstrong. John Lockhart (#A071021) born 1754 in North Carolina was a Quartermaster Sargent. Samuel Lockhart (#A071028) born 1745 was a Lieutenant Colonel in North Carolina and a member of the Provincial Congress.

*History, picture and crest of the Lockhart arms sourced from Wikipedia, Genealogy

THE BARDWELL FAMILY

The ancient history of the Bardwell's begins with the Anglo-Saxon tribes of Britain. The name is derived from the village of *Bardwell* in Suffolk, England. The first recorded name was Tedricus Baerdewaslla in 1190 of Norfolk during the reign of King Richard I "the Lionheart," 1189-1199. A Nicholas Bardwell, is recorded in Somerset in 1273. Sir William Bardwell (1361-1434), a member of the cadet branch, was a wealth landowner and owner of several Manors in Suffolk. He was a Member of Parliament in the House of Commons from 1386 to 1421. He married Margaret before 1387, the daughter of John Pakenham. John Bardwell sailed from London in 1678 on the ship "*Constant Warwick*" bound for "Virginea, New England." He was one of the earliest settlers in the Colonies.

John Bardwell was born in London, Middlesex in 1620 and died October 8, 1654 in Bardwell, Suffolk. He married Sarah Scott born August 4, 1616 in All Hallows, London Wall. She was the daughter of Samuel Scott born about 1590, who died in 1640 in England. Their son Robert was born in London, Middlesex in 1647 and emigrated to Hatfield, Massachusetts about 1675. His father paid for a commission for him and he was in charge of the Hatfield Garrison. He married Mary Gull on November 29, 1676 in Hatfield. She was the daughter of William Gull, who was born about 1620, in Billingborough, Lincolnshire, England and died December 18, 1701 in Wethersfield, Hartford, Connecticut, and Elizabeth Smith. William was the son of John Gull and Ann Annis Bench of Lincolnshire. Elizabeth Smith was the daughter of Samuel Smith, born 1602 in Suffolk England, and Anna Burleigh. Both died in Hadley, Hampshire, Massachusetts. Robert and Mary's children were Ebenezer born 1679 in Hatfield, Connecticut, Thomas, Hester and Abigail.

Ebenezer Bardwell was born October 19, 1679 in Hatfield. He married Mary Field April 25, 1706. She was born July 18, 1864 in Hatfield, the daughter of Joseph Field and Joanna Wyatt. Joseph was born 1658 in Hartford. He died 1736 in Hatfield. Joanna Wyatt was also born 1663 in Hartford and she died 1722 in Hatfield. Ebenezer and Mary later settled in Whately, Massachusetts where he had a grant for five-hundred acres in the northwest part of Montague. He was a businessman like his father and quite prominent. They had eight children, Lieutenant Ebenezer served in the Revolution (#A005960), Hannah, Joseph born 1711/1713, Remembrance (#A005987) was a Member of Committee, Jonathan (#A005972) was at Bennington Alarm, Mary, Abigail, and Esther.

Joseph, born 1711/13, married Lydia Morton on May 1, 1735 in Hatfield. In 1740, they moved to Belchertown, Massachusetts where he was involved in the community and Treasurer in 1774. They lived on Turkey Hill. Joseph #A005974 served in Revolution and was at the Lexington Alarm. (The battle was fought ten miles from Bennington, Vermont. The New Hampshire and Massachusetts Militiamen and the Green Mountain Boys, originally led by Ethan Allen, decisively defeated the British). Joseph's wife Lydia was born March 24, 1715, in Hatfield, the daughter of Ebenezer Morton and his wife Sarah, a descendant of George Morton, a Pilgrim Father. (See Morton Family). Joseph and Lydia had ten children, Catherine, Experience, Lydia, Joseph Jr. (#A005978) was a member of the Belchertown Militia in the War, Captain Elijah born 1753 in Belchertown served in Revolution, Hannah, Martin (#A005980) served in Revolution at Lexington Alarm, Obadiah (#A005985) also served and Eunice, and Lucy.

Captain Elijah Bardwell was born July 2, 1753 Belchertown, Hampshire, Massachusetts. He married Sarah Worthington Smith on December 11, 1777 in Belchertown. She was born April 21, 1752, the daughter of Elijah Smith* born January 1, 1723 in Hatfield. Elijah and Sarah had ten children, Rhoda, Sophia, Laura, Dr. Araunah, Elijah Bardwell born 1786, Horatio, Selah, Sarah, Aurelia, and Porcius. Elijah was a Captain in the Revolution #A005964. He served in the Fourth Hampshire County, Regiment as a Lieutenant under Captain Gideon Stebbens and was later a Captain. (DAR has his wife's middle name incorrectly as Wentworth). He died May 12, 1809 in Goshen, Hampshire. Sarah died in 1824. Twenty-three members of the Bardwell immediate family served in the War. Twenty-five Worthington and forty-five Hewitt family members also served. Twenty-five members of the Howes family served in the Revolution, seventeen from Massachusetts and sixty-six from the Sears family, thirty-eight from Massachusetts.

Elijah Bardwell son of Captain Elijah was born June 7, 1786 in Belchertown. He married Lavinia Howes December 8, 1811 in Ashfield, Franklin, Massachusetts. She was the daughter of Zachariah Howes, descendant of Thomas Howes born 1600 in Suffolk, England and Mary Burr. Zachariah's wife Lavinia Sears was a descendant of John Bouchier Sears born 1535 in Amsterdam, Holland, and Elizabeth Hawkins. Elijah and Lavinia had one son Elijah Bardwell, Jr. born September 4, 1812 in Ashfield. Lavinia died September 14, 1812 ten days after the birth of her son. Elijah eventually remarried. He and Elijah Jr. became Presbyterian Missionaries' to the Choctaw Indians in Mississippi. Elijah Jr. married Sarah D. Hillhouse in Oktibbeha about 1840 who, was born in 1818 in South Carolina. Their daughter Mary Aurelia Bardwell, born 1841 married Jesse Blairs Minter. (See Minter Family)

*Smith was a Captain in the French War of 1756 and deacon in Belchertown. His wife Sibyl Worthington was born 1727 a descendant of Nicholas Worthington born 1640 in Worthington, Lancashire, England. Elijah Smith descends from Joseph born about 1627 and Lydia Huitt (Hewitt) born 1635 in Warwick England, the daughter of Reverend Ephraim Hewitt a non-conformist Preacher who emigrated to the American Colonies and died in Windsor, Connecticut in 1644.
** History and pictures sourced from Wikipedia, DAR, Genealogy, and Ancestry

MAYHEW AND HEBRON MISSION

It was not until 1817 the American Board of Commissioners for Foreign Missions, (the first American Christian Missionary Organization established in 1810 by graduates of William's College in Massachusetts), began to set up a series of posts with schools among the Indians. The first one was for the Cherokees at a place called Brainerd near Chattanooga, Tennessee. Reverend Cyrus Kingsbury. Mr. and Mrs. L. S. Williams were in charge.

MAYHEW MISSION TO THE CHOCTAW INDIANS

When the Choctaw Indians in the new state of Mississippi heard about the school, two Choctaw Chiefs went to the Board to ask for a Mission school for their tribe. They said, "they wished their children to be taught the better way of life, which was found in the 'White Man's Book' and that they were equally as worthy as the Cherokees". They added, "Never had a white man's blood been shed by a Choctaw at war."

The Presbyterian Mayhew Mission was established in 1818 and Dr. Cushman was in charge. A few years later the Hebron Mission was opened about three miles from Starkville in Oktibbeha County. In 1820, Elijah Bardwell, his son Elijah, Jr. and others came from Massachusetts to work with the Choctaws. A farm was attached to every Mission. Each was placed under the charge of a northern farmer. The Indian boys were taught the art of plowing and hoeing. The wife and daughters of the farmer taught the girls to sew and knit, how to make butter and cheese, to spin and weave, and how to keep a northern kitchen. Parents of the children often visited the Mission schools. All were well attended and the pupils were subordinate and quiet.

The Superintendent's report of the Choctaw's in December of 1821 stated the workings of the school had given a favorable impression among the "full-bloods" of the tribe. There were now about seventy-four students sixty were males and the rest females. All but those who live close by live at the school and the others go home over the weekend. Fifty of the students could not speak "our language" when they entered and all have made progress in proportion to the time they have been here and several are able to speak fluent English. They are learning the alphabet, to write, and some are learning arithmetic. The students are employed on the farm when not in school. Many full-blooded Indians have made application for their children of late and are willing to submit them entirely to our direction. Strong desires were expressed to open another school. This was the first of many more mission Indian schools to open.

*History and pictures sourced from Wikipedia

THE MORTON FAMILY

The ancient people of Scotland were the first to use the name of Morton in Dumfriesshire. One of the early-recorded charters in Scotland listed Hugh de Mortoun as a prior of May in 1204. However, the Morton family is also recorded in Cheshire, Berkshire, Devonshire, Dorset, and other areas in England where they held estates from early in English history. The first recorded spelling is that of Robert de Mortone in 1130 in the "pipe rolls" during the reign of Henry I (1100-1135).

George Morton, (Pilgrim Father) was an English Puritan Separatist. He was born in 1585 and died in 1624 in Plymouth, Massachusetts. He was a Merchant and the publisher of the book, *Mourt's Relation,* the first account in Great Britain of the founding of Plymouth Colony. He was born in Bawtry, South Yorkshire, the son of George (1553-1612), and Catherine Morton whose father was Anthony Morton, supposedly a wealthy Catholic in Bawtry. George, however, converted early in life. He was a member of the Scrooby Congregation of separatists who eventually became one of the Mayflower Pilgrims. Morton moved to Leyden, Holland with the congregation, but stayed behind when the first settlers left for Plymouth. He was a financial agent and supporter of the Pilgrims and as such, he purchased *the Mayflower*. He continued to conduct business affairs in Europe and London for their cause and organized the publication and release of the Plymouth Colony account in 1622 referred to as "Mort's Journal." He then emigrated on the ship *Anne* in 1623 with his wife Juliana Carpenter and her sister, Alice Southworth, who became the second wife of the Plymouth Colony Governor William Bradford.

Some sources say George had at least one child from a previous marriage before his wife died. George married Juliana Carpenter July 23, 1612 according to the Leyden records and had nine children. His brother Thomas was one of the witnesses at their wedding.

George died a year after he arrived on August 12, 1624 in Plymouth. (His gravestone is pictured). His widow Juliana later married Manasseh Kempton who had also arrived on the *Anne* in 1623. Governor Bradford took a keen interest in helping to raise George and Juliana's children who were Nathaniel, Patience, John George, Sarah, Ephraim, a daughter (no name) who must have died at birth, Joseph, Alice, and George II who was born about May 22, 1624.* Pictured is George's Plymouth birthplace.

George II was born in Plymouth in 1624 about two months before his father died. He married Phoebe in 1640, both were age fifteen or sixteen. She was the daughter of Mr. and Mrs. Cooper (first name unknown) of Plymouth. They had one known son, Richard, who was born about 1640/41. She died May 22, 1663. George died November 23, 1686 and evidently had move to Theford, now in Orange County Vermont.

Richard married Ruth (?) about 1666 in Hatfield, Hampshire County, Massachusetts. Their children were, Richard Jr. born 1668, John, Joseph, Abraham, Elizabeth, Ebenezer born in 1682, Jonathan, and Thomas. Richard died April 3, 1710 in Hatfield.

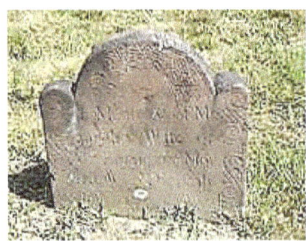
Ebenezer Morton was born August 11, 1682 in Hatfield. He married Sarah Belding February 22, 1711 in Hatfield. She was the daughter of Stephen and Mary Belding. Their children were, Dorothy, Lydia born in 1715, Elisha, Ebenezer, Oliver, Seth, Eunice, and Simeon. Ebenezer died March 4, 1760 and Sarah died June of 1749. They are buried in Hatfield. (Sarah's gravestone is pictured).

Lydia Morton was born March 24, 1715 in Hatfield. She married Joseph Bardwell May 1, 1735 in Hatfield. Their children were Joseph, Obadiah, Catherine, Eunice, Experience, Hannah, Lucy, Lydia, Martin, and Captain Elijah Bardwell born July 12, 1753 in Belchertown, Massachusetts. Lydia died July 30, 1800 and Joseph died in 1791 in Belchertown.

Captain Elijah Bardwell was born July 12, 1753 and died May 12, 1809 in Goshen Hampshire, Massachusetts. He married Sarah Worthington Smith December 11, 1777 the daughter of Elijah Smith born 1723 and Sybil Worthington born 1727.* He fought in the Revolution (See Bardwell Family). Their son Elijah was born June 7, 1786 in Belchertown. Elijah married Lavina Howes in Ashfield, Franklin, Massachusetts on December 5, 1811. Their son Elijah Jr., was born September 4, 1812 and Lavina died September 14, 1812. Elijah married second Maranda Ransom in 1818. She was from Chazy, New York. They joined a group of missionaries and in 1820, went to Mississippi to serve the Choctaw Indians. They returned to Montague, Franklin, Massachusetts in 1830 where he died in 1880. Elijah Jr. was eighteen and stayed in Mississippi. He later married Sarah Hillhouse and had one daughter, Mary Aurelia Bardwell born 1841. She married Jesse Blairs Minter in Mississippi. Elijah Jr. died at age thirty-one in 1844. (See Minter Family)

Forty-one members of the Morton family fought in the Revolution.

*Elijah Smith was born in Hatfield. Sarah was born in Belchertown.
**History, pictures, and crest sourced from Wikipedia, Ancestry, Geni, and George Morton Pilgrim Father

CHAPTER IX
THE EDMONSTONE FAMILY

The Edmonstone family (Edmiston, Edmondson, and other spelling variations) originated in Scotland in 1063. The history of Sir William Edmonstone began in Flanders with his family ancestors, the counts, and dukes of Flanders. The Counts of Flanders of Ghent, Belgium date back to the ninth century AD. The first Count was Baldwin I created about 892. He was the son-in-law of the Emperor Charles the Bald and son of King Stephen. By the reign of Baldwin V in the eleventh century, Flanders had acquired power equivalent to that of a kingdom. The Counts built a fortified stronghold in Ghent known as the Gravensteen Castle (pictured) and exercised considerable influence in the political affairs of Western Europe. Baldwin V married Adel Capet, daughter of Robert II, King of France. Their daughter, Matilda, born 1031, married William the Conqueror, King of England.

Sir William Edmonstone, younger son of the Duke of Flanders, Count de Edmont, was the "special servant" to Princess Margaret, who came to Scotland in 1063 and married King Malcolm Kenmure, King of Scotland. Count De Edmont may have been a younger brother of Baldwin IV. The Baldwin Counts are pictured on the wall in the meeting room of the Gravensteen Castle. The author toured the castle in 2001.

The ancient name of Edmonstone is derived from the lands of Edmonstone in the County of Edinburgh. It comes from Edmundus and toun, a baronial residence.

> "In the Year of God 1063, -----this King Malcolm gave the said Sir William investment of the lands of Edminstoun and Umet for his good service. He married and had by her one son called Sir William…"

Sir William's wife was not identified but it is thought that she was related to the Seton family of Abercorn, which would explain the similarity of the three crescents in both coats of arms. The family appeared next in the parish of Newton in Mid-Lothian and built a Manor House. Sir John Edmonstone married Lady Isobel, daughter of King Robert II son of Robert the Bruce and had two sons, Sir David I who succeeded him and Sir William of Culloden, ancestor of the family of Duntreath.

The Edmonstone family of Knights intermarried with the royal families of Scotland over the next several centuries and built Duntreath Castle in 1450 (pictured). Their history is documented in the book *"Edmonstone Chronicles, Royal Knights and Scottish Kings"* by Joan Wheeler LaGrone a descendant. They fought with, served the Kings of Scotland, and married their daughters. Sir William Edmonstone of Culloden married the Princess Mary Stewart in 1425, the daughter of King Robert III who gave them the land for Duntreath. The family still lives in the remodeled castle today. At first, it was only a fortified tower house, but over the centuries, it grew to a magnificent castle (pictured). It was reduce in size in 1954. Duntreath Castle is pictured above as it stands today, home of Sir Archibald Edmonstone, 7th Bart, and Lady Juliet. (Archibald Edmonstone 1st Bart of Duntreath pictured below).

Members of the family were appointed by the King to be Captains in charge of the Doune Castle. They fought at the Battle of Flodden Field in 1513 with James the IV who was killed and his baby son, James V became King. Their descendant James Edmonstone became the 1st Newton of Doune, (cadet branch). He was the fourth son of William Edmonstone, 4th of Duntreath and Captain of Doune Castle. Sir James was Master of Horse for King James the 5th and built the Tower House in the town of Doune where the family resided. (Doune Castle pictured).

His descendant, Sir James Edmonstone, 6th Newton of Doune, was a Jacobite and carried the Royal Standard for James VIII in the Battle of Sheriffmuir in 1715. The Scottish Jacobite has tried to restore the James Kings, to the Throne of Scotland after the Scots became part of England with the Union of Parliaments in 1707. (See Edmonstone Chronicles) They failed in their efforts and many Scots were either killed by the English King, George I of Hanover, or transported to the American Colonies. Sir James managed to survive in Scotland, but due to a trumpeted up charge against him for his support  of a previous duel where his friend Patrick Graeme had killed a man, he was banished from Scotland in 1696 and went to Ireland. He was forced to deed his land to his brother Patrick Edmonstone, who became the 7th Newton of Doune. James returned to support the Jacobite's in 1715. After his death, his sons, James and Mathew eventually immigrated to Pennsylvania about 1720-30 with their mother Jane Thompson, (see Thompson family) who was born in Ireland. He is probably buried near his Estate in Strathearn at Campbusbeg, another of his former properties. Doune Tower House home of the Newton's of Doune is pictured. The author, descendant of James, is pictured in the great hall of Doune Castle.

(Robert Edmonstone, son of John of Broich in Scotland is found in Prince George, Maryland in 1648. Descendants of this family provided the land on which the White House is built in Washington, D.C., but were never paid. Crest and pictures from *Edmonstone Chronicles* written by this author).

*History and pictures sourced from Author, Wikipedia, and Edmonstone Family

THE EDMISTON FAMILY IN AMERICA

James and Mathew Edmonstone/Edmiston arrived in Chester County, Pennsylvania with their mother Jane Thompson Edmonstone between 1720 to 1730. They came with members of the Thompson Family. Many Scot-Irish immigrated to Pennsylvania after 1727 when King George II was announced. Most did not stay long in Pennsylvania before moving south after 1730 along the Great Wagon Road to Augusta County Virginia. Augusta County was a huge county with no western boundary. It included most of the Shenandoah Valley, West Virginia, Kentucky, Ohio, Illinois, and the upper Mississippi River. By 1742, James and Mathew had moved to Augusta County along with other members of the Thompson family. Jane, their mother did not accompany them. She may have died in Chester County. James the eldest son was probably born about 1710-13 in Ireland and died about 1793 in Wilkes County, North Carolina. He married Sarah Hayes in 1748, widow of George Hayes, of Augusta County. She had six children and they had two more boys and three girls. The oldest Edmiston was a Robert born around 1750. James and Mathew were among the earliest settlers in the county.

Mathew was born in Donegal, Ireland about 1715 and died in 1796 in Virginia, younger son of Sir James Edmonstone Newton of Doune, Scotland and Jane Thompson of Donegal, Ireland. He was related to Sir David Edmonstone Cup Bearer to King James I of Scotland who was the brother of his ancestor Sir William of Culloden. The early records of 1742 in Augusta County show Mathew on a list of the Muster under Captains John Smith and John Moffitt. In 1743, he is listed as a witness on the lease of one-hundred and ninety-nine acres of the Borden patent to a John Stevenson. Other witnesses include John and Margaret Buchannan. In 1745, he helped open a road through Jennings Gap where he eventually lived. In 1751, James Edmondson (Edmiston) qualified as Captain of Troop of Horse and Mathew qualified as Cornet. By 1758, Mathew was Constable. In 1745, he married Margaret Patterson, the daughter of James Patterson and Ann Corry. She was born about 1720 in Chester County, Pennsylvania. Her parents were from Donegal, Ireland. Mathew and Margaret had seven children, James born October 7, 1746 and baptized at the Tinkling Springs Church by Reverend Craig. Agnes, born 1748, was also baptized at Tinkling Springs Church as well as William born 1750.

Figure XXIV
The Stone Sanctuary Constructed About 1793

David was born 1751, Mary and Ann born late 1751, probably twins, and Nancy Jean born 1753. Mathew and Margaret were among the original members of the Tinkling Springs Church. Members brought Reverend John Craig from Donegal. The church (pictured) was the first church in western Virginia built about 1740. Mathew's sons James and William served in the Revolution, William survived the King's Mountain Battle, (#A036424) and fought under Colonel Campbell. Eight Edmiston's and five Buchannan's went out from Fort Edmiston to fight in the Battle (right). Five Edmiston's were killed, two wounded and one was uninjured.

By 1751, Mathew owned two-hundred and thirty-eight acres at Jennings Gap surveyed by William Smith (his neighbor and Revolutionary Captain #A106131) and John Allen. By 1776, he had purchased another ninety-one acres. He died in 1796. His will, written June 28, 1790 was proven in Court January of 1796. It mentions all of his sons and daughters as well as his grandson Mathew Kirk and Math Magill and granddaughter Margaret Jones.

Mathew's oldest son James was born October 7, 1746 and baptized at Tinkling Spring Church (picture). He was a Revolutionary War soldier (#A036359 listed under the spelling of Edmondson) and served in the Militia. Records from the War Department Adjutant General's Office at Washington state the following:

> "It is shown by the records of this office that one James Edmonson (name also born Edmiston and Edmondson) served as a private in Captain John Hay's Company, 9th Virginia Regiment, commanded by Colonel George Matthews, Revolutionary War. His name is born on the rolls for that company for the period from April to October 1777 inclusive. The rolls from July to August, show that he was wounded, date, and place not shown."

According to family information passed down, he was wounded on the side of his face.

James settled in Greenbrier County, Virginia and married Jane Smith from Ireland, possibly relative of Captain John Smith and wife Margaret from Ulster, Ireland. (A William Smith appears in 1739 with one-hundred and thirty-five acres in the Beverly Manor next to Matthew Edmiston's land). Jane's father is unknown although William is feasible. James and Jane were married in 1769. She was born on October 17, 1746. James and Jane had eight children, Rebecca born about 1771, Margaret born 1773, William born 1775, Andrew born July 22, 1777 in Hillsboro, Pocahontas County married Mary "Polly" Gilliland, Susannah born 1779, Jane born about 1780 and married Nathan Gilliland, Matthew born in 1781, and Nancy Ann born about 1789 who married William Gilliland. James and Jane moved to Bath County where he died October 7, 1817. Bath County became Pocahontas County where several of their children were born. His executors were his trusted friends John Smith, fellow soldier, and William Edmiston.

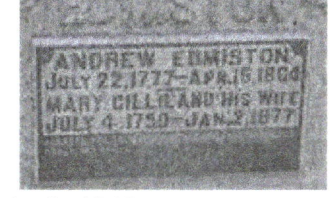

After James died in 1817, his wife Jane married James Gilliland Sr. in 1819. He also served in the Revolutionary War as a private and later promoted to Lieutenant (#A044934). He was the father of Mary "Polly" the wife of Jane's son Andrew. Jane died May 20, 1837 and James Gilliland died at age ninety-nine in 1844.

Andrew Edmiston was born July 22, 1777, married Mary "Polly" Gilliland January 8, 1807. They settled near Locust in Pocahontas County. She was the daughter of James Gilliland Sr. and the first Mrs. Gilliland, Lydia Armstrong. She was born July 4, 1790 and was a bride at age seventeen. She died January 2, 1877. Andrew and Mary "Polly" had five sons and five daughters, Lydia, Elizabeth, Jane, Martha, Mary, James, George McNeel, Matthew, Andrew Jackson, and William. Matthew became a Judge. He was admitted to the bar in 1835. He was elected to a seat in the Constitutional Convention of 1872. He was appointed to the Supreme Court of Appeals in 1886, one year before his death in Weston, Lewis County. His son Andrew followed in his fathers footsteps. He is noted in the annuals of political history of West Virginia.

George McNeel Edmiston (pictured with sons in middle of bottom row) was born May 19, 1811 in Mill Point, Pocahontas County. He married Mrs. Nancy Jordan Callison, September 20, 1840 who was born January 9, 1810 the daughter of John Jordan and Miriam McNeel. They lived many years on the Edmiston homestead. He was engaged in several business enterprises with Colonel Paul McNeel, his cousin. He and Nancy had seven sons, Matthew, Andrew, Richard, Abraham born 1846, John, Lewis, and William Russell. Nancy died August 8, 1873 in Locust Creek, Pocahontas County. She is buried in the McNeel Cemetery. George McNeel moved to Nevada, Missouri with his sons Abraham and Andrew, (who married Julie Ann Teaford), where he died August 6, 1894 and is buried in the Mount Vernon Church Cemetery near Nevada, Missouri. Four of his sons, Matthew, Andrew, Richard, and Abraham served in the Confederate Army. (Pictured above back row – Andrew and Richard, front row – Abraham, George McNeel, and Matthew) Thirty-two members of the Edmondson/Edmiston family served in the Revolution, eight from Augusta County.

Abraham (Abe) Edmiston was born January 28, 1846 in Pocahontas County, West Virginia. He married Jane Priella "Jennie" Teaford (pictured), who was born June 27, 1841 in Rockbridge County, Virginia. She was the daughter of Jacob Teaford and Philaska Greaver. Abraham (pictured) enlisted in 1863 in Early's Division of the Confederate Army and served until the end of the war. He was present at the Battle of  Winchester. He settled on a farm in Clear Creek Township and lived there until 1902 when he moved with his family to Butler County, Missouri where he purchase a large farm. Abe and Jennie had eight children, six survived to adulthood. Richard Julia (Dick) was a dentist in Oklahoma City; Henry Hillman a superintendent of schools in Johnson County, Missouri, Ella Roberta (Bertie) died young, George Teaford Superintendent of Mines in Wallace Idaho, and Malcolm Earnest an artist and businessperson in Wichita. Daughter Mary Maude died of tuberculosis at age twenty-five, Coe died young, and Lydia Jordan. Lydia was born March 24, 1881 in Nevada, Missouri. She married Roy Minter. (See Minter family) Their daughter Ruth Minter married Harry Wheeler. Jennie died May 6, 1908 in Benton, Missouri. Abe died in June 17, 1918 in Cleveland Pawnee County Oklahoma at the home of his son Richard, dentist in Oklahoma City. They are both buried in the Mount Vernon Church Cemetery in Nevada, Missouri. Lydia is buried beside her husband Roy Minter in Fort Collins, Colorado.

Left to right: Children: Richard, George, Henry, Earnest and Maude (seated died) and Lydia. Richard's first wife died in childbirth, remarried to Icy with no children. George's first wife was Lillie Maud Loving had daughter Lydia born 1896 and son Merrill born 1897 (his son George T. born 1922), married second Grace Finley in 1913. Henry married Roberta and had three children (Henry, George, and Mary Virginia); Earnest married Ella Robinson and had two children (E.K. and Roberta). Lydia married Roy Minter and had six children: Grace, Paul, Ruth, Pearl, Roy, and Carol. Pictured is the home of Abraham and Jennie. Edmiston in Nevada, Missouri painted by Earnest Edmiston.

The picture right is of the Edmiston and Minter families taken in 1938 in front of 334 East Mulberry. Back row Roy Minter Jr., Dick Edmiston, Roy Sr., Middle row, Grace wife of George, Paul Minter, Ruth Minter Wheeler, Icy wife of Dick, Lydia Minter, George Edmiston, front Donna Joan Wheeler, daughter of Ruth Minter and Harry Wheeler.

*Reference is made to early pioneer members of the Edmiston family in *Campbell's History of Virginia, Thwaite's' Dunsmore' War, Virginia History of Biography 1901-1902 and Roosevelt's Winning of the West*.

**Information on the Edmonstone/Edmiston families taken from family records, the Edmonstone records at Duntreath, Scotland, Mary (Edmonstone) McGrigor, the book *"Pocahontas County, West Virginia*" by William Price *and "Chalkleys Chronicles of Augusta County, Virginia*

THE THOMPSON FAMILY

The distinguished name of Thompson is found in Cumberland England where they held land and family estates from very early history. The first record of the term "Cumberland" appears in the year 945 when the Anglo-Saxon Chronicle recorded that the area was ceded to Malcolm I, King of Scotland by King Edmund of England.

A Thompson family from Firth, Scotland moved to Antrim, Ireland possible during the Plantation period, and members later move to the Donegal area. William Thompson born 1655 in Argyll, Scotland went to Ireland where his son Peter was born 1675 in Donegal. He was probable acquainted with Sir James Edmonstone of Doune. John Thompson, son of Alexander Thompson of Dressy, served in the King's Guard with James Edmonstone, father of James, 6th Newton of Doune. John went to Antrim, Ireland where he died in 1726. Edward Thompson was a passenger on the Mayflower in 1620.

William Thompson is found in Donegal in the early 1700's He was born in Argyll Scotland July 3, 1671 and died in County Donegal in 1725. William and his wife Margaret had five sons. Unfortunately, the daughters of these families are not mentioned. After William died, Margaret and her sons immigrated to Pennsylvania about 1720-30 where she died. Their son Mathew was born 1692 in Donegal and died in 1753 in Crosskeys, Virginia. He and some of his brothers move to Augusta County Virginia about 1741 with James and Matthew Edmonstone. William went to Maryland. After her husband James Edmonstone died, Jane Thompson and her sons, James and Matthew, went to Chester County, Pennsylvania along with the Thompson family. The Thompson family married members of the Craig family, who were associated with Reverend John Craig from Donegal. Reverend Craig was invited by members of the new Tinkling Springs Church in Augusta County to be their minister. The members included Matthew Edmonstone/Edmiston and members of the Thompson family. Jane died in Chester County. The date is unknown.

James Edmonstone a Jacobite, the father of James and Matthew, married Jane Thompson about 1710, probably in Ireland. He was banished from Scotland on a trumped up charge several years after he was indirectly involved in a duel where his friend, Patrick Graeme, killed the Master Rollo in a "fair fight." Graeme had left his sword at home and borrowed James' sword when an argument arose with Rollo. As a known leader of the Jacobite's, King William of England was persuaded by Rollo's mother, Lady Rollo" (a relative) to find a reason to expel James from Scotland. It was also known that her husband, Lord Rollo, was infatuated with James' widowed mother Isabelle. Patrick Graeme was never punished. In 1715, James returned to Scotland where he was knighted. He carried the Standard for James VIII in the Battle of Sheriffmuir where the Jacobite Army unsuccessfully tried to free Scotland from British rule. They tried again in 1745 and lost. Many Scots were killed or exiled to the American Colonies. (See Edmonstone Chronicles).

Three-hundred members of the Thompson family fought in the Revolution, seventy-seven from Virginia. James Thompson born 1742 (#A114175) a Captain from Augusta County was at the Battle of King's Mountain. Matthew Thompson (#A114406) born in Ireland gave patriotic service in Augusta County. William Thompson, Jr. (#A114657) gave patriotic service. He was born in Ireland in 1722. He married

Mary Patton about 1748 in Augusta County. Captain William Thompson (#A114682) born 1750 in Scotland was in the Artillery.

*History and crest sourced from Wikipedia, *free pages at genealogy, roots web, and ancestry*

THE PATTERSON FAMILY

The Patterson families were originally from Scotland. They are found in Ross-shire and stem from the Earl of Ross in Northern Scotland where they had family estates from very early history. Many moved to Northern Ireland during the plantation of Ireland. James Patterson was born about 1695 in Ireland, possibly Donegal. James immigrated to Nottingham Township in Chester County, Pennsylvania before 1720. By 1719, there were enough Scotch/Irish Presbyterians in Chester County to obtain the name Donegal for their Township. James Patterson was one of those first settlers. The settlers build the first Presbyterian Church, pictured.

James married Ann Corry, daughter of Matthew Corry between 1715 and 1720 in Chester County. They moved to Augusta County Virginia in 1740 and James patented two tracks of land on the Long Glade. They returned to Chester County where James wrote his will in 1740/41. His will was probated March 26, 1741. They had seven children born in Chester County. Robina, the youngest was born after James died. His will named his wife Ann and children Margaret, Mary (who married John McGill Sr.), Ann, Samuel, Rebecca, and James. Robina was not mentioned, but identified later. Ann qualified as administratrix and moved the family back to Augusta County were they settled permanently on James Long Glade property. Ann married secondly, Andrew Irvine. They had one son, Francis. Margaret Patterson born about 1720 married Matthew Edmiston. Matthew Armstrong was named guardian for Samuel and Matthew Edmiston surety. Matthew became guardian for Robina, his young sister-in-law. On June 20, 1764, Matthew and Margaret deeded Samuel a tract of land on Borden's grant. On October 15, 1765, Samuel qualified as executor of Andrew's Irvine's will, which named his wife Ann, his minor son Francis and Andrew's brothers, Edward and Francis Irvine. Ann died in 1765 in Rockbridge County Virginia.

Thirty members of the Patterson family from Virginia fought in the Revolution. James Patterson (#A08641) born 1745 in Pennsylvania was with the 12th Virginia Regiment, James (#A131457) born 1723 probable brother of Margaret furnished supplies in Augusta County. One-hundred and sixty-seven Patterson members fought in the war, seven were at King's Mountain.

*History, pictures, and crest sourced from free pages at Ancestry, Genealogy, and Wikipedia

THE CORY FAMILY

The Corry family originated in Scotland and many moved to Ireland during the Plantation by James VI. They were a landed gentry and Thomas Corry of Kellwood had a charter dated January 12, 1507 from James IV for the lands of Thomaston along with several others. The Thomaston Castle (pictured) is located near Maybole and was built in the 13th century by Thomas Bruce, the nephew of Robert the Bruce. Thomas also had a charter from James V for the lands of Newly and Clonlothry. The lands of Thomaston passed to his son John and then to his son George of Kellwood. George's son died and the land passed to his daughter Anne Corry. She married the Laird of Grimmet, John McLlvane and the lands passed to him. The rest stayed in the family.

Anne's brother, John Corry arrived in Ireland in 1641. In 1665, he purchased the Castle Coole (pictured) in the County of Fermamagh at the cost of 860 pounds and founded the Earls of Belmore and the Cole family as Earls of Ennskillen. His father was John Corry of Thomaston. John of Coole Castle died in 1708. It is unknown if any of the relatives of these men immigrated to America. Information on Matthew Corry born about 1675, father of Anne who married James Patterson, is unavailable, but is likely related to the above men possibly the son of the above George.

Fifty-two members of the Corry/Corey family fought in the Revolution, several were from New Jersey. Lieutenant James Corry and another James were killed at King's Mountain.

*Pictures and history sourced from Wikipedia and Ancestry

THE SMITH FAMILY

Steven John Conway has researched the Smith family for many years. He discovered they inherited the Viking gene. The Vikings often raided the Irish and Scottish coasts and intermarried with the Gaelic families in both countries between 795 and 1014. The Normans were also descended from the Vikings in the tenth century who conquered part of France. They came over to England with William the Conqueror in 1066 and intermarried with the Irish nobility, establishing the Norman-Irish feudal families, including Fitzgerald, Burke and Butler families, rulers of Ireland in the sixteenth century. Theobald Le Botiller Fitzwalter, the first Chief Butler (Governor) is the ancestor of the Butler family of Ireland as well as the Smith family, a common ancestor. (See Butler Family)

One of the first by the name of Smith in the Colonies was John Smith. He was a famous explorer and writer (1580-1631), who help found Virginia. He married Pocahontas the daughter of an Indian Chief after she saved him from being killed by her father. He took her to England where she died in 1622.

Osmond and Austin arrived in Virginia between 1620 and 1623. Osten Smith landed in Jamestown in 1624. Augustine Smith arrived in Virginia in 1713 and Ambrose Smith arrived in 1714. A John Augustine Smith was later President of William and Mary College.

Colonel John Smith Sr. was born in 1698 in England. He moved with his parents to Ulster, Ireland and was a Colonel in the British Army. He married Margaret Jane Harrington Schoonhester in 1719 and immigrated to America about 1730 with his wife and children. He settled first in Chester County, Pennsylvania with several other families from Ireland, including Thompson, McDowell, and Edmonstone/Edmiston. In 1740, he moved to Augusta County, Virginia, which at the time was Orange County. His sons were listed as Abraham born 1722, Henry born 1727, John born 1730, Daniel born 1739, Joseph born 1742, David 1743, Jonathan born 1744, James Jordan 1746, and daughter Margaret Louisa born 1741.

Colonel/Captain John Smith qualified in Orange County as Captain of the Militia for Augusta County and had several forts built for protection against the Indians. His seal is pictured above. One of the forts was in Botetourt on the James River, near what was to become Pattonsburg. During the French and Indian War, Smith was captured and sent to France. He returned two years later. His son Lieutenant John Smith was killed and his son Joseph died a prisoner. Colonel Smith's sons Abraham, Daniel, and Henry were also prominent in the French and Indian War. His son-in-law, Hugh Bowen, was killed at King's Mountain during the Revolution. He was one of the first members of the Vestry for the Parish of Augusta County in 1747. He received a grant of four-hundred acres of land for his service in the war. Colonel Smith had patented a total of eight-hundred acres by 1745. He and his sons owned many acres of the best land in the Shenandoah Valley. Several members of the Smith family were baptized in the Tinkling Springs Church. Colonel Smith died at age seventy-four.

Abraham Smith was born in Ulster, Ireland in 1722. He married Sarah Caldwell in 1744. Only two of his children are recorded. It might be possible they had a daughter, Jane born in 1746 who married James Edmiston. (Jane Smith's family is unclear at this time.) His son John, was born in 1755. He married Sally Moore. (More on this family is found in the book *"The History of Pocahontas County."* Son Henry was born in 1758.

Over three-hundred members of the Smith family fought in the Revolution, two-hundred and thirteen members were from Virginia. Lieutenant Benjamin Smith (#A104804), born 1761 in Augusta County, fought under Colonel Daniel Smith (#A105023) of the Virginia Militia. Daniel was born 1724 in Ireland, the son of Colonel John Smith, John Smith Ensign (#A105985) born 1755 in Augusta County fought at Point Pleasant and King's Mountain, Captain Thomas Smith (#A106029) born 1744 in Augusta County was in the Augusta Militia. Captain William Smith (#A106131), born in 1730 in Augusta County, fought at King's Mountain. Zachariah Smith (#A106184) born 1725, provided supplies. Twenty-four members of the Smith family fought at King's Mountain, only one was wounded.

*History, seal, and crest sourced from Ancestry, Wikipedia, and Smith Family. For more on the family see *"Gleanings of Virginia History."*

THE GILLILAND FAMILY

The name Gilliland originally came from Ireland. It was spelled Mac Gille Fhoalain in Gaelic. Members of the family moved to Scotland where they are found in Midlothian during the reign of King David 1324-1371. The Clan members were followers of St. Fillian, who was an Abbot near St. Andrews in eighth century Scotland. The name became almost non-existent in Ireland by the beginning of the 17th Century, but it appeared again with the Plantation of Ireland in the 16th and 17th centuries.

John Gilliland was born in Scotland about 1660 and moved to Ireland before 1685. His wife is unknown. His son Samuel was born in 1685 in Ireland. John and his family left Ireland and arrived in New Jersey about 1685-86. He died in 1750 in New Brunswick, New Jersey. Samuel married Elizabeth Smith (her parents are unknown) and they had one known son Nathan born 1720 in Chester, Lancaster, Pennsylvania. The family then moved to Virginia. Nathan married Jane Donahue in Augusta County, Virginia in 1745. Jane was born in Scotland in 1720. (Her parents are unknown). They had five children, James born in 1749, William born 1751, Samuel born 1755, and Elizabeth born 1750. Nathan died in Greenbrier, Virginia in 1790. His wife Jane died the same year. Their son James born March 16, 1749, married Lydia Armstrong in 1770. She was born in Greenbrier October 17, 1755, the daughter of James Armstrong and Sarah Dyer, both born in Virginia. Robert Armstrong, father of James, was born 1696 in Antrim, Ulster, Ireland. His wife Lydia Louden was born 1700 in Londonderry, Ireland. James and Lydia had seven children in Virginia, Robert, Jane, Elizabeth, James, Samuel, Mary Polly born 1790 in Greenbrier, and another Jane. After Lydia Armstrong died, James married Jane Edmiston, the widowed mother of Andrew Edmiston. James served as an Ensign in the Greenbrier Militia during the Revolution. He was at the Battle of Kings Mountain where he was elected Lieutenant (#A044934). Eighteen members of the Gilliland served in the Revolution, four from Virginia.

Mary Polly was July 4, 1790 in Greenbrier, Virginia and married Andrew Edmiston January 6, 1807. (See Edmiston Family). They had twelve children, James, Elizabeth, Nathan, George McNeel Edmiston born May 19, 1811 in Mill Point, Pocahontas County, Virginia, Lydia, Matthew, Andrew, Jane, Elizabeth, Martha, Mary, and William.

George McNeel G. Edmiston born 1811 married Nancy Jordan. She was born January 9, 1810 in Pocahontas County. She was the daughter of John J. Jordan, Sheriff of Pocahontas County, and Mariam McNeel. They were married 1796 in Bath County. Mariam was born May of 1778 in Pocahontas County, the daughter of John McNeel and Martha Davis. John was born 1745 in Fredrick County, Virginia and Martha was born January 28, 1743 in Wales. Nancy died December 8, 1851 in Hillsboro. She is buried in the McNeel Cemetery in Pocahontas County. George moved to Nevada, Missouri with his sons where he died in 1894.

*History and crest sourced from Ancestry, Gilliland Family History, and *"Historical Sketches of Pocahontas County"*

THE JORDAN FAMILY

The name Jordan was originally from Normandy where the name was recorded as Jordanus. The families  of Richard, Robert, and William came to Ireland with the English invaders in 1168. They accompanied the Earl of Pembroke in his invasion and acquired land from King John, the English King. The family rose to become Lords of Mayo of Roslevin Castle, (ancient Mayo crest and castle ruins pictured).

Samuel Jordan at age thirty-one was one of the "ancient planters" in Virginia. He was born in Dorsetshire, England in 1578. He was a member of the Virginia Company of London under the second charter. He sailed for Jamestown on the ship *Seaventure* commanded by Captain Christopher Newport. They were shipwrecked on an Island in Bermuda. They spent nine months building another ship. Jordan was one of the most educated men on the voyage and was chosen to keep a journal of the events. He was granted four-hundred and fifty acres of land in Jamestown and another two-hundred and fifty for his servants. He built a fortified home called Jordan's Journey on the banks of the James River. He was a member of the first Assembly of Jamestown in 1619 and listed a gentleman planter at Charles City. He survived the Powhattan Indian raid in 1622 when they tried to destroy the entire colony. He was married to his first wife Frances in England and had four children, Anne Marie, Robert, Samuel, and Thomas. He married second, Cecily Bailey and had two daughters Mary and Margaret born after her father's death in 1623. Some of his descendants are thought to have moved to North and South Carolina.

According to tradition, three brothers, Andrew, James and possibly a John or William immigrated to Virginia from County Down Ireland about 1760. Andrew settled around Bullpasture Mountain in what is now Pendleton County, West Virginia. James Jordan move to Greenbrier County were he settled and raised a family. He and his family survived an Indian attack in 1778 and took shelter in Fort Donnelly.

John Jordan was born in 1766 in County Down. His parents are unknown, but it is possible he is related to the above brothers. However, he did not arrive in America until 1783. As the result of an injury, he lost a hand while he was a young man. Prior to this, he had been a tailor. He taught school for a while, saved his money, and came to Pocahontas County as a traveling merchant dealing in Irish linen and other merchandise. He was a "hard money" man and converted all of his paper money to silver and gold. He had over a half a bushel of coins when he married Mariam McNeel on December 30, 1796 in Bath. She was the daughter of John McNeel, the first resident of the Levels in Pocahontas, County. After their marriage, John purchased several servants to help his new wife. They had eight children, Jane born in 1798, Isaac, John McNeel, Mary, Nancy born 1810 (who married first Isaac Collison and second George McNeel Edmiston), Abram, Martha (Mattie) and Franklin born 1816. After their marriage, they settled in Millstone Run between Locust and Hillsboro in Pocahontas County. In 1810, he bought the farm of his brother-in-law, Griffith Evans husband of Martha McNeel. On March 5, 1822, the County was organized. John was sworn in as High Sheriff of Pocahontas County. He gave bond of $30,000. Isaac and Abram McNeel were bondsmen. On March 6, his son Jonathan was appointed deputy.

John was one of the original ruling elders of the Oak Grove Presbyterian. His  home was open to both Methodist and Presbyterian ministers. He later donated the site for the Methodist Church near his residence. He died February 15, 1836 and buried near the ruins of the old Millstone Church marked by a neatly carved stone.

One-hundred and twenty members of the Jordan family fought in the Revolution, twenty-two from Virginia.

*History sourced from Wikipedia and Ancestry. Pictures of the old and new Oak Grove Presbyterian Church is from the history of Pocahontas County preservation

THE MCNEEL FAMILY

The windy Hebrides island of Barra and the west sea coast of Scotland are the ancestral homes of the McNeel/MacNeil family. According to 1049 records in Scotland, Niall a direct descendant of Irish King Niall of the nine hostages, landed in Barra and founded the Clan MacNeil of Barra. His younger brother Anrothan married a Princess of Dalriada from which sprang most of the early Scottish Kings and started the MacNeil house of Colonsay. This branch acquired the lands beyond the Firth of Lorne. Both branches developed independent of each other. Some branches of the McNeel family later moved to Ireland and Wales.

The MacNeil/McNeel Kiessimul Castle is located in Castle bay, Barra in the Outer Hebrides Islands and dates back to the mid sixteenth century. It sits on a rocky inlet surrounded by sea. It can only be reached by boat. It is all but impregnable and has been the stronghold of the MacNeil/McNeel's since the eleventh century. It has its own fresh water wells. It was abandoned in 1838 and deteriorated. In 1937 Robert Lister MacNeil, Chief of the McNeil Clan at the time purchased it. He made efforts to restore it. In 2001, the Chief of Clan MacNeil leased the Castle for one-thousand years to Historic Scotland for the annual sum of one pound and a bottle of whiskey. The National Records of Scotland classified the Castle (pictured twice) in the 2011 census as an inhabited island "that had no usual residents at the time."

The father of the first Virginia McNeel family was born in Wales in 1700 and died there in 1760. His son, John McNeel, born in Wales in 1725, immigrated to America before 1744. John married Elizabeth VanMeter August 2, 1744 in Pennsylvania. She was born in 1728 in New Jersey, the daughter of Abraham Van Meter, who was born in 1700 in Somerville, Somerset, New Jersey. He married Eliza (parents unknown) born 1705. John McNeel and Elizabeth moved to Virginia had two know children, John McNeel born in 1745 in Winchester, Frederick, Virginia and Thomas McNeel born in 1747. John Sr. died in 1800. He is buried in the McNeel Cemetery. Elizabeth died in 1846.

John McNeel was born 1745 in Winchester, Virginia and moved to Cumberland Valley in Maryland where he had a boxing confrontation with another young man and thought he had killed him. He fled to the wilderness of Virginia and settled in what is now known as Little Levels in Pocahontas County. He later discovered he had not killed the man. He then returned to his home in Winchester, married Martha Davis in 1768 and took her back to Little Levels. She was a Calvinist Methodist and brought a Welch Bible with her when she married John. Martha was born January 28, 1743 in St. Mary Haverfordwest Pembroke, Wales to Thomas and Ann Davis. She helped her husband build the White Pole Church and recorded as performing the first burial rites in the McNeel Cemetery. The Bible was passed down through the family and is now preserved by the Pocahontas Historical Society.

John and Martha had eight children: Abraham born 1767, Marian Phoebe born 1769 who married John Jordan, Nancy born 1769, (probably twins) Mary born 1771, Isaac born 1775, Absolem born 1776, Naomi born 1777, and Enoch born 1782.

John McNeel/McNeil served in the Militia during the Revolution and was at Point Pleasant (#A078561). His brother, Thomas born 1747 (#A078570) also served. Fourteen members of the McNeil family participated, thirteen from Virginia. John died in 1825, Martha died in 1830, and both are buried in the McNeel Cemetery. Pictured are John McNeel and his barn built in 1760, which still stands.

*History and pictures sourced from Wikipedia, free pages Genealogy and Ancestry

THE VAN METEREN FAMILY

The Van Meteren family is traced to Cornelius Van Meteren born 1475 in the Netherlands. He married Otto Van Beeste in 1500. She was born in 1479. Their fourth generation descendant, Jan Joosten Van Meteren was born in 1630 in Guilderland, Thielerwardt, Netherland and died in Burlington, New Jersey June 13, 1706. He married Maeijken Macyken crom Hendricksen December 12, 1646 in the Netherlands. Their son Joost Jan Van Meteren born 1656 in Guilderland and married Sarah Du Bois December 12, 1682 in Kingston, Ulster, New York. She was born September 14, 1662 in Hurley, Ulster, New York and christened in 1664 in the First Dutch Church in Kingston. She was the daughter of Louis Du Bois and Catherne Blanchan. Joost and his parents immigrated on April 12, 1662 on the ship *"De Vois"* (The Fox). They lived in Wiltwyck and Kingston in Ulster County.

The Minnisink Indians attacked the villages of Hurley and Kingston on June 10, 1683 and burned them taking several women and children hostage. Joost Jan and his mother were among them. After ten weeks, Captain Martin Krieger and a group of soldiers from New Amsterdam rescued twenty-three hostages. After this experience, Joost was fascinated with the Indians and later dealt well with them and gained their assistance in exploring the wilderness. He explored the South Branch of the Potomac River Valley and urged his sons to move there. Sons, John and Isaac, obtained a grant of 40,000 thousand acres in 1730 in Berkeley County, Virginia from Lieutenant Governor Gooch. His other children were Rebecca, Lysbeth, Rachel, Hendrik, Abraham (born in 1700 in Somerville, Somerset, New Jersey married Eliza (?) about 1718), Jacob, and Malinda. Joost changed the spelling of his name to John Van Metre. He died January 13, 1706 in Salem, New Jersey.

Abraham and Eliza's daughter Elizabeth, born in 1728, married John McNeel Sr. John McNeel Sr. and Elizabeth's son John, born in 1745, married Martha Davis.

*History and crest sourced from Wikipedia, Ancestry, and Clan Van Metre

THE DAVIS FAMILY

The Davis family is originally found in Flintshire, a historic county in Wales created after the English defeated the Welch Kingdom of Gwyneed in 1284. It is located in northeast Wales where the Davis family owned estates. They were descended from Cynrig Efell, Lord of Eglwysegle, the twin son of Madog ab Maredadd, who was the great grandson of Bleddyn ap Cynvin, Prince of Powys, head of the third Royal Tribe of Wales. He governed all Wales for thirteen years before his murder in 1073. The name of David, a "clericus," is recorded in Lincolnshire England in 1150.

The first recorded Davis to arrive in America in 1585 was Sir John Davis and his son. He was a noted seaman working for Queen Elizabeth, who sailed in the Hudson River. He was a navigator and explorer and tried to find a northwest passage.

William Davis was born in 1617 in Carmarthenshire, Wales. (Pictured is Carmarthen Castle). He died December 9, 1683 in Roxbury, Suffolk County, Massachusetts. He arrived in Massachusetts about 1635 from Somerset, England. He married Elizabeth, his first wife, in 1641 in Roxbury. He had two more wives and several children. His family members were active in New England for centuries.

Thomas Davis was born in Carmarthen, Carmarthen, Wales in 1718. He married Anne Meredith on June 3, 1742 in Radnor, Wales. She was born about 1721. They came to America some time after 1753. They had five children all born in Wales. Sarah and Martha (twin girls) were born in 1743 in Saint Mary Haverfordwest, Pembroke, Mary was born in 1745, Ann born 1747, and Elijah born 1753 and died 1813. Thomas died in Bridgewater, Rockingham, Virginia in 1778. It is unknown if the family of William and Thomas are related. Anne died in Hampshire County, West Virginia, date unknown. Their daughter, Martha Davis, married John McNeel in 1768. She died in Pocahontas, West Virginia in 1830

Elijah Davis, who was born in 1753, son of Thomas and Anne, was a private in the Revolution. He enlisted in the Continental Army in Virginia. According to a story passed down through his family, he was on guard duty one very cold winter night. He was not dressed for the weather, due to the lack of warm clothing for the troops and he was poorly fed. He was near freezing, and fearing he was near death, he gave the sign of extreme distress, a sign known only to members of the Order (Masonic) of whom he was a member. A young English officer among the prisoners he was guarding answered the signal. He said,

> "Let me take thy gun. I will faithfully guard my fellow prisoners whilst thou go and refresh thy self."

The British officer, saving Elijah's life, faithfully carried out the promise. After recovering, Elijah served his remaining time, taking part in several hard fought battles and several smaller actions. Following the end of the war, he married and moved to the Winchester, Virginia area with his family, where they lived in a log cabin.

This amazing story is only one among several Revolutionary War accounts of men in opposing army's helping each other. The men were members of the Order of Freemasons. Although the story does not mention the name of the Order, the behaviors is true to the Masonic tenets.

Three hundred members of the Davis Family fought in the Revolution, one hundred and twelve from Virginia and ten were in the Battle of King's Mountain.

*History, picture, and crest sourced from Ancestry and Wikipedia

THE DUFORT/TEAFORD FAMILY

The border between France and Germany changed several times do to a number of wars. France and Germany changed control of Alsace-Lorraine four times in seventy-five years shifting the people's citizenship. The Dufort name is first found in Alsace in Limousine France where the family held a seat before the twelfth century with lands and estates. Dufort is the name of a French Village in southwestern France at the southern end of the Pyrenees Mountains. It was at one time the seat of a feudal Lordship, which gave its name to this family. Although earlier lords are known, this family is only clearly traceable to Arnaud de Dufort in 1305, who acquired the "fife of Duras" by his marriage to the niece of Pope Clement V. (The Chateau de Duras is pictured). His descendant, Gaillard de Dufort, embraced the  side of the King of England and went to London in 1453. He was made Governor of Calais and a Knight of the Garter. His son Guy Aldonce married and had six sons, three became very prominent. About 1740, a descendant, Pierre Grimod du Fort was a "fermier general" and art collector under Louis XV. The branch of Dufort-Cavric dating from the sixteenth century now represents the family of Dufort in France. Henri marques de Dufort-Cavric (1812-1884) was a well-known politician and was elected several times president of the chamber of deputies. The name is also found in France near Luxemburg.

During the 1700's, wars ravaged Germany and France. Many were driven from their homes by religious disputes and they looked to the Colonies for freedom. Jacob Duffort/Teaford arrived in Philadelphia on the ship "Hero" with his wife Christenah. The spelling of the last name changed when they came to America. They signed the manifest October 27, 1764. Jacob was born January 12, 1735 in Palatinate, Alsace Lorraine, which was in Germany at the time. He married Christenah (last name unknown). His father is listed at Ancestry.com as Hans Phillip Dufort who was born 1690 in Langensoultzbach, Northern Alsace, Germany. He had at least two wives, Anna (Catrina?) and Eva Maria. He died February 1, 1767 in Morris, New Jersey. Jacob and Christenah had six known children who were Margaret, Johan Henrich Henry born 1774, Elizabeth, Jacob, John, and another Margaret. They came through Butler County, Pennsylvania, supposedly had farms in Frederick, Maryland and Woodstock Virginia (the north Shenandoah Valley) before moving to Augusta County, Virginia where Jacob bought land at the foot of Sugar Loaf Mountain about 1780. Jacob was a patriot in the Revolution (DAR #A113194). He is the only Teaford recorded in the DAR records. When he died in 1801, he owned three farms in Augusta County. After his death, Christenah lived with her youngest son George until she died in 1805.

Their son, Johan Henrich Henry Dufford/Teaford was born March 8, 1774 in Shenandoah Valley. He married Margaret Peggy Keller August 1, 1804 in Augusta County, Virginia, the daughter of George Keller. They had ten children, John Henry, Sara Sallie, Jacob B. born 1807, Sophanna, Henry M., Lewis K., Margaret, Samuel, David, and Thomas. John Henrich Henry died in April of 1881 and Margaret in January of 1886 in Augusta County.

Jacob B. Teaford was born August 4, 1807 in August County. He married Philaska Greaver October 30, 1830 in Staunton, Virginia. She was born September 22, 1810 in Augusta County the daughter of William Greaver. They had six children, Sarah Margaret, Mary Sophanna, Eliza Cathren, George William, Jane Priella (Jennie) born 1841, Henry Hileman, Julia Ann and Nancy (Nannie). Jacob built a two story home a few miles outside of Lexington in Rockbridge County on Kerr's Creek were he had a large farm, (pictured). The home eventually became an Inn and stage stop. During the Civil War, both the Union and Confederate soldiers camped there. The Union Soldiers took any food they could find. In order to hide their hams, Jacob hung them from the ceiling in the barn loft. During one of the Union Army's raids,

Jane Priella was in the apple orchard picking apples. She hid in a tree. She and her sister Julia Ann met their future husbands, Confederate Soldiers, Abraham, and Andrew Edmiston, while they were camped on the farm. Their brother George was a First Lieutenant under General Lee, (pictured). He was wounded at the Battle of Point Republic Virginia June 9, 1862. He died the next day, June 10. Jacob took a wagon to retrieve his body. He is buried in the Stonewall Jackson Cemetery in Lexington. Jacob died November 6, 1868 in Richmond, Rockbridge County, Philaska died January 30, 1889 in Lexington. Both are buried in the Stonewall Jackson Cemetery. Jane (Jennie) was born June 27, 1841 in Rockbridge County. She married Abraham (Abram "Abe") Edmiston in Lexington October 17, 1866. They had nine children. Their youngest daughter, Lydia Jordan, married Roy Minter. (See Minter Family).

A family reunion is held ever five years in Lexington Virginia. The next one will be July 3-5, 2015. The author attended a reunion and displayed the cape (handed down to her) worn by her great grandmother, Jennie Teaford, pictured. Jacob brought the clock in the background over from Germany in 1764 and it is still working. The picture was taken in the Jacob Teaford home on Kerr's Creek where his descendant lives.

*History and pictures sourced from Wikipedia, DAR, the Author, research by Nellie Woods, and Teaford family history

THE GRUBER/GREAVER FAMILY

The name Greaver stems from the name of Gruber, which is a sir name from the German state of Bavaria. They men of the family were among the warriors and knights in most of the local conflicts and battles. They gave their loyalty to nobles and princes of the early German history and aided in the struggles for control and position within the area. They married into several influential families. Otto Gruber was a Knight living in Austria in 1183. The name is the most common sir name in Austria. Many Bavarians immigrated to America in the seventeenth century to avoid religious persecution and poverty. The name has many spellings and became Greaver when the family arrived in America.

Phillip Ernest (Gruber) Greaver was born in 1703 in Lange au, Alb-Donau-Kreis, Baden-Wuerttemberg, Germany, the son of Joseph Gruber. Joseph was born in 1650 in AsselFingen Alb-Donau-Kreis. Phillip arrived in Philadelphia in 1732 and married Charlotta Frederica Charity in Virginia. She was born in 1718 in Monocracy, Maryland. Her parents are unknown. Phillip and Charlotta had four known children, Maria Elizabeth, Barbara, William born 1740, and Phillip. Phillip died June 20, 1797 at age ninety-four in Augusta, County, and Charlotte died in 1770. (A Phillip Greaver was a member of the Over the Mountain Men at the Battle of Kings Mountain).

William was born May 8, 1740 in Frederick, Virginia. He married Anna Maria (last name unknown) in Augusta County in 1769. They had ten children, George, Mary, Mary Catherine, Phillip, Mary Magdalena, Catherine, John, William born 1776, Elizabeth, and Jacob. William died January 9, 1797. Anna died in 1830 in Augusta County at the age of eighty-five. William (#A055189) was a private in the Revolution and served under Captain William Buchanan. William Greaver was born in 1776 in Augusta County. He married Elizabeth Argenbright January 14, 1802. She was born in 1781 in Augusta County, the daughter of Augustine Argenbright. William and Elizabeth had ten children, Sarah, Valentine, David, George, Phillip, Barbara, Philiska born 1810, and Jane. Elizabeth died April 14, 1816 after her daughter Jane was born. Their daughter, Phaliska, born September 22, 1810 married Jacob Teaford October 30, 1830 in Rockbridge, Virginia. Their home was in Kerr's Creek in Rockbridge County. Jacob and Philiska had nine children. Their daughter Jane (Jennie) Perelliah married Abraham Edmiston. Jennie died January 30, 1889 in Lexington, Virginia. Her daughter Lydia married Roy Minter and their daughter Ruth married Harry Wheeler.

*History and crest sourced from Wikipedia and Ancestry

THE ARGENBRIGHT FAMILY

Argenbright is the Americanized form of the German Erkenbrecht from a Germanic personal name composed of Old High German erkan meaning "pure or perfect" and berht or bright.

Hans George Erchenbrecht was the first of the family to arrive in America. He was born December 20, 1687 in Mosbach, Necker-Oddnwaldd-Kreis, Baden, Württemberg, Germany. He was the son of Hans Adam Erchnbrecht, born January 11, 1654 in Mosback and Anna Caterina Schilling born 1664. His father was Hans Erkenbrecht DeJunge born November 24, 1614 in Mosbach and his father was Hans Erkenbrecht born in 1590 also in Mosbach.

Hans George married Ursula Metzger January 18, 1706 in Mosbach, who was born in 1690 in Steinfurt, Germany. Her father was David Metzger of Steinfurt. They arrive in Philadelphia September 26, 1732 on the Palatine ship *Mary of London* pictured. They were probably Huguenots looking for religious freedom. They moved to Lancaster, Berks County where Hans died in 1752. Hans George and Ursula had nine children, all born in Germany. Their children were, Peter, Hans George Jr., Anna Catharina, Catharina, Maria, Anna, Hans Martin, Johann Martin, and Jacob born November 8, 1722 in Seinfurt, Nordrhein, Westfalen, Germany.

Jacob married Susanna Margaret Pardemer who was born in 1710. Her parents are unknown. Jacob and Susanna were married March 29, 1746 in the First Reformed Church in Lancaster, Pennsylvania. They had twelve children, Anna Maria, Anna Margaretha, John, Captain Augustine born 1755, Catherine, Jacob, John George, Elizabeth, Adam, Allan, Sally, and Jacob. They had moved to Augusta County, Virginia by 1755. He owned three-hundred and twenty-five acres between Cub Run and Peaked Mountain. Jacob died April 22, 1807 in Augusta County and Susanna died in 1807. He is buried in St. John's German Church Cemetery (pictured) in Rockingham County, Virginia. Jacob (#A096358) gave patriotic service in the Revolution by furnishing supplies in Rockingham County.

Augustine Argenbright (Captain) was born June 3, 1755 in Shenandoah Valley, Virginia. He married Barbara Hanger in 1772 who was the daughter of Johann Mechoir Hengerer and Maria Elizabeth Majer. Barbara was born October 28, 1756 in Woodstock, Frederick County, Virginia. Augustine and Barbara had fourteen children, Jacob, Catherine, Felly, Elizabeth born 1781 who married William Greaver, Valentine, Frederick, Sarah, George, David, John, Barbara, Peter, Margaret, and Polly.

In 1778 Augustine volunteered under Captain Alexander Robertson on the expedition against the Shawnee Indians who where making incursions on the Northwestern frontier, proceeding from Staunton, Virginia to Tygert's Valley, which was within the immediate County, but almost a wilderness. In 1781, he volunteered and marched with many others from Augusta County to repel the invasion of the British under Cornwallis who was then advancing into the interior of North Carolina. Shortly before the battle of Guilford, he received a furlough to enable him to visit a sick brother, who was attached to another corps of the army and had been left on the road due to his illness. Before he returned, the battle of Guilford had been fought. Shortly after the battle, Captain Smith of Staunton, commandant of the Company, discharged the troops. During the War, a contractor arrived in Staunton with an enormous number of horses. Augustine, a blacksmith, was employed for four months to shoe them working many Sundays due to the urgency of the times. Augustine was appointed Captain of the second battalion of the Militia in 1788. He applied for and received a pension in 1832 He does not have a DAR number. Five members of the Argenbrite family from Virginia are recorded, Adam (#A003024), George (#A003025), two Jacob's (#A003026 and #A096358) and John (#A003027). Four of the numbers are in chronological order and may indicate they are related.

Augustine died October 23, 1832 in Staunton, Virginia. He is buried in the old Trinity Church Cemetery, (church pictured). Barbara died in 1836 in Staunton and buried there.

*History, pictures, and crest from free pages at Ancestry, Wikimedia, and *Augustine's Revolutionary War Declaration*

THE HENGERER/HANGER FAMILY

The Princes of Schwaben were one of the most important German dynasties in the middle ages as can be seen by the fact that most of the Kings and Emperors between 1138 and 1254 were of the Staufen dynasty, the ruling family in Schwaben. The Dukes of Staufen ruled in the middle ages in what is now the State of Baden-Württemberg. The dynasty was abolished in the thirteenth century due to the change in the political climate.

Michael Huenger was born in 1618 in Baden-Württemberg. His son was Conrad born in 1638 and died in 1681 in Württemberg. His son was Hans Conrad Hengerer born July 27, 1674 and died there. He was a wine grower in 1698 in Hessigheim in the Dukedom of Württemberg. The family dates back to the 1500's. He married Eva Catharina Schweyckher November 7, 1699, the daughter of Balthas Schweyckher.* He married second Eva Maria Holdenbusch and had seven children.

Johann Melchoir Hengerer, son of Hans Conrad and Eva Catarina, was born September 9, 1700 in Hessigheim, Neckar-Kreis, Württemberg and was the first of the family to arrive in America. He was baptized in the Evangelist Protestant Church. Johann was a ducal gamekeeper, forester, and hunter. He married Maria Elizabeth Majer January 24, 1723 in Daisbach Heidelberg, Baden-Württemberg. Her father was Marx Majer. His crest is pictured. They sailed with six children from Rotterdam

December 3, 1740 aboard the ship *Robert and Alice* by way of Cowes, Isle of Wright. The Captain was Walter Goodman who was part of the Palatine Project. They arrived in Philadelphia. Their children were Maria, Johann Frederick, Johann Peter, Johann George, Johannn Phillip, Anna Barbara who married Augustine Argenbright, and Maria Frederica. Johann bought 146 acres October 26, 1746 in Lanchester, Pennsylvania and sold it before moving to Greenbrier and then to Augusta County, Virginia. Melchoir died in 1768 in Virginia. Maria death date is unknown.

Johann and Maria's sons, Frederick, (#A051072) Peter (#A01077) and George (#A051076) all served in the Revolution, Peter Jr. (#A05182) and Frederick Jr. (#A051074) served from Augusta County, Virginia.

Balthas Schweyckher was born September 27, 1624 in Besigheim, Württemberg, his father was Hans born 1586, and his father was Bernhart born about 1565 in Besigheim, Germany. Besigheim Emblem pictured.

*History, pictures and crest from Ancestry, Hanger Family history and Wikipedia

THE KELLER FAMILY

The Keller family appeared in the ancient duchy of Swabia under the Frankish Empire, which was southwest of Germany in the middle ages. It included Alsace on both side of the upper Rhine Valley and parts of Switzerland. The name comes from the German word kelner and kellaere. A kelner was the manager of a noble household and compares to the English Steward. A kellaere was "the keeper of a pantry." The first of the name mentioned in the ancient chronicles was Herman der Kelner (Keller) of Rottweil, Württemberg in 1314.

During the first part of the 18th century, a scheme was promoted for a short time in Switzerland to establish a Colony in Pennsylvania or Virginia of four to five hundred people to rid the country of undesirable paupers, members of the Baptist church, Mennonite, and other dissident religious sects. Members of the Bern Council petitioned Queen Anne to allow such a settlement. It was normally considered a crime against the Fatherland to emigrate, depriving the Country of workers and troops for the Army. Queen Anne agreed to the Colony and many Swiss immigrated. Religion was the reason many of the families moved to Bavaria and other regions before finally arriving in the Colonies.

Johannes Keller was born in 1650 in Siblingen, Kanton, Schauffenhauser, Switzerland. He married Ann Senn who was born in 1654. Their son Bastian was born in 1680. His spouse is unknown. His son George was born in 1700 in Zwibrunken, Schwarenacher, Bavaria. He married "Guth," who was born in 1704. Their son was George K. Keller born in 1719 in Bavaria. He arrived in Pennsylvania about 1732 and married Barbara Ann Hottel in 1733 in Lancaster County, Pennsylvania. She was born in Zurich, Switzerland the daughter of John Johannes Hottel.* George and Barbara had seven children, Elizabeth, Jacob, George K. born 1758 in Virginia, Anna, John, Margaret, and Barbara. George died in 1785 at Mt. Olive, Shenandoah County, Virginia. Barbara died December 5, 1815. George and Barbara's son George K. was born April 19, 1758 in Stoverstown, Augusta County, Virginia. He married Sophia Mowrey May 5, 1786 in Augusta County. Sophia was born in 1764 and died in 1864. George died in 1844. Their daughter Margaret Peggy Keller born May 3, 1791-95 married John Henry Teaford in Staunton, Virginia. She died January 8, 1881.

Forty-eight members of the Keller family served in the Revolution, thirteen from Virginia. George Keller (#A135224) was a private under Captains Thompson, Rankin, and Patterson.

*John Johannes Hottel was born in 1700 in Zurich, Switzerland. He married Margaret (last name unknown) who was born December 5, 1703 in Wisden, Switzerland. They were married in 1720 in Switzerland before coming to America. Margaret died June 1773 in Tom's Brook, Shenandoah, Virginia. John died November 5, 1780 in Tom's Brook. The Hottel name is of French origin from Orleans, France.

Four members of the Hottel family served in the Revolution. Jacob Hottel, (#A058954) born 1752 in Frederick County, Virginia and was a Private under Captain Michael Reader. George Hottel (#A058945) born 1728 in Europe gave patriotic service.

**History sourced from Wikipedia, Ancestry, Teaford Family History, and the ancient crest is from free pages at genealogy

CHAPTER X
THE IRVINE/IRVIN FAMILY

The Irvine family descends from King Duncan I, "first in the name of Eryvine," who died in the Battle of Duncrib in 965. He was the son of Crinan Irvine descendant of the High Kings of Ireland through the Abbots of Dunkeld and the daughter of King Malcolm II of Scotland. William de Irvine is the earliest recorded member of the family in Dumfriesshires, Scotland, who was an armor bearer to King Robert the Bruce.

Sometime before 373 A.D., the Clans of the Gaelic Nations came from the west coast of Spain and established themselves on the East Coast of Ireland. From there they moved on to the west coast of Scotland and the Scots called them "Erinviene's, Erin meaning "from the west" and Viene meaning a "brave, resolute, and worthy man." During the time, the Erinviene families had close relations with the Kings of Scotland. While the Erinviene's were on the west coast of Scotland, they built Irving Castle, which later became the Town of Irvine and named the Irvine River after their clan. In 373 A.D. the Erinviene's along with other Scottish Clans, fought against the Romans. King Eugenius died and all the Clans fled to Scandinavia. For many years, the Scots tried to retake their land. In 404 A.D., Fergus was made King. Fergus II led the return to Scotland and the Erinviene's along with the other clans, drove the Romans out of Scotland. Pictured is Seagate Castle in Irvine.

Three Erivine brothers, Erinus, Grim, and Duncan, grandsons of King Duncan, the first of the Erivine name, was killed at Duncrub in 965 A.D. The oldest brother, Erinus, who was ranked second to the King, inherited the family titles of Seneschal of the King's Rents, Athbane of Dule, and Abbot of Dunkeld. He married the oldest daughter of King Malcolm II.

Duncan was the ancestor of the entire Irvine Clan. Sometime before 1034, Duncan was named Prince of Cumberland by his Grandfather, King Malcolm II. Duncan took several of the Clan to the Scottish border to defend Scotland from England. His uncle brought his Clan, the Ervine's, with him. They  built the Tower of Bonshaw (pictured) along the banks of the Kirtle River along with several manors. This became the ancient home of the Irvine Clan.

Malcolm the II had no male heirs. He was assassinated in 1034 and Prince Duncan, son of Erinus, inherited the throne and became King Duncan I, (Pictured). During his reign, he was defeated by the Norseman. On his way home, he was attacked and killed by his cousin,

Macbeth "the Usurper," who took the throne. He reigned for seventeen years. Shakespeare's play "Macbeth" was written around the murder of King Duncan. Duncan's father, Erinus, was killed in 1045 by Macbeth's army while trying to avenge his son's death. The sons of Duncan went in to hiding until 1057 when Malcolm Erivine raised and army. With the help of Lord McDuff, Thane of Fife, he defeated and executed Macbeth. He also defeated Macbeth's stepson, Lulach, regained his father's throne, and became Malcolm III.

Malcolm III married Margaret, granddaughter of King Stephen of Hungary. She came to England with her father Edgar the exiled King of England, who was defeated by William the Conqueror. She escaped to Scotland with her Knight, Sir William Edmonstone of the Dukes of Flanders. (See *Edmonstone Chronicles Royal Knights and Scottish Kings* by Joan Wheeler LaGrone) Their descendants included King David I "the Saint," who created all of the offices of the royal court. This line ended with Alexander III who died without heirs. The succession was in dispute and thirteen claimants stepped forward to claim the throne, who all had ties to the Erivine line. The primary claimants were John Balliol, the great, great, great grandson of David I and Robert the Bruce the great, great, great, great grandson of David I. Edward Longshank, King of England chose Balliol as King of Scotland when he promised to be subservient to England. When Balliol could no longer tolerate following the dictates of Longshank, Baliol's nephew, John Comyn, stood between Robert the Bruce becoming King, (pictured). The two met at the Church of Grey Friars in 1306 to resolve the dispute. In the heat of the argument, Robert the Bruce stabbed Comyn in the heart and became King.

During his campaign against England, Bruce often received help and refuge from his relative, the Irvine's of Bonshaw, (pictured above). When Bruce was a fugitive from the Court of Edward I, he was forced to hide in the Castle of William de Irvine, who was his secretary and sword-bearer. Sir William de Irvine was one of his principle aids and companions. When Bruce was routed at Methven, William was one of the seven who were hidden in a corpse of Holly when his pursuers passed him by. When Bruce came into his own again, he made William Master of Rolls. William stood by Robert the Bruce during the Battle of Bannockburn in 1314, when the Scots finally defeated the English. Ten years after his service, William was given the Barony of the Royal Forest of Drum in Aberdeenshire, which was formerly owned by John Comyn. He was also given permission of use the private badge of Bruce with three holly leaves, which is still used by the Irvine family today. (See crest). He married Marjorie the granddaughter of Robert the Bruce, who was the daughter of Robert Douglas, Earl of Buchan.* William's grandson, Sir Alexander of Drum, built Drum Castle. It became the family seat. The Irvine families lived in Drum Castle, (pictured) for over six-hundred and fifty years. The fourteenth Laird of Drum was killed at the Battle of Sheriffmuir in 1715 (See *Edmonstone Chronicles*). He had no heirs and the estates passed to his uncle John Irvine of Crimond. Members of the Irvine continued to support the Jacobite cause. The Laird was forced into exile in France for seven years after the defeat of Prince Charles at Culloden in 1745.

Members of the Irvine family moved to Ireland during the Plantation of Ireland by King James VI of Scotland, (James I of England). King James intended to plant loyal wealthy Protestants, Presbyterian and members of the Church of England, in Ulster Ireland as a way to change the rebellious region, which was the most resistant to English control. Beginning in 1606 over half a million acres were confiscated from the Gaelic Chiefs, who fled Ireland in 1607 during the "Flight of the Earls" and given to King James' favorites. Two counties were privately colonized, Antrim and Down, although the others were not. The majority of the Irish were of the Catholic religion. The Lord Deputy of Ireland saw it as a scheme to anglicize the Irish. This later resulted in many of the religious wars in Ireland.

James I of England granted Sir Christopher Irvine, a Scottish Presbyterian Barrister born in 1706, land in Ennskillen, Ireland in 1613. He founded the town of Ennskillen and built the Irvine Castle of Necarne, (pictured). Rebels destroyed the Castle in 1641, but Sir Christopher restored it before he died in 1666. The Castle remained in the family until 1944 when the estate was sold. During World War II, it was used as a hospital and after was never again inhabited. It is now a large Equestrian center. (The Author visited the town of Ennskillen and the Castle in 1998 and found the Castle boarded up with blue windows. However, the Equestrian Center behind the Castle was very active).

Sir Christopher's father was John Irvine of "Camgart" and the House of Drum, who died about 1725 when his will was written. He married Rebecca Crawford, who was the daughter of William Crawford and Ann Corry whose brother John Corry purchased Castle Coole in 1656. (See Corry Family). John's will revealed that he had sons "William of Camgart" and Furnish, Dr. James of Furnish born 1715, who married Ann Armstrong, Lawrence, and John. According to a statement by Samuel Irvine in 1861, his grandfather, John Irvine, of Camgart, was married twice and had fifteen children. His brothers were James, William, and Christopher. His brother-in-law was Gerald Irvine of Greenhill. His grandson, son of Dr. James, was General William Irvine of the American Revolution. William married Ann Callender and had several children including Callender, Ann Nancy, Mary, William Neil, Elizabeth, Mary Bullen, Armstrong, Rebecca, Martha, and twins James and John. His brothers were James born 1748 who married Sarah Davis, Jerrard or Gerard, Captain Andrew of Wayne's Brigade born 1749 in Ireland, Thomas who married Ann Todd, and Dr. Matthew of Lee's Legion who married Mary Keith. This family of Irvine's was the progenitors of the Pennsylvania Irvine families. One of the brothers was the father of Andrew Irvine, who was born in Northumberland and was the father of twenty-two children. He had three wives and had children by each one. The Irvine brothers immigrated to Pennsylvania from Ireland in 1730 before the Revolution and were all prominent patriots in the war.

General William Irvine (pictured) was born in 1741 and educated in Ennnskillen, Ireland. He studied medicine under the famous Dr. Cleghorn in Dublin where he became a Doctor. He served as the ships surgeon on a Man-

O-War in the British Navy. By 1764, he had established himself as a Doctor in Carlisle, Pennsylvania, a Revolution hotbed. It is known that Molly Pitcher, Revolutionary War heroine, at age fifteen went to Carlisle to work for Dr. Irvine. It is here she met her husband William Hayes and became a camp follower serving the Revolutionary soldiers. During the battle of Monmouth, her husband, was in charge of a large artillery cannon, was wounded and Molly took his place firing the cannon.

Dr. Irvine raised and commanded the Sixth Pennsylvania Regiment and became a Colonel in 1777. He fought in the Battle on Monmouth and was in charge of Fort Pitt during most of the war, trying to keep the Indians at bay. He eventually served on General Washington's staff and became a Brigadier General in 1779, (pictured). He and General Butler a member of Washington's staff, were friends from Carlisle and remained so for the rest of their lives. After the war, William was awarded a generous land grant and was appointed head of the distribution of land promised to the troops in Northwestern Pennsylvania. He convinced the State of Pennsylvania to purchase a tract know as the "Triangle" which gave the state frontage on Lake Erie for trade purposes. He was elected Delegate to the Continental Congress of 1786-88. While in New York, he had his portrait painted (see picture) by Robert Edge Pine, an English artist visiting America. He was appointed superintendent of Military Stores and head of Indian Affairs in 1800. He held these posts until his death in July of 1804. His son Callender was overseer of the property the General owned in and around Erie. He was given the land of Brokenstraw farm. He became the Indian Agent for Six Nations. General William Irvine had a cousin, William, from Ennskillen, who also moved to Carlisle.

Three Andrew Irwin's (Irvine) served in the Revolution; one was Captain Andrew of the Pennsylvania Line, the brother of General Irvine. Private Andrew Irwin (#A060455) is cited twice as serving under two different Captains. He married Agnes Armstrong and died in 1797. His wife's sister married Robert Irwin in 1766 and later married James Irwin in 1777. Another Private Andrew Irwin (#A060454), born circa 1745 served in the Seventh Battalion, married Sarah McCullough and died in 1802. Another Captain Andrew Irwin born 1695 was commissioned in the Associated Regiment of Chester County for the French-Indian War February 8, 1747-8. He was fifty-three years of age and died the next year.

William Irvine of the Bonshaw Irvine's and his wife Ann Craig had three sons, Alexander who died in Ireland, David, and Christopher. After his wife died, William and his two sons David and Christopher went to America about 1729 and founded the southern branch of the Irvine family. William Irwin (#A060618) born 1745 in Albemarle County, Virginia was a signer of the Declaration of Independence in Albemarle County in 1779. He married Elizabeth Holt and died in 1809 in Virginia. William Irwin (#A060610) born 1738 served in Pennsylvania married Eleanor Brisbane and died in Wheeling, Virginia in 1815.

James Irvine arrived in New Jersey in 1685. He was deported from Scotland for refusing to take the oath to practice King James II's required religion and was sent to a plantation in the Colonies. At the time, King James II was persecuting the Scottish Covenanters (Protestants) and every minister was required to supply a list of all residents who did not attend the Episcopal Church or refused to take the required "Oath of Supremacy." The Covenanters could not allow any king or head of the church but Jesus Christ. The period between 1680 and 1688 were called the "killing times" and thousands of Scots were killed, sent to prison, or deported for refusing to take the "Oath" or attend church. In 1690, William II took the throne and accepted Scottish Presbyterianism with the Act of Settlement. Nothing more is found on James. Many of the deported Scots later returned to Scotland.

A George Irvine (Irwin), descendant of Alexander Irvine, tenth Laird of Drum, was born to Jared and Jane Irwin in Londonderry, Northern Ireland about 1685. He died in Honeybrook, Chester County, Pennsylvania in 1748. His children were Archibald, Jared, William, and Mary all of Chester County. Unfortunately, little more is known of the descendants of this family as the information is controlled by a "private source." However, members of the family may have served in the Revolution.

A Richard Irwin born 1740 in Armagh, Ireland, immigrated with his five brothers to Chester County, Pennsylvania. They were all sons of David Irwin and his wife Margaret Berry. Richard married Ann Steele in New London, Chester County and their sons Samuel, James, and Ninan were all pioneers in Cherry Hills Township.

A William Irwin, occupation Joiner, and John Irwin, Tanner, are listed in the 1800 cencus of Mead Township of Crawford County. John Irwin, owner of four-hundred acres of land purchased from William Butler in 1798, and George Irwin, born between 1770-75, were both living in Conneaut, Crawford County, Pennsylvania according to the 1810 census. George had two children less than ten years of age and one between ten and fifteen. He also had a daughter under ten. His wife was about his same age. By the 1820 Census, he had seven children. Andrew Irwin, possibly a brother, was also living in Conneaut in the 1810 census. He was forty-four and born about 1766. His wife was under forty-four and they had six children, two boys and a girl under ten, a boy and a girl between ten and fifteen and one between sixteen and twenty-five. It is most probably one of these men was the father of William Irvine born in 1804 in Conneaut, and highly probably it was Andrew. The Scottish naming pattern was usually followed with the oldest son named after the grandfather. In this case, Andrew's father may have been William, born about 1740-1745. (The first girl was named after the maternal grandmother).

William Irvine was born 1804 in Conneaut, Crawford County, Pennsylvania. He married Matilda Spaulding about 1828. She was born in 1809. (See Spaulding family). William and Matilda daughter of Jonathan Spaulding and Margaret Stuntz, and had six children, Harriet, Susan, Willard, Andrew, Maria, and George. William died in 1891 in Prophetstown, Whiteside, Illinois. Matilda died in 1880 in Prophetstown. Their son Willard was born in 1834 in Conneaut and married Lydia Ann Taylor born 1837 and had three children, son Marion, Cora and George. Willard died in Girard, Erie, Pennsylvania in 1905. Their son Andrew Jackson Irvin was born in 1835 in Conneaut. He married Marelda Jane Davis born 1836, daughter of Meshach Davis and Susannah Abraham. Susannah was the daughter of Lot Abraham and Susannah Griffin. (See Davis and Griffin Families).

Andrew Jackson Irvin born 1835 and Marelda Davis about 1859 and had six children, William, John W. Irvin born 1862 in Iowa, Eldora, Andrew, Margaret, and Charles. By the 1880

census, they were living in Grant, Franklin, Nebraska where he was listed as a farmer. Both Andrew and Marelda died in 1909 in Grant. Andrew served in the Civil War in Company K of the Thirty-eighth Infantry.

John Welch Irvin born 1862 in Iowa married Ida May Becker. She was born in Albion, Howard County, Iowa in 1866 to Peter Becker and Charlotte Rima. (See Becker and Rima Families). They had five  children, Roy, Geneva, Ruth, Edna, and Howard J. Irvin born 1901. John invented the automatic oiling system for the overhead cam automobile engine. The United States Patent Office issued the patent, number 1,481,962, to him on January 29, 1924. He is pictured with his six-cylinder 1924 Oakland four passenger Coupe with the first overhead cam engine and his invention of the automatic oiling system. He was a car salesman for General Motors (GM). He took his car to Detroit to sell the invention to (GM). The original 1907 founder of the Oakland Company was Edward P. Murphy. Murphy had sold part of the Company to GM in 1909 that later produced the Pontiac. When Murphy died in 1909, GM bought out the Company. (Pictured is the 1924 Oakland Blue Coup). GM took Irvin's invention, but unfortunately, claimed that their own engineer, John Delorean had invented the system and Irvine was never paid. The first car to use the system was the 1926 Pontiac. Irvin went to court to claim his invention but the attorneys for General Motors won the case. John was very disappointed and never got over the loss. He died in 1945. Ida May died in 1950 in Franklin, Nebraska. Ida May and John were devoted protestant's.

Howard J. Irvin was born November 3, 1901 in Franklin, Nebraska. He married Mary Velma Gingrich of the Catholic Faith about 1928 in Riverton. She was born May 16, 1906 in Riverton, Nebraska. Her mother-in-law, Ida May, seldom spoke to her and resented the marriage. They had three children, Howard (Cork), Thomas J. born 1932, and Catherine Anne. They moved to Fort Collins, Colorado about in 1935 where he owned a trucking deliver business. He received his Public Utilities Permit in 1936 with the help of Colorado State Patrolman, Harry Wheeler. He operated his business until about 1960 when ill health forced him to sell the business. He then worked at Colorado State University along with his wife, Velma, (pictured). They were happily married for over fifty years). Velma died February 25, 1986 and Howard died February 11, 1989 in Fort Collins. They are both buried in Fort Collins.

Thomas Jerome Irvin was born February 2, 1932 in Riverton, Franklin, Nebraska. His family moved to Fort Collins, Colorado where he grew up and attended the Fort Collins Schools. He was active in football, baseball, and swimming and was Captain of the Fort Collins High School Swim Team. He attended Colorado State University (CSU, Colorado A&M at the time) for a year before he joined the Army during the Korean conflict. He took his basic training at Fort Shafter, Schofield Barracks in Hawaii and then sent to Fort Benning, Georgia for Officer Training School (OCS). He graduated in May of 1952 and assigned to Camp

Roberts in Paso Robles, California as a Second Lieutenant where he trained troops for Korea. He became a Company Commander before he was discharged in November of in 1953. He married his high school sweetheart, Joan Wheeler* (See Wheeler Family) April 25, 1953 in San Mateo, California where her father was living. (See wedding picture). Tom and Joan moved back to Fort Collins where Tom graduated from CSU in August of 1957. He worked for the Martin Marietta Company in Denver, Colorado. He was transferred in June of 1960 to Vandenberg Missile Base at Lompoc, California where he became a supply manager in the missile launch area. The family lived in Santa Maria. In November of 1960, the Doctors discovered he had cancer of the colon. He was treated with a new chemotherapy drug, named only XYZ at the time, at the University of California Hospital in San Francisco. He recovered some, but only lived until January 30, 1961 when he died at age twenty-nine. He is buried next to his parents in the Grandview Cemetery in Fort Collins. Tom had his wife Joan had four children, Mike born in 1954, Tim born 1955, Brien born 1957, and Sean born 1960. Joan returned to Denver where she worked as a statistician at Martin Marietta. She met engineer, Clyde LaGrone, (see LaGrone Family) they eventually were married and had two more sons, David and Steven. Irvin descendants include grandchildren, Jaime, and Jenna Irvin daughters of Mike and step granddaughter Nichol and twin grandsons, Kyle and Luke Irvin and Maren Irvin children of Brien. LaGrone grandchildren are Zach and Andrew LaGrone sons of David.

*Sir John Edmonstone married Isobel, also a great granddaughter of Robert the Bruce and daughter of Robert II. Thus, the Irvine's and Edmonstone's became closely related. The families were joined again over six-hundred years later when Thomas Irvin a descendant, married Joan Wheeler in 1953, who was a descendant of Bruce through her grandmother, Lydia Edmiston/Edmonstone Minter. See Edmonstone Family.
**See book *"From Beyond the Veil"* by Joan Wheeler available at Amazon.com
+History, pictures, and crest sourced from Wikipedia, Roots web free pages, Clan Irvine, and *Edmonstone Chronicles* by this author.

THE SPAULDING FAMILY

The Spaulding family was a leaseholder in France of the Earl of Chester who was strongly tied to William the Conqueror. He held Spaulding Abby, from where the name may originate. The family moved to England following Duke William's conquest in 1066. They obtained land in Spaulding, Lincolnshire on the eastern coast. Family members also went to Scotland where they distinguished themselves as a Sept of Clan Murray in Perthshire.

Edward Spaulding landed in Braintree, Massachusetts in 1640 and Thomas Spaulding arrived in Maryland in 1657. Edward Spaulding was born September 13, 1596. He married Margaret Elliott in 1623 in Redenhall, Norfolk, England. They were parents of at least three known children, John born in 1631 in England, Edward born 1635 in Massachusetts who married Mary Brackett and Grace born 1637. They came over between 1632 and 1634 and settled first in Braintree, then Wenham and finally in Chelmsford, Middlesex County. Edward was admitted a freeman in 1640, was a Selectman for many years and a surveyor of highways in 1663. His wife died before 1640 and he married Rachael. They had five more children, Josiah, Benjamin, Joseph, Dinah, and Andrew. Members of the family later moved to New Hampshire.

Jonathan Spaulding, son of Timothy Spaulding and Lucy Skillion, was the first settler in Conneaut, Crawford County, Pennsylvania and helped to develop the area. He was born July 25, 1772 in Cornish City, Sullivan, New Hampshire and lived in Vermont before moving to Conneaut. He was a descendant of Edward Spaulding from England through his son John, who was born in 1631. Jonathan arrived in Erie County in 1795 and died in Conneaut September 24, 1855. He married Margaret Stuntz February 28, 1802 in Conneaut. She was born September 4, 1781 in Lancaster, Pennsylvania, the daughter of Conrad Stuntz and Margaret Ann Briefling. (See Stuntz Family). She died in 1861 in Conneaut. They had ten children including Matilda.

One-hundred and thirty-two members of the Spaulding family served in the Revolution. Able Spalding (#A107495) born 1755 in Massachusetts was at the Lexington Alarm. Able Spaulding, Sr. (#A107496) born 1728 in Plainfield, died 1808. Timothy Spaulding (#A107722) born November 11, 1741 in Connecticut and died in 1777. He was a member of Johnson's Connecticut men, and the father of Jonathan. Ten members of the Spaulding family including Timothy served from Plainfield with three members of the Wheeler family, Ephraim, Josiah and Jonas. Several battles were fought in 1777 including Danbury and Ridgefield Connecticut. Two Regiments and a company of Calvary were sent to help General Horatio Gates defeat British General Burgoyne on the Hudson at the Battles of Saratoga in September and October of 1777.

*History and pictures sourced from Ancestry, DAR, and Wikipedia

THE STUNTZ FAMILY

Conrad Stuntz was born 1738 in Württemberg, Germany. His father was Hermann Stuntz born January 1, 1712 in Nassau, Deggendorf, Bayem, Germany. His grandparents were Justus Stuntz and Elizabeth Weitzel. Conrad was in the German Army and one of the 17,500 German Hessian soldiers (see picture) hired by the British Government to fight for them against the Colonists during the Revolutionary War. At the Battle of White Plains, New York, Conrad, and his brother, Edward, deserted the British forces and joined the Colonists. They fought with them until the end of the War.

After the war, Conrad lived for a short time in Maryland and Virginia and then moved to Lancaster, Pennsylvania where he met his wife, Margaret Anna Briefling. They were married in 1778. She was born in 1760 in Pfalz "on the Rhine," Germany and worked four years and six months in America to pay for her passage. Conrad and Margaret had seven children John, Margaret M. born 1781, Conrad Jr., Elizabeth, Katherine, George, and Mary Magdalene. After the War, as part payment for his services, the Government gave Conrad a one-hundred acre tract of land in Crawford County. By 1807, he had a four-hundred and three acre farm patented to him by the State on August 29, 1807, which was pursuant to his improvement begun May 1, 1801. His son Conrad Jr., received the four-hundred and three acre property immediately to the south the same day. Conrad died July 24, 1810 and buried in the Stuntz Cemetery on his farm, located in Beaver Township. The Cemetery is located in the Northeast corner next to the Erie County line. Margaret died in 1830 in Erie County, Pennsylvania. Their daughter Margaret M. married Jonathan Spaulding.

Conrad is recognized by the Daughters of the American Revolution, patriot number (#A110526). The DAR emblem is pictured. They have no record of his brother, Edward.

*History and Crest sourced from Wikipedia, Ancestry, and Stuntz Family History

THE DAVIS FAMILY

The Davis family is a very ancient family found in Wales. They go back to before David ap Gryffydd, the last Prince of Wales, who was executed in 1276 by King Edward I of England. This Davis family descends from Cynwrig Aplorwerth born 1122 in Dulas, Denbighshire, and Wales. The family lived in Wales until the late 1500's.

Family members moved to Gloucestershire, England and to Marlborough, Wiltshire where James Davis II was born in 1583. He married Cicely Scissile Thayer June 11, 1618 in Saint Mary's Anglican Church parish in Gloucestershire. She was born May 1, 1600 to John Thayer and Joan Lawrence. During Charles II reign and the Bishop Wars, James and Cicely immigrated with his family and brother Thomas and family to the Massachusetts Colony in 1635 aboard the Ship *James*. They were part of the Puritan exodus from England. He and Thomas were among the Puritan Planters who eventually settled in Haverhill, Essex, Massachusetts. They followed the Reverend John Ward who obtained a grant from the government to establish Haverhill. The settlers bought out the rights of the Indians to the land. James and Thomas, both men of wealth, were two of the original twelve settlers and both were among the first five selectmen. James was awarded twenty acres of land in 1667 on which he built the Oyster Plantation. He and his wife Cicely had six children. He was active in the town government most of his life. He died in 1679 and Cicely died in 1673. Thomas, who learned masonry in England, helped to layout the foundation and build the first church. Before the Church was built, during nice weather, the congregation worshiped at the Worshipping Oak Tree still standing.

James descendant James IV moved to East Bradford, Chester, Pennsylvania where John Davis V was born October 3, 1673. He married Mary North and had five children including Abraham born 1702. His descendant, Samuel Davis son of James Davis and Keziah Phillips, moved to Franklin County Indiana where he died in 1855. Samuel's son Meshach born 1811 in Pennsylvania, eventually moved to Ohio. He married Susannah Abraham, December 18, 1834 in Butler County, Ohio. Susannah was born 1813 to Lot Abraham and his wife Susannah Griffin, a descendant of Richard Griffin (and grandson Charles) who immigrated to Roxbury Massachusetts from Norfolkshire, England about 1610-30. Richard is listed as one of the first settlers in Massachusetts. Susannah was a descendant of Noah Abraham born 1697 in Herefordshire, England, who immigrated to East Nantmeal, Chester County Pennsylvania before 1729. Meshach and Susannah had eleven children. The oldest child Marilda Jane Davis born 1835 married Andrew Irvin in Keokuk County, Iowa. She died in Franklin County, Nebraska.

Members of the above families all served in the Revolution. Three-hundred members of the Davis family fought in the War. James Davis (#A030375) born 1761, who married Keziah Phillips, served in Pennsylvania along with sixty-four other Pennsylvania members of the Davis family. Two-hundred twenty-three members of the Phillips family served, twenty-six from Pennsylvania. David Phillips (#A090428) born 1749 was in the Chester County Militia. Twelve members of the Abrahams family served, Henry Abrahams Lieutenant (#A000286) born 1747 served in Pennsylvania and died in Ohio.

One-hundred and one members of the Griffin family served. Charles Griffin (#A048130) grandson of Richard and father of Susannah, was born December 1, 1734 in Delaware was a private in the Washington County Pennsylvania Militia.

*History and pictures sourced from Wikipedia, Ancestry, and Roots web

THE BECKER FAMILY

The Becker name is of Dutch and German descent. Members of the family lived in Yorkshire England where they had lands after the Norman Conquest. Many of the immigrants to the Colonies were from Netherland. Jachem Becker arrived in New York in 1654 and Jan Jurrianse Becker in 1663. Several more members of the Becker family landed in New York in 1709 including Harts, Frederick, Albert, Anna, and Gerhard. Since New York was a Dutch Colony, it is possible they all came from Holland. However, members of the German Palatine arrived in England in 1709 and then came to New York. A Fredrick Becker age twenty-three and single was among them.

Jan Jurrianse Becker of New Amsterdam, New Netherland, immigrant in 1663, was a schoolteacher in Albany, New Amsterdam. He was licensed in 1670 by the Governor "for ye teaching of school children to read and wryte." In 1669, He was appointed notary in Albany and in 1689 was named treasurer for the city and county of Albany. He married Maria Adriens and they had three children. He was a member of the First Albany Dutch Church, pictured. Jan may be the progenitor of the Peter Becker family of Berne, Albany, New York through his son Johannas.

Peter Becker was born around 1782-86, died when his son Martin was quite young. Martin was born May 17, 1809 in Berne. He moved to Racine, Wisconsin in the spring of 1846. He married Hannah Silvernail about 1833 and they had four children, Martha, Lorenzo, Peter born July 15, 1838, and Harvey.

Peter Becker was born July 15, 1838 in Berne, Albany, New York. He moved with his father to Racine, Wisconsin in 1846. He later moved to Iowa where he met his wife, Charlotte Rima. She was born in 1843 in Sandusky County, Ohio. Her parents were Christopher Rima and Ester Storm. Peter and Charlotte were married in 1865 in Keokuk, Iowa. They had three children, Ida Mae and two others. Ida Mae was born in 1866. Charlotte died about 1908 in Bloomington, Franklin, Nebraska. Peter died in 1915 in Franklin. Ida Mae married John W. Irvin in Franklin, Nebraska. She died in 1950 in Franklin. John died in 1945. Their son, Howard J. Irvin, married Velma Gingrich. (See Irvin Family)

Thirty-eight members of the Becker Family fought in the Revolution, thirty-three from New York. Johan Joost Becker (#A205250) born 1740 was a Major from Albany and served under Colonel Peter Vrooman. Johan Peter Becker (#A206208) born 1727 in Albany was a Lieutenant in the Militia and gave patriotic service. Peter Becker (#A008321) born 1721 in Albany was a member of the Committee of Safety and gave patriotic service. Storm Becker Sr. (#A008329) born 1724 was a Captain in the 14th Albany Regiment.

*History, picture, and crest sourced from Wikipedia, Ancestry, and the Irvin Family

THE RIMA FAMILY

Jacobus Rima was born about 1760 in Pfalz, Rhine Germany. He was the son of Johannas Rima Sr. and Catherine Riemau. He immigrated to East Schuyler, Herkimer County, New York where he married Dorothea Plantz April 12, 1785 in Montgomery County. She was born in 1762, parents unknown. They were the parents of Johannes born 1788 and Christopher born July 30, 1805 in Herkimer County. Jacobus died December 24, 1819 in Rome, New York. His widow and children are listed there in 1840. Christopher married Ester Storm who was born in 1811 in Oswego New York and they moved to Ohio and eventually to Cresco, Howard County, Iowa. They had eleven children. The youngest child Charlotte was born in 1843. She married Peter Becker. There are no DAR listings under the name of Rima. Jacobus may have been the earliest immigrant to the United States and was not here during the Revolution.

*History sourced from Wikipedia and Ancestry

THE STORM FAMILY

Dirck Storm was born in the Netherland in 1630. The family lived in Leyden where they dealt in fine cloth. The Storm line goes back to Dederick Storm who lived in Wyck in 1390 and may have been descended from the Vikings. The Vikings overran the Low Countries in 1000.

Dirck's father was City Clerk for Leyden and his grandfather was a Lawyer in the Court of Justice of Holland. At age eighteen, Dirck went to work in his uncle's commercial office as a clerk. He married Maria van Montfoort in Saint Gertrude's church in s'Hertogenbosch. She was from an old family in Leyden. By 1660, he was Town Clerk of the Mayorate of s'Herogenbosh. When Protestant Holland was hit by the rescission caused by the overthrow of Cromwell in England, Dirck sailed for New Amsterdam in 1662 on the ship *The Fox*. He was an entrepreneur and dealt in real estate. He owned a Tavern on Beaver Street in New Amsterdam. He was also a farmer and later became the Town Clerk for several towns including Bedford and Flatbush. He became famous for composing the history of Dutch Community at Sleepy Hollow recording the Dutch Colonel American village life in New York Province. His record book is one of the nation's most valuable historic documents. Dirck and his wife are recorded as members of The Old Sleepy Hollow Church. He died in 1716 in Tarrytown and buried in the Old Church Cemetery. He was of the Dutch yeoman class and able to buy his land outright from the Lord of the Manor. His descendants became notable ministers and Captains of their own boats on the Hudson. Captain Jacob Storm lived in the Phillips Manor House, which is now a museum. Ester Storm who married Christopher Rima was a descendant. (Storm family history)

Several descendants fought in the Revolution. Twenty-five members of the family gave their service. Garret Storm (#A110480) born 1722 in Tarrytown, New York signed the Revolutionary Pledge on August 15, 1775 and gave $500 to purchase arms. Thomas Storm (#A110521) born 1749 in Stormville Duchess County, New York was a Member of the Duchess County Assembly and Committee of Safety. Peter Storm (#A110512) born 1754 was a member of the Duchess County Militia and sign the Articles of Association. Nicholas Storm (#A200693) born 1756 in Phillips Manor, a descendant of Jacob, was a private in the Militia.

*History and crest sourced from Wikipedia, Ancestry, and Storm Family History

THE GINGRICH FAMILY

The family can be traced to Poitou, a French province. Historically, members of the family resided in La Rochelle, France and Vienne and were part of the landed gentry with titles and manor houses. The Gingrich family name is recorded as Gundrich in Berne, Switzerland in 1389. They also lived in the German Palatine in 1669 where they were members of Mennonite religion. They were imprisoned and persecuted in both Switzerland and Germany for their religious beliefs.

Several members of the family emigrated from France to America in the early 1700's. William Gingrich arrived in Lancaster, Pennsylvania in 1724. Ulrich Gingrich came from Strasburg, Alsace and settled in Lancaster in 1747. In Chester County, they were recorded as indentured servants.

Otto Gingrich was born July 3, 1833 in Hesse-Darmstadt, Germany to Herman (Jungrich) Grinch and Maria Bachman. Otto and his brother, Sabastian, sailed for America on the ship *Splendid* from Le Havre, France. They arrived in New York March 31, 1852. Otto and Christian settled first in Butler Ohio. Sadly, Christian died, possible of typhoid fever, just six months after their arrival. They had taken out a loan for their passage and so Otto was left to work off the loan. When it was paid off, Otto moved to Putnam County, where he took out naturalization papers. Otto met and married Anna Leedolf, who was born February 21, 1836 in Hesseldornstadt, Germany. They were married in the Methodist Church on the Line in LaSalle County. Otto had been a Mennonite. Otto and Anna settled in Sheffield, Illinois where they purchased eight acres. They built a fine home and eventually had two-hundred and forty acres. The farm is one of the finest farms in the area and is still in the family. Otto and Anna had seven children, only three survived to adulthood. The surviving children were Otto, Marguerite, and Edward. Anna died in childbirth with her son Edward Julius, who was born October 29, 1867. After Anna died, Otto married Elizabeth Wagner and had six more children, four of whom survived. Otto died October 1, 1913. Otto and Anna are pictured at right.

Edward Julius Gingrich (right) was born October 29, 1867 in Illinois and moved to Nebraska where he met and married Mary Ellen Sullivan, pictured. She was born December 15, 1866 in Binghamton, Broome, New York. Her parents were Jeremiah O'Sullivan and Catherine Mahoney from Ireland. They were married May 10, 1891 in Nebraska where Edward was a farmer in Riverton. Edward and Mary Ellen had five children, John, Lucy, Catherine, Jeremiah M., and Mary Velma born in 1907. (Mary Ellen, right). Mary Ellen died March 20, 1927 and Edward died 1955.

Mary Velma was born May 16, 1907 in Riverton, Nebraska. She married Howard J. Irvin in Riverton, Nebraska in 1928. (See Irvine/Irvin Family). She died February 25, 1986 of cancer. Picture of Velma right was taken after High School. Picture left of Howard and Velma about 1940. They had three children, Howard (Cork), Tom born February 2, 1932, and Cathy. Picture of family taken about 1942, Tom, Cork and Cathy.

*History and crest sourced from Ancestry, the Gingrich family history and Wikipedia

THE O'SULLIVAN FAMILY

The O'Sullivan name is recorded in the territory of Cahir in Tipperary, which was established in the thirteenth century in south-central Ireland in the Province of Munster. The name is primarily found in Counties Cork and Kerry. The O'Sullivan's are the medieval and modern extension of the ancient sept of Cene'l Fingin descendants of Fingin mac Aedo Duib, King of Cashel, or Munster in 601 to 618. They are thus known to be of royal descent. The last king of the Cene'l Fingin/O'Sullivan line died in 847. They then became the chief princes under their close relatives, the MacCarthy dynasty successors of Cenel/Munster.

After the Norman invasion of Ireland in 1169-71, the Clan was forced from their original home in Tipperary to Cork and Kerry and divided into several branches, the main two being O'Sullivan Mor in south Kerry and O'Sullivan Beare in the Beara Peninsula of west Cork and south Kerry. Dunboy Castle County Cork (picture) on the Beara Peninsula was the home of the O'Sullivan Beare, Chief of the O'Sullivan's. It is now in ruins. The O'Sullivan's continued to be harassed by the Normans so they joined with the MacCarthy and O'Donohue Clans. Together they defeated the Normans in 1261-62 and the boundaries between the Gaelic Clans and the Normans were established. They remain so for the next three-hundred years. In the meantime, they inter-married and became friends for a time. In the 1600's all of Munster was in turmoil again and the Clans lost over 500,000 acres to the English settlers in Northern Ireland. With the plantation of the north by James I of England, Northern Ireland became Protestant while the South stayed Catholic. Friction over religion between the two continued for generations.

Jeremiah Eugene O'Sullivan, distant descendant of the O'Sullivan Beare, was born in Bunagara, Listowel, County Kerry in May of 1844. His parents were Eugene O'Sullivan and Mary Nolan (Teahan). He grew up on a farm, which is still owned by the family today. He served in the British Army (pictured) about 1863 and was stationed in Trelee, Ireland, a few miles from Listowel, where he met his wife Catherine O'Mahoney. Reverend Higgins married them in the Saint John Catholic Church in Trelee June 5, 1864. The author visited the farm in 1998 and found the old house had been replaced. The Barns were still the same.

Mary was born October 31, 1845 in Trelee, County Kerry. Her parents were Maurice (Daniel) O'Mahoney *and Mary Murphy.** Trelee is known for the yearly celebration of the "Rose of Trelee" pageant, an international completion held in August and celebrated among the Irish Communities throughout the world. It is one of Ireland's longest running festivals with rose parades, fireworks, entertainment, and live music. A talented young girl of Irish descent is selected each year as the "Rose of Trelee," (pictured).

Jeremiah and Catherine immigrated to Binghamton, New York in 1864 shortly after the Civil War. He became a Citizen of the United States on February 12, 1876 in Broome County, New York. They had eleven children; the first seven were born in New York and the last in Riverton, Nebraska. Tales of flowing grain and free land lured them to Nebraska. Her granddaughter Catherine quotes Catherine as saying, "If we'd stayed in New York, we'd be wealthy." Jeremiah was Foreman on the Burlington Railroad between Red Cloud and Oxford. Their children were Johnny, Mary Ellen born December 15, 1866, Lucy, Thomas, Catherine, Michael, Johana, Ellen Nellie, Jeremiah, Nora, and Bertha. Jeremiah died October 12, 1904 and Catherine died December 30, 1918. Both are buried in Riverton. Catherine and daughter Mary Ellen are pictured. Mary Ellen married Edward Gingrich (see Gingrich Family). Their daughter Mary Velma married Howard Irvin. (See Irvin Family).

*The O'Mahoney name comes from Mathghamban, son of Clan Mac Mael Muda, a tenth century prince and his wife Sadbh, daughter of the Irish High King Brain Boru. It is first found in County Cork where they held a family seat from ancient times. The first to arrive in America in Philadelphia was Lawrence Mahoney in 1745. Five members of the family served in the Revolution.

**The O'Murphy name is derived from O'Murch, meaning sea warrior. The Murphy's have many Septs and Cans and their achievements are numerous and wide ranging throughout the world. It is the most numerous name in Ireland. The name is first found in County Wexford, founded by the Vikings as Waesfjord in Southeastern Ireland where they held a family seat from very early times. Abraham Murphy settled in the Maryland Colony in 1674. He came as an indentured servant on the Ship *Bristol*. Fifty-five members of the family served in the Revolution.

*History, pictures, and crest sourced from free pages at genealogy, Ancestry and Wikipedia

CHAPTER XI
THE LAGRONE/LA GRONE FAMILY

The LaGrone name is recorded in Normandy, France the former Duchy of Normandy very early in French history. They had land and family estates in the seigneurie of l'Eprevier. Normandy, named after the North men or Vikings, was established about 911 AD. The LaGrone's were one of the leading aristocratic families of Normandy. They also branched into De Grondin, a village in the department of Gers in Aquitaine in the region of the midi-Pyrenees of southwest France. The various spellings of the name include Grondin and Grondian. Members of the family from Metz joined William the Conqueror when he invaded England in 1066. Most returned to France, however one family remained in England. The French name is spelled with a capitol "G."

A member of the family (a protestant Huguenot and friend of the King's) attended the second wedding of Henry IV of Navarre to Maria de' Medica in Paris in 1572. While at the Castle of Saint Germain, the gates were closed by the Catholic Noble friends of the Catherine de' Medica (mother of the bride) and the Huguenots were massacred in an attempt to kill the followers of Admiral Gaspard de Coligny, the Huguenot leader. LaGrone and a friend barely escape over the wall. He hid by day, traveling several days by foot at night to his home in Metz, France.* (for more information, see St. Bartholomew Massacre).

A descendant, Adam LaGrone born 1705 in Alsace Lorraine, Luxembourg, arrived in Charleston, South Carolina about 1725. He was to serve in the German Army, which he refused to do. His brother Tobias helped him to escape by stowing-a-way on a Merchant ship. He arrived in South Carolina where he married Mary Kinard before 1727 in Newberry where she was born in 1710. Her parents were probably Johannes Keinat/Kinard, Sr. and Lucia Koch born in Germany and died in Newbery. Both the LaGrone and Kinard families helped to settle the Dutch Fork area. (See Kinard Family) Adam and Mary (Marie) had twelve known children. Their son Tobias was born in 1730. (Adam's brother Tobias arrived in Charleston in 1552). Mary died in 1773 and Adam died in 1784 in Newberry. Tobias married Ann Mary Sptobias, born 1734 in Jamestown, Berkley County South Carolina. There is no further information on her family. They had nine known children. Tobias died in 1775 in Newberry and Ann Mary in 1785. Their son Adam William Sr. married Mary Magdaline Houseal in 1780. She was the daughter of Captain William Housel. (See Housel Family). (John) Adam fought in the Revolution under Captain Housel, his father-in-law. (No DAR number has been established for Adam LaGrone although he is listed in Captain William Houseal's roster). Adam and Mary had eleven children. Their son John Adam William Jr. was born in 1781 in Newberry. Adam William Sr. died in 1803 and Mary died in  1855. John Adam William Jr. married Christina Dominick. She was born in 1785 in Newberry, the daughter of John Dominick and his wife Elizabeth Rickard. After the War, members of the LaGrone family moved on west. John Adam and Christina had ten children. Andrew Jackson (pictured) was born

September 11, 1820. They both died in Deadwood, Texas, Christina in 1847, and John Adam in 1857. They are buried in the LaGrone Cemetery in Deadwood. Andrew Jackson LaGrone) was born September 11, 1820 in Perry County, Alabama where the family had moved from Newberry around 1813. They went on to Louisiana where they stayed a few months before going on to Texas due to the Indian unsettlement in Texas. They finally homesteaded in Deadwood, Panola County, Texas. They owned a large amount of land and helped to develop that area of Texas. Andrew Jackson married Lucinda Clementine Gibbs, daughter of Elhanan Winchester Gibbs, Sr. and Francis Polly Williams, September 6, 1846 in Panola, County. She was born February 4, 1827 in Lamar County, Alabama. (See Gibbs Family) They had seven children; the oldest Hiram was born in 1847. Andrew died March 18, 1885 and Lucinda on May 20, 1892. They are buried in the LaGrone Cemetery in Deadwood, Texas.

Hiram Clark LaGrone was born December 21, 1847 in (Linus) Deadwood. At age sixteen, he served two years in the Confederate Army during the Civil War as a message runner. He was captured and in the Union Army prison in New Orleans until the close of the war. After the war, he was a member of the Horace Randall Camp #163, United Confederate Veterans in Carthage, Texas. The Tony Smith, South Carolina Confederate Veterans Camp #38 of North Charleston, South Carolina, honored him as a true Confederate hero. Hiram's first wife was Margaret Emma Potts, whom he married June 20, 1867 in Deadwood. They joined the New Prospect Baptist Church in Deadwood on September 10, 1871. They had no children and after she died, Hiram married Ellen (Joiner) Gibbs, May 30, 1872, a young widow with a two-year-old daughter, Mattie. Hiram and Ellen had at least five more children, Ella, Judson, William, Preston, and Eva. After Ellen died in early 1885, Hiram married Sarah Salina (Sally) Bozeman May 28, 1885. (Hiram, Sally and their three oldest children are pictured). Sally was born June 28, 1864 in Spring Ridge, Caddo, Louisiana to James Richard Bozeman Jr., and Sarah Rice. (See Bozeman Family) Hiram and Sally had eight

more children; Ollie, Don, Ethel, Clarence, Emma, Ellen, Cecil and Winfred Cooper (Kip) born 1905. All of his children were college graduates. Three of his sons became preachers; son Don started the First Methodist Church in Tulsa, Oklahoma.

Hiram was a rancher, merchant and owner of several sawmills and gins. He started the Deadwood general store and he and his brother built the Deadwood Methodist Church (pictured above) next to the LaGrone Cemetery. Hiram set aside seven acres for the family cemetery built around the first LaGrone grave, which was that of his grandmother Christina Dominick LaGrone who died in 1847. He was also publisher of the Panola Watchman newspaper. His large ranch was partly in Louisiana. According to the family tradition, he died from a broken neck when he was bucked off his horse while mending fences on his ranch. After his death, oil was discovered on his land and is managed today by a family member. The ranch is still in the LaGrone family today. A family reunion is held in Deadwood every May 1st where members of the family gather each year. Hiram died in Shreveport, Caddo Parish Louisiana and buried in the LaGrone Cemetery in Deadwood beside Sally, (gravestones pictured).

Winfred Cooper (Kip) LaGrone was born July 5, 1905 in Deadwood. He graduated first from North Texas Teacher's College and then received a Masters from Texas A & M where he played end in the football team. He made the second All-American team in 1929. He was also in the Army ROTC program. He married Geraldine Beason (pictured right) on January 23, 1931. He met his wife through a relative who attended the Oklahoma Women's College with Geraldine. She was the daughter of Dr. Clyde W. Beason and Rowena Fish of Claremore, Oklahoma. (See Beason and Fish Families) When they decided to get married, they did not have the required papers for a license in either state so solved their problem by being marrying on the Oklahoma/Texas State line by his brother Don LaGrone, a minister in Oklahoma. They eventually got the papers. Kip was a teacher, Indian Agent in Oklahoma and a Thirty-Third Degree Mason. He was called into service at the beginning of World War II where he became a Lieutenant Colonel (pictured right). After the War, he continued to work for the Government in the FHA division. He earned a law degree from the University of

Arizona. He and his wife, Geraldine (Gerry) had two children, Clyde W. LaGrone and Lynn Beason, who died young in an auto accident will attending college in Tucson. Kip died March 4, 1980 in Butte, Silver Bow, Montana where he had moved to be with his son, Clyde after the death of his wife. He is buried in the Fort Gibson National Cemetery, at Muskogee, Oklahoma.

Clyde W. LaGrone was born August 14, 1932 in Tulsa, Oklahoma. He attended several schools primarily in Oklahoma (pictured right). He graduated from High School in Oklahoma City where he lettered in four sports and graduated with honors. He received an appointment to West Point where he graduated in 1954 as a second Lieutenant. He then attended Ranger training, Paratrooper school, and several others. He became an expert marksman and won the NAR Cup. He attended rifle matches through out the United Stated representing the Army. He resigned his commission in 1958 and returned to collage at the University of Colorado where he

graduated in Aeronautical Engineering. He spent the summer of 1959 traveling in Europe for the University of Colorado where he inspected the University wind tunnels. After graduation in 1959, he was hired by Martin Marietta in Denver. He worked in the Titan I project. In 1961, he met his wife, Joan Wheeler Irvin, at Martin in Denver where she was working as a statistician. Her husband, Tom Irvin who had also been with Martin, died of cancer while working in the

Titan I project at Vandenberg Air Base in Santa Maria, California. The two men had become acquainted. Joan was a widow with four boys Mike, Tim, Brien, and Sean ages seven years and under. Clyde and Joan were married March 3, 1962 (pictured) and eventually had two more sons, David born April 9, 1963 and

Steven born July 13, 1965. David graduated with masters in Civil Engineering from Colorado State University (CSU) in 1986. He is employed with the Army Core of Engineers. He married Cathy Fisher and had two sons, Zachary and Andrew. Zach graduated from Rollo Technical University in 2010 and Andrew will graduate with a Law degree in 2016 from the University of Nebraska. David was divorced and remarried to Theresa Montague with daughter Christina.

Steven graduated with a degree in Business from CSU 1989 and a Business masters from the University of Washington. He is with the United Launch Alliance in Denver. (See Wheeler addendum for more on sons).

Joan and Clyde celebrated their Fiftieth Anniversary in 2012 with their family. Their sons are pictured. Top row left to right: Mike, Brien, and Tim, second row: David, Sean and Steven, Clyde and Joan.

Family and grandchildren are pictured below.

Grandchildren, Jaime, Andrew, and Zachery are missing.

*The author and her husband a descendant researched the family in 1992 in Luxemburg and the Metz archives with the help of the archivist. Several members of the family were found. They were Huguenots and church baptisms where not recorded unless family members remained Catholic. Grady LaGrone researched the family in France in the 1950"s and his information is referenced here.

**History, crest, and pictures sourced from family records, Ancestry, and Wikipedia

THE KINARD FAMILY

The Kinard family inherited an ancient Scottish name first used by descendants of the early Picts tribe in Scotland hundreds of years ago. It is located in the barony of Kinnaird in Perthshire in central Scotland where they held properties. Members of the family eventually immigrated to mainland Europe. The name was spelled Keinat in Germany.

Passenger lists on early ships show many Keinat/Kinard immigrants to the Colonies. William Kinnaird (Kinard) arrived in Charles Town (Charleston) South Carolina in 1767 from Scotland. (John) Johannes Keinat/Kinard, born in 1667 in Winterlingen, Zollernalbkreis, Baden-Württemberg, Germany, arrived sometime in 1700-1710 with his family from Baden-Württemberg, Germany. John was the son of Hans Keinat born in Germany in 1633. His mother is unknown. John married Lucia Koch, who was born in 1677. Their son Michael was born October 31, 1697 in Germany. Other family members are not mentioned. However, Mary Kinard probably his daughter, was born in 1710 in Dutch Fork, South Carolina. Mary married Tobias LaGrone before 1727 in Newberry. John died May 10, 1747 in Dutch Forks, Newberry, South Carolina at age eighty. His son, Michael Kinard, married Anna Maria Letsche and had five sons and one daughter. Their son John was born in 1726. He married Mary Sophia LaGrone. They had five sons and one daughter. Michael died in 1750 in the Old Ninety-six District of Dutch Fork. This was the site of the first battle in South Carolina in 1775 during the Revolution. It was a small town of about one-hundred occupants. During the battle, the Loyalists captured the ammunitions and gunpowder. Outnumbered, the Colonists were unable to recapture it and had to reach a truce. It became a British stronghold during the war and remained so until near the end of the war when the British abandoned the Fort and move back to the coast. The Ninety-six was declared a National Historic Landmark in 1973.

Additional Kinard families were among a group of Protest "Palatines" who arrived in late 1744 on the ship St. Andrew commanded by Captain Brown. The Kinard families helped to settle the Dutch Fork, Newberry area and intermarried with the LaGrone family.

Three members of the Kinard (Kennard) family fought in the Revolution. Martin Kennard (#A064652) born 1730 in Newberry served in Waters Regiment. Michael Kennard born 1754 in Newberry (#A065654), the son of John also served in Waters Regiment of the Militia. John Kennard (#A064651) born around 1753-55 served under Captain Houseal in Colonel Waters Regiment. All three were probably related and descendants of (John) Johannes the immigrant.

*History and crest sourced from Kinard/Kinnaird family, Wikipedia, Clans of Scotland, and Ancestry

THE HOUSEAL FAMILY

The Housihl (Houseal) family history goes back to the very early Kingdom of Wurttemberg (crest of Württemberg right) in Germany of which Heilbronn was one of the three major towns in the provinces of Baden, Bavaria, and Hohenzollern in Suabia. The Housihl family of Heilbronn came from one of the ancient tribes of the Confederacy of Alemannic going back to before the third century. George W. Houschild, a former member of the South Carolina Newberry College faculty in 1908-10, was an authority on the Houseal name and history.

The Reverend Bernard Housihl lived in Heilbronn in the eighteenth century and became the progenitor of the Housihl (Houseal) family in America. He was a professor in the Protestant Theological Seminary in Heilbronn and minister of the Reformed church. He later moved to England were he preached the gospel as interrupted by Martin Luther. He and his wife had two sons, the oldest Bernard Michael Houseal and William Frederic Houseal born 1730. Both sons eventually went to America landing first in Philadelphia. Bernard went to New York where be became a minister in the Trinity Lutheran Church and William went to South Carolina. During the Revolution, Bernard remained a Loyalist. After the surrender of Cornwallis, he was forced to leave the country, and went to Nova Scotia. William, however, chose a different path and became a patriot and Officer in the Revolution. He went to Newberry County in South Carolina where he obtain a two-hundred acre grant on the Four-Hole now in Orangeburg.

William married Mary Elizabeth Stroman of Orangeburg, the daughter of John Jacob Stroman (born in Germany in 1728 and died in 1781) and wife Anna Margaret. (See Stroman Family). William and Mary had several children including Mary Magdalene born 1755 who married John Adam (William) LaGronne, born 1760, son of Tobias LaGrone, descendant of Adam Laurenz Le Grone a Frenchman, and Anna Marie who married Thomas Ebenezer Glass, a Scotchman. William's wife died early and he married Anna Margaret Geiselhardt. They had four sons and a daughter, John Adam, John, David, William Frederic Jr., and Mary Margaret.

William served first in the command of Militia Companies in the regiments of Colonel Lyles and Colonel Jonas Beard of the Ninety-six District and was Captain of a Calvary Troop under Colonel Philemon Waters of Newberry County. Captain Houseal (#A057537) was a gallant officer serving during many campaigns throughout the war. The roster of his Troop of Horse in his own handwriting is in the Revolutionary records of the South Carolina Historical Records in Columbia. His son in law, (John) Adam LaGrone, was among those troops. (See LaGrone Family). No other members of the Houseal family are listed in the DAR records.

*History and crest sourced from Wikipedia, Ancestry free pages and G.W. Houschild History.

THE STROMAN FAMILY

The Stroman name is established in Southern France where they belonged to the Church of St. Romanus. They also lived in northern Germany and Switzerland where members of the family acquired lands and estates. Arnold Storm and M. Stormere are both recorded in Rostock in 1283 and 1302, an old settlement near the Baltic Sea founded in 1200 by German merchants. The inhabitants were craftsmen and merchants who traded with the neighboring towns. (Ancient arms of Stroman pictured).

John (Hans) Jacob Storman was born in Waldenburg, Basel-Landschaft, Switzerland in 1721 son of Balthazar (the butcher) Stroman. The family immigrated to Orangeburg, South Carolina about 1735. John married first Anna Margaret Schaumloffel on July 18, 1741. She was the daughter of John Shaumloffel and Anna Marie During from the Rhineland-Palatine Pfalz, Germany. Anna Margret died in Orangeburg about 1757. They had several children including daughters Mary (Maria) Elizabeth who married William Fredrick Houseal, Anna Margaret, and four sons, Henry, Jacob, John, and Paul. He married second Eva Catherine Snell (Tilly?) in Orangeburg. Some sources say they had nine children.

John Jacob and two or three of his sons, Jacob, John, and Paul served with their father in the Revolution. They served in Captain Jacob Rumph's Company of Militia of independent Calvary under the command of Colonel William Thomas. John Jacob was killed in in South Carolina in 1781 during the Revolution. According to the abstract of graves of Revolutionary Patriots, John Jacob is buried in the Orangeburg Cemetery in Orangeburg, South Carolina, Patriot # (A111435). Both of his wives are buried next to him. His son Jacob, born 1751 (#A111424) died in South Carolina in 1795. John was born March 5, 1756 (DAR number not established) and died in Pennsylvania in 1843. Paul born circa 1751 (A111438) died in South Carolina September 2, 1844. He is buried in the Eutaw Springs Battleground near Orangeburg.

*History and crest sourced from Wikipedia, DAR, and Ancestry.

THE DOMINICK FAMILY

The French Dominick family arrived in England after the Norman Conquest in 1066. The name comes from the Latin Dominicus meaning "belonging to the Lord God." One of the earliest recordings of the name is a Dominicus de Buketon on the "fine rolls" in 1326 during the reign of King Edward II. Various spelling of the name is found in England during the fifteenth and sixteenth centuries.

John Dominick of Switzerland landed in South Carolina in 1738. He married Elizabeth (?) and was a Revolutionary Patriot (#A033035). He was born about 1718 in Switzerland and died in District Ninety-Six in Newberry County, South Carolina in May of 1796. During the Revolution, he furnished supplies and material aid. His son Henry (#A033032) was born in Cavern South Carolina in 1757 and served in the Revolution under Lieutenant Thomas Miller. He became a prisoner of war and survived. He died January 1, 1836 in Newberry, South Carolina. John's daughter Christina Clementine born 1785 married William Adam LaGrone, Jr. in 1803. They were of the Presbyterian faith and lived in Perry, County Alabama from 1803 until 1835 when they moved to Texas. They had seven sons and two daughters. Andrew Jackson LaGrone was born in 1820. Christina died in 1847 in Deadwood, Texas and buried beside her husband William Adam in the LaGrone Cemetery in Deadwood.

*History and crest sourced from, Ancestry, Genealogy, DAR, and LaGrone family history

THE GIBBS FAMILY

The Gibbs name is of British origin. The Pictish people of ancient Scotland were among the first to use the name Gibbs. The name is located in the ancient shire of Inverness, which was both a Pictish and Norwegian stronghold. The Gibbs Clan is recorded in early Scottish history. Members of the family also lived England. They came to the American Colonies in the early 1600's.

A Lieutenant John Gibbs was sent to Jamestown, Virginia to serve as a burgess for Captain John Ward's plantation in July and August of 1619. Later he was granted his own land in Westover. He was slain on his plantation during an Indian attack in March 22, 1622. Another John Gibbs survived the same Indian attack and eventually moved to Jorden's Journey, a fortified position for greater protection. He came over on the ship *Supply*, from Bristol England with a number of settlers bound for the Berkeley Hundred settlement. He was to receive land in exchange for his years of service. A third John Gibbs came to Virginia in 1621 on the Ship the *Abigial*. He was sent to the colony as a James Company Servant. In 1625, he was living on the south side of the Elizabeth River on the James Company land and was a twenty-four old servant in Sergeant William Barry's household. After the Virginia Company became defunct, servants and tenants were assigned to high-ranking officials. John was assigned to Governor George Yeardley, the first Governor of Jamestown. Francis Gibbs (Gibbson) was another of the first settlers in America and arrived in Virginia in 1624 aboard the ship *Sunflower*. He was a servant in the Ralph Hamer household in urban Jamestown. It is unknown if any of the above members of the Gibbs families are related.

One of above Gibbs descendants was Gregory Gibbs, born October 10, 1635 in Charles City, Charles, Virginia. His father is unknown; however, he may have been one of the above John's as he named his son John. Gregory married Mary (?) and their son John was born in October of 1680 in Christ Church, Middlesex, Virginia. Gregory died in Christ Church in 1696. Christ Church parish was established in 1653 in Middlesex County in Colonial Virginia. It is one of the oldest Counties in Virginia. John married Mary Marron and they had nine children. Their son, John Jr., was born April 5, 1716 in Christ Church. John Sr. died January 31, 1725. John Jr. married Susanne Phillipe and they were the parents of four children, Zacharias, Hanna, Phillip, and the Reverend John Gibbs. Phillip was born about 1750. John Jr. died in 1770 in Spartanburg, South Carolina.

Phillip born 1750 married Phoebe Wilcher. Two of their children were Vashti and Elhanan Winchester Gibbs born 1790 in Crawford, Georgia. (Some records state he was born in Alabama). Phillip and Phoebe's death are unknown. Their son Elhanan Winchester married Francis Polly Williams, daughter of Moses Williams. They had ten children. Their daughter Lucinda Clementine Gibbs was born in Lamar County Alabama. She married Andrew Jackson LaGrone September 6, 1846.

Elhanan Gibbs was one of the first settlers with Austin's Colony* to settle Texas. He is described in Chapter Two of Noah Smithwick's Journal, "The Evolution of a State, or Recollections of old Texas Days."

Noah and Elhanan became friends in 1827 and Noah tells a few stories of their adventures in early Texas. Elhanan died September 20, 1827 in San Felipe, Austin, Texas near the mouth of the Brazos River. Eighty-five members of the Gibbs family served in the Revolution, ten from Virginia. John Gibbs (#A044623), born in Virginia in 1756 served in Captain Walls and Colonel Rodgers Halifax Militia.

Austin's Colony was the first legal settlement of North American families in Mexican owned Texas. Samuel F. Austin, who obtained the initial grant for three-hundred families in 1821, referred to as the "Old 300," led the settlement. This opened Texas to a flood of immigrants, over 30,000 by the time of the Texas Revolution in 1835. This brought both Anglo and African settlers from the United States and exposed them to the ranching traditions of Spain and Mexico, which helped to set the course of Texas history until the discovery of oil in the twentieth century. It was one of the most successful colonization in American history. Terms of the grant requited the settlers to be loyal to the official government and the Catholic religion of Spain. A prerequisite for immigration was the reputable character of the settlers.

Soon after gaining the contract, Mexico won the eleven-year war for independence from Spain. The New Mexican government affirmed Austin's contract to settle Texas with settlers from the United States. Austin picked the rich bottomland for his settlers between the Brazos and the Colorado River. Settlers began arriving in 1821-22 transforming the unsettled wilderness into a thinly populated rural community with San Felipe the center. The promise of inexpensive land was the main reason for emigrating from the United States. It was advertised in newspapers for 12 ½ cents per acre, nearly one-tenth the cost of public land in the United States. Most of the settlers came from the southern states of Kentucky, Alabama, Mississippi, Louisiana, and Tennessee. Settlers were allotted 177 acres for farming and 4,428 if they raised stock. (The low-cost of land motivated the LaGrone families and their relatives to move Texas in the early 1800's).

Enormous herds of horses and cattle roamed the Texas plains because of the livestock lost by the Spanish missions and ranches. From these herds, integrated with those of the southern colonists, emerged the Texas longhorn cattle and the Mexican ranching traditions. The famous Texas ranching industry became the result.

Religion was a topic of controversy in the Austin Colony. The provision of the original grant required all settlers be Catholic, although the requirement was not always enforced. Most of the settlers accepted this as a business necessity and not a confession of faith. There was a lot of criticism of the Catholic Clergy that required the official church blessing on marriages and baptisms. Austin initially encouraged the settlers to comply with the law, but suggested that private devotions of any denomination could take place in the homes. Protestant Preachers were contrary to the law. However, many illegal camp meetings were held in early Texas. However, despite the efforts of the Preachers, Texans never placed a high priority on organized religion. By the end of 1845, no more than an eighth of the population was either an active or a nominal member of a Texas church. (This may have been a reason the LaGrone family eventually educated several preachers in the family and built the Church on their land in Deadwood).

Fearing the takeover of Texas by the North Americans, the Mexican government sent a military expedition to Texas to observe the colonists and their actions. Because of the report, the Mexican government passed the Law of 1830 attempting to slow down the emigration of Americans and try to balance the influx with Mexicans and Europeans. The Law was extremely unpopular and caused uneasiness and brought dissent. This led to the settler's conventions of 1832 and 1833, which eventually brought on the Texas Revolution in 1835. The settlers battled Santa Anna the Mexican General for over a year and a half before finally winning independence and establishing the Republic of Texas in 1836. Texas became a state in 1845.

**History and crest sourced from Wikipedia, DAR, Geni, Ancestry, and *Stephen F. Austin's account of the first Anglo-American settlement in Texas*

THE BOZEMAN FAMILY

The Bozeman name may have come from the Rhineland, the region around the Rhine River in Germany. The family is recorded and became well known in the district for their contributions to the social order from very ancient days. The name is also found in England as an ancient Anglo-Saxon surname and recorded around Norfolk where they had lands and family estates. There were several different spellings of the name including Basham, Bosham, and Bashum. Two of the first members of the family to immigrate to the American Colonies were Andrew Basham who sailed from England to Virginia in 1639 and Peter Bashan who went to New York in 1822.

Dr. Nathan Bozeman was born in Holland, Netherlands in 1610. He immigrated to Maryland before 1630. (Flag, pictured, found with Nathan Bozeman history on Ancestry).  His father, Nathan, and Grandfather William, born about 1560 in Holland, came to Maryland with him. Both are buried in Maryland. He married Harriet Knotts born in Georgia. Her parents are unknown. Their son Joseph Edward Bozeman was born in Maryland in 1630. Joseph married Josephine Wood, parents unknown, and had three sons, Ralph Sr. born 1653, Ambrose, and Henry. Joseph died in 1690. His son Ralph married Mary Branch (the daughter of Anthony Branch) and had two sons, Samuel Edward born in 1684 in the Isle of Wright, Virginia, Ralph Jr., and daughters Mary and Ann. Samuel Edward born 1684 married twice, first to Elizabeth and then to Mary White born 1700. Some sources say she was born in Indian Penobscot, Maine. Mary's father John White (See White Family) was born 1660-1718 on the Isle of Wright, Virginia and her mother Sarah was born 1660-65-1715, also in the Isle of Wright.* They were married about 1690. Samuel and his first wife were parents of James Edward born 1715. His sons from Mary White were Samuel Edward Jr. born 1730 in Bladen, North Carolina, Mordecai born 1735 also in Bladen and Benjamin born 1736. Samuel died in Bladen in 1735.

Mordecai married Elizabeth (?) and had six children. His son John Lewis was born in 1737 in Lunenburg, Virginia. The family then moved to Darlington, South Carolina where Mordecai died in 1765. John Lewis married Anna Tillman (See Tillman Family) the daughter of Robert Tillman born 1665 in Charles City Virginia. John Lewis and Anna had five children. Philemon the oldest was born in 1757 in Edgefield, South Carolina. Philemon married Susannah Holloway who was born 1760, the daughter of John and Sarah Holloway of Edgefield. Philemon was a Revolutionary soldier in the Ninety-Six District Militia of South Carolina. He is the only Bozeman family member listed in the DAR records (#A004053).

Philemon and Susannah had several children including Lewis, David, and James. Their son James Richard was born January 15, 1789 in Edgefield, South Carolina. Philemon died in Monroe, Alabama May 6, 1819. Susannah died in 1835. Their son James married Rachael Rowe born October 2, 1792 in Edgefield. The Rowe family descends from William Rowe born 1656 in Wales and died in Virginia in 1721. He was the grandson of Thomas Roe of Wales. Rachael was the daughter of Benjamin Rowe born 1758 in Laurence, South Carolina, Patriot (#A099049) and granddaughter of John Rowe a Patriot in the Revolutionary War (#A099172). Benjamin's wife Ruth O'Neal was born in South Carolina in 1770. She was the daughter of Hugh born 1745 Patriot (#A84078) in South Carolina and the granddaughter of Hugh O'Neal born in 1698 in Shane's Castle in Ireland. (See O'Neill Family) James and Ruth had seven children. The youngest James Richard Jr., was born 1825 in Monroe, Alabama. James Sr. was accidently killed by his brother Lewis in Monroe in a bear hunting accident. James Jr. married Sarah Rice the daughter of Jesse W. Rice and Emily (last name unknown) and they moved to Spring Ridge, Caddo, Louisiana. (See Rice Family) Their daughter Sarah Salina "Sally" Bozeman was born in Spring Ridge June 28, 1864. Sally married Hiram Clark LaGrone May 28, 1885 in Spring Ridge. (See LaGrone Family). The youngest son of Hiram and Sally was Winfred Cooper (Kip)* who married Geraldine Beson.

*According to some sources, Sarah may have been a descendant of the Penobscot Indian Tribe of Maine. The main settlement of the tribe is now on the Penobscot Indian Island Reservation. However, no connection has been found between the Maine Indians and Sarah, wife of John White. According to Ancestry, Sarah's last name was possible Clare of Cleare. The Indian name "Penobscot" may have been confused with the Pomeiooc Indian tribe in Virginia by a family researcher where Sarah was born. However, no Indian connection has been established. (See White Family).

**History sourced from Ancestry, Wikipedia, and family records

THE RICE FAMILY

The Rice name is originally from Wales where it was spelled Rhys and dates back to the ancient Celts. Rice Families lived in Carmarthenshire on the southwest coast of Wales where they had land from ancient eras. Rees is recorded in the Doomday Book of Cheshire, England in 1086. Several members of the family emigrated to the American Colonies in the early 1600's including Henry who landed in Virginia in 1622, John in 1639 and Richard Rice in 1639. Edmund Rice was an English Deacon in the Puritan Church from Suffolk who went to the Massachusetts Bay Colony in 1638. He was a prominent citizen in Concord along with the Wheeler family.

A Carlton Rice landed in Virginia in 1717 and Daniel Rice in Philadelphia in 1764. Thomas Rice arrived in Virginia on the Bristol Merchant in 1680 The Rice family is also found in Ireland in 1294 when John Rice was Lord Treasurer of Ireland. Walter Rice was Treasurer of Limerick in 1530 and other members of the family were prominent officials in other Munster towns. During the Cromwellian era, over twenty members of the family lost their estates for supporting James II's lost cause. Many members then immigrated to France and the American Colonies. Nathaniel Rice was born about 1680 in Hampshire, England. He emigrated with his wife, Ann Gibbs, and son John before 1730. He later married Mary Bursey. He died in Carven County, North Carolina in 1753. He became one of the leading planters acquiring an estate of over six thousand acres and seventeen slaves. By 1731, he was serving as secretary of the Province. He was President of the Council for over twenty years and became Governor in 1752 until his death. He had an interested in the colonist's independence. He may also have been a Mason. His son John died in Carven County in 1777. Nathaniel had several grandchildren including another John (son of Joshua) who may be the grandfather or close relative of John Rice born 1791 in South Carolina and died after 1899 in Covington County, Alabama.

John born 1791 married Catherine Cook January 30, 1818 in Mecklenburg County, North Carolina where she was born. Some family members have stated she was of Indian birth, but no proof is established. Ancestry.com lists her name as Catherine Indian Cook born 1805 in North Carolina wife of John Bryant Rice with no known parents. (See Cook Family). She was possibly connected to the Catawba Indian Tribe who was friendly with the colonists. She died in 1839 in Covington, Alabama. They had six children Bryan Bryant Reverend Rice, Jesse Willis I Rice born 1819 in Marion County, South Carolina, Fanny Phama (male) Rice, John Nelson, Nancy, Mary, and Ellen Elender Elizabeth. John received a land patent in Section thirty-four in Covington August 18, 1859. John's son Jesse born in 1819 married Emilla "Emily" Moody in 1843 in Alabama. (See Moody family) She was born January 4, 1824 in South Carolina, the daughter of Salathiel Moody and Nancy Bethea. Emily died January 10, 1910 in Grimes, Texas. Jesse and his brother John Nelson were members of the Rosehill Alabama Masonic Lodge #253. Jesse's father may have been a mason as well. The Masonic records show Jesse died February 27, 1867. Jesse had a land patent dated November 1, 1858 for eighty acres in section 23 in East Covington, almost a year before his father. His six children were all born in Alabama including Sarah Rice who married James Bozeman Jr. Their youngest daughter, Sarah Salina "Sally,"* married Hiram Clark LaGrone. Hiram had fourteen children from two of his three wives. Sally was his third wife. Hiram and Sally's youngest son Winfred Cooper "Kip" LaGrone married Geraldine Beson.   (See LaGrone and Beeson Families)

Two-hundred and fifty-nine members of the Rice family served in the Revolution, ten from North Carolina Thomas Rice (#A095156) born 1725 gave civil service and was Sheriff of Caswell County. Nathaniel Rice (#A095063) born circa 1755 in North Carolina was in the Caswell County Militia. They are probably both descendants of the emigrant Nathaniel. Aaron Rice (#A94788) born 1754 in Hanover, Virginia served in the South Carolina Militia during the Revolution. He descends from Edmund Rice immigrant to Massachusetts Bay Colony in 1638.

*A LaGrone family tradition passed down by word of mouth states that Sally Bozeman was half-Indian possibly of the Coushatta Indian Tribe of Alabama and Louisiana. This seems to be false. However, it appears she may have had some Indian blood from her great grandmother, Catherine Indian Cook, born in North Carolina in 1805. In North Carolina, the Catawba Tribe was most prevalent. The Coushatta Tribe is not found in that state.

Another LaGrone tradition also states that John M. Bozeman, founder of the Bozeman Trail in Montana Territory was a distant relative. He was born in 1835 in Georgia. Lured by gold in Colorado in 1861, he left his wife and two children in Georgia and went to Colorado. The next year he went to Montana as an explorer and founded the Bozeman trail. The Blackfeet Indians killed him in 1867 near Livingston. The town of Bozeman is named after him.

**History and crest sourced from Wikipedia, Ancestry, Genealogy, Rice Family History, N. C. Indian Tribes, History of Bozeman, and DAR

THE COOK FAMILY

The Cook name is found in Essex England. It comes from the occupational name of cook or a "keeper" of an eating-place or tavern. It comes from the old English "coc." The name was first recorded in the book of Wills dated 950. Captain Cook is one of the most famous of the name. Members of the Cook family from England arrived in the Maine and Massachusetts Colonies as early as 1622. Abraham, Charles, and Thomas Cook landed in Virginia in 1701 and 1705. Members of these families eventually moved to North and South Carolina where they had land grants. Catherine Cook's father was probably related. Three-hundred members of the Cook family fought in the Revolution, twenty-one from North Carolina.

*History and crest from free pages at Ancestry, genealogy, and DAR

THE MOODY FAMILY

The Moody name was a nickname for an impetus's or courageous person often moved quickly to anger. It is recorded in Suffolk on the early tax rolls of the Kings. The name is also established in Ireland. A Captain William Moody, Virginia emigrant, was a member of the Isle of Wight Militia in 1623. In 1635, Simon settled in the Virginia Colony and Samuel landed in New England. Robert arrived 1674 in Virginia and George Moody came in 1701. One of these emigrants is probably the ancestor of Charles Moody born 1735, Revolutionary soldier, father of Salathiel Moody who is the father of Emilla "Emily" Moody. Charles Moody (#A134692) born 1735 was a Lieutenant in the Revolution under Colonel Powell. His brother Robert (#A120095) also served. William Moody (#A079184) born 1710 in Maryland gave patriotic service and took the Oath of Fidelity. Fifty-seven members of the Moody family fought in the Revolution.

*History and crest from Ancestry, Moody family History, and DAR

THE O'NEILL FAMILY

The O'Neill name is an ancient name in Tyrone, Ireland and in Ulster, Northern Central Ireland. It was first documented here in the Middle Ages. O'Neill was Chief of Clan Dalvy and Tradree. Niall Glundub was a tenth century High King of Ireland a descendant of one of the fifth century Kings, Eogan mac Neill. From 1312 to 1318, the McNeill Clan was in Scotland and was staunch supporters of Robert the Bruce in his fight for Scottish Independence. Pictured is the ancient crest of the O'Neill's of Tyrone.

Shane Castle in Atrium, Ireland built in 1345 was the home of the O'Neill dynasty where the O'Neill Kings were crowned. The Castle grounds cover 2,600 acres on the shore of Lough Neagh. The title of Viscount O'Neill was created in 1795 and the O'Neill's served in the Irish House of Commons.

Hugh O'Neill (O'Neal) was born in Ireland in 1698. He was another of the young men "pressed" into service by the British Navy. About 1730 his ship was docked in the Delaware River. He deserted the British and jumped overboard swimming ashore. He first settled in Christiana, Delaware where he married Ann Cox on June 10, 1732. (See Cox Family). They later moved to the Susquehanna in 1750 accompanied by their six sons, William, Henry, John, Thomas, Hugh born 1745, and James all Patriots in the Revolutionary War.

The Shane Castle, pictured right, is now used extensively in the HBO TV series *The Game of Thrones.*

Twenty-seven members of the O'Neal family served in the Revolution. Hugh (#A084070) gave material aid.

*History and pictures sourced from Wikipedia, Ancestry, Geni, *The Annals of Newberry, S. C.*, and *O'Neall Family Journal*

THE WHITE FAMILY

The White name is from the old English Hwite meaning pale or white haired. Its origin is located in both Scotland and England well before 1066. The name was discovered in Berwickshire in Eastern Scotland where a member of the Hwite family witnessed the charter of Coldingham around 1100. Many members of the name Hwite, White, or Whyte may have emigrated from France, as it is also found there in early history.

Several members of the White family came to the Colonies. It is possible they were related to Sir John Whyte VII, who was born in 1380 in England and died in 1455. He was the father of Sir Richard Whyte. His son was William White and his son Sir Thomas Whyte born 1492, was knighted by Queen Mary and made the Lord Mayor of London, (pictured). He founded St. John's Oxford of the Catholic faith.

A descendant, Peter Whyte, was born in 1578. He married Mary Kebble and had several children including William born 1600 in Wiltshire. He and his family were early settlers in Virginia. William married Eleanor (or Ellen) Flowers. Their son John Sr. was born 1630 in the Isle of Wight, Virginia, located on the coast near lower Norfolk and close to North Carolina. William died in Lancaster County, Virginia in 1678. John Sr. married Eady Llewellyn of Wales and had a son John Jr. born in Isle of Wight 1660. John Jr. married Sarah Cleare also born in 1660 in the Isle of Wight. John Sr. died April 27, 1719. According to the Bath County, North Carolina land records, John was given twelve hundred acres in Bath due him for the transportation of twenty-four people from England. John Jr. and Sarah had five children including Luke, John Christopher, Mordecai, Media, and Mary White born about 1700 also in the Isle of Wight who married Samuel Bozeman. (See Bozeman Family).

John White Artist born about 1539-40 was from a prominent family in London and was an artist and early colonist. He was a participant in the first English efforts to settle the New World. Sir Walter Raleigh sent him in 1585 as Sir Richard Greenville's artist-illustrator and mapmaker on Greenville's first voyage. He served as artist to the expedition, which landed in North Carolina on Roanoke Island. John eventually became Governor of the Island in the failed attempt at a permanent settlement, which later was known as the Lost Colony. When the colonists were running short of supplies, he went back to England for help. He left his wife and daughter, who married Ananias Dare, and granddaughter Virginia, behind with the other settlers. (Virginia Dare was the first English child born in the New World). John was not able to obtain help in England at the time due to the war with Spain. When he was finally able to return, he found the colony deserted. His only evidence was that the few settlers left had joined the Pomeiooc Indian tribe for protection and moved inland. He was never able to find his family. He returned to England and died in Ireland about 1593. His

watercolor prints of the early American Indians and the Village of Pomeiooc (pictured) are stored in the British Museum along with his maps.

William White Pilgrim was born about 1580 in England and was a London Merchant according to Bradford's Plymouth Colony account. He married Susannah (?). They were passengers on the Mayflower in 1620 with their son Resolved. They had a son Peregrine born on the Mayflower in Cape Cod Harbor, who was the first child born in New England. William was the eleventh signatory to the Mayflower Compact. He died the first winter on February 21, 1621. His wife and children survived, Susannah became the wife of Edward Winslow, whose wife had also died. He later became the Governor of Plymouth County. Resolved White married Judith Vassell, daughter of William Vassell one of the founders of the Massachusetts Bay Colony. They had eight children including William born 1642, John born 1644, and Elizabeth born in 1652 who married Obadiah Wheeler Jr. in Concord in 1650. (See Wheeler Family). William's son Penegrine married Sarah Bassett, daughter of William Bassett and had seven children including Daniel and Jonathan born 1658. Jonathan married Mary Elizabeth Alexander. Their son William was born 1710 and died in 1766 in Fredrick, Virginia. He married Sarah Bond. Their son John Wesley White, born 1736 in Virginia, married Mary. Her parents are unknown.

Three hundred members of the White family are recorded in the DAR records serving in the Revolution. One-hundred and five served from Virginia including Isaac White (#A124787) from Prince William County. He died in 1777 in the Battle of Long Island. Ten Patriots with the name John White served from Virginia, one (#A125140) served in the Battle of King's Mountain. Fourteen men with the first name of William also served from Virginia, one William was from Accomack born 1745 (#A201250) gave supplies.

*History and pictures sourced White family history, Wikipedia, DAR, and Ancestry

THE TILLMAN FAMILY

The Tillman family was of English descent and found in Kent where they held land and estates. They increased their holdings by inter-marriage with other influential families of the time. The name goes back to ancient medieval records in Kent. Johannas Tilghman was born 1225 in Snodland Parish, Kent. His descendants were numerous including William Tilghman who was born at Holloway Court in the Parish of Snodland, County Kent in 1518. His fourth wife was Susan Wetenhall, a descendant of King Edward III. The Tilghman family of Virginia descended from William and his wife Susan.

Christopher Tilghman was born in 1600 in Kent, England. He married Ruth Devonshire in 1630 and had six children including Gideon, John, and Rodger. He sold his holdings in England in 1630 and was an early emigrant to James City, Virginia. He died in 1673. Christopher is listed is an original patent holder. His son Rodger was born about 1650 and married first to Winifred Austin and second to Susannah Parham. His children were Robert, Jane, Christine, John, and George. He owned 1060 acres in Bristol Parish, Charles County, Virginia. He transported twenty-two people to the Colony for which he received land. His Plantation was called Fort Tillman and located on the south side of the Appomattox River at Monk's Head. After settling in Virginia, Rodger changed his name from Tilghman to Tillman. He died in 1690 in Prince George, Virginia. His son Robert, who was born circa 1665-70, married (?) and had a daughter Anna, who married John Lewis Bozeman. Both the Devonshire and Austin families immigrated with the Tillman family.

Twenty-three members of the Tillman family served in the Revolution. John Tillman (#A115543) born 1734 in Prince George County, Virginia was a Colonel of the Carven County Militia in 1779. Trench Tillman (#A133243) born 1744 in Talbot County, Maryland was a Lieutenant Colonel and an aid-de-camp to General Washington.

*History sourced from Ancestry, Wikipedia, Genealogy, and Genealogical-gleanings

THE BEESON/BEASON/BESON FAMILY

The Beeson/Beason family dates back to the ancient tribes of Britain. Their name comes from the English variant of their residence in Beeston Castle (pictured) in the County of Cheshire. Beeson is also the name of a village near Leeds. Members of the family spelled their name Beeson, Beason and Beson.

Several members of the family immigrated to the Colonies for religious reasons. Stephen Beeson arrived in Maryland in 1666 and Thomas landed in 1679, both from England. One Beeson family settled in New England in 1773. Richard and Edward Beeson arrived around 1672 and settled first in Wilmington, Delaware. Richard eventually returned to England. Edward born 1652 in Stoke, Lancashire, son of Thomas and Ann Beeson, was a descendant of Hugh Beeson born about 1525 in Beeston, Cheshire, England. Hugh married Thomasina Copleston 1534 in Edgeford, Devonshire.

Edward is the progenitor of the Beeson family in Pennsylvania and North Carolina. He had three wives the last was Elizabeth Grubbs. She was known as the widow Holmes, born 1691, the daughter of Henry Grubb and Mary Perkins of Chester County. Edward had seven children, the oldest, William, went back to England. His sons Richard, Edward, and Isaac remained in the Colonies with both Isaac and Richard moving to North Carolina. His daughters were Ann, Elizabeth, and Rachael. Edward Sr. received a land grant from William Penn. Although his family was members of the Quaker religion, he never became a member. Edward owned land in the Brandywine One-Hundred on the Delaware River. He later drew lot eighteen, a plot of nine-hundred and eighty acres in  Nottingham, Pennsylvania, which later became Cecil County, Maryland. He was a gentleman farmer and planter. Members of this family eventually moved to North Carolina while Edward Jr. remained in Pennsylvania.

His son, Richard Beeson Sr., born 1684 in Chester County, Province of Pennsylvania died January1, 1777 in Guilford County, North Carolina. He married Charity Grubb, daughter of John Grubb II, immigrant and his wife Frances Buffington. They had eleven children, including Richard Jr. born 1711 in West Nottingham Cecil County, Province of Maryland. He was a member of Friends. Richard Jr. married Ann Brown born 1711, the daughter of Mercer Brown and Jane Richards. He died in Fredrick County, Virginia. Pictured is the home of Richard Jr. in West Nottingham. They had several children including Jacob I born June 1, 1741 in Frederic.

Jacob I had twelve children including Jacob II born October 15, 1774 and died September 13, 1823. Jacob II is possibly the father of Jacob III and may have moved to North Carolina with his brother William where his son was born in 1792.

Jacob Beason, pictured, was born December 28, 1792 in North Carolina. He moved to Tennessee where he married Martha McKendree June 1, 1824 in Sumner County. She was born 1803 in Greensville County, Virginia, a descendant of James McKendree born circa 1768 in James City County, Virginia, and his wife Martha "Patsy" Wilkinson. She was the daughter of Joel and Elizabeth Wilkinson. James was referred to as "Doctor" and was a minister of the Methodist Church. (His brother William was the first American born bishop of the Methodist Episcopal Church in America elected in 1808).

Jacob Beason and Martha had ten children, Frances, Margaret, James, William, and John Lafayette "Logan" Beason born February 13, 1833 in Sumner County, Martha, Mary, Malcena, Sarah, and Abram. Jacob is buried in the Beason Cemetery in Portland, Sumner County. Martha died November 10, 1890 in Lincoln, Logan County, Illinois. She is buried in the Union Cemetery in Lincoln.

John Lafayette "Logan," Beason born 1833 in Tennessee died July 20, 1908 in Augusta, McDonnough County, Illinois. He married Susan Ella Holmes* about 1878 in Carthage, Hancock County, Illinois. They had five children, Clyde W. Beason M.D. born August 20, 1879-81 in Illinois, John Lawrence Beason born 1881, Lula Ella, Jacob Holmes, and Nellie Faye.

Clyde William Beason was born August 20, 1879-81 in Adams County, Illinois and died September 1955 in Claremore, Oklahoma. He and his brother John are pictured. He married Romona "Rowena" Fish July 12, 1909. (See Fish Family) Rowena and Clyde are pictured below. She was born between 1881 and 1889 in Pennsylvania. He graduated about 1900 from St. Joseph College Medical School in Missouri where he played football for the College. Clyde was one of the first Doctors in Oklahoma Territory before it became a state in 1907. In 1929-31, he was Oklahoma Commissioner of Health. They had two children, Geraldine born April 3, 1911, who married Winfred Cooper "Kip" LaGrone (See LaGrone Family) and Clyde William Beson, Jr. both born in Claremore, Oklahoma. Kip and Geraldine LaGrone had two sons, Clyde Winfred born 1932 and Lynn born 1945 who died young.

*Susan Holmes' parents are unknown. However, she may descend from either Matthew Holmes who arrived in Virginia in 1635 or Jo (Joseph) Holmes who settled in New England in 1635. Both immigrants were from England.

One-hundred and thirty-six members of the Holmes family fought in the Revolution.

Eleven members of the Beeson family served in the Revolutionary War, six from North Carolina. Benjamin born 1716 in Pennsylvania (#A008558) furnished supplies and died June 14, 1794 in Randolph County North Carolina. Edward was a Captain, born January 1, 1757 in North Carolina (#A008559) and died in Alabama in 1837. The two DAR numbers are only one number different and may mean the two were related. Two Isaac's Beeson served and their numbers were close, #A008561, and #A008562. Two Richard Beeson has served; their numbers were yet again close #A008565 and #A008566. All but Edward furnished supplies. Mercer Beeson born 1744 in Virginia (#A008564) died at the Yellow Springs Hospital in Pennsylvania in 1777/8 during the war. He was in the thirteenth Virginia Regiment He was a brother of William and Jacob. Richard Beeson born 1710 (#A006567) in Nottingham, Chester Pennsylvania and his son Richard born 1755 (#A008566) both gave patriotic service. Jacob Beeson I born 1741 (#A008563) gave civil service and was Commissioner of Peace. All of the Beeson Patriot DAR numbers are in numerical order. (See DAR Patriot Index). **

**History, crest, and pictures sourced from McKendree Family History, Wikipedia, free pages at Genealogy, Roots web and Ancestry, Beson family, and DAR. There are no DAR records of McKendree family in Revolution

THE FISH FAMILY

The Fish name is from the ancient tribes of Britain. Members of the name lived in Yorkshire, England where they had lands in feudal times. Fish is an occupational name of fisherman or seller of fish. It comes from the Middle English "Fische." The first record of the name is Ernis Fish in Lincolnshire in 1202 listed as a witness in the Assize Court Rolls during the reign of King John. Members of the family left England for the American Colonies in the early 1600's. Religion, turmoil in England, and the quest for land were the main reasons behind their immigration.

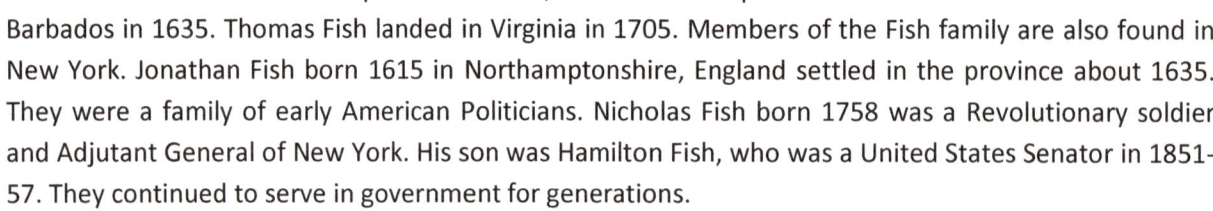

William Fish settled in Connecticut in 1630, John Fish went to Boston in 1630, Gabriel landed in New Hampshire in 1632, and a Christopher settled in Barbados in 1635. Thomas Fish landed in Virginia in 1705. Members of the Fish family are also found in New York. Jonathan Fish born 1615 in Northamptonshire, England settled in the province about 1635. They were a family of early American Politicians. Nicholas Fish born 1758 was a Revolutionary soldier and Adjutant General of New York. His son was Hamilton Fish, who was a United States Senator in 1851-57. They continued to serve in government for generations.

Ira Fish was born December 5, 1806 in Scipo, Cayuga County, New York and may be related. He died in 1868 in Racine, Wisconsin. His son Ira W. Fish was born in 1835 in Cayuga and served in the Civil War. He moved to Spartanburg, Pennsylvania where he married Diantha Coyle born 1834 in Rome Township, Pennsylvania. She was the daughter of Hugh Coyle born 1793 and Catherine Magree from Ireland. Ira and Diantha's son Leslie Fish was born September 30, 1860 in Pennsylvania and died January 5, 1925. He married Elizabeth Tipton, born January 15, 1860 and died in 1947. She was the daughter of Noah Tipton and Elizabeth May. (See Tipton Family). They had five children, Grace, Ralph, Ruth, Willard, and Rowena born September 12, 1888. Rowena married Clyde W. Beson July 12, 1909. (See Beeson Family).

Two-hundred and thirty-four members of the Fish family fought in the Revolution. They are recorded in the DAR records. Twenty–one fought in Virginia, four from New Hampshire, twenty-three from New York and sixteen in Connecticut. John Fish born 1733 (#A210832) in Dartmouth Bristol County, Massachusetts signed the Petition in 1778. He became a member of the Albany, New York Committee of Correspondence, and was a Patriot Spy. He is mentioned in Washington's papers. Ephraim Fish born 1760 in Duchess County, New York (#A041248) was a Lieutenant and died 1838 in Lyme, Ohio. (One of his descendants is Ira Oscar Fish of New York who married Rebecca Bartle). Pardon Fish (#A047769) born 1751 in Rhode Island, died 1835 in Springville, Pennsylvania. John Fish (#A041259) born 1750 in Sandwich, Massachusetts served under Captain Simon Fish. Seventy-four served from Massachusetts.

*History and crest sourced from Wikipedia, Ancestry, Archives, and DAR

THE TIPTON FAMILY

The Tipton name is found in the English Midlands. It is recorded in Doomsday Book as Tibintone, which was probably an old English settlement. They also had lands in Shropshire and were Lords of the Manor. The name was first recorded in the eleventh century. They descended from a Norman Noble, Tiptoft from France, who came to England after the Norman Conquest. His descendant was Baron Pain de Tiptoft born around 1308. A later descendant Lord John de Tiptoft became the first Earl of Worchester. He was Lord High Treasurer for King Richard in 1452.

Edward Tipton Sr. was born 1618 in Pontesford, Shropshire, England, the son of Richard Tipton and Joyce Leister a descendant of William Lyster born circa 1425 in Shrewsbury. Edward left England before 1659 and was in Jamaica a short time where his son Jonathan Tipton Sr. was born in Kingston. He was a soldier in the army of General Robert Venable who sailed in the English fleet of Admiral William Penn and conquered Jamaica from the Spanish in 1655.

Edward went to Maryland with his family in 1668.* His son Jonathan eventually owned a plantation called "Poor Man's Jamaica" where he bred horses. Both Edward and his son died in Baltimore in the Province of Maryland, Jonathan in 1757. Jonathan's obituary in the Maryland Gazette states he was one-hundred and eighteen when he died. His son Edward Sr. was born in 1703. His son Edward born 1728 served in the Revolution.

Elizabeth Tipton was the daughter of Noah Tipton born 1827 in Fairhope, Somerset, Pennsylvania, and Elizabeth May born 1829. Noah died in May of 1865 in Bedford and Elizabeth in 1885. Their daughter Elizabeth married Leslie Fish. She was a possible descendant of Edward Tipton born 1728 who gave patriotic service in the Revolution (#A134809). He died 1805 in Huntington County, Pennsylvania. John Tipton, another descendant, married Mary Butler in 1757 (See Butler Family). He moved to Virginia where he served in the Militia. His vote for George Washington to serve in the House of Burgesses is recorded in Virginia. John was elected to serve on the Committee of Safety and Correspondence where he and four other members wrote the Woodstock Resolution declaring the rights of the Colonists to resist tyranny. He was elected to the Virginia Convention in Williamsburg where they adopted the Virginia constitution. He became a Colonel of the Militia during the Revolution (#A115932). Seventeen members of the family served in the War.

*A Tipton family legend states their ancestor Anthony de Tipton was knighted by Edward I after he killed Welch Prince Llewellyn in 1282.
**History and crest from Wikipedia, free pages at Genealogy, Ancestry, and Tipton Family History

CONCLUSION

The Wheeler brothers and families came from Odell, Bedford, England in 1639. They settled in Concord in the Massachusetts Bay Colony founded in 1630 with their Puritan Ministers and helped develop the town. Later several of them moved to Fairfield and New London in the Connecticut Colony founded in 1636. The Dutch families came to the New Amsterdam Colony beginning in the 1640's, founded in 1625. In 1710, French Huguenots (Calvinists) Phillip and Nicholas Laux (Louck) arrived from the Palatine after leaving their home in Pau, France. They eventually lived in the Mohawk Valley of New York in the original Dutch Colony. The Richard Minter Family from England joined the Jamestown Colony in Virginia in 1620. Jon, relative of Richard, arrived in 1635. Jon's grandson, John, moved to Essex County in 1739. His son William Minter eventually settled in Chester County, York/Camden District, in the Provence of North Carolina, later divided into North and South Carolina. They were members of the Church of England as required and later became Presbyterians and Methodists. The Minter family is listed in the Historic Register of the First Families of Jamestown, Virginia. Mathew Edmiston (Edmonstone), his brother James and mother Jane arrived in Pennsylvania (William Penn's land grant) by 1730 and moved to Augusta County, Virginia in 1743. They were Scotch/Irish Presbyterians. Earlier relatives, John and Robert Edmonstone, arrive in the Province of Maryland between 1633 and 1650. They were all members of the Scottish Edmonstone family of Red Hall Manor in Ireland and Castle Duntreath in Scotland. The David Evans family arrived about 1740 from Wales and settled in the New Jersey Colony purchased by the Quakers from Lord Berkeley and Sir Carteret in 1702. The first members of the Evans family arrived from Wales in 1699.

The associated families of these immigrants arrived from the 1630's to the 1750's. They were the following: Baird, Boone, Butler, Clarence, (Mc)Clelland, Douglass, Gillham, Gilliland, Kirkpatrick, McMurtry, McNeal, Lutton, Patterson, Scott, Smith all from Scotland and Ireland; Babb, Bardwell, Bishop, Cheeseman, Clarke, Cox (Cock), Duffield, Grover, Greaver, Harwood, Hawks, Hillhouse, Jordan, Lockhart, Love, Miles, Newton, Phillips, Piersol (Pearsoll), Pin, Sayre, Shearer, Smith, Stiles, Topliff, Wells, Winter, and Woodward, from England. The Devoe, Gaston, and Louck (Laux) families were Huguenots from France, the Teafords were on the border of France and Germany, and Argenbright's were from Germany. The Rycken-Suydam family arrived in New Amsterdam from Holland in 1663. Other families from Holland were Baar, Van Arsdalen, Van Den Berg, (Van) Gulick, Van Neste, Van der Pool, Van Sycklin/Van Sickle, and Van der Werkin. The Wyckoff family arrived from Sweden in 1663. The Lewis and Prichard families came from Wales in 1682 and 1686. The family of LaGrone's first husband Thomas Irvin, who died young, was the Irvine's from Scotland who arrived in Pennsylvania about 1730. The associated families are included here. The family of her present husband, Clyde LaGrone, came from France arriving in South Carolina Colony in 1729. The associated families are also included. Both of these ancestors also served in the Revolution.

These immigrants were from a variety of religions, Pilgrims, Puritan, Episcopal, Methodist, Baptist, Quakers, Catholic, Lutheran, Presbyterian, and Dutch Reformed Church all looking for religious freedom and freedom from tyrannical Kings. LaGrone's ancestors came from eight different countries and ten different religions. They helped to found and develop the United States beginning in 1609 from Maine to South Carolina. One related family went to the Georgia Colony, established in 1732, just before the

Revolution thus covering the entire thirteen Colonies. Today members of the family live in all parts of the United States including Alaska and Hawaii.

During the Civil War, the Author's Wheeler and Evans great grandfathers fought for the Union while her Minter and Edmiston great grandfathers fought for the South. Andrew Irvin, great grandfather of Thomas Irvin, fought for the Union while Hiram LaGrone, grandfather of Clyde LaGrone, was in the Confederate Army.

The founding families and patriots in this book are but a small representation of all those who risk their lives and fortunes to sail to the Colonies in the 1600's and 1700's. They established the United States of America and bought freedom with their lives. *The Declaration of the Cause and Necessity of taking up Arms,* (stated below) written July 6, 1775 sums up the dedication of our ancestors.

> *"With hearts fortified with these animating reflections, we most solemnly, before God and the world declare that, exerting the utmost of those powers, which our beneficent Creator hath graciously bestowed upon us, the arms we have compelled by our enemies to assume, we will, in defiance of every hazard, with enabling firmness and perseverance employ for the preservation of our liberties; being with one mind resolved to die freeman rather than to live as slaves."*

Just as George Washington saw in his vision, the Colonies expanded across the United States. Members of the families in this book were part of the expansion and contributed to the development of the cities and states from the east coast to California and from Canada to Florida and Texas.

We, the descendants of these founding men and women must continue to honor their sacrifice by teaching the true history of our country to our children and grandchildren. We cannot allow todays "progressive" educational institutions to erode the legacy of these extraordinary men and women. We must preserve our history, freedoms, and liberty.
The Author

ADDENDUMS

Butler Addendum

Jean (or Jane) Butler, daughter of William and Eleanor, was born in 1787 in West Lancaster County, Pennsylvania and died at an unknown date in Crawford, County. Nancy was born 1790 in Chester or Lycoming County, Pennsylvania, died date and place unknown. Eleanor was born 1792 in Chester or Lycoming County died September 6, 1861 in Crawford County. Sally was born 1803 in Crawford County and died in 1855. Mary was born 1805 in Crawford County and died in 1884, and Catherine, born 1807 in Crawford County, died in 1895.

Wheeler Addendum

Albert and Sarah Jane's daughter, Ester Ann married Frank Mead who owned the general store in Prairie City. They did not have any children. She became a DAR member through her grandmother Margaret Mariah Butler who married her grandfather Oliver Cleveland Wheeler.

Son Charles Floyd was born September 22, 1872 in Lee, Fulton County. He married Kate Blanche Robinson who was born September 12, 1876 in Fandom, Illinois. They had four children, John Robinson Piersol, Charles A., Sarah, and Doris. Charles (CF as he was known) moved to Greeley, Colorado about 1914, and established Wheeler Realty in 1915. Shortly after his arrival in Greeley, he sent his nephews, Russell, Rollin, and Harry a present, a donkey shipped by train to Prairie City. Charles was very active in the community and held several elective positions. Elected to the State Senate in the early thirties, he held the office for many years. He accompanied President Roosevelt from Cheyenne, Wyoming through Greeley to the Capitol in Denver on a "whistle stop" campaign tour in October of 1936. He invited is nephew, Harry Wheeler and great niece, Donna Joan age five, to met him and President Roosevelt in Cheyenne. When the train arrived, they shook the President's hand off the back train platform.

Charles (CF) was President Pro Tem of the Colorado Senate when he died of a heart attack in 1939. He was cosigner for many bills affecting the State of Colorado. One of the Bills established the Colorado State Patrol in 1935. After his death, Charles' son, John R.P. (Robinson-Piersoll), took over the Real Estate office in 1940. John was later elected to the Colorado House of Representatives. He married Jane Conrad and had four children, Thomas, Daniel, Lorie and a younger daughter who died young. John died of a heart attack in 1992 and his son Daniel, took over the Real Estate Offices. Charles married Helen and had three children Marilyn, Jack, and Jim. Sarah married Earl Powell and had three children Charlie, Sharon and Charla. Doris married and had a daughter who died in infancy. Doris had romantic fever as a child and died of a heart attack about 1955.

Ralph Bismarck Wheeler, son of Albert, was born December 5, 1870 in Fulton County, Illinois. He married May Evans in 1895, pictured. She was born June 16, 1872, the daughter of William Evans and Cornelius Winter. (See Evans and Winter families). Ralph Wheeler was employed by his brother-in-law, Frank Mead, at the Mead General Store founded in 1866 in Prairie City. Ralph and his brother, Charles, were members of the Woodbine Athletic Club, which they organized September 29, 1892. There were twenty-five charter members. The officers were President Rob Chambers, Vice-President Ralph Wheeler, Secretary Charles Wheeler, and Treasure William Westfall. The club "leased the second floor of the Sebree's building and fitted it out for a gymnasium."

Ralph's wife, May Evans, had been a member of the Methodist Church, established in 1846, before her marriage to Ralph. The family latter attended the Methodist Church on a regular basis. May was a member of the Church Ladies Aid Society and the women put on an annual Thanksgiving Day dinner. *"People from miles around took the morning train to attend the dinner and caught the evening train home."*

About 1918 Ralph Wheeler purchased one of the first automobiles in the Village. While learning to drive it, he drove through his barn doors, yelling "Woe, Stop!" before he could find the brakes. Fortunately, the old automobiles were very sturdy and it did little harm to the car. After that incident, he taught his son, Harry to drive, who was only ten years old. During the following years, Harry often drove for his father when he delivered goods from the Mead General Store. On May 20, 1924, he and Harry were out of town at Indian Point in the City of Knox when they had a flat tire. It was a very hot day and while Ralph was changing the tire, he died of a heart attack. Harry was fifteen at the time and ran for help, but it was too late. Ralph is buried in the Prairie City Cemetery in the Wheeler Plot. May died September of 1935 at the home of her son Harry in Flagstaff, Arizona. She is buried beside her husband, Ralph, in the Prairie City Cemetery. Ralph and May had three sons Russell, Rollin, and Harry who married Ruth Minter. (Harry and Ruth's daughter, Donna Joan, is the author of this book).

Russell Clair was born September 7, 1898. He died 1971 in Houston, Texas. He joined the Army in 1918 during World War I. In 1919, he married Kathryn Whitenack and they had five sons. Russell graduated from Greeley State Teachers College and eventually became Superintendent of Schools in Riverside California. He retired and went into the Banking business with his son Richard in Houston, Texas. Russell's son Samuel, born May 6, 1920, was an engineer in the Air Force and a member of the B29 Squadron that dropped the atomic bomb on Japan that ended World War II. His plane "Strange Cargo" (plane and crew pictured), flew with the lead plane the "Enola Gay." He married Charlotte Washington and had five children, Sam Jr., and four daughters, Mary Ester, Charlotte Ann, Joan, and Patricia. Russell's son, Richard, born November 27, 1922, was not able to serve in the armed forces due a physical condition. He married Phyllis Harwell and had three children Karen, Gary, and James, Philip born August 3, 1926 served in the Navy. He married Phyllis Holmquist (*owner of the Wheeler/Whitenack family tree*) and had three children, Paul, Barbara, and Ronald. William (Bill) born March 19, 1929, served in the Army during the Korean War. He married Marilyn Kirkman and had four children, William Russell, Thomas Michael, Catherine Mary, and Steven

Captain Joseph E. Westover (Airplane Commander)
Top row, l to r—2nd Lt. John W. Dulin, 2nd Lt. Louis B. Allen, Captain Joseph E. Westover, 2nd Lt. William J. Desmond, 1st Lt. Robert M. Donnell.
Middle row, l to r—Sgt. Samuel R. Wheeler, S/Sgt. William J. Spradlin, S/Sgt. James H. Doiron, S/Sgt. William J. Cotter.
Bottom row, l to r—Cpl. Derward A. Stevens, Sgt. Cleo E. Harter, Pfc. Francis J. Merry, Pfc. John H. Hubeny, Jr., Sgt. Clyde R. Beecher, Cpl. Filbert Reynolds, M/Sgt. Robert E. Smithson.

Kirkman. Joseph born 1935 married Alice Casillas and had five sons, Mark, Matthew, Michael, Murray, and Mason.

Rollin Wayne, son of Ralph, was born March 28, 1903 and died 1998 in Flagstaff, Arizona. He married Zelpha Merriman and they had one son Ralph, born March 15, 1940. Ralph married and had three children, P.K. Cabrini and Laura. Ralph was vice-president of the Babbitt Garage and ran the company during the time his friend and owner, Bruce Babbitt, was Interior Secretary under President Clinton. His second marriage was to Maggie. Rollin graduated from Greeley State Teachers College and taught history at the Flagstaff high school his entire life. He was also the Coach and Boys Councilor. He received many honors from the School district and was beloved by his students. The community honored him many times for his life long service. He was elected Mayor of Flagstaff for four terms. He was also very active in local and State politics. The Community of Flagstaff named Wheeler Park in his honor.

Harry Louk Wheeler youngest son of Ralph and May Wheeler was born in Prairie City, Illinois September 13, 1908. His middle name comes from his grandmother Louk's maiden name. Her family ancestors arrived in the New York Colony about 1710 and were Huguenots from France. (See Louck/Laux family). He was educated in the Prairie City schools until 1924. After his father's death, his Uncle Charles (Charlie) moved him and his mother to Greeley, Colorado. His Uncle became a "second father" to him and provided help with his education. His older brothers, Russ and Rollin had already graduated from college. Harry enrolled in College High and attended Greeley State Teachers College (GSTC), which is now the University of Northern Colorado where he was involved in most sports. His basketball team won the State Championship and they went to Nationals in Chicago. He studied three years to become an athletic coach. He had a part time job driving the city bus and helped his Uncle with the driving when he toured his real estate holdings, properties, and listings. He also helped drive and entertain his cousins for his Aunt. By this time, he had become a proficient automobile mechanic as well, and kept his uncles cars in running condition.

In 1927, a group of Barnstormer pilots put on an air show in Greeley and Harry became captivated with flying. He took lessons whenever he could until his Uncle found out and *"forbid him to spend his money on flying lessons since airplanes would never amount to anything."* However, he never lost his desire to fly. He took lessons again in Fort Collins, Colorado in the 1930's, which eventually led to his employment with United Airlines during World Was II.

Harry met his wife, Ruth Minter (see Minter Family) while they were both attending Greeley State Teachers College. Ruth was on a teaching scholarship. She taught in the rural schools while studying for her degree. After she graduated, she taught in Seibert, Colorado schools where her family lived. Ruth was the daughter of Roy and Lydia Edmiston Minter, born May 23, 1909 in Dallas, Oregon. When school was out in the summer of 1930, Ruth went to California to visit her Edmiston cousins in Long Beach. Harry followed her out and they were married in Pasadena, California. They planned to find jobs in California, but it was during the Depression and unfortunately, permanent jobs were very difficult to find. In early 1931, Harry went to Flagstaff where his brother, Rollin, was teaching. He was able find a job at the Babbitt Garage as a mechanic and sent for Ruth and his baby daughter, Donna Joan, who was born March 29, 1931 in Pasadena. His older brother Russ and family also moved to Flagstaff and taught in the local schools. The brothers sent for their mother, May and moved her into an apartment next to Harry. The family was again together until their mother died in September of 1935.

In the fall of 1935, Harry's Uncle "Charlie" wrote to him and told him about the newly formed Colorado Highway Patrol. He mentioned he would have a great opportunity to join the new organization. In the meantime, Ruth's parents had moved to Fort Collins, Colorado and Ruth was anxious to see them. They made the decision to move and Harry became an officer in the State Patrol in 1936 in Fort Collins. He was again taking flying lessons. On December 7, 1941, the United States was at War with Japan. All men between the ages of eighteen and sixty-five were required to register for the draft. At age thirty-three, Harry was eligible for the draft unless he was employed in a war related job. He was deferred as a member of the Patrol for a time but Fort Collins did not have any wartime jobs for which he qualified. In 1943, he applied for employment in an opening with United Air lines for pilot training, his life long dream and considered war related. He was hired and commuted daily by bus between Fort Collins and Cheyenne, Wyoming the nearest United base. His eyesight was by now 20/22 and after several months of various treatments and gallons of carrot juice, it was determined he was ineligible to be a pilot. At that time, glasses were not allowed to correct vision to the required 20/20. He was extremely disappointed. He was then transferred to the maintenance division as a mechanic. United's Cheyenne base was soon closed and moved to the San Francisco Airport where Harry was transferred. The move was unexpected and not a welcome turn of events. Housing in the San Francisco area was extremely limited and it took six months before he was able to find housing and move his family to California.

In the summer of 1945, Harry's wife, Ruth, became ill and required a major operation. The operation was a severe shock to her system and caused her to have a complete mental breakdown. She required hospitalization for the rest of her life and died in Santa Clara, California May 27, 1954. She is buried in the Grandview Cemetery in Fort Collins, Colorado next to her parents. The war finally ended in 1946 and civilian travel once again permitted. Harry's daughter (Donna) Joan, moved back to Fort Collins where she finished High School in 1949 and lived with her Minter grandparents, aunt and uncle while attending college.

In 1949, Harry met his second wife, Shirley Wheeler (her maiden name), a nurse at the United Medical Center. She was previously a U.S. Navy Nurse stationed in Oakland, California during the War. Shirley was summoned back into service in 1950, during the Korean War. She was sent to the U. S. Naval Hospital in Yokosuka, Japan. Harry applied for, and received the job of Assistant Station Master for United Air Lines at the Tokyo Airport. He followed her over and he and Shirley were married in Japan. They had a son Jay Albert, born November 19, 1951 in San Mateo, California. Jay followed his father's example. He is employed with United Air Lines. He married Gloria Moncada, who had a daughter, Angie, whom Jay adopted. They also had a son Jay J. Wheeler born July of 1988. Harry and Shirley lived in San Mateo until Harry died in 1997. Shirley Ann Wheeler was born in Illinois in August of 1921 and died in 2000 in San Mateo. Their ashes are buried in Olivet Cemetery in Colmo, California.

Donna Joan Wheeler Irvin-LaGrone was born March 29, 1931 in Pasadena, California, (pictured). She was educated in the Fort Collins, Colorado schools until her father, Harry Wheeler, was transferred to San Francisco during World War II. She attended the South San Francisco Junior and Senior High Schools until 1946 when the War ended. Her mother Ruth was hospitalized, and she eventually went back to For Collins to live with her Minter Grandparents and her mother's sister and brother, Carol and later Roy

Minter to finish high school. She attended Colorado A & M College now Colorado State University earning the Apparel Design Award for fashions. On April 25, 1953, she married her first husband, a childhood sweetheart, Thomas Jerome Irvin, who was born February 2, 1932, in Franklin, Nebraska. They were married in San Mateo, California at Saint Gregory's Catholic Church with a reception at the home of her father. Tom was a Second Lieutenant, (pictured) serving in the army as a

Training Officer and Company Commander during the Korean War at Camp Roberts, California. After his discharge in November of 1953, they moved back to Fort Collins where Tom returned to college and graduated from Colorado State University (CSU) in August of 1957. They had four sons, Michael Jerome born March 21, 1954, Timothy Kevin born November 20, 1955, Brien Thomas born December 20, 1957 (all three born in Fort Collins), and Sean Patrick born October 13, 1960 in Santa Maria, California. After graduation, Tom was hired at the Martin Marietta Missile Company in Denver. In July of 1960, he was transferred to the Vandenberg Missile Base in Santa Maria, California where Sean was born. In November of 1960, he was diagnosed with cancer of the colon and died January 31, 1961 after extensive care at the University of California Cancer Research Hospital in San Francisco. He was buried on his twenty-ninth birthday in the Grand View Cemetery in Fort Collins, Colorado.

Joan and her sons moved back to Colorado where she hired a live-in baby sitter and worked as a Statistician for Martin Marietta Company in Littleton. She met her second husband, Clyde LaGrone, an Engineer, at Martin. He was born in Tulsa, Oklahoma August 14, 1932. He graduated from West Point in 1954 and served as a First Lieutenant during the Korean War as a Ranger and Training Officer. They were married March 3, 1962 at All Soul's Church in Englewood, Colorado.

Clyde and Joan had two sons, David Lee born April 9, 1963 in Englewood and Steven Laurence born July 13, 1965 in Littleton, Colorado. All six of her sons attended school in Littleton until 1976 when Clyde was employed with the Center for Innovation in Butte, Montana. In 1980, Clyde and Joan moved back to Fort Collins, Colorado where he opened an Engineering business and later to the Denver area. Joan spent forty years in Real Estate as a Broker and served as Vice President of Marketing at the National Women's Council of Realtors (WCR). She also served the National Association (NAR) as a member of the Political Action Committee and Strategic Planning. She followed her family's footsteps in both real estate and politics running for the Colorado House of Representatives in 1972 and as a 1972 National

Delegate. Her goal was to educate her sons. She is also an award winning author and artist. (Family pictured in New York in 1969).

Mike graduated in 1972 from Arapahoe High School in Littleton, Colorado and attended Western State College in Gunnison on a swimming scholarship. He was active in scouting, sports in high school and became an avid hunter, fisherman, and skier. He married first Becky Commins (English descent) of Englewood, Colorado in 1976 and had two daughters. Jaime Lynn born May 2, 1980, studied Nursing. Jenna Christine born March 21, 1984, graduated from college as a Vet Tech. She is employed as a Vet Hospital Pharmacists. Mike and Becky divorced in 1988. He married second Bonita (Nita) Templeton in 1990 who had a daughter, Nichole born August 1982. She married Nick Sandoval in 2011. Mike is the Senior Manager for the Sanders Wholesale Plumbing Company in Fort Collins. His wife, Nita, is his Assistant Manager who also has a separate plumbing fixture repair business. Mike raises Pinto rodeo horses on his acreage north of Fort Collins.

Tim graduated in 1973 from Arapahoe High School where he was active in scouting, the Future Farmers of America and President of the State Chapter. He graduated from North Eastern College in Sterling with a degree in Ranch Management. He then attended Colorado State University majoring in Horticulture. He lives in Wasilla, Alaska and owns a profitable Nursery business. He has developed numerous trees and plants to winter over in the Alaskan climate. He is President of the Alaskan Fruit Growers and noted authority and speaker on Alaskan agriculture. He also manages a department for the Budweiser wholesale distributing Company in Anchorage.

Brien graduated from Littleton High School in 1976 and Colorado State University with a B.A. and dual Masters in Production Engineering and Business. He was active in skiing, sports, and scouting in high school and earned his Eagle Scout. His first marriage was to classmate Donna Jo Conley (Welsh descent). On September 7, 1996, he married Geraldine (Geri) Gates (Scottish and Italian descent) in Arvada, Colorado. They have three children, twin boys Kyle Thomas and Luke Duncan born June 2, 2000 (active in sports and scouting), and Maren Christine born March 3, 2004 a gymnast and Girl Scout. Geri has been a Design Consultant for several years in Builder Design Centers. Brien an avid hunter is a Senior Production manager and Systems Engineer for the Brocade Company in the Broomfield, Colorado division. He travels worldwide.

Sean was educated in the Littleton Colorado schools before graduating from Butte, Montana High School in 1979 earning awards in debate. He attended Montana State University and graduated from the University of Northern Colorado at Greeley (formerly Greeley State Teachers College). He received a B.A. in Theater Arts. From the time he enter school, he was involved in acting in leading rolls and continued to follow that career. He was a scout for short time. Sean also studied real estate. He manages a large apartment complex in downtown Hollywood. He is a composer and lead singer in his band (and others) called *Liquid Fate* in Hollywood, California. He is also a front man, author, lyricist, and Hollywood columnist. (See Sean Patrick at vocal1@yahoo.com)

David graduated from Poudre High School in Fort Collins in 1983 and Colorado State University with a B.A. and M. A. in Engineering. He was active in scouting, sports, and spent ten years in local and state swim programs, earning his way up to work out with the US Olympic Swim team. While in college, he coached the Colorado State University girls swim team. He married Kathy Fisher (Irish descent) in 1987 and had two sons, Zackary Michael born December 16, 1989. Zach graduated from the University of Science and Technology in Rollo, Missouri and employed in the Racing Car industry in Florida. Andrew Thomas born November 4, 1991 graduated from the University of Nebraska in Lincoln in International Business and Politics. He will graduate with a degree in law in 2016. In the spring and summer of 2013, he served as an aid to his Nebraska Senator in Washington, D.C. He plans to inter politics. Kathy and David were divorced in 2002. David married Theresa Montague (English and Italian descent) in May 2004. At the time, she was employed with the US Air Force. She has a daughter, Christina who married in 2009 and has three small sons. David is an Engineer and project Manager with the Corp of Engineers in Omaha and travels in a several state division region working with local, state, and national political leaders.

Steven graduated in 1985 from Poudre High School and Colorado State University with a B.A. and a M. A. degree from the University of Washington in Business Management. In high school, he was active on the tennis team, Student Council, Drama, and show choir. He was a scout in grade school. His partner is Chris VanSickle (Greek descent), a graduate of Saint Mary's University of Maryland and Oxford, England who is a Project Manager with the National Park Service in Denver. Steve is a Senior Executive Internal Consultant Manager with United Launch Alliance of Centennial, Colorado. The Company launches satellites for the Military and Civilian users. He travels between the manufacturing, assembly, and integration plants in Decatur, Alabama and Brownsville, Texas as well as Launch facilities at Cape Canaveral and Vandenberg Air Force Base.